THE RISE AND FALL OF THE CHOCTAW REPUBLIC

THE CIVILIZATION OF THE AMERICAN INDIAN SERIES

TULLOCK-CHISK-KO *(He-who-drinks-the-juice-of-the-stone)*
CHAMPION CHOCTAW BALL PLAYER IN 1834, BY CATLIN

THE RISE AND FALL OF THE

Choctaw
Republic

Angie Debo

UNIVERSITY OF OKLAHOMA PRESS
NORMAN AND LONDON

BY ANGIE DEBO

The Historical Background of the American Policy of Isolation (with J. Fred
Rippy) (Northampton, Mass., 1924)
The Rise and Fall of the Choctaw Republic (Norman, 1934; New edition,
Norman, 1961)
And Still the Waters Run (Princeton, 1940; Norman, 1984)
The Road to Disappearance: A History of the Creek Indians (Norman,
1941)
Tulsa: From Creek Town to Oil Capital (Norman, 1943)
Prairie City: The Story of an American Community (New York, 1944;
Tulsa, Okla., 1985)
Oklahoma: Footloose and Fancy-Free (Norman, 1949; Westport, Conn.,
1981)
The Five Civilized Tribes of Oklahoma (Philadelphia, 1951)
A History of the Indians of the United States (Norman, 1970)
Oklahoma: A Guide to the Sooner State (Ed., with John M. Oskison)
(Norman, 1941)
The Cowman's Southwest, Oliver Nelson (Ed.) (Glendale, Calif., 1953)
History of the Choctaw, Chickasaw, and Natchez Indians, by H. B.
Cushman (Ed.) (Stillwater, Okla., 1962)
Geronimo: The Man, His Time, His Place (Norman, 1976)

Library of Congress Catalog Card Number: 61-7973

ISBN: 0-8061-1247-6

The Rise and Fall of the Choctaw Republic is Volume 6 in *The Civilization
of the American Indian Series.*

TO THE MEMORY OF MY BROTHER

EDWIN F. DEBO

WHOSE INTEREST IN THIS WORK AT ITS BEGINNING

FORMED THE STRONGEST INCENTIVE TO ITS COMPLETION

NANIH WAYA MOUND, WINSTON COUNTY, MISSISSIPPI

Preface to the New Edition

THE HISTORY of the Choctaw Indians records the life of a separate people with a sharply defined citizenship, an autonomous government, and distinctive social customs and institutions. It reveals a political, social, and economic existence as active and intensive and as closely circumscribed as that of any of the famous small republics of the past.

On the other hand the separate thread of Choctaw history is at all times closely interwoven with the larger fabric of American history as a whole. Choctaw law was a curious combination of ancient tribal custom and Anglo-American legal practice. Choctaw churches and schools were copied almost wholly from those of the white man's society. Choctaw economic institutions represented an adjustment of aboriginal life ways to borrowed European products and techniques. Moreover, the greatest problems of the Choctaw people were all due to irresistible forces in the life of the more numerous race surrounding them, and the main crises in their history were brought about by the same outside influences. The Choctaw story, therefore, is an interpretation of the local events in the life of the tribe as seen against the background of general American history.

The aboriginal institutions of the Choctaws have been carefully studied and described by ethnologists. The early historic period, when the Choctaw country occupied a strategic position in the imperial contest for control of North America is a well-known aspect of colonial history. The Choctaw removal and settlement in what became an "Indian Territory" in the West, the first generation of development there, and the participation in the Civil War are a part of early Oklahoma history, and have been covered fully by other writers. I thought best, however, for the convenience of the general reader and for the sake of organic completeness, to treat these phases of Choctaw history briefly in my first three chapters.

No study had ever been made of the history of the Choctaw Nation after the Civil War, and to that period the major portion of this book is devoted. The sources were found in the writings and reminiscences of the Choctaws themselves, in the official papers of Federal employees, and to a lesser extent in the recorded impressions of visitors to the Choctaw country. During the tribal period the public archives were preserved at the capitol in the care of the National Secretary. After the liquidation of the tribal government the original manuscript acts of the General Council and a few other documents were brought to the University of Oklahoma. They were in the Phillips Collection at the time of my writing, but are now in the Western History Collections of the University library. Fragments of the Senate and House journals, reports of national officers and legislative committees, proclamations and messages of the Principal Chiefs, census statistics, election returns, county records, and court records were placed in the office of the Superintendent of the Five Civilized Tribes at Muskogee, where I cited them as Union Agency Files. They have since been removed to the Indian Archives of the Oklahoma Historical Society at Oklahoma City.

The correspondence between the Choctaws and the officials of the Federal Government was in the files of the Indian Office at Washington, where I cited it accordingly. It is now in the National Archives. Many United States government documents relating to Choctaw affairs have been published and were available. Among these were the reports of the Commissioner of Indian Affairs and of the Commission to the Five Civilized Tribes, many Senate and House documents, census bulletins, and Court of Claims and Supreme Court reports. The Choctaw government also published many compilations of tribal law and occasional documents of interest to its citizens. Fairly complete files of the newspapers published in the Choctaw Nation during the tribal period have been preserved in the collections of the Oklahoma Historical Society. At the time this book was being written, a number of prominent Choctaws who had held office under the tribal government during its latter years were still living, and were able to contribute local color to the record of this vanished society.

By an evaluation and interpretation of these sources it was possible to reconstruct the history of the Choctaw people. During the generation preceding their removal to the West they consciously adopted the "civilized" institutions of the white race, and they continued this development after their expulsion from their ancient homeland and their settlement in the wild land to which they had been driven. Before the Civil War they established churches and schools and a stable constitutional government, and became fairly prosperous farmers and stock raisers under the communal system of land ownership that allowed every citizen an equal right to use the public domain. A few of them operated extensive plantations worked by Negro slaves.

Their alliance with the Confederacy and their participation in the Civil War disrupted this ordered society, and at its close they were confronted with pressing problems of reconstruction. But they gradually recovered their social and economic stability. They resumed their treaty relations with the United States by surrendering some of their land as the penalty for their "rebellion." And they solved their most perplexing problem, after twenty years of negotiation, by adopting their freedmen and granting them a limited citizenship within the tribe.

Soon after the Civil War a new era in economic enterprise began with the coming of the first railroad, and the consequent opening of their coal mines, the growth of lumbering operations, and the exploitation of other natural resources. Although this development increased the tribal income, it brought great complexity into the administration of public finance and the management of the communal estate. It also brought an increasing number of white immigrants, who as citizens of the United States were outside the tribal jurisdiction. At the same time there was a constant pressure on the Federal Government by land-hungry settlers, railroads, and speculators, who urged the abolition of the tribal institutions and the opening of the country to homesteading. Almost unanimously the Choctaws set themselves against this change, and for a generation their leaders were able to prevent hostile legislation by Congress.

By 1890 the non-citizen population outnumbered the Choctaw three to one, and the maintenance of tribal authority had become almost impossible. From that time on it became increasingly evident that the United States was determined to abolish the tribal governments of the Indian Territory, even to the extent of abrogating the treaties that had so long presented a legal barrier against white encroachment. In 1893 Congress passed the act creating the Dawes Commission, which was authorized to negotiate terms of settlement. Although several years elapsed before the Choctaws could be persuaded to surrender their tribal institutions, they finally became convinced that only by negotiating a settlement could they avoid a dictated one. They began negotiations in 1896, and accepted the "Atoka Agreement," providing for the termination of their affairs, in the Summer of 1898.

For the next few years the United States and the Choctaw governments were occupied with the working out of intricate problems of detail—the determination of citizenship, the division of the communal estate, and the gradual abdication of tribal authority. The incorporation of tribal citizenship and the merging of tribal history into the composite life of the State of Oklahoma may be said to have ended the separate history of this gifted people, who maintained for so long a distinct social and political existence in the midst of a crowding alien population.

I have carried on much research since this book was first published, but I have discovered little that would invalidate my original findings. I have detected only two serious errors. In text and index I failed to distinguish between Moshulatubbee, the great District Chief who died prior to the War of 1812, and his successor of the same name who continued to lead his people until his death in 1838. I made a more serious error on page 276 by accepting Indian Bureau population statistics, a figure obtained by adding three separate rolls of citizens living at different times.

I welcome the opportunity to incorporate the necessary corrections in this edition.

ANGIE DEBO

Marshall, Oklahoma

CONTENTS

PAGE

ILLUSTRATIONS

MAPS

THE RISE AND FALL OF THE CHOCTAW REPUBLIC

CHOCTAW EAGLE DANCE BY CATLIN, 1834

THE PRIMITIVE CHOCTAWS

I

THE Choctaw Indians constituted the most numerous branch of the great Muskogean linguistic stock. They were closely akin to the Chickasaws, who spoke a different dialect of the same language, and more distantly related to the Creeks and Seminoles. At the beginning of the historic period they occupied the central and southern part of the present state of Mississippi, and a large tract of territory in southwestern Alabama. Their lands were bounded on the north by the hunting grounds of the Chickasaws, and on the east by the Creek settlements.

The sacred traditions of the tribe were closely centered around the great fortified mound of Nanih Waya,[1] the most imposing structure in the Choctaw country. It was located on the northern frontier of Choctaw settlement in what is now Winston County, Mississippi, and apparently was designed to serve as an outpost against the Chickasaws. According to the earliest descriptions it was an oblong mound forty to fifty feet high, and covering at the base about an acre. It was protected by a circular earthen rampart, ten feet in height and thirty to forty feet in width, with several entrance gaps, and enclosing an area of about one square mile. Within this enclosure and about 250 yards from the great mound was a lower conical mound evidently used as a burial place. Between these two large mounds were the traces of several smaller ones. Two deeply worn trails, now grown up with forest trees and almost obliterated, led away from this prehistoric stronghold to the southeast and north.

These mounds and ramparts were first described by James Adair in 1775. The place had been abandoned before that time, but the great

[1]The name, *Nanih Waya*, clearly signifies "leaning" or "sloping hill," but the meaning of this designation has been lost.

1

number of stone artifacts noticed in the vicinity by the earliest observers indicates that it was a center of population until a comparatively recent period. The walls and smaller mounds are now being rapidly obliterated by the white man's plow; but the large mound with its sides overgrown by great forest trees still stands as an impressive landmark of ancient Choctaw culture.[2]

The legendary history of the tribe is closely woven around this sacred spot. According to their most widely accepted creation myth, their ancestors issued from a hole or cave under the great mound, and ranged themselves around its sides to dry before dispersing to occupy the surrounding country. Sometimes the legend is varied to represent the neighboring tribes as issuing from the same subterranean source, before they moved off to their respective locations leaving the Choctaws, the last comers, to remain in the vicinity.[3]

According to another widespread tradition the Choctaws came originally from a land far distant in the West. They were miraculously guided by a sacred pole, which was carried by their leader during the day and planted by night in their place of encampment. Every morning it was found to be leaning toward the east as a signal for them to continue their journey; but when they reached the site of Nanih Waya, it remained in an upright position. In consequence they settled there, built mounds and ramparts, and made it the ceremonial center of their Nation. This legend usually accounts for the Chickasaws by showing that the two tribes were originally one people who became separated during the migration; a common version relates that the leaders were two brothers named Chahtah and Chikasah, who became the founders of their respective tribes.[4]

The later Choctaws tried to reconcile these contradictory traditions, and several ingenious explanations were evolved. One old Indian is quoted by Schermerhorn as saying that when the migrating Choctaws first arrived in Mississippi, they fortified the area around their cornfields and settlement to protect themselves against their unknown and probably hostile neighbors. When their scouts reported that there was

[2]John R. Swanton, *Source Material for the Social and Ceremonial Life of the Choctaw Indians*, Bureau of American Ethnology, *Bulletin 103* (Washington, 1931), pp. 6-10.

[3]*Ibid.*, pp. 5-7, 35-37, 201; Thomas Nuttall, *A Journal of Travels into the Arkansas Territory during the Year 1819*, Reuben Gold Thwaites, *Early Western Travels* (Cleveland, 1905), XIII, 304-5.

[4]*Ibid.*, pp. 5, 6, 10-30, 32-35; H. B. Cushman, *History of the Choctaw, Chickasaw, and Natchez Indians* (Greenville, Texas, 1899), pp. 62-66, 361-62; Israel Folsom, "Choctaw Traditions," a series of articles running in the *Vindicator*, November 10, 1875.

no danger from invaders, they issued from the fort to settle in different parts of the country; the tradition therefore arose that they sprang from the mound within the fort.[5] The missionary, Alfred Wright, reported that an aged Choctaw interpreter explained the discrepancy by saying that the Choctaws destroyed the original inhabitants of the land where they settled, and then invented the creation myth to erase from their history the record of their injustice and violence.[6] A legend related by Peter P. Pitchlynn, a Choctaw statesman of the middle nineteenth century, apparently makes an attempt to unite and consolidate the two stories. According to this version, the Choctaws came from under the ocean (apparently the Gulf of Mexico), and were guided north by their sacred pole. They crossed the Mississippi and settled in their home land, and became the ancestors of the other Southeastern tribes.[7]

Since these myths were not collected until the nineteenth century, it is possible that they were inspired in part by missionary influence; the story of the migration, for instance, with its sacred pole pointing the way reminds one somewhat of the Hebrew exodus and its pillar of cloud and fire. Even more similarity is seen in the version of the flood, where the Choctaw Noah and his party were saved by building a raft or boat.[8]

Many of the incidents of this story, however, are not Biblical; and the descriptions show not only the vivid contact with nature so characteristic of Indian life, but the most exuberant native fancy. The version by Israel Folsom, an early Christian convert, is fairly characteristic. He concluded his story of the flood (Oka falama) and the preservation of Noah (Oklatabashih) with the following incidents:

"Finally Oklatabashih sent a dove to see if any dry land could be found. She returned with her beak full of grass, which she had gathered from a desert island. Oklatabashih to reward her for her discovery mingled a little salt in her food. Soon after this the waters subsided and the dry land appeared; then the inmates of the great boat went forth to repeople another earth. But the dove having acquired a taste for salt during her stay in the boat continued its use by finding it in the salt-licks that then abounded in many places, to which the deer and cattle frequently resorted.... One day, however, after having eaten some grass seed, she unfortunately forgot to eat a little salt as usual. For this

[5]Swanton, *Choctaw Social and Ceremonial Life*, pp. 6-7.
[6]*Ibid.*, p. 11.
[7]*Ibid.*, pp. 31-32.
[8]*Ibid.*, pp. 202-8; Cushman, *History of the Choctaw*, pp. 282-87, 365-66; George Catlin, *North American Indians* (Edinburgh, 1926), II, 145.

neglect the Great Spirit punished her and her descendants by forbidding them forever the use of salt.... From that day to this in memory of this lost privilege, the doves everywhere, on the return of spring, still continue their cooing for salt, which they will never again be permitted to eat..... [But Oklatabashih had been unable to capture a pair of *biskinik* (sapsuckers), *fitukhak* (yellow hammers), or *bakbak* (large red-headed woodpeckers).] *".... They flew high in the air at the approach of Oka falama, and, as the waters rose higher and higher, they also flew higher above the surging waves. Finally, the waters rose in near proximity to the sky, upon which they lit as their last hope. Soon, to their great joy and comfort, the waters ceased to rise, and commenced to recede. But while sitting on the sky their tails, projecting downward, were continually being drenched by the dashing spray of the surging waters below, and thus the end of their tail feathers became forked and notched, and this peculiar shape of the tails of the biskinik, fitukhak and bakbak has been transmitted to their latest posterity.*[9]*...."*

The borrowings here are evident — the use of a boat, the mention of cattle, the conception of the Great Spirit, and the incident of the dove's return; but the Choctaws had certainly incorporated it into their own experience.

The belief in the immortality of the soul was certainly aboriginal, although the system of rewards and punishments was no doubt modified by Christian conceptions of heaven and hell. It seems to have been the primitive belief that the spirit, or *shilup*, remained for some time about the body, and then set out on its long journey to the "happy hunting ground," from which only murderers and possibly those who had died by violence were excluded. Later the idea developed that at the end of the journey the *shilup* had to walk a slippery foot log across a swirling river under a bombardment of rocks from the guardians of the "happy hunting grounds"; only the good were able to effect a happy crossing, while the wicked were dislodged and condemned to eternal wandering in the abyss below.[10]

The fundamental character of the belief in immortality is shown by its appearance in the burial customs, the most curious and the most distinctive of all Choctaw ceremonials. When a member of the tribe

[9]Swanton, *Choctaw Social and Ceremonial Life*, p. 205.
[10]*Ibid.*, pp. 215-20; David I. Bushnell, Jr., *The Choctaw of Bayou Lacomb St. Tammany Parish, Louisiana*, Bureau of American Ethnology, *Bulletin 48* (Washington, 1909), pp. 28-29; Catlin, *North American Indians*, II, 145-46; Folsom,*Vindicator*, November 17, 1875.

4

died, the body was covered with skins and bark and placed upon an elevated platform which was erected near the house for that purpose. Even if the death had occurred far from home, the body was carefully brought back and placed near the house. Beside the corpse were placed food and drink, a change of clothing, and favorite utensils and ornaments which would be needed by the spirit in its long journey to the other world. A dog was killed to provide the deceased with a companion, and after the introduction of horses, ponies were also sacrificed so that the spirit might ride. For the first few days a fire was kept constantly burning to furnish light and warmth for the journey.

The body remained upon the scaffold for a fixed period, which, however, seems to have varied from one to four or even six months according to local custom. During this time the relatives frequently resorted to the foot of the platform to wail and mourn, although in warm weather the stench from the decomposing body became so intolerable that the women sometimes fainted while performing this respect to the deceased.

Among the honored officials of the Choctaws were men — and possibly women — who were known as bone-pickers. These undertakers were tattooed in a distinctive manner, and allowed their finger nails to grow long for their revolting occupation. When the body had remained upon the scaffold the specified time, a bone-picker was summoned, and all the relatives and friends were invited for the last rites. These mourners surrounded the scaffold, wailing and weeping, while the grisly undertaker ascended the platform, and with his long finger nails thoroughly cleaned the bones of the putrified flesh. The bones were then passed down to the waiting relatives, the skull was painted with vermilion, and they were carefully placed in a coffin curiously constructed of such materials as bark and cane. The flesh was left on the platform, which was set on fire; or it was carried away and buried.

The hamper of bones was borne with much ceremonial wailing to the village bone house, a rude structure built on poles and surrounded by a palisade. There it was placed in a row with other coffins, and the mourners returned to the house, where all participated in a feast over which the bone-picker presided (without having washed his hands, as shocked white observers were wont to state).

Apparently it was the custom at stated intervals once or twice a year, to hold a mourning ceremony at which the entire settlement participated. The hampers of bones were all removed at this time, but they were returned at the close of the ceremony. When the charnel house became full, the bones were buried; sometimes the earth was placed over it to form a mound, and sometimes the bones of several villages were carried out and placed in one heap and covered with soil.[11] This custom accounts for the burial mound at Nanih Waya, and for the many smaller mounds that form such a distinctive feature of the old Choctaw country.

Aside from their elaborate mourning rites, the Choctaws apparently were inferior to the neighboring tribes in the development of native ceremonials. Their religious conceptions also were rudimentary. They believed vaguely in the existence of a great number of supernatural beings, both beneficent and harmful; but they do not seem to have propitiated them by complicated ceremonies. Their belief in a Great Spirit was almost certainly borrowed from the white people, but a certain recognition of the Sun — with his companion, the Fire — as a universal deity seems to have been a native conception. Prayer to this deity, however, appears to have been of only minor and incidental importance in the tribal songs and dances.[12]

The Choctaw depended largely upon magic, which seems to have had little reference to any supernatural beings. Every warrior carried a "medicine" bag, which he had prepared after a long period of seclusion spent in fasting and meditation. It was filled with such articles as earth of various colors, ashes of weeds, and bones of birds, all cooked together over a fire and placed in the little bag with much care and ceremony. If the contents became known to anybody except the wearer, it lost its potency, and another had to be prepared. The tribe also had its sacred "medicine"; this was kept in the custody of the Chief, who carried it in time of war, and in time of peace guarded it from profanation. If it

[11]The unusual features of the Choctaw burial customs have attracted the notice of many white observers. These accounts have been collected in Swanton, *Choctaw Social and Ceremonial Life*, pp. 12-20, 170-88. Other sources are Cushman, *History of the Choctaw*, pp. 203-4, 225-28, 363-64, 367, 389; Folsom, *Vindicator*, November 24, December 1, 1875; James Adair, *The History of the American Indians* (Johnson City, Tennessee, 1930), pp. 192-93; Nuttall, *Travels into Arkansas Territory*, Thwaites, XIII, 304; Jedidiah Morse, *Report to the Secretary of War of the United States on Indian Affairs* (New Haven, 1822), p. 183; John R. Swanton, "An Early Account of the Choctaw Indians," *Memoirs of the American Anthropological Association*, V (1918), No. 2, pp. 64-65.

[12]Swanton, *Choctaw Social and Ceremonial Life*, pp. 149, 194-99; Adair, *History of the American Indians*, p. 24n; Cushman, *History of the Choctaw*, pp. 176, 362-63; Morse, *Report to the Secretary of War*, p. 183; John R. Swanton, "An Early Account of the Choctaw Indians," p. 61; Adam Hodgson, *Letters from North America* (London, 1824), I, 246.

was captured by an enemy, the most strenuous efforts were made to recover it.[13]

Certain men and women among the Choctaws were supposed to possess occult powers for both good and evil. The Choctaw *alikchi*, or "doctor," combined unscrupulous cunning in the use of magic with a real knowledge of the properties of certain herbs; his "remedies" consisted of incantations, singing, pretending to suck balls of skin or other foreign substances from the affected part, bleeding through a hollow horn, administering emetics and cathartics, and sweating. As he was liable to punishment for failure, he usually found it safer to discover evidence of witchcraft, which made death inevitable. If necessary he took measures to insure the fatal outcome which he had predicted, and the enraged relatives thereupon killed some unpopular old woman whom he had identified as the culprit.[14] Under these circumstances witches and wizards naturally were very numerous in the Choctaw country; they were believed to project their intestines from their bodies and hang them over the branches of trees while practicing their unhallowed rites.[15] They were sometimes employed by the Choctaws to use their occult power to injure enemies, but they were usually held in disfavor. Still another class of men supposed to have supernatural powers were the rainmakers or fair weather makers, who managed to maintain their ascendency by shrewd understanding of psychology and an accurate knowledge of weather signs.[16]

Although religious white people interpreted these magical practices in the light of belief in a Christian God or devil, there is no reason to believe that the Choctaws connected them with the worship of any supernatural being. The same may be said of their numerous feasts and dances, which seemed to be more recreational than ceremonial and religious.

Among the most important of these dances were the green corn dance, the dances in honor of various animals and birds, the dance of the young people, the war dance, and the scalp dance. Every village

[13]Swanton, *Choctaw Social and Ceremonial Life*, pp. 11, 165; Cushman, *History of the Choctaw*, pp. 158-59.
[14]Swanton, *Choctaw Social and Ceremonial Life*, pp. 226-39; Swanton, "An Early Account of the Choctaw Indians," p. 64; Cushman, *History of the Choctaw*, pp. 60, 230-31, 258, 367-68; Folsom, *Vindicator*, December 8, 1875; Hodgson, *Letters from North America*, pp. 214-15; Bushnell, *The Choctaw of Bayou Lacomb*, p. 23.
[15]*Niles' Weekly Register* XXXVII (1829), 181, copied from *Alexandria Gazette*.
[16]Swanton, *Choctaw Social and Ceremonial Life*, pp. 196, 240-41; Cushman, *History of the Choctaw*, pp. 260-61.

of any size was built around an open space, which was used for dances, councils, and other community gatherings. Elaborate preparations were made for the feasts, at which the hunters furnished the meat and the women prepared the corn and other vegetable foods. For the musical accompaniment of their dances they used a drum made of a hollowed log with skin drawn tightly across the ends. The Choctaws enjoyed camping, and they assembled frequently for games, dancing, feasting, and social intercourse.[17]

Of all their community activities they entered most heartily into their native ball game, or *ishtaboli*. The ball was made of deer skin, and was handled by means of two *kapucha*, or hickory sticks about three feet long, with one end trimmed flat and bent back into an oblong loop across which a web of raccoon skin thongs was laced to form a sort of cup. Two goals were erected at a distance of about two hundred or three hundred yards from each other; each consisted of two halves of a split log planted in the ground about six feet apart with the split side toward the playing field, and held in position by a transverse pole. The players scored by scooping up the ball with the *kapucha* and tossing it against their own goal post; and the score required to win was sometimes fixed as high as one hundred points. Games were matched against neighboring settlements or even neighboring tribes, or two men were selected as champions with the privilege of choosing the players alternately through the whole tribe. Almost any number of players could participate, and almost any means of stopping an opponent was legitimate.

The match was planned a long time in advance, and runners were sent over the country with bundles of sticks to assist in calculating the date; one stick was discarded from the bundle each day, and when only one remained, the eve of the contest had arrived. People assembled at the appointed place from all directions, and much excited betting took place, especially among the women.

The night before the contest was spent in the wild and picturesque ball play dance, with the players dancing, singing, and rattling their sticks around their respective goals, while the women who had participated in the betting formed two lines between them and danced encouragement to their men. The old men who were to act as referees took their places in the center of the field; all night they sat impassively

[17]Swanton, *Choctaw Social and Ceremonial Life*, pp. 21, 161, 221-26; Catlin, *North American Indians*, II, 144-45; Swanton, "An Early Account of the Choctaw Indians," pp. 58, 68-69; Folsom, *Vindicator*, December 8, 1875.

smoking, strongly impressed with the importance of their responsibility. The stake-holders sat to one side and guarded the articles that had been put up as wagers, which usually consisted of all the movable possessions of both parties. During the whole night the medicine men of the opposing sides pitted their magic charms against each other, striving to bring the unseen forces to the assistance of their party.

The players were gorgeously painted and entirely naked except for a belt and breech-clout and a fantastic tail and mane. When it was time for the game to begin, they took their places, and one of the judges tossed up the ball in the center of the field. White observers were invariably impressed with the savage beauty of the spectacle, in which the players ran together, literally leaped over each other's heads, and tripped and dodged and foiled their opponents in every possible combination of agility and grace. When a point was made, the successful players taunted their rivals by gobbling like a wild turkey, a sound which is even yet a characteristic Choctaw call of defiance. The medicine men worked as hard as the players, frantically invoking the powers of magic by their occult signs and formulas.

Serious injuries, even resulting in the death of the contestants, were not uncommon, and the wagers often involved all the earthly possessions of the defeated party; but although poor sportsmanship was not unknown, it was very unusual. The losses were accepted with an absence of the vindictive feeling which the Choctaws were wont to show on other and less important occasions.

The women of the opposing sides often engaged in a game after the men had finished. These games were as hotly contested as those of the men, and the women played with great agility and skill.[18]

A Choctaw game similar to *ishtaboli* was played with a larger ball, which was caught or carried with the hand. Men and women played promiscuously in this game.[19] There was also *ulth chuppih*, or *alhchah-pi*, in which a rounded stone about six inches in diameter was rolled down a smooth clay alley. The players were provided with poles, which they hurled after the moving stone. The object was to strike the

[18]Swanton, *Choctaw Social and Ceremonial Life*, pp. 140-51; Swanton, "An Early Account of the Choctaw Indians," p. 68; Cushman, *History of the Choctaw*, pp. 184-93; Hodgson, *Letters from North America*, pp. 217-22; Catlin, *North American Indians*, II, 140-44; Stewart Culin, "Games of the North American Indians," *Twenty-fourth Annual Report Bureau of American Ethnology* (Washington, 1907), pp. 598-99; William H. Goode, *Outposts of Zion* (Cincinnati, 1864), p. 164; Baldwin Möllhausen, *Diary of a Journey from the Mississippi to the Coasts of the Pacific* (London, 1858), I, 47.

[19]Swanton, *Choctaw Social and Ceremonial Life*, pp. 141, 148-49, 151-52.

rolling stone of the opponent, who for his part sought to protect his stone by striking the flying pole of his adversary.[20] Minor games were: the *naki lohmi*, where a small object was hidden under one of several articles of clothing and the opponent was supposed to guess its location;[21] the *baskatanje*, where kernels of white corn charred black on one side were thrown as dice;[22] and a game played by the women, in which they tossed up a small ball and tried to pick up a stick or other object from the ground before it struck the earth, very much as modern children play jackstones.[23]

Although the most important of these games were common to all Southeastern Indians, it appears from the impression they made on white travelers that the Choctaws entered into them with more abandon than the other tribes. It seems that the Choctaws, who were noticeably deficient in religious conceptions and ceremonials, were the most active of all the tribes in recreational and social activities. This same interest in the practical and immediate rather than the mystical probably accounts for their advanced economic condition, in which they surpassed all their neighbors at the time of the first coming of the white man.[24]

They were primarily an agricultural people, raising corn, beans, pumpkins, and melons in the little plots by their cabins. Their method of cultivation was similar to that practiced all through the Southeast. They cleared their fields by burning the underbrush and girdling the larger trees. Their agricultural implements consisted of crude hoes made of a bent stick, the shoulder blade of a bison, or a piece of flint. Although they owned less land than any of the surrounding tribes, they raised more corn and beans than they needed for their own use and sold the surplus to their neighbors.[25]

So important was corn in their economic life that they invented legends to account for its origin. According to one story it came as the gift of a beautiful woman to a couple of Choctaw hunters who shared their last meal with her. According to another story a child was playing in

[20]*Ibid.*, pp. 156-58; Cushman, *History of the Choctaw*, p. 190; Culin, "Games of the North American Indians," pp. 485, 598.

[21]Swanton, *Choctaw Social and Ceremonial Life*, p. 158; Bushnell, *The Choctaw of Bayou Lacomb*, p. 19.

[22]Swanton, *Choctaw Social and Ceremonial Life*, p. 159; Culin, "Games of the North American Indians," p. 146; Bushnell, *The Choctaw of Bayou Lacomb*, p. 19. Some of these grains may be seen in the museum of the Oklahoma State Historical Society.

[23]Swanton, *Choctaw Social and Ceremonial Life*, p. 159.

[24]*Ibid.*, pp. 1-2.

[25]*Ibid.*, pp. 46-47; John R. Swanton, "Aboriginal Culture of the Southeast," *Forty-second Annual Report Bureau of American Ethnology* (Washington, 1928), p. 691.

the yard when a crow flew over and dropped a single grain; the child planted it and in this way became the discoverer of their most important article of food.[26]

Each family's supply of corn was stored in a rude crib raised on poles about eight feet from the ground. Fruits, nuts, seeds, and roots that grew in the woods were also gathered, and stored in the houses. They ground their corn into meal with a wooden pestle, in a mortar which they made by burning a hollow in the side of a fallen tree.[27]

Although hunting, with the primitive Choctaws, was an occupation secondary in importance to agriculture, it was an important source of their food supply. In his knowledge of woodcraft, and his skill in stalking and killing game, the Choctaw hunter showed characteristic Indian strategy. The bison had disappeared at an early period, and the deer was the main source of meat and clothing. The bear was prized for his fat, which was rendered and stored in deerskins. Turkeys, pigeons, squirrels, beaver, otter, raccoon, opossum, and rabbits also abounded in the Choctaw country. The men, of course, used the bow and arrow; but the little boys became adept at killing birds and small animals with a blowgun made of cane and loaded with little arrows.[28]

Fishing was also an important occupation. The Choctaws did not use fishhooks until the coming of the white man, but they killed fish to some extent with spears and arrows. The favorite method was dragging the pools with a net made of brush fastened together with creepers, or poisoning them with winter-berries, buckeye, or devil's shoestring. The Choctaws never wasted either fish or game; any surplus over the needs of one band was invariably divided with others.[29]

The Choctaws' weapons were made of stone, as were also the axes and knives. Dishes and spoons were made of wood, bison horn, or shells. They also made pottery, which seems to have been of a rather inferior sort.[30] From the canes which grew abundantly in their country they

[26]Swanton, *Choctaw Social and Ceremonial Life*, pp. 208-10; Cushman, *History of the Choctaw*, pp. 276-78.

[27]Swanton, *Choctaw Social and Ceremonial Life*, pp. 38-39, 48; Swanton, "Aboriginal Culture of the Southeast," pp. 689, 691-92; Swanton, "An Early Account of the Choctaw Indians," p. 57.

[28]Swanton, *Choctaw Social and Ceremonial Life*, pp. 49-52, 54; Swanton, "Aboriginal Culture of the Southeast," pp. 692-93; Cushman, *History of the Choctaw*, pp. 180-81, 234.

[29]Swanton, *Choctaw Social and Ceremonial Life*, p. 54; Swanton, "Aboriginal Culture of the Southeast," p. 694.

[30]In the museum of the Oklahoma State Historical Society are specimens of Choctaw pottery which were brought from Mississippi during the removal period, 1831-33. They are of ungraceful shape and only slightly decorated.

wove baskets of various shapes and sizes according to the use for which they were destined, and dyed them yellow, brown, and purple with native dyes. The canes were also woven into the sieves which they used for sifting their meal. For crossing the rivers they made rafts of logs fastened together with vines.[31]

A French writer of the eighteenth century has given the most complete description in existence of the Choctaw domestic economy. He says in part:

"*The house is merely a cabin made of wooden posts of the size of the leg, buried in the earth [at one end], and fastened together with* lianas, *which make very flexible bands. The rest of the wall is of mud and there are no windows; the door is only from three to four feet in height. The cabins are covered with bark of the cypress or pine. A hole is left at the top of each gable-end to let the smoke out, for they make their fires in the middle of the cabins, which are a gunshot distant from one another. The inside is surrounded with cane beds raised from three to four feet from the ground on account of the fleas which exist there in quantities, because of the dirt.....These beds serve them as table and chair. They have by way of furniture only an earthen pot in which to cook their food, some earthen pans for the same purpose, and some fanners or sieves and hampers for the preparation of their corn, which is their regular nourishment. They pound it in a wooden crusher or mortar, which they make out of the trunk of a tree, hollowed by means of burning embers.....After it is thus crushed they sift it in order to separate the finer part. They boil the coarser in a great skin which holds about three or four buckets of water, and mix it sometimes with pumpkins, or beans, or bean leaves. When this stew is almost done they throw into it the finest of the corn which they had reserved for thickening, and by way of seasoning they have a pot hung aloft in which are the ashes of corn silk, beanpods, or finally oak ashes, and having thrown water upon this they take the lye collected in a vessel underneath, and with it season their stew, which is called* sagamité. *This serves as their principal food,....*

"*They sometimes make bread without lye, but rarely, because that consumes too much corn, and it is difficult to make, since they reduce it to flour only with the strength of their arms; after which it is kneaded, or they boil it in water, or wrap it in leaves and cook it in the ashes, or finally, having flattened the paste to the thickness of two crowns*

[31]Swanton, *Choctaw Social and Ceremonial* Life, pp. 40-41; Swanton, "Aboriginal Culture of the Southeast," p. 689; Folsom, *Vindicator*, December 22, 1875.

(*ecus*), *and the diameter of the two hands, they cook it on a piece of a pot on the embers. They also eat it with acorns. Having reduced the acorns to flour they put them in a cane sieve placed near the bank of a stream, and from time to time throw water upon them. By means of this lye they cause it to lose its bitterness, after which they put the paste around a piece of wood which they cook in the fire. When they have meat they boil it in water, without washing it, however dirty it is, saying that [washing] would make it lose its flavor. When it is cooked they sometimes put some of the acorn flour into the broth. They also cook unpounded corn with their meat, and when it is dry they reduce it to bits by pounding. This they boil along with the corn. It has no taste and one must be a savage to eat it.*

"While the corn is green is the time when they hold the most feasts and they prepare it in different ways. First they roast it in the fire and eat it so; .... When it is very tender they pound it and make porridge of it, but the [dish] most esteemed among them is the cold meal. It is corn, considerably mature, which they boil, then roast in order to dry it, and then pound; and this flour has the same effect in cold water as wheat flour put into hot water over the fire and has a fairly agreeable taste; .... They also have a species of corn which is smaller than the other and comes to maturity in three months. That they dry and then without pounding it boil it with meat. This 'little corn,' boiled with a turkey or some pieces of fat meat, is a favorite dish with them."[32]

The Choctaw dress was not materially different from that of other Southeastern tribes of Indians. The men always wore a belt and breech-clout, usually of deerskin. In addition they usually wore an upper garment of skin, or of feathers woven into a network of cords. In winter they wore skin leggings with the lower ends tucked into the moccasins and the upper ends coming high enough to be fastened with thongs to the belt; these were held in under the knee with ornamented garters. They wore moccasins when traveling, but often went barefoot at home. The invariable female garment was a short skirt, usually made of deer-skin. In winter the upper part of the body was protected by a shawl of skin, or woven feathers, or the inner bark of the mulberry tree, fastened

[32]Swanton, "An Early Account of the Choctaw Indians," pp. 57-58; Swanton, *Choctaw Social and Ceremonial Life*, pp. 37-38. *See* also John Edwards, "The Choctaw Indians in the Middle of the Nineteenth Century," *Chronicles of Oklahoma*, X(1932), 404-8.

over the left shoulder leaving the right breast exposed. The women wore moccasins similar to those of the men.[33]

For ornaments they wore wooden beads as large as acorns, or dyed chinquapin nuts strung together, or even winter berries and the seeds of the red haw. Bones, shell gorgets, and colored stones were also worn. The ears and nose were often pierced for the display of pendants. Feathers were worn in the hair, the kind depending upon the rank or condition or accomplishments of the wearer.[34]

Although like most Indians the Choctaw men removed their scanty beards, both sexes allowed their hair to grow long. For this reason they were distinguished from the other Southeastern tribes by the name of *Pa"s falaya,* or "Long Hairs."[35] Another distinctive Choctaw custom, shared only by the minor tribes of their vicinity, was the practice of flattening the head. The newborn infant was encased in a wooden cradle with his head tilted back and immovably fixed so that the weight rested upon the crown; a bag of sand was then placed on the forehead. The result, as one traveler described it, was a "head somewhat the form of a brick," with a high and lofty forehead "sloping off backwards."[36] They also practiced tattooing, and apparently each clan had its distinctive quarterings, which decorated the bodies of the warriors and the handles of the war clubs, and were sketched along the trail to signify what party had passed over it.[37]

Although animals and plants were used for these pictorial representations, they seem to have had no totemic significance. They were, however, the symbols of a complex system of moiety, clan, and local divisions that played an important part in the social organization.

[33]Swanton, "Aboriginal Culture of the Southeast," pp. 681-83; Thwaites, *Early Western Travels* (an account by an anonymous writer who visited New Orleans in 1799, in Fortescue Cuming, *Sketches of a Tour to the Western Country*), IV, 365-66.

[34]Swanton, *Choctaw Social and Ceremonial Life,* pp. 44, 102; Swanton, "Aboriginal Culture of the Southeast," p. 685. Numerous Choctaw ornaments are in the collection of the Oklahoma State Historical Society.

[35]Swanton, *Choctaw Social and Ceremonial Life,* p. 57; Swanton, "Aboriginal Culture of the Southeast," pp. 683, 716.

[36]Swanton, *Choctaw Social and Ceremonial Life,* pp. 116, 118-19; Henry R. Schoolcraft, *Information Respecting the History, Condition and Prospects of the Indian Tribes of the United States* (Philadelphia, 1852), II, 324; Adair, *History of the American Indians,* p. 305; Catlin, *North American Indians,* II, 127; Möllhausen, *Journey from the Mississippi to the Pacific,* I, 35.

[37]Swanton, *Choctaw Social and Ceremonial Life,* pp. 57, 163, 181; Swanton, "An Early Account of the Choctaw Indians," p. 66; James H. Malone, *The Chickasaw Nation* (Louisville, Kentucky, 1922), opposite p. 16; Garrick Mallery, "Picture Writing by the American Indians," *Tenth Annual Report Bureau of American Ethnology* (Washington, 1893), p. 347.

The entire tribe was divided into two great moieties, the *I^nhulata*, and the *Imoklasha* or *Kashapa okla*. Although the members of these divisions lived together promiscuously throughout the tribe, every Choctaw knew his own classification. Marriage within the moiety was strictly prohibited, and as descent was from the female line, it necessarily followed that every family was divided, the mother and children and the father belonging to opposite groups. When the men were assembled in council, they were seated according to their respective moieties, and when a crime had been committed serious enough to be brought to the attention of the public the accused was defended by his own division and prosecuted by the opposite one. The separation was strictly observed in the funeral ceremonies: at the periodical mourning periods the two divisions wailed and feasted on alternate days; the burial offices were performed by one group for the members of the other; and at the mourning feasts the two divisions ate separately. On all such ceremonial occasions the man of a family would, of course, be seated at one fire, while his wife and children took their places at the other.[38]

The moieties were further subdivided into six or eight clans, which were of fundamental significance in the social organization, but which present a hopeless confusion to the modern investigator. There were also local groups, which appear sometimes to have embraced several towns, at other times to have corresponded with the town organization, and more often to have divided the village into several bands. As the Choctaw used the word *iksa* to designate not only moieties, clans, and local groups, but at a later period even the various Christian sects, it seems impossible to reconstruct in a systematic manner these ancient divisions.[39] At the same time there is reason to believe that they persisted long after the Choctaws had adopted civilized customs, and that they were often the source of the obscure feuds and group loyalties so baffling to the student of Choctaw history.

Choctaw family life was subordinated to the iksa. The father had no authority over his own children, who were under the control of their oldest maternal uncle; hereditary chieftainships passed from uncle to nephew rather than from father to son; and when a man died, his property was claimed by his brothers or other members of his iksa to the exclusion of his own children.

[38]Swanton, *Choctaw Social and Ceremonial Life*, pp. 76-78, 176, 179, 192, 193; Cushman, *History of the Choctaw*, pp. 367, 389.
[39]Swanton, *Choctaw Social and Ceremonial Life*, pp. 79-84; Folsom, *Vindicator*, December 1, 1875.

Choctaw courtship was brief, but the wedding was accompanied by the inevitable feasting and dancing. After some preliminary advances to the maiden to determine the state of her feelings, the young Choctaw purchased the bride from her family. Although some writers speak of presents to the parents, it is probable that the young man's mother conducted the negotiations, and that consent to the marriage was obtained from the girl's maternal uncle. Both the young people seem to have been allowed the utmost freedom of choice so long as they observed the moiety taboo.[40]

The relatives and friends of both parties assembled for the wedding. A characteristic feature of the ceremony was the flight of the bride and the pursuit and capture by the groom or his female relatives. This custom offered the girl a second chance to refuse her consent, for if she had changed her mind since the presents were given to her family the pretended flight became a real one. Such instances, however, seldom occurred. After the capture, the girl was seated on the ground, while presents were showered upon her head by the man's friends and relatives, and immediately snatched off and distributed among the women of the opposite party, often to the damage of the girl's hair and clothing. The ceremony was ended by a feast and dance, after which the groom conducted the bride to the home he had prepared, unless the youth of the couple made it expedient that they should live for a time in one of the parental homes.[41]

A curious feature of the family life was the taboo that forbade the mother-in-law to look upon her daughter's husband. This custom was very inconvenient during the frequent periods of traveling or camping in the open, for the women were obliged to keep their eyes cast down or closed for fear they would fall upon the interdicted object.[42]

Polygamy was tolerated, but was not universal; and the plural wives were usually sisters or at least close relatives. Separation was not disapproved, but it seems to have occurred but seldom. When the home was broken up by separation or death, the children belonged to the family of their mother. Adoption of children was common, and was

[40]Greenwood LeFlore testified in 1843 that a woman could be given in marriage or even taken from her husband by her oldest maternal uncle without her consent—Grant Foreman, *Advancing the Frontier* (Norman, Oklahoma, 1933), p. 307. It seems to have been customary, however, for the uncle to act in accordance with the woman's wishes.

[41]Swanton, *Choctaw Social and Ceremonial Life*, pp. 127-28; Swanton, "An Early Account of the Choctaw Indians," p. 60; Cushman, *History of the Choctaw*, pp. 369-70.

[42]Swanton, *Choctaw Social and Ceremonial Life*, pp. 127, 129; Cushman, *History of the Choctaw*, pp. 201-2; Josiah Gregg, *Commerce of the Prairies*, Thwaites, XX, 314.

indicated by the simple process of allowing the adopted child to eat from the family bowl.[43]

The children grew up in almost unrestrained freedom. Such slight control as was imposed upon them was vested in the mother in the case of the girls, while the maternal uncle had authority over the boys. Neither boys nor girls were allowed to carry burdens, but they were encouraged to exercise freely to make them active. The boys roamed through the woods from village to village, shooting at birds and small animals with their blow guns, or, with the innate cruelty of little savages, tormenting dogs and other animals that fell into their hands. They began at an early age to play at the two games of ball, and to engage in violent feats of wrestling and running. They also practiced the use of the bow and arrow, and their skill was noticed and praised by the older men. Even the little boys took delight in proving their hardihood by self-inflicted pain, and when a youth was recognized as a warrior he was required to submit to a severe beating without flinching or showing any sign of suffering.[44]

Choctaw children were usually named after animals, or for some incident connected with their birth. Later in life they received new names as a recognition of some special achievement, or from some incident or adventure, or as an indication of some personal characteristic. Speeches and ceremonials usually accompanied the bestowal of this second title. The word *humma* or *homma,* meaning "red," was often added to a man's name as a mark of distinction, and a great proportion of the war names carried the termination *àbi,* signifying "killer," which was corrupted by the whites into the "tubbee" so frequently found in later native Choctaw names.[45]

The Choctaw was extremely reluctant to pronounce his own name. The wife was also forbidden to speak the name of her husband; when it was necessary for her to distinguish him, she referred to him by the name of her child, as "Ok-le-wo-na's father." An even stricter taboo

[43]Swanton, *Choctaw Social and Ceremonial Life,* pp. 127, 131; Swanton, "An Early Account of the Choctaw Indians," p. 61; Henry C. Benson, *Life among the Choctaw Indians* (Cincinnati, 1860), pp. 31-32; Morse, *Report to the Secretary of War,* p. 183; Foreman, *Advancing the Frontier,* pp. 306-7.

[44]Swanton, *Choctaw Social and Ceremonial Life,* pp. 124-27, 162-63 ; Swanton, "An Early Account of the Choctaw Indians," pp. 61, 66; Folsom, *Vindicator,* December 22, 1875; Cushman, *History of the Choctaw,* pp. 213-16, 218-19.

[45]Swanton, *Choctaw Social and Ceremonial Life,* pp. 119-24; Cushman, *History of the Choctaw,* pp. 202, 236-37; Cyrus Byington, *A Dictionary of the Choctaw Language* (Editors, John R. Swanton and H. S. Halbert), Bureau of American Ethnology, *Bulletin No. 46* (Washington, 1915); Benson, *Life among the Choctaw Indians,* p. 53.

forbade them to name their dead. United States Commissioner Claiborne found in allotting land, that the only way in which the parents could be induced to present claims for their deceased children was by asking them to arrange their families in a line according to ages; they invariably left a vacancy where the deceased would have stood.[46]

Although the Choctaws held no strict notions of sexual morality, it would appear from the testimony of those who lived among them in later years that they were a relatively chaste people whose family life was pure. In cases of adultery the woman was subject to punishment by her husband. If her family chanced to be stronger or more numerous than his own, she usually escaped; otherwise she was cast off by her husband and exposed at a public place in the town as the victim of all the men who chose to be present. To a shocked French visitor the Choctaws explained that "the only way to disgust lewd women is to give them at once what they so constantly and eagerly pursue."[47]

It is evident from all accounts of Choctaw society that the women occupied an honored and important position within the tribe. Sensitive white observers sometimes spoke of the unequal division of labor between the sexes, where the women performed all the drudgery and the men occupied themselves in such pleasurable occupations as hunting and fishing; but such a generalization fails to take into account the importance and difficulty of the chase. The women performed a large part of the labor of the fields, made the clothing, prepared and stored the food, and carried the burdens; the men provided the game, built the houses, manufactured the wooden and stone implements, carried on the governmental activities, and protected the tribe in war.[48]

As might have been expected from their interest in agriculture and their devotion to practical concerns, the Choctaws were an unwarlike people. They rarely made hostile excursions into the territory of their neighbors, but when their own country was invaded they defended their homes with great courage. The women sometimes accompanied their husbands to battle, standing beside them, handing them arrows, and exhorting them to fight bravely. Like other Indians the Choctaws depended more upon cunning than open combat, and they exercised a

[46]Swanton, *Choctaw Social and Ceremonial Life*, pp. 120-21, 178, 180, 182, 187; Cushman, *Life among the Choctaw*, pp. 228, 246; Gregg, *Commerce of the Prairies*, Thwaites, XX, 314.

[47]Swanton, *Choctaw Social and Ceremonial Life*, pp. 110-11; Swanton, "An Early Account of the Choctaw Indians," p. 61.

[48]Swanton, *Choctaw Social and Ceremonial Life*, p. 139; Folsom, *Vindicator*, December 22, 1875.

18

patience and skill in surprising their enemy that to white men seemed almost supernatural. Their military expeditions were always preceded by much dancing and "medicine," and the return of a successful party with scalps was the occasion of village hilarity. They practiced less cruelty to captives than most Indian tribes; they adopted the women and children, and burned the warriors or dispatched them quickly with a blow of the hatchet.[49]

The peace making ritual is described by an early French writer as follows:

"When they have promised to conclude a peace five or six leading men of the nation come, bearing a calumet or pipe made of a stone, red like coral, which is found in rocks in the Illinois country. This calumet has a stem about two or three feet in length surrounded by red feathers artistically worked, and from which hangs eight or ten black feathers. This serves them as a war standard, as a seal in alliances, as a mark of the continuation of faithfulness among friends, and as a sign of war with those with whom they wish to break. It is true that there is one which is the calumet of peace and another that of war. They are both made similarly. When they have concluded the peace the master of ceremonies lights this calumet and has all those who are in the assembly smoke two or three whiffs. Then the treaty is concluded and inviolable. They deliver this calumet to the chief with whom they make this contract which is as a hostage of their good faith and the fidelity with which they wish to observe the articles on which they have agreed."[50]

A red calumet was also presented to a tribe to invite them to form an alliance against a common enemy, and its acceptance was equivalent to a promise of assistance.[51]

The Choctaw towns on the Chickasaw and Creek frontiers were compactly built and strongly fortified;[52] but in other parts of the country the cabins and fields of a village were scattered over an area of several miles, so that "A stranger might be in the middle of one of their

[49]Swanton, *Choctaw Social and Ceremonial Life*, pp. 5, 162-69; Cushman, *History of the Choctaw*, pp. 253-54; Swanton, "An Early Account of the Choctaw Indians," pp. 65-67; Edward Gaylord Bourne, *Narratives of the Career of Hernando de Soto* (New York, 1922), I (Diary of Rodrigo Ranjal), 96-97, II (Fidalgo of Elvas), 126-27,

[50]Swanton, *Choctaw Social and Ceremonial Life*, pp. 169-70; Swanton, "An Early Account of the Choctaw Indians," p. 67.

[51]Swanton, *Choctaw Social and Ceremonial Life*, p. 167.

[52]*Ibid.*, p. 76; Bourne, *Narratives of De Soto*, I, 90, 98; II, 115.

populous extensive towns, without seeing half a dozen of their houses, in the direct course of his path."[53]

Ethnologists believe that in early times the towns were grouped together to form four geographical divisions: the Sixtown Indians, *Okla Hannali,* and their neighbors in the south, who spoke a distinctive dialect, tattooed blue marks around their mouths, and were shorter and heavier in build than the other Choctaws: the Big People, *Okla Chito,* a small group in the center, who in the early eighteenth century furnished the principal officials of the Nation; the Long People, *Okla Falaya,* in the west, whose dialect was destined to become the standard Choctaw language; and the People of the Opposite Side, *Okla tànnàp,* on the east, sometimes known as *Ahepat okla* or *Haiyip atokolo.*[54] But when Europeans first began to know the Choctaws intimately, the central division, if it had ever existed, had disappeared, and three districts with definitely recognized boundaries became the most fundamental part of their constitutional structure.

French writers of the eighteenth century speak of a Head Chief over the entire Nation, whose power depended more upon personal influence than prerogative; and their maps designate the village of the Head Chief as the "Choctaw capital."[55] But in view of the hostility which the Choctaws during the period of their constitutional development showed to the idea of a central executive, one is reluctant to accept this statement; it is probable that white observers, unfamiliar with the district organization, upon coming in contact with a District Chief overestimated the extent of his authority.

Each district had a Chief, whose position depended partly upon personal prowess and partly upon inheritance. In war and other enterprises where the whole Nation was involved, the three acted in concert. There was no capital in the modern sense, since a Chief might be succeeded by one from another village. Each Head Chief had one or more assistants who were regarded as second chiefs.

Each town also had its chief who was somewhat under the authority of the Head Chief. Besides the town chief, each village had, according to one French writer, the following officers: the *Tichou mingo,* who acted as the chief's speaker, and arranged the ceremonies, feasts, and

<hr />

[53]Swanton, *Choctaw Social and Ceremonial Life,* pp. 76, 166. The quotation is from Bernard Romans, *A Concise Natural History of East and West Florida.*

[54]Swanton, *Choctaw Social and Ceremonial Life,* pp. 55-75; Grant Foreman, *Indian Removal* (Norman, Oklahoma, 1932), 84n.

[55]Swanton, *Choctaw Social and Ceremonial Life,* pp. 90-92; Swanton, "An Early Account of the Choctaw Indians," p. 54.

dances; the war chief, who led the men of his village when the Nation went to war; and two *Taskaminkochi,* who were the assistants of the war chief. In later times all the village chiefs were known as captains.[56]

The same French writer divided Choctaw society into the following classes: the Head Chiefs, village chiefs, and war chiefs; the distinguished warriors, or beloved men (*hommes de valleur*); the common warriors; and those who had not yet struck blows, or who had killed only women or children.[57] Though there was no rigid order of nobility, the primacy of a few leading families was such a distinctive feature of later society that it seems almost certain that the leaders of primitive times also came from this class.

Councils of the district were called by its Head Chief, and Councils of the entire Nation by the Head Chiefs acting in concert. Runners carrying bundles of sticks to reckon the time of meeting, were sent to summon all the town chiefs to the assembly. Apparently only these officials were admitted to participate in the Council, but the common people also came to listen to the speeches and to join in the inevitable feasting, games, and dances. The Councils were distinguished by the decorum with which they were conducted, and by the wild eloquence of the native orators. The members were greatly influenced by the judgment of the Head Chiefs and guided by their recommendations, but the decision was democratic and in accord with the wishes of the assembly.[58]

The Council usually dealt with such matters of public policy as peace, war, or foreign relations, but apparently it sometimes exercised a certain judicial power.[59] It was not a legislative body, for the Choctaws like other primitive people thought of law as a universal custom rather than a legislative enactment.

Murder, or even accidental killing, was the one great crime recognized among the Choctaws, and was invariably avenged by the relatives of the victim. The murderer seldom attempted to escape, making it a point of honor to submit to his fate; but if he did exhibit some unmanly

[56]Swanton, *Choctaw Social and Ceremonial Life,* pp. 91, 96; Swanton, "An Early Account of the Choctaw Indians," p. 54.

[57]*Loc. cit.*

[58]Swanton, *Choctaw Social and Ceremonial Life,* pp. 96-102; Folsom, *Vindicator,* December 22, 1875.

[59]Swanton, *Choctaw Social and Ceremonial Life,* p. 95.

reluctance, any member of his family could be accepted as a substitute.[60]

Witchcraft involving the death of the victim was also regarded as murder, although the supernatural fears connected with such unholy powers caused the Choctaws to regard it with particular abhorrence. In this case the medicine man who had attended the patient made the accusation, and the relatives of the deceased lost no time in enforcing the law of retaliation upon the witch.

When a Choctaw became angry at an opponent, he was likely to challenge him to a duel in which it was understood that both should die. When such a challenge had been given, it was impossible to refuse except at the penalty of everlasting degradation and disgrace.

These duels were carried out in various ways. Sometimes the principals shot at each other, and if one survived he was immediately dispatched by the relatives of the dead man. More often the principals stood unarmed facing each other, and both were dispatched by their seconds. It is told of Pushmataha, the great and beloved District Chief of the early nineteenth century, that when a white man once called him a coward he purchased a barrel of gunpowder, carried it to the village, lighted a firebrand, calmly seated himself on top of the barrel, and invited his accuser to join him while he applied the match to the powder. Needless to say, the white man declined the challenge.[61]

These curious duels may be classed as a form of suicide, in which the Choctaw upheld his honor by demonstrating to his opponent that he was not afraid to die. Suicide in the usual sense was also very common, and was brought about by discouragement or humiliation.[62]

The punishment visited upon a woman for unfaithfulness to her husband has already been given. Incest, which included the marriage of close relatives as well as marriage within the iksa, was a major crime, but the punishment is not known. Sodomy seems to have been common, but apparently was not punished; the male prostitutes are said to

---

[60]Ibid., pp. 104-10; Cushman, History of the Choctaw, pp. 263-64; Adair, The History of the American Indians, p. 307; Benson, Life among the Choctaw Indians, p. 30; Niles' Register, XXIV (1823), 248; Gregg, Commerce of the Prairies, Thwaites, XX, 311-12; Nuttall, Travels into the Arkansas Territory, Thwaites, XIII, 305; Bushnell, The Choctaw of Bayou Lacomb, p. 25; Hodgson, Letters from North America, p. 222; Charles Gayarre, Louisiana—its History as a French Colony (New York, 1852), p. 65.

[61]Swanton, Choctaw Social and Ceremonial Life, pp. 108-9; Cushman, History of the Choctaw, pp. 199-201; Niles' Register, XVI (1819), 104.

[62]Swanton, Choctaw Social and Ceremonial Life, pp. 105, 110, 155; Cushman, History of the Choctaw, p. 265; Bourne, Narratives of De Soto, II, 126; Goode, Outposts of Zion, p. 52.

have worn a short skirt like the women, and to have been held in supreme contempt. Stealing, of course, was a virtue when the property of people outside the tribe was involved, but it seems to have been almost unknown within the tribe. Although treachery to a foe was a recognized strategem, the Choctaws seems to have had a contempt for falsehood and a high sense of honor in dealing with their friends.[63]

Physically the Choctaws were a small and active people with graceful hands and feet. The men were handsome and well proportioned, but the women showed a tendency to be stout in later life. In their primitive state, deformity was unknown.[64]

In attempting to evaluate the characteristics of the aboriginal Choctaws it is hard to differentiate between those common to all primitive people and those traits that were distinctive. But compared with other Indians they seem to have been distinguished for their peaceful character and their friendly disposition; their dependence on agriculture and trade; the absence of religious feeling and meaningful ceremonial; and their enjoyment of games and social gatherings. A mild, quiet, and kindly people, their institutions present little of spectacular interest; but to the very extent that they were practical minded and adaptable rather than strong and independent and fierce, they readily adopted the customs of the more advanced and more numerous race with which they came in contact.

[63]Swanton, *Choctaw Social and Ceremonial Life*, pp. 110-15.
[64]Adair, *History of the American Indians*, p. 6; Benson, *Life Among the Choctaw Indians*, pp. 54-55; Hodgson, *Letters from North America*, p. 218.

THE COMING OF THE WHITE MAN

2

FOR the first two and a half centuries of their intercourse with the white man the Choctaws made no radical change in their fundamental social and political institutions. They were quick, however, to grasp the economic importance of trading with the foreigners, and they eagerly acquired the domestic animals and plants and the superior implements and weapons of Western Europe. They also secured a remarkable training in diplomacy from the imperialistic powers that sought to dominate their territory. From 1800 on, they definitely sought to adopt the white man's institutions, and during the next generation they established churches, schools, and a constitutional government. The culmination of this intercourse was their expulsion from their ancient homes in Mississippi and their establishment in a remote region where they hoped to be free from white encroachment.

Their first contact with Europeans is recorded by De Soto's chroniclers, who had ample cause to remember it as the most disastrous encounter of the whole expedition. In the battle that followed, native courage proved to be almost a match for Spanish steel, and De Soto's men barely escaped annihilation.

As the Spaniards, coming from the east, entered the Choctaw country, they were hospitably welcomed by Tuscaloosa, who was evidently a District Chief —"the suzerain of many territories, and of a numerous people." He is described as a tall, fine looking man, who carried himself with the dignity of a European monarch. He was wearing a long mantle of feathers, and an impressive headdress, and was preceded by an attendant who held over his head a sort of parasol of tightly-stretched deerskin.[1]

[1]Bourne, *Narratives of De Soto,* I, 87-88; II, 120-21.

24

De Soto visited his town, also called Tuscaloosa, and demanded carriers and women. Tuscaloosa furnished the carriers, and promised to secure the women at Mabila, near the present site of Mobile. De Soto then ordered canoes; the Indians had none, but they built rafts of cane and dried wood. In the meantime Tuscaloosa sent one of his people on to Mabila ostensibly with orders to collect provisions and assemble carriers for the Spaniards, but actually to summon all the warriors in that vicinity.[2]

With some outward show of courtesy the Spaniards forced Tuscaloosa to accompany them. They dressed him in a scarlet coat, and mounted him on one of their horses — those unknown beasts that inspired the Choctaws with such superstitious awe. For three days they traveled through a rich and populous country with numerous villages palisaded with tall stakes driven into the ground, interlaced with long withes, and plastered with clay. Messengers from Mabila met them with an abundance of bread made from chestnuts, and the soldiers foraged freely in the several villages as they passed.[3]

They reached Mabila, October 18, 1540. As they approached, a Spanish scout reported to De Soto that the Indians appeared to be making preparations for defense; many warriors had assembled in the town, weapons had been collected, and work had been done to strengthen the palisades. The Spaniards had scattered somewhat to plunder the neighboring villages, but in order that "the Governor might not show weakness" he entered the town in state with Tuscaloosa and a guard of forty soldiers. The Indians immediately started a dance.[4]

Tuscaloosa then requested his release since he had guided the Spaniards to the town, but De Soto delayed giving his answer. The Chief thereupon joined a group of his head men in one of the cabins and refused to come out. The Choctaws then attacked the Spaniards with such desperate courage that they drove them out of the town, and seized the baggage which the carriers had deposited within the walls before the battle began. Believing that the enemy was completely routed, the Indians started in pursuit. Here they were at a disadvantage because their arrows failed to pierce the Spanish armor and because they were thrown into such supernatural terror at the sight of the Spanish horses. The Spaniards wheeled and charged, killing a great many Choctaws with their lances and setting fire to the stockade. Here

[2]Ibid., I, 89-90; II, 121-22.
[3]Ibid., I, 90; II, 115, 122-23.
[4]Ibid., I, 90; II, 115, 123.

all the Choctaws perished, the last survivors hanging themselves with their bowstrings within the burning walls. The Spaniards lost their baggage, consisting of about two hundred pounds of pearls which they had plundered from other tribes, their food and wine and clothing, their sacramental vessels, and part of their arms and ammunition; wisely "they considered the loss less than the injury they might receive of the Indians from within the houses, where they had brought the things together."[5]

The Spaniards estimated that twenty-five hundred to three thousand of the Choctaws had been killed in the battle and fire, figures no doubt grossly exaggerated, but indicating the terror which the native warriors had inspired. Twenty-two of their own men had been killed, and 148 of the survivors had received a total of 688 arrow wounds. De Soto remained in the vicinity until November 14, so that his wounded might recover. Then having burned over much of the country, he seized sufficient corn for his journey and marched to the northwest, crossing the entire Choctaw country, and entering the domains of the Chickasaws.[6] Thus ended the Choctaws' first experience with the ruthless and conquering race that was so profoundly to influence their destiny.

For the next century and a half the Choctaws were undisturbed by white encroachments. De Soto had failed to discover the wealth and glory that he sought, and the few settlements that Spain planted in Florida were too distant and too feeble to be a menace. Before the end of the seventeenth century, articles of English manufacture had penetrated to their country from the Atlantic seaboard, and from 1700 on, the French were close neighbors because of their settlements in the region around the lower Mississippi.[7] It was probably during this period that they began to plant European grains and garden vegetables and to raise horses, cattle, hogs, and barnyard fowls.[8] The single-file trails that had connected their settlements and marked the routes of

[5]*Ibid.,* I, 91-97; II, 124-27.
[6]*Ibid.,* I, 97-98; II, 127-28.
[7]Biloxi, 1699; St. Louis, Mobile Bay, 1702; Mobile, present site, 1710; New Orleans, 1718.
[8]Swanton, *Choctaw Social and Ceremonial Life,* pp. 46-47, 67—an anonymous French writer of 1755, or earlier, said that they raised chickens and hogs for their food and Romans, writing in 1770-71, said that they raised hogs, that they sold leeks, garlic, cabbage, and other garden vegetables to the traders, and that they carried poultry 150 miles to market at Mobile; *ibid.,* p. 175—Milfort, whose book was published in 1802, represents them as killing as many as three horses of the deceased for the mourning ceremonies; Adair, *History of the American Indians,* pp. 340-41—this writer, who visited them in 1746-47, described Choctaw ponies as a distinct breed, and he believed that they were descended from the Spanish horses brought by De Soto.

inter-tribal trade before the coming of the white man, now became the thoroughfares of a more important commerce. Three main trails led from the Chickasaw Nation to Mobile Bay, but the most important highway crossed the Choctaw country from east to west and later became the famous Camino Real of the Spaniards, leading from St. Augustine to Mexico City.[9]

The eighteenth century presents a complicated story of French, English, Spanish, and lastly American intrigue. The Choctaws occupying a strategic position between the rival European settlements, were subject to the persuasive advances of colonial officials, who earnestly entreated them to fight the white man's battles. They were induced to wage several wars in defense of their European allies, and their Nation was divided in even more unfortunate internecine strife between the adherents of rival empires. But it was probably these experiences that gave them the training in diplomacy that was such a conspicuous trait of the civilized Choctaw.

These wars lasted during the entire French occupation of Louisiana. From the very beginning the French governors sought to buy Choctaw favor by presents and distinguished honors to the Chiefs, and rival English and French traders stirred up hostility between them and the neighboring tribes.[10]

The war seems to have started between the French and the Natchez Indians. The Choctaws assisted the French, and the unfortunate Natchez were almost exterminated. The Chickasaws, incited by the English traders, then came to the assistance of the Natchez, and the Choctaws and Chickasaws thus became involved in a long and bloody war against each other. In a battle that took place in 1736, it is said that an English flag floated over the Chickasaw fort, and that Indian allies of the French from the Illinois country and even from Canada came from their northern homes to help the Choctaws.[11]

In the early Forties a peace party developed among the Choctaws. The leader was Chief Shulush Homa, or Red Shoes, whose wife had been seduced by the French, and who was therefore inclined to accept the presents and overtures of the English. In 1744 the Chickasaws and Choctaws almost succeeded in settling their differences, but Vaudreuil,

[9]William Edward Myer, "Indian Trails of the Southeast," *Forty-second Annual Report, Bureau of American Ethnology* (Washington, 1928), pp. 743, 823-24, 828-30, map opposite p. 748.

[10]Gayarre, *Louisiana*, p. 21.

[11]Cushman, *History of the Choctaw*, pp. 74-79; Swanton, "An Early Account of the Choctaw Indians," pp. 55-57; Nuttall, *Travels into the Arkansas Territory*, Thwaites, XIII, 179n, 359-61.

the French governor, managed to defeat the negotiations. It was Vaudreuil's belief that the Chickasaws should be systematically and completely exterminated, leaving a unified Choctaw Nation wholly subservient to French interests; but he was not sufficiently backed up by his home government, which failed to furnish the soldiers needed to annihilate the Chickasaws, or the presents necessary to satisfy the increasing demands of his Choctaw allies.[12]

The effect of Vaudreuil's policy in defeating the peace negotiations was the division of the Choctaw Nation into French and English factions. In 1748 the hostility between these two parties ran so high that a civil war broke out. The tribal divisions played an important part in this alignment, the Okla Falaya siding with the English, the Okla tannàp with the French, and the Okla Hannali being divided between the two parties. The war was waged with more deadly thoroughness than was common in Indian battles, and the losses were heavy on both sides. Finally the Choctaws began to realize that they were annihilating their own Nation for the benefit of European rivals, and attempted to reconcile their differences at a Council. This gathering seems to have been under the influence of the French party, for it was decided to sacrifice Shulush Homa for the sake of harmony, and he was accordingly killed. But the English won back their partisans by means of presents, and under the leadership of Shulush Homa's brother they renewed the war. This party made attacks on French settlements, while their opponents plundered the establishments of English traders. But although the Okla tànnàp division, according to a statement of Governor Vaudreuil, had originally been the weakest, the French party with the assistance of its European ally completely crushed its opponents in September, 1750.[13]

Peace was made by the Grandpré Treaty, which virtually reduced the Choctaw Nation to a French dependency. The death penalty was prescribed for any Choctaw who should kill a Frenchman, and it was further provided that if the family or friends of the culprit should seek to protect him the whole Nation would take up arms against them. The death penalty would be visited upon any Englishman who should enter any Choctaw village and upon any Choctaw who invited him, and retaliation would never be sought for their deaths. The whole Choctaw Nation would continue to make war on the Chickasaws, and

[12]Gayarre, *Louisiana*, pp. 20-22; Adair, *History of the American Indians*, pp. 335-38.

[13]Gayarre, *Louisiana*, pp. 30-49; Cushman, *History of the Choctaw*, p. 86; Adair, *History of the American Indians*, pp. 354-56.

would "never cease to strike at that perfidious race as long as there should be any portion of it remaining." All fortifications would be destroyed in the villages that had supported the English party, and the prisoners and slaves captured by both sides would be restored.[14]

The Chickasaws also made peace overtures at this time, but Vaudreuil temporized and gave them no definite answer. He wrote to his government that the only feasible policy was to postpone all action until the French should be prepared to annihilate them.[15] But the required aid from France was not forthcoming, and in 1752 the baffled Chickasaws, incited by the English, renewed their depredations on the French settlements.[16]

After the Grandpré Treaty Vaudreuil was greatly embarrassed in retaining the favor of his Choctaw dependents. They had become so accustomed to receiving French presents that the distribution at Mobile became a regular event of their calendar. Vaudreuil reported that it was essential to purchase their continued friendship and thus forestall the English who were known to be holding conferences with them. At the same time the Intendent Commissary wrote to the home government that the Choctaws had already become a source of enormous expense through bad administration.[17] In 1753 Vaudreuil was succeeded by Kerleric, who was at first favorably impressed by the Choctaws. He wrote: "It seems to me that they are true to their plighted faith. But we must be the same in our transactions with them. They are men who reflect, and who have more logic and precision in their reasoning than it is commonly thought." But the French Government continued its neglect, and early in 1754 he reported that he had no merchandise to trade with his Choctaw allies and no presents to give them, and the Indians having been disappointed three times were becoming impatient and threatening to call in the English. In December of the same year the Choctaws were invited to Mobile for a great festival and the distribution of presents, and the disillusioned Kerleric wrote to his government, "I am sufficiently acquainted with the Choctaws to know that they are covetous, lying, and treacherous. So that I keep on my guard without showing it."[18]

At the time Kerleric wrote this letter the French and English with their Indian allies had already begun the great war that was to decide

[14]Gayarre, *Louisiana*, pp. 49-50.
[15]*Ibid.*, p. 50.
[16]*Ibid.*, p. 64.
[17]*Ibid.*, pp. 58-59; Swanton, "An Early Account of the Choctaw Indians," pp. 55-57.
[18]Gayarre, *Louisiana*, pp. 69, 74, 77, 89.

the fate of a continent, and the French Government, engaged in a world struggle on land and sea, was too busy to conciliate its Choctaw protectorate. The Choctaws became increasingly insolent in their demands and loud in their threats to join the English,[19] but they seem to have remained at least nominally loyal to French interests until the end of the war. Then in 1763, by the Peace of Paris, which marked the doom of French colonial ambitions, the Choctaws were handed over without their knowledge or consent to become members of the British Empire.

During this period in which the Choctaws were not only the victims but the ready pupils of the white man's diplomacy, they were also invited to adopt the white man's religion. A Roman Catholic mission is known to have been established in the Six Town district in 1726, and another was opened the next year at Yazoo on the Mississippi.[20] For some reason these efforts were without result, as is proved by the entire absence of any Roman Catholic influence or bias when the Protestant missionaries began their work almost a century later. Apparently the Choctaws regarded the white man's religion as a magic medicine, which they distrusted as inferior to their own. An instance is given of a Choctaw who had accepted baptism, to the detriment, as he believed, of his prowess in the chase. He finally went to the Jesuit who had administered the rite, told him his new medicine was worthless, and demanded to be unbaptized. The Jesuit, to escape his resentment, pretended to comply, and the debaptized savage became again a successful hunter.[21]

As soon as the English succeeded the French in their imperial control, they realized that one of their major problems was the conciliation of the proud and warlike tribes who had unwittingly become their subjects. The Creeks with their strong military spirit presented the most serious menace; but the Choctaws were estimated to have a potential strength of six thousand warriors, and they had shown that they could fight desperately when sufficiently aroused. The French had already invited the Creeks and Choctaws to convene at Mobile in November, 1763, to receive their usual gifts; and the British officers decided to continue the custom.[22] It will be remembered also by the historical student

[19]*Ibid.*, p. 89.
[20]Charles O. Paulin, *Atlas of the History of the United States* (Washington, 1922), Plate 37.
[21]Swanton, *Choctaw Social and Ceremonial Life,* p. 239, from the account of Bossu, published in Paris, 1768.
[22]Clarence E. Carter, "The Beginnings of British West Florida," *Mississippi Valley Historical Review,* IV (1917), 335-36.

that Virginia, the two Carolinas, and Georgia at that time claimed the land west of their settlements as far back as the Mississippi. The governors of those colonies accordingly called a council of the Indians that by this claim were under their jurisdiction. This meeting was held at Augusta, Georgia, in 1763, and Chiefs of the Choctaws, Chickasaws, Cherokees, and Creeks were in attendance.[23]

At Mobile, March 26, 1765, the British governor, Johnstone, made a treaty with the Choctaws which defined their eastern boundary and forbade the encroachments of English settlers within their territory.[24] But while the Choctaws were encamped at Mobile, the Creeks fell upon them, murdered ten, and captured several, whom they refused to surrender. A devastating war ensued, which lasted for six years. Johnstone feared the Creeks, and he followed the policy of inciting the Choctaws, Chickasaws, and Cherokees to war against them.[25]

These events show that the Choctaws passively accepted the new relations that had been arranged for them by the diplomats of Europe in the Peace of Paris. The English, however, did not succeed in winning their active friendship, and when the American Revolution broke out, Choctaw scouts served under Washington, Morgan, Wayne, and Sullivan.[26] With the peace that ended that war, the new American Republic succeeded to English interests in the Southwest, and English influence passed forever from the Choctaw country.

During the period of English control, the Choctaws were also brought into close proximity to the Spanish. The historian will remember that the Peace of Paris confirmed the cession of Louisiana to Spain; the Spanish empire thus joined the Choctaw country on the west across the Mississippi, and Spanish officials governed from New Orleans, which was immediately south of the Choctaw lands. Spain does not seem to have made systematic overtures to the Choctaws, however, until England was forced to cede Florida to her in 1783 at the close of the American Revolution, an arrangement that placed the entire southern part of the Choctaw country within the Spanish dominions.

It is apparent that the end of the American Revolution thus marked for the Choctaws the beginning of a new period of intrigue. Spain with

[23]Cushman, *History of the Choctaw*, p. 87.

[24]Carter, "Beginnings of British West Florida," p. 337; Cushman, *History of the Choctaw*, p. 93; Charles C. Royce, "Indian Land Cessions in the United States," *Eighteenth Annual Report Bureau of American Ethnology* (Washington, 1899), p. 559.

[25]Carter, "Beginnings of British West Florida," pp. 337-38; Cushman, *History of the Choctaw*, p. 87.

[26]Cushman, *History of the Choctaw*, p. 299.

her control of Louisiana and the Gulf settlements had succeeded France, and the United States with her settlements along the Atlantic and her claims to the hinterland had succeeded England, as rivals for Choctaw favor.

Spain, fearing the expansion of the new American Republic, planned to build a barrier state in the Southwest by trading alliances with the Choctaws, Chickasaws, and Creeks. In the Summer of 1784 she made treaties at Pensacola in which these tribes acknowledged themselves under her protection and agreed to exclude traders who could not show Spanish licenses.[27] When it is remembered that the greater part of the territory occupied by these tribes lay within the boundary of the United States, the significance of these intrigues becomes apparent.

The Americans on their part, were vigilant in seeking to counteract the effect of Spanish influence. In 1786 at Hopewell, on the Keowee River, in South Carolina, the United States and the Choctaws made the first of the many treaties that were to occupy such a conspicuous place in the relations of the two peoples. It established perpetual peace and friendship, a pledge which was never broken until the Choctaws joined the Confederacy in the Civil War; it gave the United States the right to establish three trading posts within the Choctaw Nation, a provision which was not carried out at that time; it defined, but did not survey, the eastern boundary along the line fixed by the British treaty of 1765; and it provided that a citizen of the United States who should settle within the Choctaw Nation would forfeit the protection of his government and become subject to tribal jurisdiction.[28]

The individual states with Southwestern interests were also active in seeking Choctaw friendship. Joseph Martin, who had been appointed by Georgia as agent to the Chickasaws and Cherokees, wrote to the governor of Virginia, March 25, 1786, that Spanish influence was increasing among the Choctaws. The same year Georgia appointed emissaries to win their favor and to incite them against the Creeks. In 1787 Col. Arthur Campbell, who was Virginia's agent to the Indians, reported favorably to Governor Randolph regarding the request of a Choctaw

[27]Walter H. Mohr, *Federal Indian Relations* (Philadelphia, 1933), pp. 144-46. *See* also Anna Lewis, *Along the Arkansas* (Dallas, 1932), p. 195, where "Gifts to the Choctahs," constitutes an important item of the expense of Spanish administration in 1783.

[28]Royce, "Indian Land Cessions," p. 650; *United States Statutes at Large*, VII, 21; *see* also Charles J. Kappler, *Indian Affairs—Laws and Treaties* (Washington, 1904), II, 11-14.

Chief for the establishment of a trading post on the Tennessee near Muscle Shoals.[29]

The Spanish also increased their efforts to extend their influence with the Indians. They managed to secure a tract of land from the Choctaws and Chickasaws near the mouth of the Yazoo at the site of a former English post. There they built Fort Nogales, and at this place on May 14, 1792, they concluded a treaty of friendship with the Choctaws, Chickasaws, Creeks, and Cherokees.[30] They also induced the Choctaws to cede a tract of land on the Tombigbee in the eastern part of their country. Their consent was difficult to obtain, but the Spaniards gave them two thousand pesos worth of provisions, and pointed out to them the advantage of having a fort as a means of protection against the United States, as well as a meeting place and a place to store their corn. The fort erected at this place was named Fort Confederation to perpetuate the memory of the treaty of friendship signed at Nogales. The Spanish governor, Baron de Carondelet, reported to his superiors that he had established the post "in order to assure myself of that nation [the Choctaws] and of all that most fertile country, which is much envied by the Americans[,] located between the Mississippi, Yazoo, Chickasaw and Mobile Rivers and the sea."[31]

With these accomplishments Governor Carondelet believed that the Spanish ambition of extending a protectorate over the Choctaws was virtually realized. He depended upon the Indians in the vicinity of Nogales to defend that fort against attack. He also recommended the construction of another fort, on the Iberville between Nogales and New Orleans, which would be protected by 150 militiamen and a body of Choctaws. When he issued provisions to the Choctaws at the establishment of Fort Confederation, he reported that "That warlike nation, which has not less than fourteen thousand men will always be well affected toward Spain, which will relieve them in their necessities." He also planned to garrison thirty men at Fort Tombigbee, near a Choc-

[29]Mohr, *Federal Indian Relations,* pp. 153, 156, 189.

[30]James Alexander Robertson, *Louisiana under the Rule of Spain, France, and the United States, 1785-1807* (Cleveland, 1911), I, 279, 281, 305, 339, "Political Condition of the Province of Louisiana," by Col. Don Manuel Gayosa (De Lemos), governor of Louisiana, 1797-99, and "Military Report of Louisiana and West Florida," November 24, 1794, by Governor Baron de Carondelet.

[31]*Ibid.,* I, 332, 339, 340. Spain at this time claimed a line drawn east from the mouth of the Yazoo as the northern boundary of west Florida, which would thus embrace most of this territory.

taw town which furnished Mobile with corn, and which might be useful as a source of supply to Fort Confederation.[32]

The opening years of the nineteenth century, which brought the retrocession of Louisiana to France and its subsequent transfer to the United States, also marked a series of treaties between the Choctaws and the American Government. In 1801 at Fort Adams, on the Mississippi, the eastern boundary fixed by the treaty with Great Britain was reaffirmed; the United States secured the right to construct a road from Natchez northeast across the Choctaw country to Nashville, Tennessee; and the Choctaws surrendered their claim to a triangular tract of land on their southwestern frontier.[33] The next year a treaty made at Fort Confederation provided for marking the eastern boundary, and the Choctaws relinquished a small circular tract of territory north of Mobile;[34] and in 1803, another treaty again defined the boundary.[35] In 1805, by the Treaty of Mount Dexter, the Choctaws ceded a large tract extending across the southern part of their territory,[36] and in 1816 they surrendered the remainder of their land east of the Tombigbee.[37]

The inducements offered by the United States to persuade the Choctaws to grant these concessions established precedents which were to have a great influence on later Choctaw history; there was the idea of compensation to those who had suffered individual loss, the beginning of a permanent tribal income, and the pernicious practice of systematic corruption of the Chiefs. The Treaty of 1801 granted two thousand dollars in money and merchandise, and three sets of blacksmith's tools to the Choctaws whose homes were in the ceded land. The Treaty of 1802 carried no compensation. The Treaty of 1803 provided the following gifts to the Chiefs who signed it: 15 pieces of strouds, 3 rifles, 150 blankets, 250 rounds of powder, 250 pounds of lead, 1 bridle, 1 man's saddle, and 1 black silk handkerchief. The Treaty of 1805 carried the first provision for a permanent tribal income, an annuity of $3,000 to be expended under the direction of their Chiefs; it also made appropriations of $48,000 to be paid to white men for debts owed them by Choctaws, and $2,500 to John Pitchlynn, a white interpreter, "to compensate

[32]*Ibid.*, I, 305, 308, 339, 340.
[33]Kappler, *Laws and Treaties*, II, 56-58; Royce, "Indian Land Cessions," pp. 660-61; Schoolcraft, *Indian Tribes of the United States*, II, 594.
[34]Kappler, *Laws and Treaties*, II, 63-64; Schoolcraft, *loc. cit.*
[35]Kappler, *Laws and Treaties*, II, 69-70.
[36]*Ibid.*, II, 87-88; Schoolcraft, *Indian Tribes of the United States*, II, 598; Royce, "Indian Land Cessions," pp. 684-85.
[37]Kappler, *Laws and Treaties*, II, 137; Schoolcraft, *loc. cit.*; Royce, *loc. cit.*

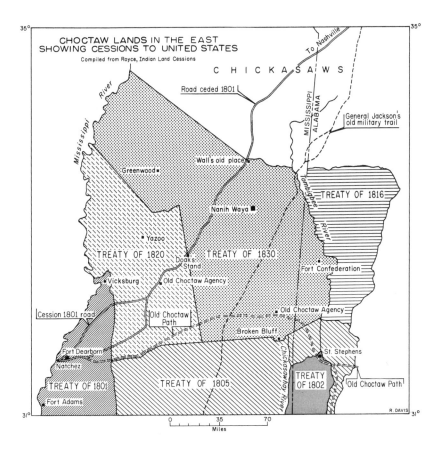

CHOCTAW LANDS IN THE EAST
SHOWING CESSIONS TO UNITED STATES
Compiled from Royce, Indian Land Cessions

35°

C H I C K A S A W S

To Nashville

Road ceded 1801

Mississippi River

MISSISSIPPI
ALABAMA

General Jackson's old military trail

Wall's old place

Greenwood ■

TREATY OF 1816

Tombigbee River

Nanih Waya ■

Yazoo ●

Doak's Stand

TREATY OF 1820

TREATY OF 1830

Fort Confederation

Vicksburg ●

Old Choctaw Agency

Cession 1801 road

Old Choctaw Path

Old Choctaw Agency ■

Broken Bluff

Chickasawhay River

Fort Dearborn

St. Stephens

Natchez

TREATY OF 1801

TREATY OF 1805

TREATY OF 1802

Old Choctaw Path

Fort Adams ●

31°

R. DAVIS

31°

0   35   70
Miles

35

him" for unspecified losses and services; and it provided that the District Chiefs, Apukshunnubbee, Pushmataha, and Moshulatubbee, should each receive a cash payment of $500 in consideration of his past service to the Nation and a salary of $150 a year during his continuance in office.[38] Moshulatubbee soon died. The date is unknown, but by the time of the War of 1812 he had been succeeded by a Chief of the same name, designated by white officials as his "son," but more probably his nephew; and the salary was transferred by a subsequent treaty to this successor. It would be unfair to class as corrupt officials the Chiefs who were induced to cede tribal land for such a personal consideration as was granted by the Treaty of 1803, for they could hardly have been expected to hold a civilized conception of disinterested public service; but the whole practice of special favors to individuals was demoralizing, and may have been the origin of that official corruption that white men were so ready to condemn in the later Choctaw government.

During this period when the United States was gradually absorbing Choctaw territory, Spain's influence had almost disappeared. She had lost her province of Louisiana, and she was not able to hold West Florida against American aggressions. But Jefferson's proposed amendment to the Constitution authorizing the purchase of Louisiana had proposed the removal of the Indians to the region beyond the Mississippi, and the Louisiana Territorial Act of 1804 had empowered the President to carry on negotiations with the natives for that purpose.[39] The watchful Spanish officials welcomed this policy as an opportunity to build a barrier state upon the new Spanish frontier, by consolidating the exiles into one body devoted to Spanish interests and united by their resentment against the aggressive people who were crowding them from their homes.[40] But these hopes were destined to disappointment; the anticipated removal was postponed for a generation, and when it finally occurred, the Choctaws accepted their fate with sorrow, but without resentment, and made it their proudest boast that they had never taken up arms against the United States. The transfer of the Louisiana territory to the United States in 1803 ended the intrigues of rival powers for Choctaw friendship.

[38]Kappler, *Laws and Treaties*, II, 57, 69-70, 87-88.

[39]Annie Heloise Abel, *The History of Events Resulting in Indian Consolidation West of the Mississippi* (Washington, 1906), p. 242.

[40]Robertson, *Louisiana under Spain, France, and the United States*, II, 191, 341, Marquis de Calvo to Don Pedro Cevallos, May 18, 1804, and "Reflections on Louisiana," about 1804 by Vincente Iolch, governor of West Florida.

Although the Choctaws had been subject to these intrigues for a century, the series of land treaties with the United States indicates that for the first time in their history they were being seriously crowded by settlers. But this contact also brought about a definite decision to adopt the white man's institutions, and the same generation that saw them driven from their ancient homes also marked the period of their greatest educational, religious, and political development.

A strong factor in this decision was the influence of a few intermarried white men of great ability and force of character, who identified themselves fully with their adopted people. Among the most prominent of these were the Folsom brothers, who came from South Carolina;[41] John Pitchlynn, the son of an Englishman, who had grown up in the Choctaw country;[42] and the French Canadians, Louis and Michael LeFlore.[43] These men settled among the Choctaws during the last quarter of the eighteenth century, and their sons became leaders of progress and education within the tribe.

Another source of white influence was the increasing activities of traders, and the construction of roads in the Choctaw country. The most important trading post was St. Stephens, established by the United States in 1802. It was located on the Tombigbee close to its junction with the Alabama, on the old east-west Indian trail from the Natchez to the lower Creeks; it thus tapped the trade of the old Spanish Camino Real, and could compete for all the trade coming down the Alabama and Tombigbee rivers, and all the trails converging towards Mobile. George S. Gaines, a native of Virginia, who came to this place in 1805 and served first as assistant, and later as principal factor, was greatly loved and trusted by the Choctaws. Gaines was assisted by a clerk, a skinsman, and an interpreter, all of whom received substantial salaries from the United States. The Choctaws brought bears' oil, kegs of honey, beeswax, bacon, groundnuts, kegs of tobacco, and all kinds of furs, which they traded for the cloth, iron tools, arms and ammunition, and plows kept in stock by the Federal Government.[44]

[41]Czarina C. Conlan, "David Folsom," *Chronicles of Oklahoma*, IV (1926), 340-55; Muriel H. Wright, "Tryphena," *ibid.*, IX (1931), 182n.

[42]Czarina C. Conlan, "Peter P. Pitchlynn," *ibid.*, VI (1928), 215-24; Cushman, *History of the Choctaw*, p. 392; Myer, "Indian Trails of the Southeast," p. 826.

[43]Mrs. Lee J. Langley, "Malmaison, Palace in a Wilderness," *Chronicles of Oklahoma*, V (1927), 371-80; Cushman, *History of the Choctaw*, pp. 400, 402, 403, 410.

[44]Myer, "Indian Trails of the Southeast," p. 824.

At first the Choctaw products were shipped from Mobile, but the United States soon secured permission from the Chickasaw tribe to carry them on packhorses to Colbert's Ferry on the Tennessee, in the extreme northwestern part of Alabama. This route, known as Gaines's Trace, followed the Tombigbee to the mouth of the Okibbeha; it was probably identical with a primitive trail from the Chickasaw settlements in the north, through the Choctaw country, to the lower Creek towns.[45] The road constructed under the Treaty of 1801 crossed the Choctaw country from southwest to northeast from Natchez to Nashville.

The white people who traveled these trails found the Choctaws hospitable and friendly, willing to welcome them in their homes or accept employment as guides. Public inns were established in some places, but apparently these enterprises were usually conducted by the mixed bloods or white citizens. The most famous was Pitchlynn's Place on Gaines's Trace, where the goods brought up the Tombigbee were unloaded for the overland part of the journey. John Pitchlynn and his sons, Peter and John, owned most of the land in that region, and their home was a favorite stopping place for travelers. Pitchlynn was employed by the United States as interpreter, and was a good friend of both Indians and whites. The white citizen, Nathaniel Folsom, also entertained numerous travelers; he told Adam Hodgson, who visited him in 1820, that there were scarcely five days in the year when he failed to have guests, and that seventy or eighty often stopped in one day.[46]

The relations between the Choctaws and the white people were regulated by a series of Indian Intercourse Acts passed by the Federal Congress in 1790, 1793, 1796, and 1802. Hunting, herding, or settling on Indian lands, or entering the Indian country with hostile intent was prohibited under pain of fine or imprisonment. It was illegal to enter an Indian reservation without a passport from Federal officials. Licenses were required of traders, who were forbidden to purchase from the Indians any guns or weapons used in hunting, any instrument of husbandry or cooking utensil, or any article of clothing except furs. United States soldiers were authorized to enter the reservations and remove white intruders.[47]

[45]*Ibid.*, pp. 825, 827.
[46]*Ibid.*, p. 826; Hodgson, *Letters from North America*, pp. 215, 217, 224; Morse, *Report to the Secretary of War*, p. 183.
[47]*United States Statutes at Large*, I, 137-38, 329-32, 469-74, 743-49; II, 139-46.

The United States also maintained an agent to the Choctaws, who was supposed to protect them from intruders, encourage them to adopt civilized customs, and represent the Federal Government in the negotiation and execution of treaties. The Intercourse Laws were especially difficult to enforce against the lawless frontiersmen. Agent Silas Dinsmore, in particular, incurred the wrath of intruders in 1811-12, by his insistence upon passports from travelers in the Choctaw country. Andrew Jackson, especially, became so enraged that he threatened to burn both the agency house and the agent.[48]

The influence of all this white intercourse is shown by the modification of the Choctaws' most important and most distinctive ceremonial, their mourning rites. The scaffolding of the bodies and the bone picking was suddenly abandoned by most of the tribe about 1800, though the custom persisted for a generation longer in some places, notably among the Six Town Choctaws.[49] According to the new custom, they dug a grave close to the house, in which they placed the body with such individual belongings as clothing and ornaments, favorite weapons for a man or pots and kettles for a woman, and sometimes slain ponies and dogs. At the sides of the grave they planted six poles smoothed and painted red, and at the head was a taller pole flying a white flag and decorated with grapevine loops. During a stated time, which seems to have varied from thirty days to thirteen months, the family of the deceased repaired to the grave two or three times a day to wail and weep. At the expiration of the mourning period, all the relatives and friends having been summoned by the usual bundles of sticks, assembled for the final rites, which consisted of protracted weeping and the pulling and removal of the poles. The ceremonies closed with a feast, and the mourning period was ended.[50]

The Choctaws also, yielding to pressure on the part of the Indian agent, began to modify their ancient law of retaliation. Some white hunters had wantonly murdered a peaceful Choctaw in the Chickasaw country, and the Choctaws, in accordance with their old custom, had satisfied the demands of justice by killing an innocent white trader. Agent Dinsmore then demanded the life of the man who had retaliated upon the trader. A conference was called in September, 1812, at

[48]*Niles' Register*, XXXIV (1828), 110-13.

[49]Swanton *Choctaw Social and Ceremonial Life*, pp. 175-77, 189; Nuttall, *Travels into the Arkansas Territory*, Thwaites, XIII, 304.

[50]Swanton, *Choctaw Social and Ceremonial Life*, pp. 177-78, 183-86, 189-94; Cushman, *History of the Choctaw*, pp. 364-65; Hodgson, *Letters from North America*, pp. 216-17; Gregg, *Commerce of the Prairies*, Thwaites, XX, 314-15.

the Chickasaw council house, at which Apukshunnubbee, Moshula-tubbee, and other Choctaw leaders were present, as well as John Pitchlynn and other interpreters, and the Chickasaw agent with two Chiefs of that tribe. This Council abandoned in principle the law of retaliation by agreeing to the death of the Choctaw who had killed the trader; but the Chiefs cannily delayed the execution of the sentence until the white people should have punished their murderer. A treaty was made, however, between the Choctaw leaders and a group of Cherokees who had migrated to the region beyond the Mississippi, by which if a murder were committed by a citizen of one tribe against a citizen of the other, only the guilty person, and not any innocent member of the offending tribe, should be subject to the law of blood revenge. The Chickasaws also subscribed to the same agreement.[51]

The Choctaws made rapid material progress during this period. Many of them had extensive herds of cattle, and they had learned to raise cotton, which they carded, spun, wove, and made into clothing. A visitor in 1820 described the crowd assembled at a ball play as wearing cotton dresses with beaded belts and deerskin moccasins and feathered cotton turbans. They were richly loaded with silver ornaments hanging from their necks and arms, and even depending from the cartilage of their noses.[52]

The Choctaws were invited to abandon this peaceful progress when Tecumseh visited them on his journey south in 1811 in the interest of his Indian confederacy; but they wisely, if ignobly, refused. With thirty warriors he came first to the Okla Falaya or Upper Towns District, of which Apukshunnubbee was Chief. As he passed from town to town trying to arouse the Choctaws, he made many converts. But Pushmataha, Chief of the Six Towns District, used all his influence to maintain friendly relations with the United States. Finally, at Molasha Town, the residence of Chief Moshulatubbee, in the Okla tánnáp or Lower Towns District, the Choctaws—with some visiting Chickasaws, if one man's memory can be trusted—assembled for one of the greatest Councils in their history.

At the east edge of the town stood a hill which commanded the whole savage scene. Here the oldest chiefs formed an inner circle, with the younger chiefs next, the tried warriors surrounding them, and the

[51]*Niles' Register*, III (1812), 166.
[52]*Ibid.*, XV (1818), 186; Morse, *Report to the Secretary of War*, p. 182; Hodgson, *Letters from North America*, p. 218; Cushman, *History of the Choctaw*, p. 44.

inexperienced young men on the outer edge. No sound disturbed the dramatic intensity of the occasion as the crowd and circle parted to let Tecumseh and his delegation pass to the center. Tecumseh spoke with his usual headlong eloquence, as he urged his hearers to rise against the white intruder while there was yet a chance of success. Then one after another of the Choctaw and Chickasaw warriors gave his opinion. Some were undecided, others leaned definitely toward the alliance, and the issue was in doubt. Finally Pushmataha, who had remained silent, rose and began to speak with an eloquence equal to that of the great northern visitor. His words carried weight, for he was trusted as the wisest statesman in the tribe, and he had hunted the buffalo and taken Osage and Comanche scalps far beyond the Mississippi. He reminded the Choctaws of their unbroken friendship for the United States, and pointed out the danger of arousing the hostility of a stronger and more numerous people. The final decision was left to the divinations of a medicine man, who prudently discovered that the supernatural forces were on the side of Pushmataha. The council then ordered Tecumseh to leave the Choctaw Nation under pain of death, and David Folsom and a group of warriors undertook to escort him across the Tombigbee into the country of the Creeks.[53]

Pushmataha then returned to his home, which was in the vicinity of St. Stephens, and told Gaines he was ready to join the United States in the war against the Creeks who had joined Tecumseh. Thus Pushmataha and Moshulatubbee with several hundred warriors joined the American forces and Apukshunnubbee brought a small contingent from his district. They fought with Andrew Jackson against the Creek hostiles at Horseshoe Bend, and against the British at the Battle of New Orleans. A few Choctaws aided the Creeks, but upon their return they were put to death as traitors by their fellow tribesmen.[54] The War of 1812 thus demonstrated that the Choctaw people had definitely joined their future with that of the growing American Republic.

Only three years after the Battle of New Orleans, the Choctaws made another decision that consolidated the interests of the two races, when they invited missionaries to establish stations in their country.

[53]Draper Collection, Tecumseh Manuscripts (copies in Phillips Collection, University of Oklahoma, Norman, Oklahoma), IV, 9; Flora Warren Seymour, *The Story of the Red Man* (New York, 1929), pp. 110-12; Cushman, *History of the Choctaw*, pp. 297-99, 306–307, 316–18, 320–21. Cushman's account of the Council seems to have been inspired by the reminiscences of John Pitchlynn, who was present.

[54]Draper Collection, Tecumseh Manuscripts, IV, pp. 46–48; Cushman, *History of the Choctaw*, pp. 322-23, 325; Seymour, *The Story of the Red Man*, pp. 117-18.

This request seems to have been due to the influence of the younger generation of Folsoms, LeFlores, and Pitchlynns, whose fathers had given them some schooling, and who felt that the only hope for their people lay in education and the adoption of civilized institutions; but there is no doubt that the Choctaw people as a whole were ready for this further acquisition of the white man's customs.

In 1817 the newly organized American Board of Commissioners for Foreign Missions had established a station among the Cherokees near Chattanooga, Tennessee, the Missionary Ridge of Civil War fame. The Choctaws then requested a similar work among their people, and as a result the Presbyterian, Cyrus Kingsbury, an instructor in the Cherokee school, was sent to their country. In August, 1818, he established a mission at Eliot, on the Yalobusha River, about thirty miles above its junction with the Yazoo.[55]

A letter written by David Folsom, son of Nathaniel Folsom, a month before the mission was established, throws light upon the motives of the Choctaw people in their response to missionary efforts, as well as the influence of the mixed blood element and the attitude of the people in general. Folsom apologized for his bad English, saying he had attended school only six months; but he said that education was vital to the survival of his people, since the hunting had declined until those dependent upon it had come to want. "I have been talking to my people, and have advised them for the best, turn their attention to industry and farming, and lay our hunting aside. And here is one point of great work, is just come to hand, before us which is the establishment of a school; and the Choctaws appear to be well pleased."[56]

Within a year Kingsbury and four assistants with their wives had cleared land for a demonstration farm, erected buildings, and established a school. In August of 1819, he attended a Council of the whole Nation and presented the needs of the mission; and the assembled warriors appropriated their annuities amounting to $3,000 a year, and donated $1,800 in money and eighty cows and calves for its support.[57]

The next year, Kingsbury, aided by John Pitchlynn and David Folsom, located a mission and school at Mayhew, which was opened in the Fall of 1821. During the Winter of 1820 seven new missionaries arrived with their families. Among these recruits were Calvin Cush-

[55]*Niles' Register*, XVI (1819), 399; XVII (1819), 192; Cushman, *History of the Choctaw*, pp. 135-36.

[56]*Niles' Register*, XVI (1819), supplement, pp. 96-98.

[57]*Ibid.*, XVII (1819), 192; XXIII (1822), supplement, p. 63; S. C. Bartlett, *Sketches of the Mission of the American Board* (Boston, 1872), p. 179.

man, whose son became such a sympathetic student of Choctaw institutions, and Cyrus Byington, who with the aid of the Folsoms translated hymns and portions of the Bible into Choctaw, wrote a speller and an almanac in that language, and compiled a Choctaw grammar and a dictionary.[58] In 1821 three white men with Choctaw families, whose children had been in school at Eliot, proposed to erect buildings in their own neighborhood, and board and clothe the children if the American Board would furnish the teacher. As a result the Newell Station was established, which enrolled fifteen pupils, and seems to have been the beginning of the Choctaw system of neighborhood schools.[59]

An incident that occurred at this time shows not only the attitude of the Choctaws toward the schools, but it shows that the old system of family relationships was beginning to break down. A member of the prominent McCurtain family, who had five children in school attempted to enter the sixth; but the school was full, and Kingsbury was obliged to refuse. McCurtain became offended, and exercising a prerogative not justified by Choctaw custom, withdrew all his children. Robert Cole, the maternal uncle and therefore the guardian, wrote to Kingsbury that although he had given way to the father, the loss of education to the children had given him "great dissatisfaction of mind," and he requested Kingsbury to reinstate the boys at least, and to do as he thought best about the girls. Eight other Choctaws appended their marks to this letter, expressing their sorrow that Cole had been made so unhappy by the loss of his nephews' educational opportunities.[60]

The activities and general atmosphere of these schools is shown in a report by the head of the Eliot Mission, dated December 21, 1820; and an account by Adam Hodgson, an English traveler who visited it in May of the same year. Eighty pupils were in attendance, of whom ten lived at their homes in the vicinity and seventy boarded with the mission family. Of this number, fifty had spoken only Choctaw when they entered. The children rose at daybreak and began their work; they assembled at seven o'clock for reading, prayer, and breakfast; after an interval of play, they came together for school, which opened with

[58]William B. Morrison, "The Choctaw Mission of the American Board of Commissioners for Foreign Missions," *Chronicles of Oklahoma*, IV (1926), 175; Bureau of American Ethnology *Bulletin No. 46* (Washington, 1915), pp. vii-viii; Cyrus Byington, *A Grammar of the Choctaw Language* (Philadelphia, 1870); Cushman, *History of the Choctaw*, pp. 140, 144; Morse, *Report to the Secretary of War*, p. 191, from Kingsbury's report to the Secretary of War, January, 1822.

[59]Morse, *Report to the Secretary of War*, p. 194.

[60]*Ibid.*, pp. 186-87.

prayer, singing, and reading of a chapter of the Bible and examination in the chapter read the previous morning, after which they were instructed in the three R's; after school was dismissed, the boys worked at agricultural tasks and the girls at sewing and other domestic employments until supper; then a chapter was read from the Bible with Scott's *Practical Observations,* and they joined in singing and prayer, after which they retired to their little rooms in the log cabins of the mission settlement.[61]

Hodgson arrived just as David Folsom, who had come sixty miles from his home to visit the school, was preparing to speak to the children. Folsom began by translating into their language a letter which he had received from some friends in the North who had sent them a missionary box; he then spoke to them for some time in Choctaw. Before he left, he shook hands with Hodgson, and expressed his gratification that the white people in England were interested in their red brethren.[62]

Hodgson was greatly impressed with the sincerity and practical attitude of the missionaries. As the buildings were not yet completed, the teachers and their families were living in tents, with wolves howling and panthers screaming in the surrounding forest, and the men were obliged to swim their horses over several streams every time they made a trip to the settlements for supplies; but they said they were enduring no more privations than any sailor, soldier, or frontier trader.[63]

These devoted workers received no salary, but their maintenance was provided by the American Board. The Federal Government made a small appropriation from the Civilization Fund, and benevolent white friends of the mission made donations, but the main expense was borne by the Choctaw Nation.[64]

The Choctaws also made an arrangement with Col. Richard Mentor Johnson, by which he established an academy for boys at a site which they selected in Kentucky. This school was initiated by the Baptists, and was under the patronage of the Baptist general convention. The Choctaws supported this institution enthusiastically from the entrance of the first group of twenty-five boys in the Fall of 1825 until the Fall of 1841, when they decided, chiefly through the influence of Peter

[61]*Niles' Register,* XXII (1822), supplement, p. 53; XXIII (1822), supplement, p. 63; Hodgson, *Letters from North America,* pp. 227-28.

[62]Hodgson, *Letters from North America,* pp. 226-27.

[63]*Ibid.,* pp. 234, 237.

[64]Cushman, *History of the Choctaw,* p. 145; Morse, *Report to the Secretary of War,* pp. 188, 193, 195; Kappler, *Laws and Treaties,* II, 193, Articles VII, VIII, Treaty of 1820.

Pitchlynn, to discontinue their support in favor of schools in their own country. During the time it was in existence, many of the future leaders of the Nation were trained in this school.[65]

In 1830 it was reported that there were 11 schools in the Choctaw Nation, with a total of 29 teachers, and an enrollment of 260 children; and in addition, 250 adults had been taught to read their native language. There were also 89 boys enrolled in the Choctaw Academy.[66] Thus was established the educational system, that was to be the greatest pride of the Choctaws during all the rest of their tribal history.

It is apparent that the Choctaws' support of the missionary activities was due to their educational and economic, rather than their religious interests. Few converts were made during the first ten years, but in 1828 a great revival movement swept the country. The wealthy and prominent mixed bloods became active converts, and large numbers of the more humble citizens came into the church in a great wave of emotional excitement. This religious movement may have been due in part to the evangelistic efforts of the Methodists, who began their work in 1825, and who reported a thousand members in 1830.[67]

The missionaries used their influence to encourage the legal and constitutional development that was already in progress, and punishment by the tribe began to supplant the old custom of private vengeance. Chief Aboha Kulla Humma writing to Kingsbury, October 18, 1822, from the Six Towns to request the establishment of a mission there, reported that his district had prescribed a punishment of thirty-nine lashes for parents who should murder their infants, wives or husbands who should abandon their homes in favor of other partners, and hog and cattle thieves.[68] A body of enforcement officers was created in each district, under the influence, it is said, of Greenwood LeFlore and David Folsom. These lighthorsemen, as they were called, served as judge, jury, and sheriff. They rode over the country settling difficulties that arose among parties and individuals, and arresting, trying, and inflicting punishment on all violators of the law. Young Peter Pitchlynn, who had just returned from Nashville University, was made the

[65]Carolyn Thomas Foreman, "The Choctaw Academy," *Chronicles of Oklahoma,* VI (1928), 453-80; *ibid.,* X (1933), 77-114; *Niles' Register,* XXI (1821), 159; XXIX (1825), 226-27.

[66]*Indian Affairs, Annual Report,* 1830, Table B. *See* also *ibid.,* 1829, pp. 176-78.

[67]William B. Morrison, *The Red Man's Trail* (Richmond, 1932), p. 51; John Ross MSS and Papers (Phillips Collection, University of Oklahoma, Norman, Oklahoma), Choctaws, pp. 2-10; Cushman, *History of the Choctaw,* pp. 135-71.

[68]Cushman, *History of the Choctaw,* p. 150.

head of this force in 1824, and the next year a treaty with the United States provided a permanent annuity for its maintenance.[69]

Under the influence of their advancing civilization the Choctaws also began to modify their belief in witchcraft. Shortly after the establishment of the first mission of the American Board, a Choctaw girl died after a woman "doctor" had predicted her recovery. The "doctor" then accused a Chickasaw woman of thwarting her skill by projecting a ball of poison into the girl's body, and the enraged father accordingly took the life of the accused witch. Kingsbury assisted in the burial of this victim of superstition, and used the occasion to preach a strong sermon against the belief in witchcraft.[70] It may have been on this same occasion that Adam Hodgson saw fifty or sixty Choctaws assembled in the woods to avenge the death of a woman who had been killed as a witch;[71] the incident at least shows that the Choctaws were beginning to question and resent the irresponsible accusations of their "doctors."

In 1829 a law was enacted giving a person accused of witchcraft the benefit of a trial. This law illustrates the curious, and sometimes amusing, combinations which resulted when the primitive beliefs and customs of the tribe were joined with the borrowed phraseology of Anglo-American legal procedure.

"Council House, September 18, 1829

"Whereas, it has been an old custom of the Choctaws to punish persons said to be wizzards or witches with death, without giving them any fair trial by any disinterested persons; and many have fallen victims under the influence of this habit—

"We do hereby resolve; in general council of the north, east, and southern districts, that, in future, all persons who shall be accused of being a wizzard or witch, shall be tried before the chiefs and committees, or by any four captains; and if they be found guilty, they shall be punished at the discretion of the court.

"Be it further resolved, that if any person or persons shall find at any place the entrails of a wizzard or witch, the said entrails going from or returning to the body, the said body shall be put to death at the place where it may be discovered, and the said body shall be cut open, by a

[69]*Ibid.*, pp. 217, 219, 392-93; Kappler, *Laws and Treaties*, II, 193, Article XIII, Treaty of 1825; Swanton, *Choctaw Social and Ceremonial Life*, p. 107n.

[70]Cushman, *History of the Choctaw*, pp. 137, 139.

[71]Hodgson, *Letters from North America*, p. 215. This incident occurred in May, 1820.

*proper person, and an examination be made to see whether it has in it
any entrails, and a report be made of said body.*

*"And it is hereby further resolved, that no doctor shall have the
power to pass sentence of death upon any person or persons that may
be accused of being a wizzard or witch: and any doctor so offending
shall suffer the penalty of death."*[72]

This law also indicates that the judicial functions formerly exercised
by the lighthorsemen had been displaced or at least were shared by an
irregular court consisting of the District Chiefs and their assistants, or
by the head men of the towns.

As the primitive Choctaw murderer had made it a point of honor
to await the stroke of the avenger of blood, so the criminal convicted
under the new laws now presented himself for the execution of his
sentence. White observers were deeply impressed by the stoical manner
with which the Choctaw would receive a severe whipping, or the non-
chalance with which he would accept a sentence of death. Occasionally
a sentence would be postponed until after a projected ball play or
dance or until growing crops could be harvested; then the accused
would voluntarily report at the place appointed for his execution. The
criminal was always dispatched with a rifle, for the Choctaws regarded
hanging with superstitious horror as a mode of death that condemned
the spirit to eternal wandering.[73]

During this period of developing law the Choctaws also took steps
to protect themselves against the liquor traffic. Like other Indians they
seemed unable to resist the pleasurable stimulation of the white man's
oka humma—"red water"— and helpless to protect themselves against
its demoralizing effects. Travelers frequently drew unpleasant pictures
of Choctaw camps near the white settlements where both sexes were
singing, drinking, and rolling on the ground in the last stages of
intoxication.[74]

Although the missionaries naturally opposed the sale and use of
liquor, it appears that the initiative came from the Choctaws themselves.
In 1770 Don Francisco de Masilleres, the Spanish official in charge of
Arkansas Post, wrote to his superiors requesting a liquor allowance
for the Choctaws; he said they always expected to be furnished liquor

[72]*Niles' Register*, XXXVII (1829), 181.

[73]Cushman, *History of the Choctaw*, pp. 217-19.

[74]Thwaites, *Early Western Travels* (an anonymous writer who visited New Orleans
in 1799), IV, 366; *Niles' Register*, XXXVIII (1830), 345; Morse, *Report to the Secretary of War*, p. 196, Kingsbury's observations in 1822.

when they visited the Post, but he made this significant statement —
"Their Grand Chief says the Government should deprive them of this
liquor altogether."[75] In 1833 Elbert Herring, Commissioner of Indian
Affairs, made the following statement in his report: "The Choctaws,
on the other hand, are now, as they were in 1801 and in 1820, almost
unanimously opposed to the introduction and sale of ardent spirits in
their country. 'We came here [to the Council] sober,' said the Chiefs
to the commissioners of the United States in 1801, 'we wish to go
away so — We therefore request that the strong drink, which we
understand our brothers have brought here, may not be distributed.' "[76]
In 1822, Chief Aboha Kullo Humma, in the letter previously mentioned, informed Kingsbury that his district had a law by which all
liquor brought into the country was to be destroyed; and in 1826 a
General Council outlawed the traffic for the entire Nation.[77] The
Choctaws thus seem to have been the first people in the United States
to enact a "prohibition law."

The federal intercourse laws of March 30, 1802, and May 6, 1822,
also forbade the introduction of intoxicating liquor into the Indian
country,[78] and the Treaty of Doak's Stand, made with the Choctaws
in 1820, authorized the United States agent to destroy all liquor except
such as had been brought in with his consent, or with the consent of
the District Chiefs.[79] But the Federal Government made little attempt
to enforce these laws, and as long as the Choctaws remained in Mississippi they were greatly demoralized by liquor dealers, and even by
United States commissioners who used their well known susceptibility
in order to secure their approval of governmental projects.

At the same time that the Choctaws were beginning to build their
legal code they also began to modify their ancient government in accordance with the constitutional practices of their white neighbors. Two
of their District Chiefs — Apukshunnubbee and the great and statesmanlike Pushmataha — had died in 1824 while on a trip to Washington.[80] This circumstance may have hastened the constitutional change

[75]Anna Lewis, "Oklahoma as a Part of the Spanish Domain," *Chronicles of Oklahoma*, III (1924), 48-49, translation of letter in the Archives of the Indies at Seville.

[76]*Report Commissioner of Indian Affairs*, 1833, p. 203.

[77]*Ibid.*, 1853, p. 421; John Ross MSS, p. 6; Cushman, *History of the Choctaw*,
pp 141, 150, 171.

[78]*United States Statutes at Large*, I, 139-46; III, 682-83.

[79]Kappler, *Laws and Treaties*, II, 193, Article XII.

[80]Draper Collection, Tecumseh Manuscripts, X, 162, letter of David Folsom to
Cyrus Kingsbury, December 24, 1824; Cushman, *History of the Choctaw*, p. 336.

that took place in 1826 when a Council of the entire Nation adopted a system of elective Chiefs who should hold office for four years. At the same time the Council adopted a code of written laws.[81]

But the old customs were hard to displace. It was very difficult for Moshulatubbee and his adherents to relinquish the idea of life tenure, and there was also a tendency to revert to the ancient principle of inheritance through a natural assumption of authority on the part of a sister's son. The immediate result of this change was an unstable executive, with an unseemly scrambling for office and considerable uncertainty as to who constituted the legal officials.[82]

The proximity of white settlement that influenced the Choctaws to adapt themselves so rapidly to civilized customs also subjected them to the encroachments of the landseekers who were thronging in to establish cotton plantations on the rich soil of the lower South. During the decade from 1820 to 1830 they were induced to surrender their ancient homes to the white men, and to agree to removal beyond the Mississippi.

By the Treaty of Doak's Stand, signed in 1820, they exchanged the southwestern portion of their territory for a wild tract of country between the Red River on the south and the Arkansas and Canadian rivers on the north, constituting what is now the southern half of Oklahoma and a section of southwestern Arkansas. The United States offered them inducements to emigrate to the new home by promising them supplies for the first year and the assistance of an agent and a blacksmith.[83]

Before the Choctaws had time to enter into possession of their new territory, it was discovered that the eastern portion was already occupied by white settlers. The Federal Government, realizing the difficulty of dislodging these families, therefore decided to induce the Choctaws to relinquish that portion of their land. A Choctaw delegation of which Moshulatubbee, Apukshunnubbee, Pushmataha, Daniel McCurtain, David Folsom, and Pitchlynn were prominent members, was invited to Washington in 1824 to negotiate a treaty that would correct the blunder that had been made when the land was sold. Strangely enough the trip proved fatal to two of the three great District Chiefs who had guided the Nation for almost a generation of the most critical period

[81]Joseph B. Thoburn and Muriel H. Wright, *Oklahoma, A History of the State and its People* (New York, 1929), II, 788.

[82]Foreman, *Indian Removal*, pp. 29-30.

[83]*United States Statutes at Large*, VII, 210; also Kappler, *Laws and Treaties*, II, 191-95.

of its history; Apukshunnubbee died at Maysville, Kentucky, as the result of an accident, and Pushmataha, after he reached the capital.

It is impossible to escape the conviction that the Federal officials systematically corrupted and even more systematically intoxicated Indian leaders as an economical method of securing land cessions. Apparently this negotiation was no exception, for the official expense account for entertaining the delegation was as follows: bar bill $2,149.50; board and lodging, $2,029; oysters and liquor, $349.75; suit of clothes for each, $1,134.74. Some of these items were too much even for the sturdy constitution of old Chief Pushmataha, and he succumbed to the effects of the white man's firewater.[84]

The treaty was adopted in 1825. By its terms the present boundary between Oklahoma and Arkansas was established, and the Choctaws ceded back to the United States all the land lying east of that line. For this cession they were to receive $6,000 a year for sixteen years and a permanent annuity of $6,320.[85]

The Federal officials hoped that the Choctaws would voluntarily remove to this new location. If their earlier traditions are based on fact, they had come originally from that direction; they had long been sending war parties and hunting parties into what is now Oklahoma; and they had numerous settlements in Arkansas and Louisiana.[86] In fulfilment of the treaty provisions Major William McClellan was appointed agent to the Western Choctaws in 1826, and the next year he began to erect buildings for his agency fifteen miles above Fort Smith at what was later known as Skullyville. By 1829 about 150 Choctaws had been induced to settle in their new territory.[87]

This gradual emigration was too slow, however, for the land-hungry white men. In 1826, United States commissioners held a council with the Choctaws at Florence, Alabama, and made an unsuccessful attempt to secure the remainder of their lands in Mississippi.[88] The next year Colonel McKinney, the Superintendent of Indian Affairs,

[84]Cushman, *History of the Choctaw*, p. 336; Grant Foreman, *Indians and Pioneers* (New Haven, 1930), p. 184; Draper Collection, Tecumseh Manuscripts, X, 162, 164, letter from David Folsom to Cyrus Kingsbury, December 24, 1824. Folsom with his strong religious convictions might easily have overestimated the ill effects of the Chief's drinking, but the expense account bears out his evidence.

[85]Kappler, *Laws and Treaties*, II, 211-14.

[86]Foreman, *Indians and Pioneers*, pp. 25-26, 31-34; Nuttall, *Travels into the Arkansas Territory*, Thwaites, XIII, 128-29; Lewis, "Oklahoma as a Part of the Spanish Domain," p. 48.

[87]Foreman, *Indians and Pioneers*, pp. 302-3.

[88]*Niles' Register*, XXXI (1826), 259, 283.

made a special trip to the Choctaw country to induce them to remove, but the Indians, although courteous, were firm in their refusal—"It always gives us pain to disagree to a friend's talk."[89] John H. Eaton, Secretary of War, then (May 30, 1829) instructed the commissioners, Carroll and Coffee, to bribe the Chiefs and head men by offers of "extensive reservations in fee simple, and *other rewards.*"[90]

But the people of Mississippi did not wait for the success of these Federal schemes for the removal of the Choctaws. In 1829 the legislature provided for the extension of the state laws over Choctaw and Chickasaw lands adjacent to organized counties; and on January 19, 1830, the Indians were granted Mississippi citizenship, and the tribal governments were abolished under penalty of fine and imprisonment for any Indian who should exercise the "office of chief, mingo, head man, or other post of power established by the tribal statutes, ordinances, or customs of the said Indians."[91]

It must have been an attempt to reconcile the Indians to this law that caused the suggestion to be made to former Chief Moshulatubbee that he was now eligible to serve his district in Congress. On April 1, he issued the following appeal to the voters of Mississippi:

"Fellow citizens:—I have fought for you, I have been by your own act, made a citizen of your state; I am a freeholder, nature my parent. I am unsophisticated in the wiles of foreign nations or my own. . . . . In my youth I was a hunter, in manhood a warrior, I always battled on the side of this republic. My feet now fail in the chase, and my arm can no longer bear the burthen of my bow. While in a state of nature my ambition was alone in the shade — my hopes to be interred in the mounds of my ancestors. But you have awakened new hopes; your laws have for me brightened my prospects. I know no man who has suffered more than myself, whether you or myself time will tell. I have been told by my white brethren that the pen of history is impartial, and that in after years, our forlorn kindred *will have justice and 'mercy too.'*

"This, fellow citizens, is a plain talk. Listen, for I have spoken in candor. According to your laws I think that I am qualified to a seat in the councils of a mighty republic, ... I have no animosity against any of my white brethren, who enter the list against me, but with Indian

[89]*Ibid.*, XXXIII (1827), 274.

[90]*Speeches on Passage of the Bill for the Removal of Indians* (New York, 1830), p. 4.

[91]*Laws of the Colonial and State Governments Relating to Indians and Indian Affairs from 1633 to 1831 inclusive* (Washington, 1832). pp. 242-43; *see* also *Niles' Register*, XXXVIII (1830), 73.

sincerity, I wish you would elect me a member of the next congress of the United States."[92]

But if old Moshulatubbee had been persuaded to think of this grant of citizenship only as a boon to politically minded Choctaws, he was soon to be disillusioned; for it precipitated the most serious division that had occurred within the tribe since the civil war between the French and British factions nearly a century before.

The Methodist missionaries actively supported the removal schemes of the United States Government, apparently because they dreaded the demoralizing contacts with white people, and especially the effect of the liquor traffic, to which the Choctaw country was thrown open by the Mississippi law abrogating the tribal government. They were seconded in their efforts by Greenwood LeFlore, Chief of the Upper Towns, who was an active convert and who apparently cherished schemes of personal advancement.

In March, LeFlore called a Council of his supporters, to which the Methodist missionaries were also invited. At this meeting David Folsom, Chief of the Lower Towns, and John Garland, Chief of the Six Towns, resigned their positions in favor of LeFlore as single executive. Apparently Folsom and Garland were influenced in this action by their fear of the penalty prescribed by the Mississippi statute for those who should hold office under the tribal government; while LeFlore, who had decided to emigrate to the West, was unaffected by this threat. LeFlore then presided over the Council as Chief of the whole Nation, and presented his views in favor of emigration. A treaty in the handwriting of Alexander Talley, the Methodist missionary, was then adopted providing for the cession of the remaining lands in Mississippi and Alabama, and removal to the West.[93]

This treaty was carried to Washington by D. W. Haley. At the same time the faction opposed to removal sent a strong protest against its ratification. The treaty was rejected by the United States Senate, apparently not so much through considerations of justice, but because the administration believed it to be too favorable to the Choctaws.[94] At the same time Congress enacted the Indian Removal Bill, expressing

[92]*Niles' Register*, XXXXVIII (1830), 362-63.
[93]*Ibid.*, XXXVIII (1830), 457; Abel, *Indian Consolidation West of the Mississippi*, p. 375.
[94]*Indian Removal, Senate Docs.*, 23 Cong., 1 Sess., No. 512 (Washington, 1834-35), II, 240, 257; *Niles' Register*, XXXVIII (1830), 216.

the settled purpose of the Government to locate the eastern Indian tribes on lands beyond the Mississippi.[95]

In the interest of this policy, President Andrew Jackson himself planned to come West to negotiate with the Choctaws and Chickasaws, his former allies in the War of 1812. On June 1, four days after the passage of the law, Secretary Eaton wrote to the Choctaws inviting them to meet with him and the President at Franklin, Tennessee, and professing the benevolent purpose of the Government to remove them from the hostile jurisdiction of Mississippi. "Congress has passed a law manifesting a desire that you should remove and have liberally prepared the means for taking care of you. They will not, because they cannot, interfere to prevent the States extending their laws over you." In view of the professed impotence of the Federal Government, the Indians were therefore under the alternative of losing their tribal autonomy in Mississippi or removing to the West where they could develop their own laws "with none to interrupt you."[96]

At the same time Eaton received a petition from the Choctaws expressing gratification that the LeFlore treaty had been rejected, and requesting at least the privilege of sending an exploring party to investigate the possibilities of their unknown purchase in the West before surrendering their homes. They did, however, express a willingness to treat with commissioners that should be sent to them.[97]

Jackson and Eaton arrived at the latter's home in Franklin early in August, but the Choctaws failed to meet them there.[98] The President then returned to Washington, leaving Eaton with John Coffee to visit the Choctaws and carry on the negotiations in their own country.

It was in fact impossible for the Choctaws to treat with the President in August, for at that time their Nation was torn with such bitter internal dissension that civil war was narrowly averted. The fullblood element in the tribe, deeply resentful of LeFlore's attempted coup, elected Moshulatubbee as Chief of the Lower Towns, and Nitakechi, the nephew of Pushmataha, in the Six Town District. They took the name of Republican Party, and for a time were decidedly anti-Christian. LeFlore continued to assert his authority as Chief of the whole Nation. His followers made up largely of the mixed blood element and those who had come under the influence of the missionaries were

[95]*United States Statutes at Large,* IV, 411-12, May 28, 1830.
[96]*Senate Docs.,* 23 Cong., 1 Sess., No. 512, II, 3.
[97]*Ibid.,* II, 58-59.
[98]*Ibid.,* II, 240, Jackson to the Chickasaws, August 23, 1830.

known, at least by their opponents, as the Despotic Party.[99] The indiscreet action of the Methodist missionaries has already been mentioned; but although the Presbyterian missionaries of the American Board refrained from taking any part in the controversy, there is no doubt that in spite of the alignment of their followers, their secret sympathies were with the party that opposed removal.[100]

The trouble came to a head during the last of July or the first of August, while the people of the two eastern districts were assembled at the factory to receive their annuities from the Federal officials. Moshulatubbee and Nitakechi with several hundred armed followers surrounded the building and attempted to prevent the Christian party from sharing in the distribution. But LeFlore marched quickly from his district with a much larger force of armed and painted warriors, and demanded Moshulatubbee's instant resignation. For a few minutes a battle was imminent, but partly through the dread of civil war and partly through the influence of George Gaines, who was greatly respected by the Choctaws, a compromise was effected. Nitakechi was retained as Chief of the Six Towns, on condition that he would "walk straight," and Moshulatubbee was induced to resign with the understanding that his successor would be elected.[101] It is evident, however, that as soon as LeFlore returned to his own district, Moshulatubbee quietly resumed his office.[102]

Soon after these disturbing events, the Federal commissioners arrived for the negotiation of a removal treaty. The Council convened at Dancing Rabbit Creek on September 18, and remained in session until September 28. The Choctaws were conciliated by generous presents and general feasting;[103] the goodwill of their leaders was purchased by valuable land grants;[104] and they were systematically bullied by Secretary Eaton, who reminded them of their helplessness in the face of hostile state legislation against which the Federal Government declined

[99]Ibid., II, 58-59; Niles' Register, XXXVIII (1830), 457-58.
[100]Senate Docs., 23 Cong., 1 Sess., No. 512, II, 252, 254-56.
[101]Niles' Register, XXXVIII (1830), 457-58.
[102]Kappler, Laws and Treaties, II, 315, Moshulatubbee's signature to the Treaty of Dancing Rabbit Creek.
[103]Senate Docs., 23 Cong., 1 Sess., No. 512, V, 251-55, expense account of commissioners, including $1409.84 for such items as calico, quilts, razors, soap, etc.; $569.67 for supplies; and $155 for entertainment of Chiefs and head men at commissioners' table. See also ibid., II, 251, for distribution of rations.
[104]Kappler, Laws and Treaties, II, 312, 314-15, 317-18, Articles XV, XIX, and supplementary articles, I and II. When the outline of the treaty was submitted to the Choctaws, these articles were proposed first—Senate Docs., 23 Cong., 1 Sess., No. 512, II, 259, official report of Eaton and Coffee. See also ibid., II, 392-93, 477, 517.

to intervene. It is apparent that in spite of Choctaw susceptibility to presents and special favors, it was this last consideration that finally influenced them to consent.[105] The treaty was concluded, September 27, and a supplement was adopted, September 28.

Besides the land grants to leading individuals, the Choctaws received numerous temporary annuities for the support of their government and schools; but they received no permanent grant of money or land, although they ceded to the United States the remainder of their lands in Mississippi and Alabama. They did, however, receive a guarantee that for nearly three-quarters of a century was to be the Magna Carta of their national existence. This clause, which was quoted many times in later years by able Choctaw leaders, provided that the United States would secure to them *"the jurisdiction and government of all the persons and property that may be within their limits west, so that no Territory or State shall ever have a right to pass laws for the government of the Choctaw Nation of Red People and their descendants; and that no part of the land granted them shall ever be embraced in any Territory or State; but the U. S. shall forever secure said Choctaw Nation from, and against all laws except such as from time to time may be enacted in their own National Councils, not inconsistent with the Constitution, Treaties, and Laws of the United States; and except such as may, and which have been enacted by Congress, to the extent that Congress under the Constitution are required to exercise a legislation over Indian Affairs."*

The Treaty also gave every Choctaw head of a family the opportunity of remaining, selecting an allotment, and becoming a citizen of the United States. Those who should elect to remove were to be paid for their cattle and other property left behind, and to be provided with transportation to their new homes, and with food for twelve months after their arrival.[106]

As soon as the treaty was signed, the Nation fell into a state of anarchy. There was a strong undercurrent of resentment, which expressed itself in frequent meetings where attempts were made to depose the Chiefs who had consented to the removal, and to petition the President and Senate against ratification. But the Federal Government was able to overawe the discontented, and to prevent concerted action.[107]

[105]*Senate Docs.* 23 Cong., 1 Sess., No. 512, II, 256-61, report of Eaton and Coffee.
[106]*United States Statutes at Large*, VII, 333; also Kappler, *Laws and Treaties*, II, 310-19.
[107]*Senate Docs.*, 23 Cong., 1 Sess., No. 512, II, 183, 581.

The main removals took place during 1831, 1832, and 1833. The sufferings of the emigrants were almost beyond belief. It was a difficult journey at best — 350 miles through a wild unsettled country of vast swamps, dense forests, impenetrable canebrakes, and swollen rivers. Added to this was a great deal of blundering and inefficiency on the part of the War Department. Additional suffering and loss of life was caused by one of the worst blizzards in the history of that region, which broke upon the emigrants who were removed during the Winter of 1831-32; and the cholera epidemic, which swept down the Mississippi and caught those who were crossing the following Summer.[108] The population of the tribe was permanently decreased by the losses sustained during this terrible experience.

White Americans, with their more mobile habits, have never been able to appreciate the hopeless grief of this despoiled people when they abandoned their ancient homes, and in a strictly literal sense, the bones of their beloved dead. George W. Harkins, nephew and successor to Greenwood LeFlore, made a statement at Natchez while en route to the new country that is fairly typical of this feeling:

"The man [Andrew Jackson] *who said that he would plant a stake and draw a line around us, that never should be passed, was the first to say he could not guard the lines, and drew up the stake and wiped out all traces of the line. . . . . Amid the gloom and horrors of the present separation, we are cheered with a hope that ere long we shall reach our destined home, and that nothing short of the basest acts of treachery will ever be able to wrest it from us, and that we may live free."*[109]

There is more restraint, but no less bitterness in this letter from Peter Pitchlynn to a Federal official:

"I beg, sir, that for a whole nation to give up their whole country, and remove to a distant, wild, and uncultivated land, more for the benefit of the Government than the Choctaws, is a consideration which, I hope, the Government will always cherish with the livliest sensibility. The privations of a whole nation before setting out, their turmoil and losses on the road, and settling their homes in a wild world, are all calculated to embitter the human heart."[110]

[108]Foreman, *Indian Removal*, pp. 31-104.
[109]*Niles' Register*, XLI (1832), 480.
[110]*Senate Docs.*, 23 Cong. 1 Sess., No. 512, III, 396, Pitchlynn to Lewis Cass.

Although these words were written by educated Choctaws, there is no doubt that they expressed the sentiments of the inarticulate majority of the tribe.

The three centuries of the Choctaws' intercourse with the white man had thus culminated in their expulsion from their native forests. It now remained for them to develop in the distant region to which they had been driven, the new institutions which they had adopted as the result of this intercourse. For a generation after the removal they were left unmolested to work out this problem, and to adapt themselves to the customs of the more numerous race that was eventually to absorb them.

LIFE IN THE NEW LAND

3

BEFORE the Choctaws left Mississippi, they had agreed that the Six Town people should settle west of the Kiamichi, the Upper Towns to the east of that river, and the Lower Towns in the northern part of their country, along the Arkansas.[1] Soon after their arrival they divided the country into definite districts: the *Okla Falaya*, or *Red River*, soon changed to *Apukshunnubbee*, in the southeast; the *Moshulatubbee* in the north; and the *Pushmataha* to the west of the Kiamichi.

Greenwood LeFlore, for some reason, changed his mind and decided to remain in Mississippi. He had become increasingly unpopular after the negotiation of the removal treaty, and the disaffected element in the tribe deposed him in favor of his nephew, George W. Harkins. The United States Government refused to recognize this change, but Harkins apparently continued to exercise the office of Chief. Thomas LeFlore, a cousin of Greenwood, later succeeded to the position and became Chief of the Apukshunnubbee District.[2] Moshulatubbee removed with his people of the Lower Towns and continued as Chief of the northern district until his death in a smallpox epidemic in 1838. He was succeeded by his nephew, Joseph Kincaid, who had been his active assistant during the last few years of his life.[3] Nitakechi also removed with his people, and continued as Chief of the Pushmataha District. He died in 1845 in Mississippi, where he was serving as a

[1]Foreman, *Indian Removal*, p. 46.
[2]*Senate Docs.*, 23 Cong., 1 Sess., No. 512, II, 46, 580-81, 890; *Niles' Register*, XLI (1832), 480; Thoburn and Wright, *Oklahoma*, I, 220n; Foreman, *Indian Removal*, p. 203n; Cushman, *History of the Choctaw*, p. 403.
[3]Catlin, *North American Indians*, II, 140; Foreman, *Indian Removal*, p. 203n; Kappler, *Laws and Treaties*, II, 435-39—Moshulatubbee signed the Treaty of Camp Holmes, August 24, 1835.

member of a delegation sent to induce the remaining Choctaws to join their brethren in the West.[4]

As soon as the shock of the removals was over, the Choctaws began to prosper in their new home. Through the streams and woods and mountains of their wild, but beautiful country, roads and trails were soon established and settlements sprang up. Boggy Depot grew up at the intersection where the road that later carried many gold-seekers to California crossed the highway used by the Texas emigrants; it became the trading center of that part of the country. In the southeastern part, a mile from Fort Towson, was Doaksville, the largest town in all the Indian Territory. The Federal Government established a postoffice there in 1832. Other postoffices were established at Skullyville, 1833; Eagletown, 1834; Perryville, 1841; and Boggy Depot, 1849.[5]

These towns were small, but thriving, with hotels, blacksmith shops, stores, and produce markets. They were located on important highways where great streams of emigration flowed through to Texas or California. The *Choctaw Telegraph,* established at Doaksville in 1848 by Daniel Folsom, seems to have been the first newspaper; it was succeeded in 1850 by the *Choctaw Intelligencer.*[6] A meeting held in Skullyville in 1847 took up a collection of $710 to assist the victims of the Potato Famine in Ireland. Agent William Armstrong presided, and traders, missionaries, and agency officials contributed, but the greater part of the money was subscribed by the Indians themselves.[7]

The Choctaws were mainly an agricultural people. A few had been slaveowners in Mississippi. Some of the leaders who had received special land grants under the Treaty of Dancing Rabbit Creek sold these

[4]Foreman, *Indian Removal,* pp. 103-4n, 203n.

[5]W. A. Carter, *McCurtain County and Southeast Oklahoma* (Idabel, Oklahoma, 1923), pp. 134, 137-42; Carolyn Thomas Foreman (editor), "Report of Captain John Stuart on the Construction of the Road from Fort Smith to Horse Prairie on Red River," *Chronicles of Oklahoma,* V (1927), 333-47; James Culberson, "The Fort Towson Road," *ibid.,* V (1927), 414-21; Muriel H. Wright, "Old Boggy Depot," *ibid.,* V (1927), 4-17; William B. Morrison, "A Visit to Old Fort Washita," *ibid.,* VII (1929), 175-79; William B. Morrison, "Fort Towson," *ibid.,* VIII (1930), 226-32; Muriel H. Wright, "Additional Notes on Perryville, Choctaw Nation," *ibid.,* VIII (1930), 146-48; Goode, *Outposts of Zion,* p. 187; *Report Commissioner of Indian Affairs,* 1842, p. 446.

[6]Thoburn and Wright, *Oklahoma,* I, 250; II, appendix, 786-87. The second reference gives advertisements and market quotations copied from the *Choctaw Intelligencer.* The advertisements tell of shipments of goods just received from New Orleans, and quote prices on dry goods, saddles and harness, hardware, and groceries. The following prices were offered for farm produce: $1 a bushel for corn, 75 cents a bushel for Irish potatoes, 50 cents a bushel for sweet potatoes, 12.5 cents a dozen for eggs, and 12.5 cents a pound for butter.

[7]*Niles' Register,* LXXII (1847), 139.

farms and purchased slaves with the proceeds. These thrifty individuals brought their slaves to the new land and established extensive cotton plantations along the Red River. Along the Arkansas and Canadian rivers were prosperous farms with fine orchards and extensive cornfields, well stocked with cattle, hogs, and fowls. The poorer citizens lived back in the hills, where they cultivated small patches of corn for their own food, while their cattle, hogs, and ponies, of which they owned a large number, were left to shift for themselves in the woods. Corn and pecans and large quantities of cotton were exported from the Choctaw country in exchange for manufactured goods. The shipping was carried on by means of steamboats which came up the Arkansas and Red rivers. Robert M. Jones was probably the wealthiest Choctaw citizen; he is said to have owned more than five hundred slaves, an interest in a trading establishment at Doaksville, a number of steamboats, and five large Red River plantations, of which the largest comprised more than five thousand acres.[8]

As soon as the Choctaws established their homes in the new country, they began to build their school system. The initiative was taken by the missionaries of the American Board, who in 1836 reported 11 schools with an enrollment of 228 Choctaw children. Agent F. W. Armstrong also encouraged the Choctaws to construct log buildings and organize the schools provided by the treaty annuities. Apparently some of these were opened during the Winter of 1833-34. In 1836 the agent reported that there were five schools with an enrollment of 101, supported by the Choctaw Nation; and one school in each district with a total enrollment of 51, maintained by the annuity provided by the Treaty of Dancing Rabbit Creek.[9]

The greatest step forward in Choctaw education was taken in 1842, only nine years after the removal, when the Council provided for the establishment of a comprehensive system of schools. As a result of this legislation, Spencer Academy was located ten miles north of Doaksville, and opened in February, 1844; Fort Coffee, at an abandoned military post on the Arkansas, five miles from Skullyville, was opened

[8]Thoburn and Wright, *Oklahoma*, I, 297-301; Benson, *Life among the Choctaw Indians*, pp. 33-34; Möllhausen, *Journey from the Mississippi to the Pacific*, I, 27-52; Muriel H. Wright, "Early Navigation and Commerce along the Arkansas and Red Rivers in Oklahoma," *Chronicles of Oklahoma*, VIII (1930), 65-88; Albert D. Richardson, *Beyond the Mississippi* (Hartford, Connecticut, 1867), pp. 219-22; Grant Foreman (editor), *A Traveler in Indian Territory* (Cedar Rapids, Iowa, 1930), pp. 259-61; *Report Commissioner of Indian Affairs*, 1836, p. 391; 1837, pp. 541-42, 545; 1843, p. 336; 1852, p. 412.

[9]*Report Commissioner of Indian Affairs*, 1833, p. 197; 1836, p. 421.

CHOCTAW BALL PLAY DANCE AT SKULLYVILLE BY CATLIN, 1834

PUSHMATAHA BY C. B. KING, 1824

at the same time; Armstrong Academy in the Pushmataha district, and New Hope, near Fort Coffee, were opened two years later. The Council also appropriated money for the support of Pine Ridge, Stockbridge, Goodwater, and Wheelock, which had been established earlier by the American Board.[10] In 1848 the Choctaws had nine boarding schools supported by tribal funds, and usually operated under a contract with a mission board, which furnished the teachers and paid their salaries.[11] When they established these schools in their own country, the Choctaws withdrew their support from the academy in Kentucky;[12] but they began the practice of sending a number of selected graduates from their boarding schools to attend college in the "States" at public expense, and several of the future Choctaw leaders received degrees from Dartmouth, Union, Yale, and other colleges.

Besides the boarding schools, day or neighborhood schools were established rapidly in the various communities. At first these were the result of local enterprise or missionary encouragement, but very soon they were supported by public appropriations.[13] In 1860 the Choctaws reported five hundred children enrolled in these neighborhood schools, which with the boarding school attendance brought the total school enrollment up to nine hundred.[14]

Provision was also made for adult education through the "Sunday Schools," a project initiated by the missionaries, but aided by appropriations by the Council. Whole families came and camped near the church or schoolhouse, attended school on Saturday and Sunday, and received instruction in the rudiments of arithmetic, and reading and

[10]*Ibid.*, 1842, pp. 499-501, 521; 1843, pp. 332-36, 386-87; 1844, pp. 375-77, 386-89; 1846, p. 343; Benson, *Life among the Choctaw Indians*, pp. 60-65, 99, 181, 186-87, 191-96; Thoburn and Wright, *Oklahoma*, I, 198-99, 214, 224; J. W. Bryce (editor), "Our First Schools in the Choctaw Nation," *Chronicles of Oklahoma*, VI (1928), 354-94; *Niles' Register*, LXVII (1844), 19, 178; Goode, *Outposts of Zion*, pp. 130, 183-85, 255; Joseph P. Folsom, *Digest of Choctaw Law* (*Report of the Committee on Indian Affairs of the United States Senate*, Vol. IX, Part 2, appendix—Washington, 1886), p. 489. Folsom's *Digest* was also printed by the Choctaws as a separate document (New York, 1869).

[11]*Report Commissioner of Indian Affairs*, 1847, p. 407; 1848, pp. 497, 501; Thoburn and Wright, *Oklahoma*, I, 224.

[12]Goode, *Outposts of Zion*, p. 240; Benson, *Life among the Choctaw Indians*, p. 38; John D. Lang and Samuel Taylor, Jr., *Report of a Visit to Some of the Tribes of Indians Located West of the Mississippi River* (Providence, 1843), p. 41.

[13]*Report Commissioner of Indian Affairs*, 1849, p. 1103; 1857, p. 232; 1860, p. 129; Folsom, *Digest of Choctaw Law*, pp. 501, 502, 506; *Acts and Resolutions of the General Council of the Choctaw Nation at the Called Sessions thereof held in April and June, 1858, and the Regular Session Held in October 1858* (Fort Smith, Arkansas, 1859), pp. 52-53.

[14]*Report Commissioner of Indian Affairs*, 1860, pp. 129, 135.

writing in the Choctaw language. The adult Choctaws experienced little difficulty in learning to read. Unlike the Cherokee, their language had few aspirated gutturals, and the missionaries found that most of its sounds could be indicated by the Roman alphabet. Before they had been in their new home for a generation, the Choctaws became, at least so far as their own language was concerned, a literate people.[15]

Although publications in the vernacular did not offer a wide variety of reading matter, the number of religious books and tracts published through the efforts of the indefatigable Byington and his co-workers of the American Board seems almost incredible. Besides the *New Testament* and portions of the *Old Testament,* these publications consisted of hymn books, moral lectures, biographical sketches of pious Indians, the Westminster catechism, and numerous doctrinal tracts on such formidable subjects as "Regeneration, Repentance, and Judgment," "Sinners in the Hands of an Angry God," "Salvation by Faith, and Other Pieces," and "Fraud Detected and Exposed." In 1837 the number of tracts published in the Choctaw language during the year reached a total of 30,500, embracing 576,000 pages. The American Board also compiled a Choctaw definer, and published spellers, arithmetics, and collections of Bible stories for children in the vernacular; and from 1836 to 1843 they issued a Choctaw almanac, which contained all manner of statistical information about the tribe, and used a measure of time more effective than the familiar bundles of sticks.

The *New Testament* was published in New York by the American Bible Society, under the direction of Byington and his assistant, Alfred Wright; but nearly all the other material was printed at a press that had been set up in the Cherokee Nation soon after that tribe emigrated to the West. The Methodists also used the Cherokee press to print a Choctaw edition of their Discipline; and at least as early as 1843, the Choctaw Nation used the same medium for the publication of the tribal constitution and statutes in the native tongue.[16]

But in spite of these publications in the vernacular, the Choctaws were anxious for their children to learn English, and all the regular schools were conducted in that language. Although the parents did not

[15]*Ibid.,* 1841, pp. 249, 336; 1842, p. 502; 1843, p. 337; 1844, p. 383; 1845, p. 589; 1849, p. 1115; 1856, pp. 153, 246; 1857, p. 246; 1858, p. 166; Benson, *Life among the Choctaw Indians,* pp. 40-41; *Acts of the General Council for 1858,* pp. 52-53; Acts and Resolutions of the General Council for the Regular Session of 1860, and the Called Session of 1861 (Phillips Collection, University of Oklahoma, Norman, Oklahoma), p. 96.

[16]*Report Commissioner of Indian Affairs,* 1837, p. 561; 1843, pp. 340, 350; 1844, p. 399; 1845, p. 594; 1846, p. 361; 1851, pp. 374, 376; *Niles' Register,* LXXIV (1848), 118.

appreciate the importance of regular attendance for their children, and allowed their gypsy-like fondness for camping to interfere with the school program, they were deeply interested in education. As soon as the first school was opened in Mississippi, the men, and especially the tribal officials, began the practice of frequent visits. During the day they walked quietly about the grounds or sat in the shade smoking, watching the activities of their young people; and when night came, they rolled themselves in their blankets and lay down on the ground to sleep. Before they left they always made a speech to the children in Choctaw.[17]

At least as early as 1842 the tribal schools were under the control of a board of trustees, consisting of one member from each district, appointed by the District Chiefs. Each trustee was responsible for the establishment of neighborhood schools in his district, and the appointment of the teachers; and the board as a whole made contracts with missionary societies for the operation of the boarding schools. An act passed in 1853 provided for a Superintendent of Schools, who should be *ex-officio* president of the board, and who with the trustees should be elected by the General Council for a four year term.[18]

The close coöperation between the Choctaw government and the mission boards in the management of their schools is an indication of the confidence they felt in the missionaries. This relationship made it inevitable that their conversion to Christianity would parallel the development of their educational system.

The Methodist missionaries, who had been so strongly in favor of removal, took an active part in the emigration. Alexander Talley took charge of a party during the Winter of 1830-31, and assisted them to settle on the Little River, and on the Kiamichi near Fort Towson.[19] This region was for a time the center of their educational and evangelistic work.

The Presbyterian missionaries of the American Board were less active in the removals; but Kingsbury, Byington, the physician Alfred Wright, and a few other workers joined the Indians in their new home before 1835. They settled in the southeastern part of the country, where

[17]W. B. Morrison, "The Choctaw Mission of the American Board of Commissioners for Foreign Missions," *Chronicles of Oklahoma*, IV (1926), 173; Cushman, *History of the Choctaw Indians*, p. 147; Benson, *Life among the Choctaw Indians*, p. 222; *Report Commissioner of Indian Affairs*, 1846, p. 343; 1856, p. 151; 1857, p. 251; 1858, p. 165.

[18]Benson, *Life among the Choctaw Indians*, pp. 60-62; Folsom, *Digest of Choctaw Law*, pp. 502, 505; *Report Commissioner of Indian Affairs*, 1848, pp. 1105, 1107.

[19]Foreman, *Indian Removal*, pp. 40-41; John Ross MSS, p. 10.

they established stations at Stockbridge, Pine Ridge, and Wheelock. The Wheelock Church was organized under the trees by Alfred Wright, December 9, 1832. It was a solemn and dramatic occasion for the exiles who were attempting to reëstablish their institutions in the new land. The men with their long black hair and colored blankets, and the women with their deerskin dresses and moccasins came from their scattered settlements in the woods, to join in the familiar services. At the close thirty members of the old church in Mississippi and seven others united to form the new Wheelock Church.[20]

The Baptists began their work among the Choctaws through a graduate of the Choctaw Academy, who had become a convert and had been ordained as a Baptist preacher. He began his ministry among his own people in the Fall of 1833. Shortly after his arrival, two Baptist missionaries with their wives were employed by the Federal Government to teach in the schools established by treaty funds, but their work was not subsidized by their church.[21] The Baptist work among the Choctaws did not become important during this period.

Chief Moshulatubbee, embittered by the removal experiences, determined that white influences in the way of missionary propaganda should not follow the Choctaws to their new home. Before they left Mississippi, the old Chief, with Joseph Kincaid and other irreconcilables, wrote to President Jackson that during the twelve years the mission schools had been in existence they had not turned out a "scholar" capable of keeping a grog shop book. They therefore requested the President to see that no more tribal money should be wasted on an experiment that had proved a costly failure.[22]

Under the influence of Moshulatubbee, the anti-Christian party settled in the northern district, which became for a time the center of a pagan reaction. On June 14, 1831, shortly after their arrival they sent another petition to the Federal officials requesting that Alexander Talley be expelled from their country, and that the missionaries of the American Board be forbidden to enter.[23] But the Choctaws were naturally a peaceable people, and it was difficult for them to retain any lasting resentment against the white Americans or their institutions. When the Council voted to establish the Fort Coffee and New Hope boarding

[20]Morrison, The Red Man's Trail, pp. 62-63; Morrison, "The Choctaw Mission," p. 14; Cushman, History of the Choctaw, p. 178; W. F. Dunkle (editor), "A Choctaw Indian's Diary" (Diary of Willis F. Folsom), Chronicles of Oklahoma, IV (1926), 61-69; Report Commissioner of Indian Affairs, 1843, p. 341.
[21]Isaac McCoy, History of Baptist Missions (Washington, 1840), pp. 485, 549, 574.
[22]Senate Docs., 23 Cong., 1 Sess., No. 512, II, 205, letter dated December 23, 1830.
[23]Ibid., II, 474.

schools in the Moshulatubbee District, the contract to operate them was secured by the Methodist Church. The workers came out in 1843, and began training the children in the two schools, and preaching at camp meetings in the community. Moshulatubbee by that time had died, and the people listened to the missionaries as eagerly as though there had never been any pagan sentiment among them. As a result, that district soon became Christian. By the opening of the Civil War, the Choctaw Nation may be said to have been a Christian nation in the usual acceptance of the term: 20 to 25 per cent of the people were members of Presbyterian, Methodist, or Baptist churches; Sunday observance was general; and sessions of the Council opened and closed with prayer.[24]

A great deal of temperance sentiment also developed among the Choctaws at this time, and the prohibition policy which they had adopted in Mississippi was again put into operation. An amusing story, which may or may not be true, relates the manner in which this policy was initiated. At a Council soon after their arrival in the West, many speeches were made against the evils of drink, and it was voted by acclamation that any citizen who should introduce intoxicating liquors into the Nation would be punished by one hundred lashes and the destruction of his stock. The law, however, was not made retroactive, and after adjournment the members of the Council began to realize that the liquor traffic would continue for some time until the stock on hand should be exhausted. Accordingly, they decided to drink up the available supply, a feat which they accomplished in two hours. The immediate effect upon those who performed this necessary public service is said to have been rather appalling.[25]

The legislation was strengthened and modified by the developing legal technique of the Choctaws, but the prohibition policy was continued, and the laws were well enforced by the tribal officials.[26] Many of the Choctaw leaders, especially the native preachers, were active temperance workers, and temperance societies were organized in connection with the churches and schools. Apparently there was at this time very little drunkenness in the Choctaw Nation, but many of the Choctaws habitually succumbed to temptation whenever they crossed

[24]Morrison, "The Choctaw Mission"; Benson, *Life among the Choctaw Indians;* Goode, *Outposts of Zion;* Baxter Taylor, "An Early Day Baptist Missionary," *Chronicles of Oklahoma,* IV (1926), 296-98; Folsom, *Digest of Choctaw Law,* pp. 493, 504; *Report Commissioner of Indian Affairs,* 1848, pp. 504, 508; 1851, p. 374; B. F. McCurtain, "The Indians of Oklahoma," *Sturm's Oklahoma Magazine,* XI (1910), 23.

[25]Gregg, *Commerce of the Prairies,* Thwaites, XX, 313.

[26]*Report Commissioner of Indian Affairs,* 1853, p. 421.

the Red River into Texas or the Arkansas line at Fort Smith.[27] In 1858 they actually persuaded the Texas legislature to pass a law prohibiting the sale of intoxicants to their citizens,[28] but it is apparent in all accounts of life in the border towns that no attention was ever paid to its enforcement.

While the Choctaws were building their institutions, they were establishing friendly relations with their new neighbors in the Indian Territory. At first there was some apprehension of raids from the wild tribes of the plains, and Federal troops were stationed for a short time at Fort Towson and Fort Coffee; but no serious trouble developed.[29] In 1835, a council was held at Camp Holmes, in the Creek Nation, and a treaty of peace was made between the Osages, Comanches, Wichitas, and other native tribes, and the newly arrived Creeks, Cherokees, and Choctaws.[30] The culmination of inter-tribal action was the council of the Five Civilized Tribes, as the Cherokees, Choctaws, Chickasaws, Creeks, and Seminoles soon came to be called, at North Fork Village, in the Creek Nation, November 8-14, 1859. A code of inter-tribal law was adopted, which provided that criminals fleeing from justice might be requisitioned by the nation where the crime was committed, that citizens of one nation might be admitted to citizenship in another by the consent of the proper authorities, that a citizen of one nation who should commit a crime or harbor a runaway slave in another nation would be subject to the jurisdiction of the local laws, and that the five nations would coöperate in suppressing the sale of strong drink.[31]

The Federal Government encouraged these inter-tribal conferences, hoping thereby to further a favorite project that embraced the union of all the recent immigrants and the wild tribes of the region into a consolidated territorial government. This plan was approved by genuine friends of the Indians, who believed that it would enable them to protect themselves more effectively when white encroachment should again menace their homes. It was also promoted by the frontier settlers,

[27]*Ibid.*, 1842, pp. 500, 503, 504, 505; 1851, p. 366; 1852, p. 412; Benson, *Life among the Choctaw Indians*, pp. 131-32, 223-25.

[28]*Report Commissioner of Indian Affairs*, 1851, p. 277; 1858, p. 162.

[29]Foreman, *Advancing the Frontier*, pp. 15-180.

[30]Kappler, *Laws and Treaties*, II, 435-39.

[31]The text of this important agreement was published in the *Vindicator*, December 22, 1875. For an instance of the naturalization process, *see* application of one Wash Red, a Creek, to Chief Samuel Checote in 1883 for a letter of recommendation so that he might become a citizen of the Choctaw Nation, Union Agency Files (Muskogee, Oklahoma), Creek—Foreign Relations. For example of requisition of criminals and punishment of citizens of other nations *see, infra*, p. 178.

who already coveted the land the Indians had won at the cost of such appalling suffering, and who hoped that a territorial government with ultimate statehood would bring about individual allotments that would eventually pass into the possession of the whites.[32]

In 1834, a commission which had been appointed two years before by the Federal Government, to study the problems of the recent immigrants, presented a plan to Congress for a territorial organization of all the Indians in the region. The commission was actively assisted by Isaac McCoy, a Baptist missionary, who believed that union of the Indian tribes was essential for self defense.[33] In 1837 the Indian Office authorized McCoy to select a site for the capital of the proposed territory, and he chose a location on the Osage River close to the Missouri line.[34]

Proposals for creating an Indian territory or state continued to come up in Congress, but no legislation was enacted.[35] The Government seems to have been restrained by the inconvenient pledges of the removal treaties, and by the opposition of the Indians, who were devoted to their tribal autonomy and determined not to relinquish it. The feelings of the Choctaws are shown by the desperate eloquence with which their delegate, Peter Pitchlynn, fought the proposal in 1849 —"It may be thought that I write with too much feeling; but let it be remembered, that the history and character of nearly all these tribes are familiar to me — that I have spent my life among them, and hence my anticipations of the future are based upon the history of the past, and not upon mere speculation, and my country, my people, my home and my children — all that can stimulate a man, are at stake in this matter."[36]

But although the Choctaws objected to the loss of their national identity through a consolidation of all the tribes, they worked actively for territorial privileges for themselves. At the Dancing Rabbit Creek council ground they had requested that they might have a delegate to

[32]*Niles' Register*, LXIX (1845), 87; *Report Commissioner of Indian Affairs*, 1858, pp. 127-28; John Warner Barber and Henry Howe, *Our Whole Country* (Cincinnati, 1861), II, 1477-78.

[33]Foreman, *Advancing the Frontier*, pp. 182-85.

[34]Thomas J. Farnham, *Travels in the Great Western Prairies the Anahuac and Rocky Mountains*, Thwaites, *Early Western Travels*, XXVIII, 120.

[35]Annie Heloise Abel, "Proposals for an Indian State," *American Historical Association—Annual Report*, 1907, I, 95-100; Roy Gittinger, *Formation of the State of Oklahoma* (Berkeley, California, 1917), pp. 44-55; Foreman, *Advancing the Frontier*, pp. 180-94.

[36]*House Misc. Docs.*, 30 Cong., 2 Sess., No. 35.

the House of Representatives, and at their earnest solicitation, an article presenting this request was included in the treaty.[37] But Congress never carried out the recommendation, although the Choctaws continued to petition for its adoption. Their reasons for desiring this representation are strongly brought out in a resolution of the General Council, dated November 17, 1853.

"Resolved . . . . by the General Council of the Choctaw Nation assembled, That whereas, our nation and people having many interests both of public and private character to represent at Washington: and whereas, it has been repeatedly asserted by the citizens of Arkansas that they would sooner or later extend the jurisdiction of her territorial limits to some place near the mouth of the Kiamichi, and thereby force the government of the United States to again request a portion of our country: Therefore our General Council and chiefs are hereby requested by memorial, or otherwise, to ask the government of the United States to allow the Choctaw people a delegate on the floor of Congress, to warn and guard the interests of our people as a Nation, and at the same time to represent such other matters as our citizens may from time to time wish to bring to the notice of the government."[38]

Taught by their bitter experience, the Choctaws exercised eternal vigilance to protect their new homes in the West from alienation. A law passed in 1839 prescribed the death penalty for any Chief, captain, or citizen who should sign a conveyance of Choctaw land. In 1842 they secured a confirmation of their title by a patent from the United States Government, which they guarded carefully during all the rest of their tribal history, and which is still preserved in the archives of the Oklahoma State Historical Society. This important document contained the following guarantee:

"NOW KNOW YE, That the United States of America, in consideration of the Premises, and in execution of the agreement and stipulations in the aforesaid Treaty [of Dancing Rabbit Creek], HAVE GIVEN AND GRANTED, *and by these Presents* DO GIVE AND GRANT, *unto the said Choctaw Nation, the aforesaid 'Tract of Country West of the Mississippi,'* TO HAVE AND TO HOLD *the same, with all the rights, privileges, immunities, and appurtenances of whatsoever nature, thereunto belong-*

[37]Kappler, *Laws and Treaties*, II, 315, Article XXII.
[38]*Acts and Resolutions of the General Council of the Choctaw Nation, 1852-1857 inc.* (Fort Smith, Arkansas, 1858), p. 65. See also *Niles' Register*, LXVIII (1845), 325; LXIX (1854), 51; *Report Commissioner of Indian Affairs*, 1856, p. 147.

ing, as intended 'to be conveyed' by the aforesaid Article, 'in fee simple, to them and their descendants, to inure to them, while they shall exist as a Nation, and live on it,' liable to no transfer or alienation, except to the U. States, or with their consent."

The Choctaws believed that their only hope for retaining possession of their land was through tribal tenure rather than individual ownership. They had good reason to fear allotment. It will be remembered that the Treaty of Dancing Rabbit Creek had given them the option of selecting allotments and remaining in Mississippi. Apparently it was assumed at the time that few would claim the benefit of this provision, and the government officials were deeply chagrined to learn that in spite of their utmost persuasion more than one-third of the whole tribe elected to remain and become citizens of the United States.[39] William Ward, the Federal agent to the Choctaws in Mississippi, was an habitual drunkard and notoriously inattentive to duty; but he carried out the policy of his superiors by neglecting to file the applications for allotment, and by threatening with personal violence those who became too persistent in presenting them.[40] At the same time the white settlers had not waited for the removal interval, specified by the treaty, to elapse, but began moving at once into the Choctaws' land and taking possession of their improvements.[41] For several years after the removals proper were over, large numbers of these despoiled people, driven by white purchasers from the farms which they had supposed to be registered as their homesteads, made their way to their brethren in the West.

The population of the Choctaw Nation in Alabama and Mississippi had been variously estimated,[42] but the number was probably about twenty thousand. A census taken by the Federal Government in 1831 just before the removal, was apparently more accurate than the usual statistics of the Indian Office; according to these figures, LeFlore's district had a population of 7,505, Nitakechi's had 6,106, and Moshulatubbee's, 5,943, making a total of 19,554, which included 97 white citizens and 248 Negro slaves.[43] It was estimated that 18,000 emigrated during 1831-33, but these figures do not take account of the appalling number of deaths on the trail, and for the first few years after arrival. Bying-

[39]*Senate Docs.,* 23 Cong., 1 Sess., No. 512, I, 290-91, 325-26; II, 493.
[40]*Ibid.,* IV, 556; *Senate Reports,* 35 Cong., 2 Sess., No. 374.
[41]*Senate Docs.,* 23 Cong., 1 Sess., No. 512, II, 628, 697; III, 193, 363.
[42]John R. Swanton, *Early History of the Creek Indians and their Neighbors,* Bureau of American Ethnology, *Bulletin No. 73* (Washington, 1922), pp. 452, 454-55.
[43]*Senate Docs.,* 23 Cong., 1 Sess., No. 512, III, 149.

ton's *Choctaw Almanac,* which was rather carefully compiled, gave the population as 12,690 in 1843.[44]

For a whole generation after the main removals, there was a gradual movement of Mississippi Choctaws to the "New Nation." Small parties came on their own initiative, but by far the greater number came in larger groups as the result of special effort on the part of the United States Government. The distrust which they felt toward the proposals of the Federal officials is shown by the reply of Chief Cobb to Capt. J. J. McRea, who had addressed them in Council in 1843, urging them to remove.

> *"Brother: When you were young we were strong; we fought by your side; but our arms are now broken. You have grown large. My people have become small.*
>
> *"Brother: My voice is weak; you can scarcely hear me; it is not the shout of a warrior but the wail of an infant. I have lost it in mourning over the misfortunes of my people. These are their graves, and in those aged pines you hear the ghosts of the departed.—Their ashes are here, and we have been left to protect them. Our warriors are nearly all gone to the far country west; but here are our dead. Shall we go too, and give their bones to the wolves?*
>
> .   .   .   .
>
> *"Brother: Our hearts are full. Twelve winters ago our chiefs sold our country. Every warrior that you see here was opposed to the treaty. If the dead could have counted, it could never have been made, but alas! though they stood around, they could not be seen or heard. Their tears came in the raindrops, and their voices in the wailing wind, but the pale faces knew it not, and our land was taken away.*
>
> *". . . . When you took our country, you promised us land. There is your promise in the book. Twelve times have the trees dropped their leaves, and yet we have received no land. Our houses have been taken from us. The white man's plough turns up the bones of our fathers. We dare not kindle our fires; and yet you said we might remain and you would give us land."*[45]

But a large number of the Eastern Choctaws finally consented to emigrate, and the most important removals since 1833 took place during 1845-47. It was reported that 3,824 joined their Western kinsmen at

[44]Gregg, *Commerce of the Prairies,* Thwaites, XX, 317n; *Report Commissioner of Indian Affairs,* 1844, pp. 321, 456; *House Reports,* 42 Cong., 3 Sess., No. 94.

[45]*Niles' Register,* LXIV (1843), 131-32.

that time, and in the Fifties a few hundred more followed them to the new home.[46] The population of the "New Nation" toward the close of the period is usually placed at about 15,000, but this estimate is probably too high.

Besides these accessions of their own people, the Choctaws also received the Chickasaws into their country during this period. Almost as soon as the Treaty of Dancing Rabbit Creek was signed, and before the Choctaws had hardly begun to emigrate, the Federal officials approached them regarding the cession of a portion of their Western land to this kindred tribe. The harassed Choctaws were too demoralized over the removal to meet in Council, and one of them bluntly informed the commissioners that they had hoped at least to set foot on their new land before they should be asked to part with it.[47] But the Chickasaws ceded their lands to the United States in 1832, and in 1837 they signed a treaty with the Choctaws at Doaksville, by which for a consideration of $530,000 they secured the right to settle in the Choctaw country.[48] Here they found themselves in a minority, outvoted in the government, and treated as intruders by their new neighbors; and the two tribes were finally separated by the three-cornered Treaty of 1855, signed by the Choctaws, the Chickasaws, and the United States. By this treaty the Chickasaws were to establish an independent government over their district, which was located in the central part of the country between the Canadian and Red rivers, and bounded on the east by the Island Bayou and a line drawn due north from its source, and on the west by the ninety-eighth meridian. The tribal moneys were to be kept separate but the title to the land was to be held in common, and the citizens of either nation were privileged to settle within the jurisdiction of the other, and enjoy the "rights, privileges, and immunities" of citizenship.

The same treaty also provided for the settlement of several outstanding disputes between the United States and the Choctaws.

When the Choctaws had purchased their lands in the West, the western boundary was somewhat vague. It had also been discovered later that their purchase overlapped lands already occupied by the

[46]Ibid., LXV (1844), 339; LXVII (1845), 369; LXVIII (1845), 36, 64; LXX (1846), 18; LXXI (1847), 355; LXXII (1848), 299; Report Commissioner of Indian Affairs, 1845, p. 459; 1846, p. 267; 1847, pp. 411, 877; 1848, p. 490; 1853, p. 405; 1854, p. 130.

[47]Senate Docs., 23 Cong., 1 Sess., No. 512, I, 932; II, 273-75, 301, 359-60, 570, 624, 690, 697, 700, 739, 787; Foreman, Indian Removal, p. 49.

[48]United States Statutes at Large, XI, 573.

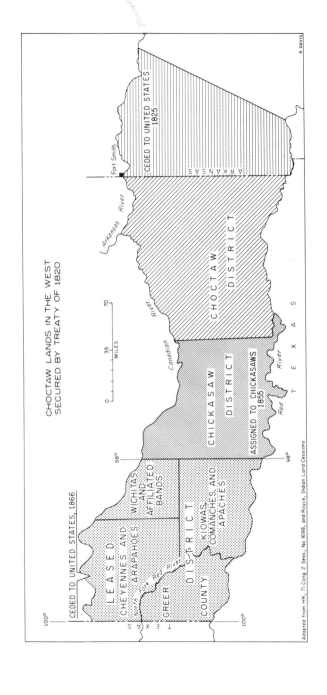

CHOCTAW LANDS IN THE WEST
SECURED BY TREATY OF 1820

Wichitas and other bands. This treaty settled the boundary definitely at the hundredth meridian, and provided that the land between this boundary and the Chickasaw District should be leased to the United States as a permanent home for the Wichitas and their neighbors. For this "Leased District" the Choctaws and Chickasaws were to receive from the United States the sum of $800,000 to be divided between the two tribes respectively in the ratio of three to one, and were to retain their privilege of settling there. For some time the Choctaws had been dissatisfied with the survey of their eastern boundary, which had been fixed by the Treaty of 1825. The United States now undertook to check the accuracy of this line.

The Choctaws also claimed that they had been wronged by the failure of the United States to fulfil the obligations assumed by the Treaty of Dancing Rabbit Creek. They had never been paid for the cattle and other property abandoned at the time of their removal. Those who had paid their own expenses of removal had never been reimbursed. Those who had chosen to remain in Mississippi had lost their allotments through the hostility of the Federal officials. Finally, after all the expenses of removal had been deducted, the United States had realized a large profit from the sale of their Mississippi lands to white settlers. Since 1853 a delegation[49] of which P. P. Pitchlynn was the head, had been in Washington pushing this claim; they maintained that the Government should reimburse each individual Choctaw defrauded in the course of the removals, and should pay the Nation the "Net Proceeds," or the amount realized from the sale of the lands after subtracting the cost of the removals and survey. The Treaty of 1855 now referred the whole question to the arbitration of the United States Senate, and stipulated that the decision should be final.[50]

The Senate made its award in 1859. It was found that many individual Choctaws had indeed suffered wrong, but the determination of the amount was too detailed and complicated a question for a legislative body to decide. The Senate, therefore, made an award of $2,981,247.30 on the basis of the Net Proceeds, leaving the Choctaw government the adjudication and payment of individual claims. Although by this decision the Choctaws received no allowance for the live stock and household property they had left behind in Mississippi, and were charged

[49]*Acts of the General Council, 1852-1857*, pp. 54-55, law creating the delegation. *See* also pp. 74, 91-93, 100-1, 103.

[50]*United States Statutes at Large*, XI, 611; *see* also Kappler, *Laws and Treaties*, II, 706-14.

for all the legitimate and illegitimate expenses of their removal, it was, nevertheless, a substantial victory for them.

On March 2, 1861, Congress began the payment of this award by appropriating $250,000 in cash and an equal amount in bonds to be delivered to the Choctaw Nation. As the unprecedented drought of the previous Summer had brought many of the poorer Choctaws to the verge of famine, the General Council appropriated a large share of this sum for relief; but the Civil War began at that time, and nearly the whole amount was lost or dissipated in the general confusion. The United States Government never delivered the bonds, because the Choctaw Nation joined the Confederacy.[51]

While the Choctaws were winning diplomatic victories in their controversies with the United States, they were at the same time developing their organic law. In 1834 they wrote a new constitution, which vested all legislative power in a General Council. This body was composed of twenty-seven elected members, who were paid for their services from the tribal annuities. The three District Chiefs were regarded as *ex-officio* members of the Council, and any two of them could veto legislative enactments unless they were repassed by a two-thirds majority. The laws were in written form, and a copy was deposited with the United States agent.[52] In the central part of their settlements near the present site of Tuskahoma, they built a commodious log council house, which was given the sacred name of Nanih Waya. This building was used for the first time during the Council session of 1838.[53]

When the Chickasaws were incorporated within the Choctaw Nation, changes in the government became necessary, and a new constitution was adopted in 1838. A fourth district was created west of the older settlements, where most of the new arrivals had established their homes; and the number of Council members was increased to forty. There were now four District Chiefs, who were elected for four years, and who were eligible for reëlection.[54] In 1843 the constitution was changed again to make a bicameral Council, with a Senate of four members from each district holding office for two years, and a House of Repre-

[51]*House Misc. Docs.*, 45 Cong., 2 Sess., No. 251; *Miscellaneous Documents Relating to Indian Affairs* (Indian Office Library, Washington), XV, 11935-60; Acts of the General Council, 1860, pp. 82-85, 105.

[52]*Report Commissioner of Indian Affairs*, 1836, p. 391.

[53]*Ibid.*, 1838, p. 509.

[54]*Ibid.*, 1838, p. 509; 1840, p. 310; 1842, p. 447; Gregg, *Commerce of the Prairies*, Thwaites, XX, 310-11; Farnham, *Travels in the Great Western Prairies*, Thwaites, XXVIII, 123; Thoburn and Wright, *Oklahoma*, II, 806-7.

sentatives elected annually and apportioned among the districts according to population.[55] The experimenting Choctaws soon became dissatisfied with this constitution, because it proved difficult of amendment, and from 1853 to 1857 they held numerous conventions and elections in an attempt to form a new organic law.[56] While this movement was in progress, the separation of the Choctaws and Chickasaws by the Treaty of 1855 made some change in the government really necessary. Finally in January, 1857, a new constitution was drafted at Skullyville, which abolished the office of District Chief and created a Governor for the Nation. Conservative citizens objected to this constitution saying it had been illegally adopted and that it created a State in place of their old tribal government. They met at Doaksville, in May, 1858, wrote a new constitution, and proceeded to elect a rival set of officers. For a time there was danger of civil war between the factions, but a compromise satisfactory to all was reached by the constitution of 1860, which retained the district organization with its District Chiefs and courts, and provided for a national government with a Principal Chief and other executive officers, a General Council of two houses, and a Supreme Court. This constitution with very few amendments was the fundamental law of the Choctaw Nation throughout the rest of its tribal history.[57]

Although the Skullyville constitution was short-lived and was accepted by only a part of the Choctaw people, the legislation enacted under its provisions was recognized as official and became a part of the Choctaw legal code. It was this government that adopted the official seal, with its bow and crossed arrows and combined pipe and hatchet, which now forms a part of the Great Seal of Oklahoma.[58]

During this period of constitutional experimentation, the Choctaw capital also was changed back and forth several times from Nanih

[55]*Report Commissioner of Indian Affairs*, 1843, p. 410; 1853, p. 407; Möllhausen, *Journey from the Mississippi to the Pacific*, I, 40-41.
[56]*Acts of the General Council, 1852-1857*, pp. 55-56, 57, 58, 82, 99-100, 102.
[57]*Acts and Resolutions of the General Council of the Choctaw Nation for the year 1859* (Fort Smith, 1860), pp. 7-25, constitution of 1857; *Acts of the General Council, 1858*, pp. 31-33, 43, 45, 64-67; *Report Commissioner of Indian Affairs*, 1857, pp. 231-32; 1858, pp. 130-31; 1859, p. 188; 1860, p. 128; Seth K. Corden and W. B. Richards, *The Oklahoma Red Book* (Oklahoma City, 1912), I, 211-23, text of constitution of 1860.
[58]Acts of the Choctaw Nation (Phillips Collection), October 26, 1857—a manuscript collection consisting of the original acts as endorsed by the presiding officers of the two Houses, approved by the executive, and filed with the National Secretary.

Waya to Doaksville, Skullyville, Fort Towson, and Boggy Depot.[59] Finally a constitutional amendment, adopted in 1862, provided that in the Fall of 1863 the Council should meet at Armstrong Academy, which should be the permanent capital of the Nation with the name of Chahta Tamaha.[60]

The Choctaws also built up a comprehensive law code out of a curious mixture of English law and savage custom. Before they left Mississippi, they had established two important principles that became the basis of their developing legal system. When they instituted the lighthorsemen with their informal trials and summary punishments, they accepted the principle that law enforcement was a matter of tribal concern rather than of private revenge. When they began to modify their ancient customs by decisions of their warriors in council, they recognized the legislative character of their legal code. Now they established a system of courts, and adopted jury trial and the court procedure of the neighboring states; and their General Council became strictly a law-making body in the Anglo-American sense.

Under the constitution of 1838 each district had three elective judges, who held inferior and superior courts within the district, and trial by jury was guaranteed in the Bill of Rights.[61] In 1850 the judicial system was changed: county courts were created for the trial of minor cases; instead of a local court for each district, a circuit judge held court three months a year in each of the four districts;[62] and there was a national court composed of one supreme and three associate judges sitting at the council house six months of the year. Both the circuit and national court had appellate jurisdiction.[63] The lighthorsemen by this time had lost their judicial functions, but they continued to make arrests and carry out the sentences of the courts.

According to the testimony of friendly observers, Choctaw court procedure was smooth and regular, and the laws were well enforced.[64] The punishments consisted of fines, whipping, and death by shooting.

[59]Muriel H. Wright, "Historic Spots in the Vicinity of Tuskahoma,"*Chronicles of Oklahoma*, IX (1931), 27-42; Möllhausen, *Journey from the Mississippi to the Pacific*, I, 40; *Acts of the General Council, 1852-1857*, p. 85.

[60]Folsom, *Digest of Choctaw Law*, p. 468.

[61]Farnham, *Travels in the Great Western Prairies*, Thwaites, XXVIII, 123; *Report Commissioner of Indian Affairs*, 1840, pp. 310-11. It is possible that the judges at this time were appointed by the Chiefs.—*See Report Commissioner of Indian Affairs*, 1842, p. 447; 1843, p. 410.

[62]The Chickasaws, of course, constituted the fourth district.

[63]*Report Commissioner of Indian Affairs*, 1851, p. 367.

[64]*Ibid.*, 1843, p. 410; 1846, p. 268; Benson, *Life among the Choctaw Indians*, p. 29.

For a long time prisons were unnecessary, but the proud stoicism of the old time Choctaw who presented himself on the appointed day for the execution of his sentence, broke down under the demoralizing influences of civilization, and before 1860 it was necessary to build jails and to provide for the guarding of prisonsers.[65] In general the Choctaws were a quiet and law abiding people, but they did not seem to set a very high value upon human life, and murder and suicide were frightfully common.

Choctaw marriage customs also underwent considerable legal modification at this time. A law of 1835 provided for a brief marriage ceremony consisting of a mutual admission of intention before a captain or preacher; and in 1849 all couples living together were required to conform to this custom. In 1836 the most fundamental of all the primitive taboos was abolished, when it was made lawful to marry within the iksa. Polygamy still existed as late as 1845, but it was not approved; and it was made illegal in 1849.[66] Family life was pure, and the laws regarding property and marriage gave the wife complete equality with her husband.[67]

The Choctaws also began to regulate the intermarriage of white men within their tribe. A law passed in 1849 provided that any white man living with a Choctaw woman should enter into a legal marriage with her or be expelled from the country, and that no white man of bad character would be permitted to marry a Choctaw woman "under any circumstances whatever."[68]

At this time there was very little white immigration, and only a slight admixture of white blood. The mixed blood ascendency that had been so apparent in Choctaw councils just before the removal had declined; and the government was carried on by the fullbloods, or by men like the third generation of Folsoms who had forgotten that they had one white ancestor. The mixed bloods often served as school trustees or in some other appointive position but it was very difficult for them to secure an elective office. The Choctaws were eager to adopt civilized

[65]*Acts of the General Council, 1852-1857; Acts of the General Council 1858; Acts of the General Council, 1859;* Acts of the General Council, 1860-61; Folsom, *Digest of Choctaw Law,* legislation enacted from 1834 to 1869; Benson, *Life among the Choctaw Indians,* pp. 213-15. Acts were passed 1858-1860 substituting hanging for shooting as a means of capital punishment, but they were soon repealed.

[66]Folsom, *Digest of Choctaw Law,* pp. 486, 498.

[67]*Ibid.,* pp. 496-97; Benson, *Life among the Choctaw Indians,* pp. 31-32. Women, of course, had not yet attained equality before the law in the white societies of America and Europe.

[68]Folsom, *Digest of Choctaw Law,* p. 499.

customs that they considered superior to their own, but they had a strong clannishness that made them desire to live by themselves and work out their own destiny.[69]

Among themselves they were a sociable people, and rode their hardy little ponies to many neighborhood and tribal gatherings, where they usually camped out for several days under the trees. They joined heartily in the religious camp meetings conducted by their white missionaries or their native preachers. They entered actively into the political campaigns, and large numbers visited the Council sessions to listen to the speeches of the Chiefs and legislators. At first the regular annuity payment at the agency was a festive occasion, with the happy disorder of an Indian encampment mingled with the alluring displays of the traders; but after the Choctaws appropriated their money for education, the per caput distributions declined, and finally ceased. They soon abandoned the pole pulling ceremony at their burials, but the "funeral cry" where relatives and friends assembled to pay their respects to the dead by wailing and feasting was still observed and widely attended. The most exciting gathering was the ball play, which was of semi-official character, and usually took place between districts or counties.[70]

At the time of the removals a large proportion of the Choctaws wore their native costume, but by the close of the period they dressed much like the frontier white people of their day. They had begun to adopt European names before they left Mississippi, and the custom was rapidly extended after education became more general; their white teachers found it more convenient to rechristen their pupils in honor of some "pious friend of the Mission," or some prominent historical character, than to stumble through the complicated syllables that made up the average Choctaw name.

Taken as a whole the generation from 1833 to 1861 presents a record of orderly development almost unprecedented in the history of any people. The Choctaws had settled a wild and remote frontier, accepted an alien religion and code of morals, established an educational system completely foreign to their aboriginal conceptions, adopted the constitutional and legal system of an unrelated racial experience, and modified their agricultural and commercial practices to conform to a complex economic system; and these innovations had been so eagerly

[69]Benson, *Life among the Choctaw Indians*, pp. 101-5; *Acts of the General Council, 1852-1857*, p. 78.

[70]Goode. *Outposts of Zion*, pp. 154, 164-65, 193-95; Benson, *Life among the Choctaw Indians*, pp. 154-56, 292-95; Möllhausen, *Journey from the Mississippi to the Pacific* 1, 40-41.

accepted that they had become fundamental in their social, political, and economic life. Strangely enough they never showed any resentment against the Government that had driven them into exile, and they desired nothing more than autonomous development under its protection. Engrossed in the satisfying activities of their remote society, they seemed unconscious of the menace that lay across the future of the great Republic with which their fate was so closely joined.

THE CIVIL WAR AND RECON-
STRUCTION

4

THE idyllic calm of this remote society was rudely shattered by the Civil War. Almost to a man the Choctaws sided with the Confederacy, and they continued their support until the end. There were many reasons why they should have felt that their fortunes lay with the South. Their laws supported slavery, and a few of them were large slave owners. Douglas H. Cooper, who had been for eight years their loved and trusted agent, was an active Southern sympathizer. They feared the Republican Party, for during the campaign of 1860 Seward had openly advocated the policy of seizing their land and filling it with white settlers. When the war began, they were neglected by the United States, while men from Arkansas and Texas carried on an active, and sometimes threatening, propaganda among them.[1] It is evident from the tone of their official pronouncements that they believed the United States Government on the verge of collapse.

Quickly and almost lightly they entered the conflict. The General Council, called in special session, passed an act, approved February 6, 1861, instructing their delegates at Washington to confer with the authorities there regarding the safety of their invested funds, and to withdraw them if necessary and deposit them in Southern banks.[2] The next day the Principal Chief was authorized to appoint delegates to any inter-tribal convention that might be called to determine their relations with the United States "so long as said Government is in existence,

[1]Annie Heloise Abel, *The American Indian under Reconstruction* (Cleveland, 1925), p. 234; Thoburn and Wright, *Oklahoma*, II, 297-301, 832-34; Acts and Resolutions of the General Council 1860, and January-February Session, 1861, pp. 86, 88-89, resolution, October 31, 1860, asking that Cooper be retained as agent in spite of the change in administration.

[2]Acts and Resolutions of the General Council, 1860 and January-February Session, 1861, pp. 129-30.

otherwise to urge a renewal of such relations with such Confederacy as may be framed among the Southern States."[3] A resolution of the same date, which the Principal Chief was instructed to communicate to the governors of the Southern states, expressed regret over the "present unhappy political disagreement" between the North and South, and declared that if dissolution of the Union should result, the "natural affections, education, institutions, and interests" of the Choctaws would bind them to the South.[4]

The next day, February 8, it was provided that the Council should elect twelve delegates who, with the Principal Chief, were to meet a similar Chickasaw delegation in joint convention at Boggy Depot, March 11, "to consult for the common safety of these two tribes, in the event of the dissolution of the American Union."[5] This convention met on the appointed day, and former Governor Walker of the Choctaw Nation was elected chairman. A delegation of Texas citizens visited and addressed this meeting; they were highly pleased with the unanimity of Southern sentiment displayed by the delegates and the parliamentary skill and decorum with which they conducted their deliberations. Resolutions were passed recommending the raising of a company of minute men in each county of the two nations to be drilled for actual service when necessary.[6]

The Net Proceeds delegates, however, who represented the Choctaw Nation at Washington, hoped to keep their country out of the war. In April they assured the Commissioner of Indian Affairs that their people would remain neutral,[7] and Pitchlynn returned home and worked so actively for neutrality that he was threatened by a Texas vigilance committee. George Hudson, the Principal Chief, prepared a neutrality message to deliver at a special session of the Council which he had called to convene on June 1. Robert M. Jones, who was one of the most ardent secessionists in the Nation, learned of his intention through Douglas H. Cooper. At a secession meeting held in Doaksville, which was at that time the capital, Jones made a furious speech attacking all who opposed secession. The Chief became convinced or intimidated, and when he appeared before the Council he advised the appointment

[3]*Ibid.*, pp. 131-32.

[4]*The War of the Rebellion, a Compilation of the Official Records of the Union and Confederate Armies* (Washington, 1880-1901), First Series, I, 681.

[5]Acts and Resolutions of the General Council, 1860 and January-February Session, 1861, pp. 121-22.

[6]*War of the Rebellion*, Fourth Series, I, 322-23.

[7]Annie Heloise Abel, *The American Indian as Slaveholder and Secessionist* (Cleveland, 1915), p. 74.

of commissioners to treat with the Confederacy, and the raising of a regiment for the Confederate army.[8]

On June 10 the Council declared the Choctaw Nation free and independent, and appointed commissioners to make a treaty of alliance with the Confederate states.[9] These commissioners proceeded to North Fork Village in the Creek Nation, where they met Albert Pike, the Confederate Commissioner. Here on July 12 they signed a very favorable treaty, by which the Confederate Government assumed all obligations owed by the United States, and guaranteed the Choctaws a large measure of independence and protection.[10]

The Choctaws did little active fighting during the war, although with the Chickasaws they raised three regiments, which, under the command of Tandy Walker, constituted the Second Indian Brigade.[11] The Choctaw troops took some part in the fighting in Arkansas and Missouri, and they were engaged with the Federal forces in the Creek Nation at the battle of Honey Springs; but most of the time they were stationed in the southern part of their own country in temporary camps, or at Fort McCulloch, an elaborate defense that Albert Pike constructed on the Blue River. Their country did not suffer seriously from invasion by the enemy, although in 1863 the Union forces penetrated to Perryville, and destroyed the Confederate stores there. The Union forces, however, captured Fort Smith, Arkansas, with its Choctaw outpost of Skullyville, and they occupied the Cherokee and Creek nations during the last two years of the war.[11a] The defeat of their Indian allies brought the Choctaws a distressing food shortage, for the Confederate forces of the Creeks and Cherokees were stationed in the Choctaw country, and thousands of destitute civilians who had fled from their homes before the invaders established refugee camps on the Boggy, Blue, and Kiamichi rivers, where they remained until the termination of the war.[12]

[8]Thoburn and Wright, *Oklahoma*, II, 823-34; Abel, *The American Indian as Slaveholder and Secessionist*, pp. 75-79.

[9]*War of the Rebellion*, First Series, III, 593-94, proclamation of Chief Hudson, June 14.

[10]*Ibid.*, Fourth Series, I, 445-66, text of treaty.

[11]*Ibid.*, First Series, XXX, Part IV, 694.

[11a]For a complete account of the Civil War in the Indian Territory *see* Annie Heloise Abel, *The American Indian as a Participant in the Civil War* (Cleveland, 1919). *See* also Thoburn and Wright, *Oklahoma*, I, 353, 359, and Muriel H. Wright, "Additional Notes on Perryville, Choctaw Nation," *Chronicles of Oklahoma*, VIII (1930), 146-48.

[12]Angie Debo, "Southern Refugees of the Cherokee Nation," *Southwestern Historical Quarterly*, XXXV (April, 1932), 255-66.

The Choctaws coöperated actively with the other Indian allies of the Confederacy through a Grand Council of all the tribes, which from 1863 on was usually held at Chahta Tamaha. The Nation also sent a delegate to the Confederate Congress,[13] a privilege which the United States had always denied to its Indian protectorates. The Choctaws were greatly displeased by the intricate quarrels and conflicts of authority that characterized the Confederate command in their country; they desired that the Indian Territory, which was regarded as an appendage of Arkansas, should constitute a separate department, and that Douglas H. Cooper should be placed in supreme command.[14]

As the fortunes of the Confederacy declined, there was some apprehension that the Choctaws were weakening in their support.[15] That they were, in fact, becoming discouraged is indicated by a letter from Jackson McCurtain, an officer in their army, to General McNeil, who was in command of the Union forces at Van Buren, Arkansas. He said that he was using his influence to induce his people to make peace with the United States, but that he hoped to prevent a division within the tribe—"As we dont wish to be divided like other Nations if we can be saved any other way. As we all come out together and we should all like to come in together." He felt that it would be difficult for all the Choctaws "to turn over at the same time" while the Southern forces occupied the Nation, but "by working the thing slowly it will succeed in time."[16]

It was probably this fear of the internecine strife that had devastated the Cherokee and Creek nations that held the Choctaws so steadily to the Confederate alliance, for there was never any serious defection. In February of 1864, Colonel William A. Phillips invaded the Chickasaw Nation and penetrated almost to Fort Washita. He distributed copies of Lincoln's Amnesty Proclamation and carried on an active propaganda to detach the Indians from the Confederate alliance. On February 15 he addressed a message to the Choctaw Council bidding them "choose between peace and mercy and destruction," but they refused to treat.[17] In the Summer of 1864 the First Choctaw Regiment reënlisted for the duration of the war; it prepared a statement that its mem-

---

[13]*War of the Rebellion*, Fourth Series, III, 1189,1191. Robert M. Jones was the Choctaw delegate to the Confederate Congress.

[14]*Ibid.*, First Series, XXII, Part II, 1122 1124-25.

[15]*Ibid.*, First Series, XXII, Part II, 1016, 1024, 1031, 1046, 1106-7.

[16]Abel, *The American Indian under Reconstruction*, pp. 15-16n. This letter was dated December 16, 1863.

[17]*Ibid.*, First Series, XXXIV, Part I, 110-12.

bers would support no man for the Council in the coming election who would not come out in favor of universal conscription.[18]

Toward the close of the war a few Choctaw citizens who claimed to be loyal to the Union tried to advance their importance by claiming recognition from the United States as the *de jure* government. They met in 1864, first at Doaksville, and later at Skullyville and New Hope. At New Hope on March 14 they drew up a provisional government and chose Edward P. Perkins, a recently intermarried citizen, as delegate to Washington, and Thomas Edwards, also an adopted citizen, as governor. Colonel Phillips refused to recognize them, saying that the Nation was "still *de facto* rebel" and that if no inconvenient promises were made the land would be subject to confiscation at the close of the war.[19] Phillips was correct in saying that the Choctaws were still loyal to the South, for they continued their support until its government collapsed. They were then left completely at the mercy of the Federal Government, for they had violated the most fundamental principle of their "foreign" policy when they had taken up arms against the United States. The people of Kansas were clamoring for the removal of the Indian tribes who owned land in that state, and millions of liberated Negroes were trustfully expecting "forty acres and a mule" from the authorities at Washington. The homes of the "rebel Indians" might be confiscated as a cheap and convenient solution of these two problems.

Tenacious of the independent position of their Nation as an ally of the Confederacy they denied the right of its military authorities to include them in the terms of surrender.[20] But they fully realized their peril at the hands of the Federal Government, and joined forces with the other Indians for the diplomatic struggle that lay before them. At Camp Napoleon on May 24 representatives of fourteen tribes entered into a "solemn league of peace and friendship" to maintain the integrity of the Indian Territory as the future home of the Indian race, upon the principle that "An Indian shall not spill another Indian's blood." A called session of the Grand Council held at Chahta Tamaha on June 15 adopted resolutions accepting these principles and inviting Union Indians to unite with them in joint negotiation of a peace treaty.[21]

[18]*Ibid.*, First Series, XXX, Part IV, 694-95.
[19]Abel, *The American Indian under Reconstruction*, pp. 17-21, 28n; Indian Office Files (Office of Commissioner of Indian Affairs, Washington), Choctaw, 1868, B583, V15.
[20]*War of the Rebellion*, First Series, XLVIII, Part II, 1095.
[21]*Ibid.*, First Series, XLVIII, Part II, 1103-4.

General F. J. Herron, the Federal officer in command of the Northern District of Louisiana, authorized commissioners to treat with this Council, but they arrived after its adjournment, and made a separate armistice with each tribe.[22] The war closed officially for the Choctaws on June 19, 1865, when Chief Pitchlynn surrendered the military forces of the Nation to this commission at Doaksville. The armistice was to remain in force until a treaty of peace should be ratified; the Choctaws were to lay down their arms, and the United States undertook to protect them from whites and Union Indians.[23]

The regular session of the Grand Council was to convene at Chahta Tamaha on the first Monday in September. The Confederate Indians were extremely anxious for the peace negotiations to take place there, but in spite of their protests the United States decided on Fort Smith. As it was too late to notify the wild plains tribes of the change of plans, it was decided that the Grand Council should convene at the appointed time and then adjourn to meet the United States commissioners.[24] Israel Folsom of the Choctaw Nation was President of the Grand Council, and representatives of the Five Civilized Tribes and the Osages, Comanches, Caddoes, and Arapahoes were in attendance.[25]

A called session of the Choctaw General Council also convened at Chahta Tamaha, which it will be remembered was now the capital of the Nation, and on September 6 provided for the appointment of seven men from each district, who with Chief Pitchlynn should constitute the Choctaw delegation at Fort Smith.[26] Robert M. Jones was selected as the president of this delegation, and all its members were Southern men.[27]

The Fort Smith Council convened September 8 with D. N. Cooley, Commissioner of Indian Affairs, as president, and Charles E. Mix, chief clerk of the Indian Bureau, as secretary.[28] The Choctaw delegation, delayed by the Grand Council, did not arrive for some time, but William S. and Robert B. Patton were present, having been appointed by the United States agent to represent the few Union Choctaws.[29]

On the second day of the session the United States commissioners

[22]Abel, *The American Indian under Reconstruction*, pp. 146-47.
[23]*War of the Rebellion*, First Series, XLVIII, Part II, 1105, proclamation of Chief Pitchlynn; *ibid.*, 1106, text of the armistice.
[24]Abel, *The American Indian under Reconstruction*, pp. 153n, 167-71.
[25]*Ibid.*, pp. 186-87n.
[26]Folsom, *Digest of Choctaw Law*, pp. 581-82.
[27]*Report Commissioner of Indian Affairs*, 1865, p. 306.
[28]*Ibid.*, p. 297.
[29]*Ibid.*, pp. 120, 316.

delivered their ultimatum to the Council. The Indians were to abolish slavery and incorporate the freedmen into their tribes upon equal footing or make some other suitable provision for them; and to surrender part of their lands for the location of friendly Indians from Kansas. The United States undertook to form one consolidated government for the Indian Territory, and prevent all white persons but employees of the Government, or of internal improvement corporations from settling therein.[30]

The Pattons replied for the Choctaws two days later. They said that they were not authorized to speak for their government, but that they personally approved of all the provisions except the one which restricted only white men from settling among the Indians, and they suggested that the prohibition should include Negroes also.[31] Even this hand-picked delegation opposed the scheme to colonize Negroes from the Southern states within the Indian Territory.

On September 13 the United States commissioners presented their demands in the form of a preliminary treaty. The preamble stated that the Indians having been "induced by the machinations of the emissaries" of the Confederacy to throw off their allegiance to the Federal Government were now ready to make peace and acknowledge the "exclusive jurisdiction" of the United States. The provisions of the treaty then followed very closely the terms of the ultimatum presented on September 9.[32]

The official Choctaw delegates reported to the Council on September 16.[33] Two days later, with the Chickasaws, they replied to the proposals of the United States in a statement so lucid, so able, and so dignified that it deserves to rank with the greatest state papers produced by this gifted people. They said they had not joined the South because of the "machinations" of Confederate emissaries, but because such a course had seemed to offer the best means of preserving their national identity. Believing that separation was an established fact they had felt free to treat with the South, with whom their interests were more closely identified than with the North. Now that the Confederacy had ceased to exist they were willing to resume their relations with the United States. They offered their previous record of unbroken friendship as proof of their fidelity to the American Government, and expressed a hope that "the established relations between the sections of

[30]*Ibid.*, pp. 318-19.
[31]*Ibid.*, pp. 320-21.
[32]*Ibid.*, pp. 330-31.
[33]*Ibid.*, p. 305.

the United States may be lasting, and that we may never be again forced to cast our fortunes with one of two contending sections."[34]

On September 20, the day before adjournment, they presented another statement, still dignified but more conciliatory in tone; the allusion to Confederate "machinations" was allowed to pass unchallenged, and several of the bolder expressions of the earlier statement were moderated. They were ready to accept the propositions of the commissioners as the basis of negotiations, with the understanding that in acknowledging the "exclusive jurisdiction" of the United States they were not admitting the right of interference in any of their internal affairs except slavery.[35]

A draft treaty embodying these general principles was submitted to the Choctaws and Chickasaws. They were to abolish slavery, and declare a general amnesty to protect their citizens who had supported the North. They should surrender not more than one-third of their occupied territory for the settlement of Indians from Kansas and other places at a compensation to be fixed by the United States. The United States might settle any tribes within the Leased District without restriction. At the next meeting of their legislatures they would present and recommend the bill then before Congress for the consolidation of the Indian Territory into one government. The United States would protect them against white immigration, and would restore their tribal annuities and other moneys except such as had been expended for the support of loyal Indians. Finally the United States Senate might make any amendment, which would be as binding as though "formally submitted to and ratified by such parties."[36]

It is evident that the Choctaws and Chickasaws were facing ruin — the loss of the Leased District and the forced sale of one-third of their remaining territory, the unrestricted colonization of freedmen among them, the extinction of their tribal autonomy, and any other punishment the United States Senate might see fit to inflict. Their escape constitutes a triumph of diplomacy almost unexampled in the history of the relations between a weak people and a strong.

This treaty was never accepted by the Choctaw Nation.[37] The Preliminary Treaty was ratified on October 7 with a specific reservation

[34]*Ibid.*, pp. 345-46.
[35]*Ibid.*, pp. 349-50.
[36]Folsom, *Digest of Choctaw Law*, pp. 581-82.
[37]Folsom, *loc. cit.*; *Report Commissioner of Indian Affairs*, 1865, p. 36. There is no reason to believe Cooley's statement that it was accepted by the delegates at Fort Smith; it bears no signature and no record of ratification.

accepting the interpretation the delegates had placed upon the acknowledgment of the "exclusive jurisdiction" of the United States.[38] On October 17 the Council provided for the appointment of five delegates who, with the Chickasaw delegation, should negotiate the final treaty at Washington.[39] Two days later secret instructions were drawn up for these delegates.[40] Under no conditions were they to cede any portion of the occupied territory; if the United States commissioners should insist, they were to refer them directly to the people. They might make concessions, however, regarding the Leased District, though they were to exact payment for its relinquishment if possible, or seek to retain their ownership of the land while surrendering their jurisdiction. But as a last resort they might give up the Leased District without compensation, or surrender all of their tribal monies, or even submit to the settlement of Kansas Indians within their occupied territory. Finally, they were to "demand" compensation for the emancipation of their slaves — a claim obviously advanced for bargaining purposes, to be surrendered in exchange for the undisturbed possession of their lands exclusive of the Leased District.[41]

Allen Wright, who was at that time National Treasurer, Alfred Wade, John Page, James Riley, and Robert M. Jones were appointed as delegates. Jones for some reason did not act and his name does not appear on the treaty, while Chief Pitchlynn, who was still a member of the Net Proceeds delegation, took a leading part in the negotiations.[42]

At Baltimore they secured the services of the attorney, John H. B. Latrobe, by an agreement that was later to cause them much embarrassment. Douglas H. Cooper and John D. Cochrane were associated with Latrobe, but as they had been Confederates it was deemed wiser that their names should not appear in official communications. Latrobe always claimed full credit for the discovery that the Treaty of 1855 had not been abrogated by the war, and he maintained that he wrote and secured the adoption of the peace treaty.[43]

The negotiations took place at Washington during the Winter of

[38]Folsom, *Digest of Choctaw Law*, pp. 580-81.

[39]*Ibid.*, pp. 584-85.

[40]*Ibid.*, p. 587.

[41]Abel, *The American Indian under Reconstruction*, pp. 327-29n, text of instructions.

[42]*Court of Claims Reports*, LIX, 799; Kappler, *Laws and Treaties*, II, 918, 931.

[43]John H. B. Latrobe, *An Address to the Choctaw and Chickasaw Nations* (Baltimore, 1873), pp. 7-8; John E. Semmes, *John H. B. Latrobe and his Times* (Baltimore, 1917), pp. 544-45. In view of the conspicuous ability of at least two of the delegates—Pitchlynn and Wright—it would seem that Latrobe over-estimated the value of his services.

1865-66. The closest possible coöperation existed between the Choctaw and Chickasaw delegations, and a joint treaty with the two nations was adopted. It was finally signed on April 28.

During the negotiations the Leased District and the Negro questions became joined; the United States hoped to induce the Choctaws and Chickasaws to adopt their freedmen, or failing in this to secure the Leased District for the establishment of a Negro colony.[44] The treaty as finally completed provided for the surrender of this territory; the United States was to pay $300,000 for the cession, to be divided between the two tribes in the three-to-one ratio if they should adopt the freedmen, or to be expended for the benefit of the Negroes if the Indians, by failing to adopt them within two years, should decree their removal.

The treaty also granted right of way for a north-south and east-west railroad across the Indian Territory, and gave the nation through which the road might pass the right to subscribe to the stock, and pay for it by land grants. Elaborate provision was made for an annual council of the nations of the Indian Territory, which it was hoped would in time absorb the tribal governments. The United States also hoped to induce the Indians to accept allotments, and the treaty contained minute specifications to govern the survey and division of the land, provided the two nations should adopt the system of private ownership. The Indians also consented to the incorporation of not more than ten thousand Kansas Indians within the two tribes, and the establishment of United States courts, which, however, should not interfere with the functioning of the tribal judiciary. The Indians were allowed full jurisdiction over their intermarried or adopted citizens, and almost complete control of white immigration. Though there was no prohibition against Negro immigration it seemed to be the sense of both the United States and the Indians from this time on that if the United States should undertake any Negro colonization it would be confined to the Leased District. A commission to be appointed by the President of the United States was to adjudicate the claims of the loyal Indians and licensed traders who had been forced to abandon their property during the war. The trust funds which the two tribes had accumulated through various treaties were to be restored as they were in 1861, and the United States would resume the payment of their regular annuities on June 30.[45]

[44]Union Agency Files, Choctaw—Federal Relations, printed circular dated July 12, 1866, sent out by Chief Pitchlynn of the Choctaw Nation and Governor Winchester Colbert of the Chickasaw Nation urging ratification of the Treaty.

[45]U. S. Statutes at Large, XIV, 769; Kappler, Laws and Treaties, II, 918-931.

Considering the temper of the United States Government and the helpless position of the Indians this treaty was surprisingly favorable. They had come to Washington prepared to fight every concession, but if forced to the last extremity, to surrender everything except their homes. They conceded only the relinquishment of the Leased District, a possible restitution to loyal Choctaws and traders, the admission of Kansas Indians — a provision which was never carried out — and the loss of their property in slaves. They retained their occupied lands, their invested funds, their tribal autonomy, and, should they so desire, the removal of their former slaves. It was probably due to the firmness and unity of the Choctaw Nation that this treaty with the most steadfast of the Indian allies of the Confederacy was the least "reconstructive" of all those negotiated at the close of the Civil War.

Unfortunately the history of this brilliant negotiation is marred by an unpleasant financial transaction. Latrobe and his associates were employed with the secret understanding that they would divide their fee with the Choctaw delegates. Allen Wright as National Treasurer accordingly paid the attorneys $100,000, for which Latrobe gave him a receipt. Latrobe and his colleagues retained half of this money, which they divided among themselves, and returned the other half to Wright, who distributed it in $10,000 shares among the four acting delegates (including himself) and the Principal Chief. The delegates also received $2,843 each, as legitimate pay for their services, and for some time it was not known by their constituents that they had participated in a division of the attorneys' fee[46] When the transaction became public, and the Choctaw people realized that Latrobe's fee had been inflated to the extent of $50,000 to benefit the delegates at the expense of the Nation, it created a tribal scandal, and it seems to have ruined the political career of Allen Wright.

The treaty was ratified by the United States Senate on June 28, and proclaimed by the President on July 10. The Choctaw General Council ratified it on December 21, with the exception of the optional provisions regarding the adoption of the freedmen, participation in the intertribal council, and the allotment of lands in severalty; decision of these questions was deferred until the wishes of the people should be expressed at the next general election.[47]

[46]*Court of Claims Reports,* LIX, 775-76, 799, 806.

[47]Folsom, *Digest of Choctaw Law,* p. 589. Though the act of ratification was carelessly drafted, the interpretation given above is the only one possible. It is in the form of a simple resolution approving the report of the delegates; the Choctaws, however, were in the habit of enacting legislation by the mere acceptance of a committee report.

As soon as the conditions of their national existence were defined by this treaty, the Choctaws were able to concentrate their efforts upon rebuilding their ravaged country. Although they had escaped the internal feuds and repeated invasions that had reduced the lands across the Arkansas to a desolate waste, the war had brought them much suffering. Many of their men had been in the army where they could not provide adequately for their families, and they had received very little of their pay from the Confederate Government. Part of Stand Watie's Cherokee Brigade and other Confederate troops had been quartered in the Choctaw country as other parts of the Indian Territory passed under Federal control, and their requisitions upon the inadequate food supply had brought the poorer people to the verge of starvation. At the Fort Smith council the Choctaw delegates reported that one-third of their people were entirely destitute.[48]

The food situation was complicated by the presence of large numbers of Cherokee and Creek refugees who had fled from their homes when the Federal forces occupied their country. The Southern Cherokee government had built camps for its own people along the Boggy, Blue, and Kiamichi rivers, and had made appropriations, supplemented by loans from the Confederate Government, for their support. After the war ended, relief was distributed by United States agents at Boggy Depot.

The refugees were too destitute and too disheartened to return immediately to their ruined homes upon the close of the war; in the Fall of 1865 it was reported that six thousand Cherokees and a large number of Creeks were still in the Choctaw country.[49] It was inevitable that some of these starving people should commit depredations, and after the war ended, the more irresponsible among them showed a tendency to remain and form a lawless element in the Choctaw Nation.

The Choctaws had been sympathetic and had made voluntary contributions to their support, but on October 19, 1865, an act of the Council stated that "many and serious complaints" had come in regarding the "wanton destruction" of live stock and other property by

[48]*War of the Rebellion*, First Series, LIII, supplement, 1034-35, Chief Pitchlynn to Major General Maxey, December 29, 1864, and Maxey to Brigadier General W. R. Boggs, December 31, 1864; Folsom, *Digest of Choctaw Law*, p. 577, act passed Fall of 1862 appropriating $25,000 for support of destitute Choctaw citizens; Union Agency Files, Choctaw—Auditor, report of National Auditor William Robuck to Council, October, 1871; *Report Commissioner of Indian Affairs*, 1865, pp. 257, 280.

[49]Debo, "Southern Refugees of the Cherokee Nation"; *Report Commissioner of Indian Affairs*, 1865, pp. 36, 280, 347; Arthur Fairfield Chamberlin, personal interview. Chamberlin, a Cherokee refugee, was entertained in the home of Allen Wright.

refugees, and instructed the Chief to address the head men of the Cherokee and Creek nations urging "immediate and strenuous measures" of restraint, after which notification the offenders would be dealt with by Choctaw law to the detriment of the good feeling that had long existed between the tribes.[50] Allen Wright, who became Principal Chief in the Fall of 1866, in his inaugural address called upon all law-abiding citizens among his own people and "those who are making their temporary residence among us" to unite in establishing industry and good order; he said the law would recognize no difference of nationality within the jurisdiction of the Choctaw Nation.[51] Early in 1867 he issued a proclamation warning those who were "abusing the privileges, which for the sake of humanity, have been extended to them"; and refugees were required to secure temporary permits upon the recommendation of their Choctaw neighbors or they would be subject to removal as intruders.[52] On June 17 he instructed the chief of the Moshulatubbee District to remove certain specified intruders including eleven Cherokees, six Creeks, and one Creek freedman family.[53] By the Fall of 1867, although the refugee problem still existed, the Choctaw government had the situation under control.[54]

The Choctaws also suffered from the activities of cattle thieves, who during the war had established an organized business of running cattle from the country and selling them to Union commissaries.[55] After the war ended, these depredations continued. In the Fall of 1865, Agent Colman reported that droves of stolen cattle were continually passing out of the Choctaw country over all the public thoroughfares, especially the highways leading to Fort Smith and Little Rock.[56] During the next two Summers droves of Texas cattle passed through on their way to Kansas or Missouri, and the Choctaws complained bitterly that some of the drovers adopted the practice of adding Choctaw cattle to their herds as they passed by.[57]

These depredations and the legitimate requirements of soldiers and refugees almost swept away the large herds of cattle which had once

[50]Folsom, *Digest of Choctaw Law*, p. 586.
[51]Union Agency Files, Letters of Chiefs Wright, McCurtain *et. al.*, pp. 3-9. This was in harmony with the inter-tribal code drawn up at North Fork Village in 1859.
[52]*Ibid.*, pp. 18-19.
[53]*Ibid.*, p. 45.
[54]*Ibid.*, pp. 53-63.
[55]*Report Commissioner of Indian Affairs*, 1864, pp. 305-6, 320; Abel, *The American Indian under Reconstruction*, pp. 281-82n.
[56]*Report Commissioner of Indian Affairs*, 1865, p. 280.
[57]Union Agency Files, Letters of Chiefs, pp. 40-41; Acts of the Choctaw Nation, October 21, 1870.

PETER P. PITCHLYNN, PRINCIPAL CHIEF, 1864–66
PAINTING BY CATLIN, 1834

MOSHULATUBBEE *(He-who-puts-out-and-kills)* BY CATLIN, 1834

constituted so large a part of the national wealth. But cattle stealing as an organized business ceased soon after the war. The cattle drives were soon regulated by the Choctaw government, which established the right to collect a tax upon all live stock passing through the country. As law and order were reëstablished the diminished herds were built up by natural increase, and within ten years from the close of the war Choctaw citizens were shipping to outside markets.[58]

The activities of cattle thieves constituted only one phase of the general demoralization that existed in the Choctaw country, where for a time it seemed that all the restraints of civilized society had broken down. Many of the county governments had entirely ceased to function, and there was nobody to enforce the laws. Gangs of outlaws roamed at will over the country, committing murders and other crimes without hindrance. White renegades and roving bands of freedmen from neighboring states were finding the Nation a convenient rendezvous. There was truth in the bitter words of Chief Wright's inaugural address: "This was the second time in our history that the bright future prospect for the Choctaws in the rapid march to civilization — progress of education, and wide spread of religion among them have been impeded and paralyzed by direct and indirect acts of the Government of the United States," the direct act being the removal from "their ancient and much loved homes" in Mississippi, and the indirect, "their own unfortunate intestine war" in which the Choctaws became involved.[59]

Conditions at first seemed hopeless. During the Fort Smith council, Chief Pitchlynn even appealed to Cooley for assistance from the United States in maintaining "domestic tranquility pending the adoption of definitive treaties."[60] The Choctaws, however, solved their own problems, and they restored order with surprising rapidity. A semi-military auxiliary force created at the close of the war to aid the civil officers in enforcing the law was abolished as no longer needed by the end of 1866.[61] Chief Wright was able to report to the Council in the Fall of 1867 that every county in the Nation now had its full complement of officers, and that appreciable progress had been made in suppressing

[58]Acts of the Choctaw Nation, October 27, 1870; *Report Commissioner of Indian Affairs,* 1871, p. 570; *Vindicator,* June 14, 1876; *Report of the Productions of Agriculture, Tenth Census* (Washington, 1883). Chief J. F. McCurtain made the following estimate of the growth of the cattle business from 1845 to 1880: 1845, 25,000 head; 1860, 62,000 head; 1870, 15,500 head; 1875, 40,000 head; 1880, 65,000 head.
[59]Union Agency Files, Letters of Chiefs, pp. 39, 53-63.
[60]Abel, *The American Indian under Reconstruction,* pp. 217-18.
[61]Folsom, *Digest of Choctaw Law,* p. 588.

crime.[62] The appalling number of executions shown by the court records of the time[63] would indicate that one of the main methods of decreasing crime was decreasing the number of criminals.

One reason for the breakdown of government was the chaotic condition of the public finances. The Choctaws had never adopted any system of taxation; they had supported their government and schools solely by the income from their invested funds. During the war the United States had suspended the payment of their annuities and diverted the money to the support of refugee Indians of Union sympathies.[64] By the Treaty of Alliance the Confederacy had assumed these obligations, and for a time made payment in specie,[65] but later payments were made in depreciated paper, and the amount remaining in the Choctaw treasury at the close of the war was a total loss.[66] Moreover, there is reason to believe that the Choctaws were not entirely free from that official corruption that has been known to attack larger nations during the confusion of war, and that the manipulation of Latrobe's fee was not the only instance of the diversion of public money to private gain.[67]

It was impossible for the Choctaws to compute their national debt at the close of the war.[68] An unknown sum in national warrants was outstanding, and a special form of paper issued the last three years of the war under the name of treasury warrants was also unpaid.[69]

After the ratification of the Treaty of 1866 the United States resumed the payment of annuities, and made a large payment on the Leased District, but at least part of these payments was made in "Greenbacks," which at that time were greatly depreciated.[70] Moreover, it seems to

[62]Union Agency Files, Letters of Chiefs, pp. 53-63.

[63]These court records are in the files of the Union Agency.

[64]Abel, *The American Indian under Reconstruction*, p. 251n.

[65]*The Statutes at Large of the Provisional Government of the Confederate States of America* (Richmond, 1864), p. 232; Abel, *The American Indian as Slaveholder and Secessionist*, pp. 323-35. These references show that a payment of $50,000 in specie was made in the Fall of 1862.

[66]Folsom, *Digest of Choctaw Law*, p. 585.

[67]The $250,000 appropriated by Congress as first payment on the Net Proceeds award was never satisfactorily accounted for (*Court of Claims Records*, LIX, 803). The appropriations made by the Council during the War seem rather reckless in some cases, even when the deterioration of the Confederate currency is taken into account (Folsom, *Digest of Choctaw Law*, pp. 573-79), but this may not have involved official misconduct.

[68]Acts of the Choctaw Nation, October 28, 1869; Union Agency Files, Choctaw—Auditor, report of National Auditor William Robuck to Council, October, 1871. Robuck estimated the indebtedness at that time at eighty to one hundred thousand dollars.

[69]Folsom, *Digest of Choctaw Law*, pp. 584, 585.

[70]Union Agency Files, Letters of Chiefs, pp. 27-8, Chief Wright to Geo. L. Williams, March 18, 1867.

have been the custom of the Indian Office to expend part of the money for the supposed benefit of the Choctaws instead of turning it over to them.[71]

When finances had become somewhat stabilized, the National Treasurer began to make *pro rata* payments on all warrants that were presented at the time of the semi-annual annuity payments. By 1870 the Treasurer was able to pay twenty-eight cents on the dollar in January, and twenty-three cents in June; the holders of the warrants received certificates for the balance.[72] It was frequently necessary to borrow money during this period, especially to defray the expenses of the Council sessions. These sums were usually obtained by making an agreement with the lender to cash for him a specified number of old warrants, usually to the amount of the loan.[73] Wealthy citizens seemed willing to lend their money on these terms and by the cashing of their warrants to exchange an old for a new indebtedness, and the Nation avoided the payment of ruinous interest.[74] It was some years before the Choctaw Nation returned to the solvent financial condition that had existed before the war.

As a result of the loss of tribal revenue the entire system of tribal schools closed down in 1861 and remained closed throughout the war. The large two-story brick building at Armstrong Academy became the capitol, the Fort Coffee Academy was burned by raiding Union Indians from across the Arkansas, other buildings were used for barracks or refugee quarters, and the rest fell into decay. Many of the missionaries and teachers were forced to leave. A whole generation was growing up entirely without schools.[75]

Almost the first measure of reconstruction taken up by the Choctaw

[71]*Ibid.*, p. 9; *Report Commissioner of Indian Affairs*, 1865, p. 40; Acts of the Choctaw Nation, October 15, 1867; October 23, 1869. The first two references relate to relief work administered by the Indian Office which was surely carried on with tribal funds; the acts of the Council are protests against disbursements of Choctaw money by the Commissioner of Indian Affairs.

[72]Union Agency Files, Choctaw—Treasurer, report of Treasurer Basil LeFlore to the Council, October 1, 1870.

[73]Union Agency Files, Choctaw—Treasurer, report of Treasurer LeFlore to Council, November 3, 1868, November 6, 1868, October 1, 1869; Acts of the Choctaw Nation, October 26, 1869; Folsom, *Digest of Choctaw Law*, p. 592.

[74]Acts of the Choctaw Nation, March 19, 1872, act authorizing L. S. W. Folsom to go to Boggy Depot to negotiate a "lone" of $5,000 for the "use of the present Council" at a "reasonable rate of interest" not exceeding twenty per cent.

[75]Union Agency Files, Letters of Chiefs, pp. 3-9, Chief Wright's inaugural address, 1866; Mrs. Flora Paine Eichenberger, "A Reminiscence of a Methodist Minister's Daughter," *Chronicles of Oklahoma*, VII (1929), 260-65; Thoburn and Wright, *Oklahoma*, I, 347n.

government was an attempt to rebuild its educational system. An act bearing the same date (October 19, 1865) as the secret instructions to the delegates who were to negotiate the peace treaty, was passed by the Council providing for the appointment of a committee to make an educational survey and report a plan for reëstablishing the school system upon a permanent basis.[76] Nothing was done that year, however. In fact nothing could have been done; there was no national revenue, and with the terms of peace unsettled no one could predict the future.

When the Council convened the following year, economic and social conditions were still in the most extreme demoralization, but the treaty had been negotiated and the existence of the Nation was assured. A special day of the session was set apart for exclusive discussion of the school situation, when the two houses were to meet together and the school officials of the Nation and other prominent citizens were requested to attend and participate in the discussion. The people of the community were also invited to be present.[77]

The neighborhood schools were put into operation by an act of December 21[78]—the date which marked also the ratification of the Peace Treaty. As a result of this legislation the first week in January, 1867, saw the Choctaw children, who had been running wild for five years, once more gathered for instruction in the rude log cabins that housed the neighborhood schools.[79] In the Fall of 1869, or possibly the year before, the Choctaw government resumed the practice of supporting a selected group of young people at colleges in the "States."[80] Within the next two years, two of the boarding schools — Spencer for the boys, and New Hope for the girls — had been repaired and were in operation under contracts with Methodist and Presbyterian mission boards.[81]

According to the report of Superintendent Forbis LeFlore there were eighty-four neighborhood schools in operation during the Winter of 1869-70 with an enrollment of 1,764. About one-third of the teachers were white; the rest were Choctaws educated in the old tribal schools

[76]Folsom, *Digest of Choctaw Law*, p. 585.
[77]*Ibid.*, p. 587.
[78]*Ibid.*, p. 589.
[79]Union Agency Files, Letters of Chiefs, pp. 53-63, annual message of Chief Wright, October 8, 1867.
[80]Acts of the Choctaw Nation, October 30, 1869. The exact date when the Choctaw government resumed this practice is not clearly indicated in this document.
[81]Acts of the Choctaw Nation, November 2, 1870, October 30, 1871; *Report Commissioner of Indian Affairs*, 1870, pp. 293-95; 1871, p. 572.

or in the "States." Attendance was irregular because of the extreme poverty of the people; the majority of the children suffered the handicap of knowing no language but Choctaw; and many of the teachers were not properly qualified; but the people were pitiably eager for the establishment of schools. However, when the two boarding schools were opened, the number of neighborhood schools had to be reduced to meet the increased expense. "Sunday Schools" were once more maintained by the churches in various parts of the Nation. The Choctaw school system, although far inferior to that existing before the war, may be said to have been reëstablished in all its essential features by 1871.[82]

Another reconstruction problem was created by the obligation assumed under the Treaty of 1866 to indemnify the so-called "loyal Choctaws." A few members of the tribe had been loyal to the Union all through the war; they had been forced to leave their homes and some of them had served in the Union army. Others, apparently under the leadership of intermarried whites, had hoped to secure an advantage for themselves by intriguing with the Federal commander after the capture of Fort Smith.[83] At the time of the Fort Smith Council the number of loyal Choctaws was estimated at 212.[84]

The treaty provided that a commission appointed by the President should adjudicate the claims of these people and make an award which should be paid out of tribal moneys in the hands of the United States.[85] E. W. Rice of Iowa and A. H. Jackson of Nebraska were chosen to constitute this commission. The hearings were held at Fort Smith in September of 1866. General James G. Blunt was the attorney for the claimants, and John H. B. Latrobe and Campbell LeFlore defended the Choctaw Nation.[86]

[82]*Report Commissioner of Indian Affairs,* 1870, 1871, *loc. cit.*

[83]This apparently harsh judgment is fully borne out by documents in the Indian Office Files. There are many letters from "Governor" Thomas Edwards requesting payment of his salary from March 14, 1864, to June 20, 1865, also a statement from General James G. Blunt saying that Edwards had been adjutant of Colonel Sampson Folsom's regiment before he changed his allegiance, and that he had stolen the rations which Blunt had entrusted to him for distribution to the loyal Choctaw refugees at Fort Smith (Choctaw, 1868, B583, E48). *See* also the complaint of Robert B. Patton to Commissioner Parker, January 1, 1870, asking that the tribal annuities be paid to the "loyal Choctaws" instead of the regular Choctaw government, and that he be made their representative (Choctaw, 1870, P283).

[84]*Report Commissioner of Indian Affairs,* 1865, pp. 257, 316, 320.

[85]Kappler, *Laws and Treaties,* II, 930, Art. 49.

[86]Abel, *The American Indian under Reconstruction,* p. 336n; Acts of the Choctaw Nation, October 28, 1872; November 4, 1879; October 22, 1883; Folsom, *Digest of Choctaw Law,* p. 589; Indian Office Files, Choctaw, 1869, P85.

The damages assessed by the commission reached a total of $109,-742.08.[87] The Nation protested to the Secretary of the Interior against the confirmation of this award, and finally effected a compromise with Blunt which reduced it slightly, but Secretary Browning ruled that it should stand.[88] The amount was accordingly taken from the half-million-dollar trust fund which had been created under the Treaty of 1855 as part payment for the use of the Leased District.[89] This trust fund was now reduced to $390,257.92, and the annual income from the invested funds was correspondingly decreased.[90]

Samuel S. Smoot, the special agent appointed by the United States, paid out the individual awards in the Fall of 1868.[91] Judging from the stream of complaints that poured into the Indian Office for the next few years it would seem that most of the money was swallowed up in attorneys' fees and expenses of payment, and that the claimants received very little benefit from the award.[92]

The treaty also stipulated that the commission should adjudicate the claims of loyal traders who had been forced to abandon their property at the outbreak of the war, provided that the total award should not exceed $90,000. The commission disallowed all the claims except those of Joseph G. Heald and Reuben Wright of Massachusetts, between whom the $90,000 was prorated. The Choctaws made a compromise with these traders by which certain accounts, buildings, and other property were turned over to the Nation to balance this award.[93]

With the payment of this indemnity to loyal citizens and white traders, the Choctaws may be said to have completed the reconstruction process so far as it involved the renewal of their former relations to the Federal Government. The adjustment of the refugee problem, the gradual restoration of prosperity, the establishment of law and

[87]Indian Office Files, Choctaw, 1868, 1888.

[88]Indian Office Files, *loc. cit.;* Folsom, *Digest of Choctaw Law,* pp. 589-90; Union Agency Files, Letters of Chiefs, pp. 53-63.

[89]Kappler, *Laws and Treaties,* II, 708-10, Arts. 8, 10, 13.

[90]Indian Office Files, Choctaw, 1868, 1981, 1993; Union Agency Files, Choctaw—Treasurer, report of National Treasurer Basil LeFlore to Council, October 1, 1870.

[91]Indian Office Files, Choctaw, 1868, 1981, 1993; *Report Commissioner of Indian Affairs,* 1868, pp. 275-76.

[92]*See* for instance Indian Office Files, Choctaw, 1869, P61, P85, ff.

[93]Abel, *The American Indian under Reconstruction,* p. 337n; Union Agency Files, Choctaw—National Council, message of Chief Wright to Council, October 19, 1869; *ibid.,* Choctaw—Federal Relations, Franceway Battice to Commissioner Parker, July 3, 1869; and statement from Chief Wright, July 25, 1869; Acts of the Choctaw Nation, report of Sampson Folsom to Chief Wright, September 30, 1869; *House Exec. Docs.* 40 Cong., 2 Sess., No. 204.

order, and the reopening of the tribal schools completed the process of social and economic rehabilitation. There still remained the question of what to do with the freedmen — the most perplexing of all the problems of reconstruction, and the one that remained unsettled for the longest period after the conclusion of peace. The Choctaws immediately accepted the economic fact of emancipation,[94] but the political and social adjustments were much more difficult.

Slavery was officially abolished by legislation enacted October 14 and 19, 1865, regulating the employment of "such persons as have, to the present time, been considered as slaves." They were required to choose an employer and make a written wage agreement with him before a county judge. Vagrants who should be found without employment were to be arrested by the sheriffs or lighthorsemen and their services sold to the highest bidder, who should compel them to work. The money thus secured was to be put in a special fund for the support of any "freed person" in need of financial assistance. The payment of wages should begin after January 1, and a standard scale was fixed for eight classes of laborers including children, with wages ranging from two dollars to ten dollars a month, and specified items of food and shelter. The working day was limited to ten hours in Summer and nine in Winter, with Saturday afternoon and Sunday holidays except when forced labor was necessary to save the crop. The wages of laborers constituted a first lien on the crop and the property on the plantation. The former masters were required to make provision in their contracts for the support of the aged, crippled, and infirm whom they had held as slaves. The freedmen were guaranteed full protection of person and property, and were given civil and criminal protection in the courts equal to that enjoyed by citizens. Former slaves who had voluntarily left the Nation were not to be permitted to return.[95]

This change from a slave system to a wage system was not effected without a certain amount of disorder, which was increased by the general disorganization of Choctaw society existing at the time. Choctaw freedmen, joined by roving bands of Negroes from Texas, formed settlements in the Red River Valley, where they lived by stealing from their Indian neighbors. To check these depredations a secret organization called the Vigilance Committee, which seems to have antedated the Ku Klux Klan, was formed with a small group in each locality

[94]*Report Commissioner of Indian Affairs,* 1865, p. 281.
[95]Folsom, *Digest of Choctaw Law,* pp. 583-84, 586. Some of the contracts made under this law in the Spring of 1866 may be found in Indian Office Files, Choctaw, 1868, S710.

communicating very closely with other groups by a system of mounted couriers. These self-constituted police patrolled the country, warning vagrants, hanging cattle thieves, and disbanding the most disorderly of the freedman settlements.[96] It must have been rumors of these activities that reached the ears of the United States officials at Fort Smith, and caused them to report during the Winter of 1865-66 that the Negroes were suffering from a reign of terror in the Choctaw country.[97]

In the Fall of 1865, Major General John B. Sanborn was appointed as special commissioner to the Indian Territory to guard the interests of the freedmen. Considering it unsafe to venture into their country he sent out circulars from Fort Smith warning the Choctaws that the freedmen were under his protection. At the same time he sent reports to the Indian Office describing the atrocities committed by the Choctaws against the freedmen, and advising that the whole country be placed under martial law.[98]

The Choctaw government seems to have made every possible effort to coöperate with the United States officials in providing for the establishment of the freedmen. While he was still at the Fort Smith Council, Chief Pitchlynn wrote to Cooley that in abandoning their property rights in slaves the Choctaws were not abandoning their interest in their welfare, and requested that an agent of the Freedmen's Bureau be sent to assist them.[99] When Sanborn finally dared to visit the Choctaw country, he must have been treated with the utmost consideration, for the tone of his official reports changed completely. Though he still lightly recommended an Indian policy that would have meant nothing less than the extinction of the Choctaw Nation,[100] he said that conditions had never been so bad as might be inferred from his previous report, that the rights of the freedmen were generally recognized, and that they were receiving fair wages or rents for their labor on the plantations.[101] He seems to have approved the Choctaw law regulating

[96]Thoburn and Wright, Oklahoma, pp. 375-77.

[97]Abel, The American Indian under Reconstruction, p. 273n; Report Commissioner of Indian Affairs, 1866, pp. 283-85.

[98]Report Commissioner of Indian Affairs, 1866, pp. 55, 283-85; Abel, op. cit., pp. 290-92n.

[99]Letter given in Abel, op. cit., p. 285.

[100]His policy for the entire Indian Territory was the allotment of 160-acre tracts to Negroes and eighty acres to Indians, liberal grants to railroads, the segregation of tracts for the settlement of Kansas Indians, and the opening of the remainder to homestead entry.

[101]Report Commissioner of Indian Affairs, 1866, pp. 56, 285-87.

the employment of freedmen, for he transmitted to the Indian Office numerous wage agreements made between the Negroes and their former masters.[102] In April, 1866, he asked to be relieved from duty, on the ground that the freedmen were no longer in need of his services. The commission was accordingly discontinued, leaving the final status of the Negroes to be determined by the Choctaws under the terms of the treaty, which by this time had been negotiated.

The treaty, it will be remembered, gave the Choctaws and Chickasaws the alternative of adopting the freedmen and receiving $300,000 for the Leased District, or having them removed by the United States at the expiration of two years, in which case the Negroes would receive the Leased District money.[103] At first some of the tribal leaders were inclined to favor adoption. Governor Colbert of the Chickasaw Nation and Chief Pitchlynn expressed the opinion that the freedmen were needed as laborers; that their number was too small to constitute a menace if they should remain with their former masters; and that if they were removed and colonized in the Leased District, freedmen from the "States" would settle with them and create a large Negro nation upon the borders of the Choctaw-Chickasaw country.[104]

The majority of the people, however, favored removal. When the treaty was ratified in the Fall of 1866, the question, as has been previously stated, was postponed until it could be referred to the people through their selection of representatives at the next election. The Council that met after this popular mandate formally requested the Commissioner of Indian Affairs to remove the freedmen.[105] The Chickasaw Nation took similar action.

The United States, in the meantime, had not waited for the Indians to make their decision. Apparently with the intention of influencing them in favor of adoption, Congress on July 26, 1866, made an appropriation of $200,000 to be divided between the two tribes as a payment on the Leased District. The Choctaw share, or $150,000, was paid to Treasurer Wright on September 3; evidently it was from this source that Latrobe received the $100,000 fee that was to create such a tribal scandal. Congress at the same time seemingly for no logical reason appropriated $15,000 as interest, the Choctaw share of which was paid on August 13. Even after both tribes had definitely decided not to

102Indian Office Files, Choctaw, 1868, S710.
103Kappler, *Laws and Treaties,* II, 919-920, Arts. 2-4.
104*See* Pitchlynn and Colbert's circular urging ratification of the peace treaty.
105Folsom, *Digest of Choctaw Law,* pp. 594-95, November 20, 1867.

adopt their freedmen, an additional $15,000 was appropriated and paid in 1869.[106]

It does not seem to have occurred to the Choctaws that the United States would refuse to remove the freedmen upon the expiration of the two-year period fixed by the treaty; it was expected that the removal would take place as a matter of course during the Summer of 1868.[107] When the Federal Government failed to act, they made a formal request on August 15 that the terms of the treaty be carried out.[108] Agent Chollar also urged the removal before cold weather should set in.[109] No action was taken, however, and the question was left unsettled.

For twenty years the freedmen remained in the Nation with no clearly defined legal status. The Choctaws at first attempted to give them the equal protection of their courts provided by their act of emancipation,[110] but the United States first denied,[111] and then demanded[112] that the tribal jurisdiction be extended to freedmen. In general after 1868 they were treated as United States citizens, and were therefore under the criminal jurisdiction of the Federal district court at Fort Smith and entirely outside any civil jurisdiction.[113] They had no rights in the public domain, but by common consent they were allowed the use of all the land they cared to cultivate.[114] The most serious disadvantage of their anomalous position was the absence of all school privileges for their children.

In spite of reports of occasional friction, which were magnified and circulated by enemies of the Choctaws, there is strong proof of the

[106]Indian Office Files, Choctaw, O.I.A., May 21, 1869.

[107]Union Agency Files, Letters of Chiefs, p. 101, Chief Wright to Sheriff J. H. Minehart of Skullyville County, June 17, 1868. In this letter Wright instructed the sheriff not to disturb a certain Creek freedman intruder, since all the freedmen would be removed within ninety days. "The freedman question has been a great source of annoyance, but it will soon be disposed of, and hereafter that class of persons will be treated like other citizens of the United States, which will be some relief to us."

[108]*House Misc. Docs.*, 42 Cong., 2 Sess., No. 46.

[109]*Report Commissioner of Indian Affairs*, 1868, p. 280.

[110]Union Agency Files, Letters of Chiefs, p. 27, Chief Wright to Judge George L. Williams, of the Second Judicial District, March 18, 1867.

[111]Abel, *The American Indian under Reconstruction*, pp. 290-92n, circular sent out from Fort Smith by General Sanborn, January 27, 1866; *Report Commissioner of Indian Affairs*, 1871, pp. 570-71; 1877, p. 111.

[112]Indian Office Files, Choctaw, O.I.A., May 21, 1869, instructions to Agent Tufts, September 10, 1880.

[113]*Report Commissioner of Indian Affairs*, 1877, p. 111; *Report Senate Committee on Indian Affairs*, IX, 230.

[114]Acts of the Choctaw Nation, October 27, 1877; Indian Office Files, Union, 1880, C925; *Report Commissioner of Indian Affairs*, 1873, p. 209.

friendly feeling existing between the two races in the fact that with no legal or political rights the Negroes prospered in the Choctaw country and were determined to stay there. During the whole period, Washington was deluged by freedmen petitions,[115] but the requests for removal were more than balanced by such frightened, pathetic appeals as the protest to "Mr. onebel Prsident Greant" from the "collord Poplation of the Choctaw and ChickSaw nation" that "We ar doing So well and we dont want to be out of hom." What the majority of the Negroes really desired was an arrangement by which they could remain in the country under the special protection of the United States; they were suspicious of Choctaw citizenship, and were unwilling to submit themselves to the jurisdiction of Choctaw law.[116]

Many of the petitions supposed to have originated with the freedmen are clearly not genuine expressions of their opinions, but are artificial demands inspired by scheming white men who sought to influence them for their own purposes. V. Dell, editor of the Fort Smith *New Era,* and a member, apparently of "carpetbag" antecedents, of the Arkansas legislature, sponsored a number of meetings of Choctaw freedmen during 1869 and 1870 and secured the adoption of resolutions demanding full citizenship, with equal property rights in land and tribal moneys, the allotment of the land, and the opening of the whole country to white settlement. The exasperated Choctaws tore down some of the announcement posters, and by threats prevented one of the meetings, and the United States agent, Captain Olmstead, arrested one Negro who was carrying a letter inciting the freedmen to attend. The Negroes were then influenced to demand the removal of Olmstead for his sympathy with the "rebel element." Dell used these resolutions in every possible way to bring pressure upon the Government at Washington against the "semi-barbarous" "rebel Indians" who had the misfortune to own valuable lands.[117] Major S. N. Clark, a special agent of the Freedmen's Bureau, also gave his approval to these inspired resolutions.[118]

The Indians were in some danger that this propaganda would have the desired effect. In 1874 the Interior Department prepared a bill and submitted it to Congress giving the freedmen all the rights of Choctaw

[115]Indian Office Files, Choctaw, 1869, C86; O.I.A., May 21, 1869.
[116]Indian Office Files, Choctaw, 1872, P758; *House Misc. Docs.,* 42 Cong., 2 Sess., No. 46, pp. 11-12; *Report Commissioner of Indian Affairs,* 1869, pp. 408-9; 1872, pp. 237-38.
[117]*Senate Misc. Docs.,* 41 Cong., 2 Sess., No. 106.
[118]*House Misc. Docs.,* 42 Cong., 2 Sess., No. 46, p. 15.

and Chickasaw citizenship including an equal share of the "annuities, moneys, and public domain." When Pitchlynn and his colleagues defended their treaty rights in an able argument against the bill, Secretary Delano informed Congress that the freedman were "as meritorious, to say the least as the average" Choctaw and Chickasaw, implying that the Negroes had earned the lands by their labor, while the undeserving Indians had received them as a free gift from the Government.[119]

As the question continued to drag on with no prospect of settlement, the Federal Government finally took steps to establish schools for the freedmen. Pathetic, illiterate appeals had been coming into the Indian Office, bearing eloquent testimony to the eagerness as well as the need of the Negroes for educational privileges.[120] The first school was opened at Boggy Depot in 1874. It was supported by the Government under contract with the Baptist Mission Board.[121] Certain lawless white people who were living in the country under permit were so opposed to the establishment of the school that they sought to embarrass and intimidate the teachers, and were probably responsible for its destruction by fire in the Fall of 1875.[122] Another building was secured, however, and additional schools were established at Skullyville, Doaksville, Fort Coffee, and other places.[123] The freedmen were extremely anxious for the establishment of schools, but very unwilling to bear any of the burden of their support.[124]

The Choctaws continued to petition the United States for the fulfilment of the treaty,[125] but when it was apparent that such a policy would never be carried out, a sentiment began to develop in favor of adoption. From 1875 on, Choctaw and Chickasaw commissioners met together in many attempts to effect a joint settlement, but their efforts failed, chiefly because the Chickasaws still stood out uncompromisingly against adoption.[126]

Finally, the Choctaws resolved to take independent action. In the Fall of 1880 the Council adopted a resolution signifying to the United

119*House Misc. Docs.,* 43 Cong., 1 Sess., No. 294; Indian Office Files, Choctaw, O.I.A., May 21, 1869.

120For example *see* Indian Office Files, Union, 1879, C74.

121Indian Office Files, Choctaw, 1874, P143; *Report Commissioner of Indian Affairs,* 1882, p. 89.

122Indian Office Files, Choctaw, 1875, I780, I781, I1608.

123*Ibid.,* Union, 1876, M1300; 1877, C220; 1879, C239, ff.

124*Ibid.,* Union, 1879, L710; 1880, L151.

125*Report Commissioner of Indian Affairs,* 1869, p. 400; Acts of the Choctaw Nation, March 14, 1872.

126Acts of the Choctaw Nation, October 14, 1875; November 12, 1875; November 8, 1878.

States their willingness to adopt the freedmen according to the lapsed provisions of the treaty,[127] but Congress took no action, and the Choctaws were unable to act in the absence of legislation. In 1882 Congress appropriated $10,000 of Choctaw and Chickasaw money for the support of the freedman schools provided that if either Nation should adopt the freedmen it should be reimbursed from the unpaid balance of the Leased District money.[128] After ignoring the Choctaw overtures of two years before, Congress thus sought to force adoption by the misuse of tribal funds. The law, however, gave the Choctaws, for the first time an opportunity to act independently of the Chickasaws.

Accordingly on May 21, 1883, the Choctaws passed a law adopting their freedmen. All former slaves of the Choctaws and Chickasaws residing in the Choctaw Nation at the date of the Preliminary Treaty signed at Fort Smith September 13, 1865, together with their descendants were granted all "the rights, privileges, and immunities, including the right of suffrage of citizens of the Choctaw Nation, except in the annuities[,] moneys, and the public domain of the Nation." They were limited to forty-acre shares in the public domain under the same title as was held by the Choctaws. They were to receive educational opportunities equal to those of the Choctaws so far as neighborhood schools were concerned. Those who should elect to remove were each to receive one hundred dollars to be paid out of the Leased District balance; those who should decline to become citizens and fail to remove were to be classed as intruders and subject to removal like other citizens of the United States.

All these provisions were in close harmony with the lapsed stipulations of the Treaty of 1866. In addition the law provided that the freedmen should be ineligible to the offices of Principal Chief and District Chief, and that intermarried citizenship should not be conferred upon non-citizen Negroes who should marry Choctaw freedmen.[129] The Commissioner of Indian Affairs objected to these two provisions on the ground that they were in violation of the treaty. The Council then repealed the article that made Negroes ineligible to the office of Chief, and provided for the appointment of two delegates who were to proceed to Washington and work for the adoption of the bill as thus amended.[130]

[127]*Ibid.*, November 2, 1880.

[128]*Report Commissioner of Indian Affairs*, 1882, p. 196.

[129]Acts of the Choctaw Nation, May 21, 1883; May 22, 1883; Kappler, *Laws and Treaties*, II, 919-20, Arts. 3-4.

[130]*Branding Iron*, March 15, 1884; Acts of the Choctaw Nation, November 1, 1883.

Campbell LeFlore and J. S. Standley, who were selected as delegates, prepared a very able paper showing that the refusal to grant citizenship to intermarried Negroes was not in violation of the treaty, and was necessary for the protection of the Nation in view of the temporary character of the marriage relation among the freedmen. If they could not retain this article they threatened to return the payments they had received on the Leased District and leave the whole question as it had stood at the beginning. Secretary Teller became convinced, and ruled that since the restriction was placed upon Negro non-citizens rather than Negro citizens it did not conflict with the treaty.[131] On March 3, 1885, Congress appropriated $52,125 to be placed to the credit of the Choctaws as their share of the balance of the Leased District money.[132] This ended the diplomatic aspects of the question after twenty years of negotiation.

The government officials would have been chagrined if they could have known how the astute Choctaw leaders had outwitted them by their ready repeal of the provision that made the freedmen ineligible to the office of Chief. Their constitution already limited this office as well as membership in the Council to lineal descendants of the Choctaw or Chickasaw race.[133] This provision, designed to prevent their white citizens from securing undue weight in their councils at a time when no man could have foreseen the emancipation and enfranchisement of their slaves, could be made to apply also to the freedmen, limiting their political privileges more surely than any mere legislative enactment could have done.

The Choctaw government undertook the enrollment of the new citizens during the Summer of 1885.[134] They were very reluctant to register. In some cases they were cultivating as much as one hundred acres of the public domain, and they feared that their holdings would be reduced to forty acres. They desired high schools in addition to the neighborhood schools guaranteed them by the act of adoption. They complained of their ineligibility to office, which they seemed to understand better than the officials of the United States did, and they objected to the denial of citizenship to intermarried Negroes. A subcommittee of the Senate Committee on Indian Affairs, which happened to be making an inspection of the Indian Territory that Summer,

[131]*Branding Iron*, March 1, 1884.
[132]*Report Commissioner of Indian Affairs*, 1885, pp. 275-76; 1887, p. lxii.
[133]Art. VII, Sec. 2.
[134]*Indian Champion*, April 11, 1885, proclamation of Chief Edmund McCurtain.

soothed the freedmen who appeared before it, and advised them to trust the Choctaws and register without protest.[135]

When the registration was completed it was found that eighty-three of the freedmen had expressed a desire to remove. The Choctaws accordingly requested the United States to appropriate $8,300 of the Leased District money for their benefit.[136] The cases of those Negroes who had not been able to convince the registration commission of their right to Choctaw citizenship were referred to the Council, with the privilege of an appeal to the Indian agent.[137] The rolls as finally completed were deposited in the national archives, and a copy was sent to the Department of the Interior.[138]

Although the Choctaws had been determined to grant only a limited citizenship to their freedmen, the grant so far as it went was made in good faith, and was scrupulously observed. No attempt was made to prevent their voting, as has been the case in so many Southern states, and, as they were numerous enough to hold the balance of power in a close election, it was customary for political parties to bid for their support.[139]

The Choctaws even took their obligations to their new citizens so seriously that they insisted that under the reciprocal citizenship arrangement of the Treaty of 1855 the Chickasaws were bound to grant the right of suffrage and the use of the tribal land to such of the Choctaw freedmen as were living in their district.

The Chickasaws, possibly because of their numerical inferiority, had never been as liberal in interpreting these provisions as had the Choctaws. While the Choctaws had given absolute political equality to persons of Chickasaw blood living in their nation, the Chickasaw constitution had stipulated that only members of that tribe were eligible to fill the office of Governor or member of the Council. The Chickasaws had been upheld in this discrimination against Choctaw citizens by Attorney General Caleb Cushing, who ruled, January 7, 1857, that the "rights, privileges, and immunities" of citizenship guaranteed by the Treaty of 1855 did not necessarily include suffrage or the right to hold office.[140]

[135]*Report Senate Committee on Indian Affairs*, IX, 295-300.

[136]Acts of the Choctaw Nation, November 5, 1885.

[137]*Report Commissioner of Indian Affairs*, 1886, p. 155; Acts of the Choctaw Nation, October 30, 1886; October 23, 1888.

[138]Acts of the Choctaw Nation, November 5, 1885.

[139]For example *see Indian Citizen*, July 19, 1890; July 16, 1896; July 12, 1900.

[140]*Official Opinions of the Attorneys General of the United States* (Washington, 1872), VIII, 300-3.

The Chickasaws were, therefore, within their rights when they refused to grant any political privileges to the Choctaw freedmen. The Choctaws, however, undertook to protect the interests of their new citizens, and an extended dispute between the two tribes resulted. In the Spring of 1886 the Choctaws lodged a formal complaint against the Chickasaws with the Commissioner of Indian Affairs, but apparently he took no action.[141] When the Council convened the following Fall, a delegation consisting of C. E. Nelson, A. R. Durant, and J. S. Standley was appointed to negotiate with the Chickasaws. The delegates were instructed to maintain the principle that any discrimination against Choctaw citizens living in the Chickasaw district would apply with equal force to Chickasaws living in the Choctaw country. The representatives of the two nations met at Atoka on October 28, and an agreement was signed on November 1. During the negotiations the Chickasaws "earnestly contended" for their right to determine political qualifications within their own jurisdiction, and the Choctaws were forced to yield. An agreement was drawn up which accepted the Chickasaw principle on condition that if the Chickasaws living in the Choctaw Nation should continue to enjoy political and economic equality with the Choctaws, this practice should "be regarded as a matter of sufferance of the Choctaw Nation, and not as of treaty right," and should be a subject completely within Choctaw jurisdiction.[142] With this empty victory the Choctaws were forced to be content; it is apparent that the Chickasaws, who held out against adoption through their entire tribal history, could hardly have been persuaded to grant privileges to the Choctaw freedmen which they withheld from their own.

The Choctaws found some occasion to enforce the constitutional provision that prescribed Indian blood as a condition of eligibility to the Council. In 1890, five years after the adoption, a Negro who wished to be a member of the lower house appealed to the Indian Office against this discrimination, but nothing appears to have been done.[143] In 1895 when a colored citizen was actually elected as a Representative from Kiamitia County, this provision seems to have been invoked to prevent him from taking his seat.[144]

[141]Indian Office Land File, 1886, 10258, brief by Campbell LeFlore before Commissioner of Indian Affairs, March 31, 1886. The document is endorsed with the one word *filed,* and the most diligent search has failed to locate any record of official action.
[142]Acts of the Choctaw Nation, October 22, October 26, November 6, 1886.
[143]*Indian Citizen,* August 2, 1890, Washington letter.
[144]*Ibid.,* August 22, 1895. The writer has been informed by leading Choctaws that the House refused to seat him.

CHOCTAW LAND PATENT GRANTED BY PRESIDENT TYLER, 1842

CHOCTAW BALL PLAY AT SKULLYVILLE BY CATLIN, 1834

The Choctaws carried out their agreement to establish schools for the freedmen as scrupulously as they safeguarded their right to vote. The Council which met in the Fall after their registration made an appropriation for colored neighborhood schools, and directed that they be opened immediately.[145] During that first Winter thirty-four neighborhood schools were established with an enrollment of 847 children.[146] In 1891 the Nation went beyond the obligation assumed by the act of adoption by establishing a colored boarding school.[147]

Although the freedmen had feared that they would be restricted to the use of forty acres of the public domain, no attempt was ever made to limit their holdings; they enjoyed equal rights with the Choctaws to as much land as they cared to cultivate. The Choctaws, however, interpreted the control of white immigration guaranteed to them by the Treaty of 1866 to apply to all citizens of the United States and they strove to prevent Negro immigration.[148]

The Choctaws never mingled socially with the Negroes. Their schools were separate. They constituted a distinct political group. They were racially apart. When intermarriage became possible by the incorporation of the freedmen into the tribe, a law was immediately passed making it a felony.[149] Adoption, to the Choctaws, meant the granting of specific privileges that would regulate the relations between the two races in a definite way, but never amalgamation.

The granting of citizenship to the freedmen may be said to end the reconstruction period. Order had been reëstablished, the schools had been restored, public finances had been stabilized, the obligations imposed by the Peace Treaty had been carried out. All these developments were interrelated with the great economic changes that will be taken up in the next chapter.

[145]Acts of the Choctaw Nation, November 10, 1885.
[146]Ibid., October 30, 1886.
[147]Ibid., October 21, 1891.
[148]Indian Citizen, November 7, 1891, text of law of October 22, 1891.
[149]Acts of the Choctaw Nation, November 6, 1885.

ECONOMIC DEVELOPMENT

5

THE entire structure of the Choctaws' economic life was based upon the ancient tribal system of common ownership of land. Any citizen was entitled "to open up a farm" in any portion of the public domain, provided he did not encroach upon the property of another citizen. He might construct improvements, and hold the land as long as he cared to use it for agricultural purposes; if he should abandon it the title would revert to the Nation.[1]

Grazing land was held by the same tenure until 1883 when an act of the General Council limited the size of a pasture to one mile square, and provided that no citizen should hold more than one such pasture in any one county.[2] The fences ran across the country in all directions without regard for points of the compass, but after 1887 legislative regulations provided for at least a twenty-foot lane between neighboring pastures.[3] As the law regulating the size of pastures had not been retroactive, a few citizens continued to enjoy larger holdings, the two largest being about ten and six miles square respectively.[4]

Under this system of land ownership some Choctaws became very wealthy. The richest citizen was Wilson N. Jones, who began farming in 1849 with no capital at all. In the early Nineties he was reported to have about 17,600 acres of land under fence, of which 550 acres was cultivated and the remainder in pasture; and he was said to own 5,000 cattle, 75 horses, and important mining interests, besides a cotton gin and a store at Caddo. More representative of this class of well-to-do

[1]Folsom, *Digest of Choctaw Law,* p. 487, law of October 11, 1839; Acts of the Choctaw Nation, October 24, 1873; *Report Commissioner of Indian Affairs,* 1887, pp. 102, 111; 1888, p. 134.

[2]Acts of the Choctaw Nation, November 6, 1883; October 28, 1884.

[3]*Ibid.,* November 8, 1887.

[4]*Report Senate Committee on Indian Affairs,* IX, 227, 228, 247, 270.

citizens were Edmund McCurtain, who had 300 acres of land under cultivation, and owned 500 head of live stock and other ranching interests; J. C. Folsom, who had 2,040 acres of land, of which 1,500 was under cultivation; Napoleon B. Ainsworth, with 400 acres of land and extensive ranching and mining interests; and B. F. Smallwood, with a store and a well stocked farm.[5]

The labor on these farms was usually performed by several white or Negro tenants, who lived in small cabins and cultivated the land for a share of the produce. If a Choctaw wished to extend his holdings he would employ a "laborer" for a period of five to ten years and locate him on some unimproved portion of the public domain. In this case the white man paid no rent, but he was expected to break the land, fence it, and erect a house. At the end of the time the improvements became the property of the Indian. This custom also enabled thrifty Choctaws to provide improved farms for their children when they should come of age. The leasing of the public domain to non-citizens was made illegal in 1877, but the law was generally evaded by the simple fiction of classing the lessees as laborers.[6]

These well-to-do Choctaws usually lived in large rambling houses of the Southern type, practicing a careless hospitality and accepting by a sort of natural right the responsibility of leadership in local and tribal affairs. In the absence of economic statistics it is impossible to discover their number, but it is probable that less than two hundred families belonged to this class.[7]

Although all citizens theoretically owned an equal interest in the land, there was a great contrast between the extensive holdings of these prosperous families and the small patch of land that satisfied the average Choctaw. These poorer people lived near a stream or spring at some isolated spot in the hills. Their homes were rude log cabins or crude board huts without plaster or sheeting, and their furniture was

[5]*Ibid.*, IX, 227-28, 246-48, 268-70; J. H. Beadle, *The Undeveloped West* (Philadelphia, 1873), p. 401; Stanley Pumphrey, *Indian Civilization* (Philadelphia, 1877); *Report Commissioner of Indian Affairs,* 1876, p. 62; 1887, p. 115; O'Beirne, *Leaders and Leading Men,* I, 28-29, 70, 106-7, 178-79. *See* also advertised brands in the *Branding Iron* during 1884.

[6]*Report Commissioner of Indian Affairs,* 1874, p. 71; 1887, p. 112; 1888, pp. 134-35; *Report Senate Committee on Indian Affairs,* IX, 246; *Extra Census Bulletin—The Five Civilized Tribes in Indian Territory* (Washington, 1894), p. 57; Acts of the Choctaw Nation, October 30, 1877.

[7]Union Agency Files, Choctaw—Census. The Choctaws took a census regularly and collected agricultural statistics of all kinds, but most of the data have been lost. The estimate given above is based upon fragments of these census returns.

primitive. Their live stock and corn furnished them with a scanty food supply which they supplemented by hunting and fishing, and they added to their meagre income by the sale of snake root and furs.[8]

They carried their corn to the grist mills, which were numerous in the Choctaw country, and had it ground into meal for their family use. To a certain extent they still used native recipes in preparing food. The most characteristic Choctaw dish was the *to falla* or "Tom Fuller," which was made of corn cracked in a wooden mortar and then boiled. Other native foods were *pashofa*, made of cooked meal mixed with finely cut meat and again cooked; *walusha*, of grape juice mixed with meal and sugar or cane syrup; *bahar*, of hickory nuts and walnuts beaten to a pulp to which cracked parched corn, sugar, and water were added to make a thick dough; and *abunaha*, cooked corn beaten into a dough, mixed with cooked beans, wrapped in corn shucks and then boiled, and laid away in the husks until needed.[9]

The poorer Choctaws lived such a hand-to-mouth existence that a crop shortage always threatened them with starvation. The food situation became especially acute in 1875, 1882, 1897, and 1902.

A crop failure in 1874 brought such serious distress during the following Winter that in February Peter P. Pitchlynn, the Choctaw delegate at Washington, requested the United States to appropriate $200,000 of the invested funds of the Nation for relief purposes. Congress gave the necessary authority, but Secretary Delano refused to diminish the Choctaws' principal in this way.[10]

When, in 1881, another crop failure occurred, Chief Jackson McCurtain advised the Council to forestall famine by authorizing relief measures, but no action was taken. Great suffering resulted, and the people, exercising their constitutional right of petition, assembled to appeal to the Chief for "redress of their sore grievances." It was agreed at this meeting that six thousand dollars should be expended for relief, and the Chief carried out the distribution on his own responsibility. When the Council convened the following Fall, it commended McCurtain for his "timely and patriotic action," and made an appropriation to cover the amount of his unauthorized expenditure.[11]

[8]*Extra Census Bulletin*, pp. 58-59; John James, *My Experience with Indians* (Austin, Texas, 1925), pp. 55-57, 84; H. F. and E. S. O'Beirne, *The Indian Territory; its Chiefs, Legislators and Leading Men* (St. Louis, 1892), pp. 53-54, 65-67, 483-85; *Report Commissioner of Indian Affairs*, 1884, p. 100.

[9]*Vindicator*, February 2, July 26, 1876; James, *My Experience with Indians*, p. 105; G. A. Crossett, "A Vanishing Race," *Chronicles of Oklahoma*, IV (June, 1926), 100-15.

[10]Indian Office Files, Choctaw, 1875, 1225, 1345.

[11]Acts of the Choctaw Nation, October 19, 1882.

When Chief Green McCurtain was confronted by a similar crisis early in 1897, he first asked the National Treasurer to advance money for the purchase of corn. When that official declined to take such irregular action, McCurtain borrowed $2,600 upon his own responsibility, which he afterwards repaid from tax money turned in by the revenue collectors. He then appointed an enumerator in each county to make a list of needy citizens and take charge of the distribution, and D. N. Robb was authorized to superintend the entire program of relief. The work was carried on with a high degree of efficiency, and 9,200 bushels of corn was purchased and hauled from the railroads to the different counties where it was distributed. The amount dispensed to individuals varied from one to six bushels, and the value of the corn was charged to the recipient to be deducted from some future per caput payment. Apparently about half of the population of the Nation received assistance at this time. All these emergency measures were legalized by the Council at the next regular session.[12]

In 1902 Chief Dukes requested Congress to make an appropriation for relief purposes from a sum which the Federal Government had collected for the Choctaws from the sale of townsites. Congress then appropriated $20,000 with the provision that the amount advanced to each individual should be deducted from his share of the townsite money in the final per caput distribution. A commission consisting of Chief Dukes, National Treasurer Scott, and ex-Chief McCurtain investigated the situation and listed the destitute families, and contracts were made with merchants to furnish groceries to those whose names appeared on the list. The amount of aid extended to each needy family was grocery credit to the extent of $9.09. Again, as in 1897, it appears that fully half the population of the Nation received this assistance.[13]

In years of plenty the average Choctaw family, exclusive of the wealthy citizens, apparently owned about four or five ponies, six or eight cattle, and ten to twenty hogs, and raised about one hundred bushels of corn. A very little wheat and oats was raised in the Choctaw country, but the amount was negligible. Some of the more progressive citizens raised mules, and there were a few thousand sheep owned by

[12]Union Agency Files, Choctaw—Principal Chief, annual message of Chief McCurtain; *ibid.*, Choctaw—Indigents, reports from the county enumerators; Acts of the Choctaw Nation, November 11, 1897.

[13]Union Agency Files, Choctaw—Indigents,—among these documents are the contracts made with the merchants, and the list prepared by the special commission; *Report Commissioner of Indian Affairs*, 1902, p. 488.

Choctaws. The main export was cotton, which was produced mainly on the large farms of the well-to-do citizens, especially in the Red River region. Any estimate of the value of the cotton crop must be based on the most fragmentary data; the Choctaw census in 1867 placed the year's production at 211,595 bales, but this enumeration came too soon after the Civil War to represent a normal yield. The number of cattle shipped out of the Nation was also considerable, although it is equally difficult to determine; Chief McCurtain estimated in 1880 that the Choctaws had shipped out 6,500 head during the year and had slaughtered 3,250 for home consumption.[14]

In a society where the average citizen secured his living by the most elemental agriculture the financial structure was necessarily simple. Apparently there was not even a bank in the Nation until after 1890.[15] United States money was, of course, in circulation, but the poorer Choctaw was able to satisfy most of his simple needs by barter. The wealthy citizens, with their extensive financial interests, were in the habit of going to Texas towns to transact their banking business. The government also deposited its money in Texas, and the public officials were expected to draw it from the banks and carry it in their saddle bags or hide it in their homes, guarding it from outlaws until they could pay it out to the school teachers and other employees of the Nation.[16]

Transportation, until the coming of the railroads, was also very primitive. The roads were mere trails winding around pastures and fields, and fording rivers.[17] As a citizen could enclose any part of the public domain, it was provided by law that a person who would build a fence across any road leading to a church or school should be required

[14]Union Agency Files, Choctaw—Census—among these papers are the complete returns of the census of 1867 for the entire Nation, with the exception of San Bois County, but apparently the returns of only one or two counties have been preserved from any later census; *ibid.*, Choctaw—Principal Chief—Chief Cole's annual message, October 8, 1878, includes the census statistics of that year for Eagle County; *Report of the Productions of Agriculture, Tenth Census*, Chief McCurtain's estimates for 1880; *Reports Commissioner of Indian Affairs*—the statistics given in these reports are too inaccurate to be of much value—for instance the number of horses reported was 18,000 in 1872, and 100,000 in 1873—*Report*, 1872, pp. 402-3 and 1873, Plate No. 80, opposite p. 346; *Vindicator*, February 16, June 14, 1876, shipments of cattle and hogs.

[15]*Extra Census Bulletin*, p. 13; *Indian Citizen*, January 18, 1890; March 28, 1892; December 3, 1896.

[16]O'Beirne, *Leaders and Leading Men*, I, 190-93; B. L. Phipps, "Banking in Indian Territory during the '80's," *Chronicles of Oklahoma*, VII (June, 1929), 186-87; James, *My Experience with Indians*, pp. 91-103.

[17]John Laracy, "Sacred Heart Mission and Abbey" (Diary of Joseph Lanchet, 1884), *Chronicles of Oklahoma*, V (June, 1927), 239.

"to make a good substantial road around such fences, or to make a lane, or to make gates at the point where the original road comes in and out."[18]

The only public provision for improving the roads was the law that required all male citizens between the ages of eighteen and fifty, except certain exempted professional classes, to turn out for six days each year "with their hoes, axes, and other utensils" to work the roads under the direction of overseers appointed by the county judge.[19] Although white travelers, probably judging by appearances, frequently made the statement that Choctaw roads were never worked, this law seems to have been fairly well enforced.[20] The obligation to work the roads was also extended to non-citizens who were living in the Choctaw country, but as there was no way of enforcing this provision of the law, it was nearly always ignored. This caused much bad feeling on the part of the Choctaws who felt that the white residents used the roads more than the citizens did, and it caused a tendency for the Indians themselves, to become delinquent in performing their road work.[21]

The Choctaw Nation never appropriated money for highway improvement. In view of the fact that several important thoroughfares led across the Nation, the building of toll bridges and turnpikes, and the maintenance of ferries were profitable enterprises. Franchises were granted by special legislative enactment, and the rates for various classes of traffic were specified — always with the provision that citizens should be exempt.[22] The Nation thus developed its highways at the expense of travelers, and enterprising Choctaw citizens enjoyed a good income from their road improvements. Some indignant white men protested bitterly to the Interior Department about the expense of cross-

[18]Acts of the Choctaw Nation, October 29, 1881; see also Folsom, Digest of Choctaw Law, p. 486, act of October 8, 1836.

[19]Ibid., November 7, 1878; November 12, 1881; October 29, 1884; Union Agency Files, Letters of Chiefs, p. 35, Chief Allen Wright to District Chiefs, April 25, 1867.

[20]In the Union Agency Files are lists of citizens of the various counties showing the amount of work done by each, and also instructions from the county judge directing the sheriff to sell the property of certain delinquents, to pay their fine for failing to observe the law. For a white observer's impression of Choctaw roads see Extra Census Bulletin, p. 57.

[21]Acts of the Choctaw Nation, November 7, 1878; Report of the Select Committee to Investigate Matters Connected with Affairs in the Indian Territory (Washington, 1907), I, 929; Indian Citizen, October 5, 1889, "Canadian Clippings."

[22]For examples of such laws see Acts of the Choctaw Nation, April 8, 1870; October 20, 1874; October 24, 1889; April 11, 1891; October 23, 1895. The rates usually ranged from twenty-five cents for each team hitched to a wagon, to one cent a head for cattle in a drove. The charge to a pedestrian was usually five cents.

ing the Indian country; they said that in a few cases the bridges and turnpikes were a convenience to travelers and the expense was, therefore, legitimate, but than in many instances the wily Indians built bridges over fordable streams, fenced up the fords, and compelled the traveler to pay toll.[23] The Nation as a whole seems to have profited very little from this system of road improvement; as there was no inducement to build a bridge or construct a turnpike except where it would be used by non-citizens, the only improved roads seem to have been the through highways from the "States."[24]

The coming of the railroads was the strongest influence in destroying the isolation of the Choctaw country, at the same time that it brought many perplexing problems to the Choctaw people.

The Treaty of 1855, which separated the Choctaws and Chickasaws, had provided that the right of way would be granted to the United States or to any incorporated company to construct railroad or telegraph lines across the lands of the two nations.[25] The Peace Treaty of 1866 stipulated that the right of way should be granted to any company authorized by Congress or the legislatures of the two nations with the express consent of the Secretary of the Interior, to construct one north-south and one east-west road across the Indian lands. The nation through which such road might pass was permitted to subscribe to stock and pay for it by the sale of alternate sections of a six mile strip on each side of the track, but the railway company might dispose of this land only to citizens of the nation.[26] The treaties made with the other tribes of the Indian Territory at the close of the Civil War also contained provisions for grants to railroads.

The Choctaw Nation very soon took steps to promote railroad building under the stipulations of the Treaty of 1866. The two houses of the Council met in joint session in the Fall of 1869 and gave special consideration to several railroad propositions that were presented for their approval.[27] At a special session the following Spring, charters were granted to two railroads — the Choctaw and Chickasaw Central Railway Company, and the Choctaw and Chickasaw Thirty-fifth Parallel Railway Company. The Nation voted to subscribe to stock, paying for it by the sale of alternate sections of land as provided by the treaty.

[23]Indian Office Files, Choctaw, 1874, P38, P89; *ibid.,* Union, 1879, W121.
[24]*Ibid.,* Choctaw, 1874, P89.
[25]Kappler, *Laws and Treaties,* II, 710, Art. 18.
[26]*Ibid.,* II, 920-21, Art. 6.
[27]Acts of the Choctaw Nation, October 21, 1869; October 23, 1869.

The Chickasaws, however, refused their assent, the Secretary of the Interior withheld his approval, and, as a consequence, the enterprise was abandoned.[28]

The United States Government, indeed, had not waited for the Indians to act. On July 25, 1866, even before the Peace Treaty had been ratified by the Choctaws, Congress passed a law providing that of three specified Kansas railroads the one that should first reach the boundary of the Indian Territory should be the beneficiary of the treaties. It made a free grant of the right of way, and a conditional grant of every alternate section in a ten mile strip on each side of the track "whenever the Indian title shall be extinguished by treaty or otherwise . . . . . *Provided,* That said lands become a part of the public lands of the United States."[29]

According to the treaties the United States could never grant these alternate sections to the railroad, for the Choctaw-Chickasaw title was as strong as the faith of a nation could make it; the land could never "become a part of the public lands of the United States" except in the improbable event "that said Indians and their heirs become extinct or abandon the same."[30] The provision did, however, have the mischievous effect of creating in the railroad company that should secure the right of way, a powerful enemy to tribal autonomy and the integrity of Indian titles.[31]

Immediately upon the passage of the act the three railroads began a race for the border. The winner was the Union Pacific, Southern Branch — soon to be known as the Missouri, Kansas, and Texas, or "Katy"— which reached the line, June 6, 1870.[32] It crossed the Cherokee and Creek nations during the next two years, reached the northern boundary of the Choctaw country in the Spring of 1872, and crossed the Red River into Texas early in December of the same year.[33] It followed approximately the line of the old "Texas Trail" from Muskogee in the Creek Nation to Denison, Texas, traversing the entire Choc-

[28]*Ibid.,* April 8, October 10, October 21, 1870; Indian Office Files, Choctaw, 1870, I1428, I1629; Union Agency Files, Letters of Chiefs, p. 140, Chief Bryant to J. D. McCoy, October 21, 1870.

[29] *U. S. Statutes at Large,* XIV, 236–39.

[30]Kappler, *Laws and Treaties,* II, 707, Treaty of 1855.

[31]*Report Commissioner of Indian Affairs,* 1872, p. 77; Resolutions of Okmulgee Council, December 5, 1873; May 14, 1874; May 13, 1875—found in Acts of the Choctaw Nation, 1875.

[32]Edward King, *The Southern States of North America* (London, 1875), p. 195.

[33]*Report Commissioner of Indian Affairs,* 1872, p. 76; Thoburn and Wright, *Oklahoma,* II, 480.

taw country from north to south and cutting across a spur of the Chickasaw Nation just north of the Red River.

As the road advanced into the Indian Territory a succession of roistering tent cities sprang up at the temporary terminals, only to be abandoned as the construction moved on. Whisky peddlers, with their cargo smuggled in the baggage car, gamblers, and other notorious "bad men" flocked to these places, and crimes of all sorts were of almost daily occurrence. The criminals were outside the jurisdiction of the Indian courts, and the authority of the Federal Government was too remote to trouble them.

Some amusement was occasioned by the experience of the Secretary of the Interior, who came on a tour of inspection just as the road had reached the boundary of the Choctaw country. On the day he arrived at the terminal, a robbery was committed a few feet from the track, and during the night a man was murdered close to his sleeping car. He showed more excitement over these occurrences than it was customary to exhibit in that lawless community, and telegraphed to President Grant for troops. The Tenth Cavalry from the Department of Missouri soon arrived and expelled the outlaws, and for a time the lurid camp on the Canadian became an orderly community.[34] But the War Department refused to coöperate, and before the road was completed across the Choctaw country the troops, in spite of the frantic protests of the Indian agent, were removed, on the ground that the "Department is unable to spare troops for that country, even if they were necessary for its protection, which is not established."[35] As soon, however, as construction advanced beyond the Red River, the last terminal camp in the Indian country was abandoned, and the "bad men" departed.

As soon as the railroad entered the Choctaw country, it became involved in controversies with the tribal government. It made no payment for the right of way; it secured exemption from taxation; and it purchased timber and stone from individual citizens in violation of the law that placed such sales under the control of the Nation.

Individual citizens also complained bitterly regarding their losses when live stock were injured by the trains. The company did not fence the right of way, alleging that the random arrangement of Choctaw fences and roads made such protection impossible. The trainmen made

[34]Beadle, *The Undeveloped West*, pp. 398-402; King, *The Southern States of North America*, pp. 206-7.
[35]Indian Office Files, Choctaw, 1872, G1, G310, G455, W51.

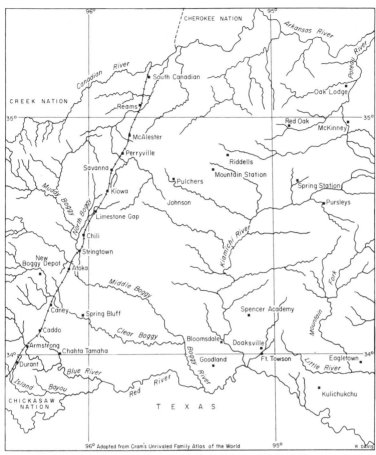

CREEK NATION

CHEROKEE NATION

Canadian River

Arkansas River

Poteau River

South Canadian

Oak Lodge

Reams

35°   35°

Red Oak

McAlester   McKinney

Perryville

Savanna   Riddells

Pulchers   Mountain Station

Kiowa   Spring Station

Johnson   Pursleys

Muddy Boggy

North Boggy

Limestone Gap

Chili

Kiamichi River

New Boggy Depot   Stringtown

Atoka

Middle Boggy

Fork

Caney   Spring Bluff   Spencer Academy

Mountain

Caddo

Clear Boggy

Bloomsdale   Doaksville

34° Armstrong   Chahta Tamaha   Goodland   Ft. Towson   Eagletown 34°

Durant

Blue River   Boggy River   Little River

Island Bayou   Red River

CHICKASAW NATION   Kulichukchu

T E X A S

96° Adapted from Cram's Unrivaled Family Atlas of the World   95°   R. DAVIS

TOWNS OF THE CHOCTAW NATION ABOUT 1872

119

an effort to drive live stock from the track by blowing the whistle, but many accidents occurred. An arrogant letter from Claim Agent J. D. Hollister regarding some hogs killed by a train seems to have been characteristic of the attitude taken by the railway officials. He bluntly refused to entertain any claim for damages — "The stand which I take relative to hogs is that if men through that section of the country wish to keep that class of animals, they should see that they are thoroughly protected, as it is utterly impossible for us to do anything to further the safety of that class of animals."[36] Since the majority of the Choctaws depended for their meat supply upon hogs which ran almost wild in the woods, the losses from this source were particularly exasperating.

The excessive freight and passenger charges exacted by the railroad also aroused much bitter feeling on the part of the Choctaws. Manager Stevens always said that in building the railroad across the Indian Territory he had built it through two hundred miles of tunnel. It is true that the shipping through that region was very light, but the discriminatory rates levied against the Indian country were almost prohibitive. It was generally believed that the railroad officials controlled certain mining companies, notably the Osage Coal and Mining Company,[37] and that these companies enjoyed concessions in the matter of rates.

Shippers and passengers were charged double fare to Indian Territory points; it cost less to buy a ticket through the territory than to points within it.[38] Early in 1876 the passenger fare was reduced from seven to five cents a mile, and it remained at that figure until 1900, in spite of memorials of the General Council, protests to the Secretary of the Interior, and threatened reduction by Congress.[39] At the same time other railroads that had *paid* for their right of way through the Choctaw Nation were charging the three-cent fare customary in neighboring states.

In 1876 Chief Coleman Cole drew up a paper which he submitted to the Secretary of the Interior as embodying his ideas of a correct railroad policy. He made the following suggestions:

[36]Indian Office Files, Special Case No. 136, Hollister to R. L. Fite, June 5, 1889.

[37]A certain amount of interlocking ownership was admitted by T. C. Sears, attorney for the railroad, in the suit before the Commissioner of Indian Affairs—Indian Office Files, Special Case, No. 136.

[38]*The Vindicator*, November 3, 1875.

[39]Acts of the Choctaw Nation, November 2, 1888; Indian Office Files, Special Case No. 136, act of Council, October 23, 1889; *Indian Citizen*, May 19, 1892; January 3, 1895; *Antlers Democrat*, November 2, 1900.

1. Railroad, telegraph, and express companies should pay taxes to the Nation.

2. Railroad employees engaging in any pursuit other than their railroad work should be subject to the same regulations as other non-citizens engaged in similar pursuits.

3. Crossings should not be obstructed by standing trains.

4. The railroads should pay at least three-fourths of the value of any property destroyed.

5. Railroads should not engage in mining, or in the manufacture and sale of lumber except as carriers.

6. Passenger and freight rates should be the same as in the "States."

7. The amount of land claimed for right of way and station grounds should be limited and defined by act of Congress and treaty stipulations.[40]

It must have been some satisfaction to the old Chief to observe that subsequent railroad grants were more nearly in line with what he considered sound railroad policy. The Missouri, Kansas, and Texas was the only road in the Choctaw country constructed under the terms of the Treaty of 1866, and no later treaty was made with the Choctaws. In 1871 Congress passed the law that terminated the fiction maintained for almost a century that Indian nations or tribes were independent sovereignties capable of entering into treaty relations with the United States. From this time on, any road, unless accepted as the east-west road of the Treaty of 1866, would secure its charter through an act of Congress.

The granting of the franchise for the next railroad represents a transition from the old custom of negotiating a treaty to the method subsequently adopted of granting a charter by Congressional enactment. The Choctaws were consulted freely at every stage of the proceedings, and yet there was a recognition that in the last analysis the United States held the right of eminent domain.

The St. Louis and San Francisco, or "Frisco," negotiated with the Choctaws to secure their consent to the right of way, and the question was considered by the Council in the Fall of 1880, and entered into the election of 1881. When the newly elected Council met, Chief J. F. McCurtain recommended in his message that the franchise be granted.[41]

At the same time the Chicago, Texas, and Mexican Central was seeking the approval of the Interior Department. The Department

[40]Indian Office Files, Choctaw, 1876, U77.
[41]*Senate Exec. Docs.*, 47 Cong., 1 Sess., No. 15, pp. 11-12, 21.

was inclined to favor this application, and sent Uri J. Baxter as a special agent to secure the consent of the Choctaws.[42] Baxter proceeded to Chahta Tamaha, where he found the officials of the Nation in favor of making the grant to the other road. Instructed by the Department to show no favoritism he presented both applications. The representatives of the companies then compromised, and the Chicago, Texas, and Mexican Central withdrew.[43]

Chief McCurtain then recommended to the Council that a committee be appointed to meet with Baxter to draft a bill, pointing out to the irreconcilables that disapproved of railroads in general that the United States Congress had power to grant a franchise to the road without Choctaw consent. The committee was then appointed, and the bill drafted, but B. F. Smallwood, the Speaker of the House of Representatives, claiming the right to vote as a member of that body, cast his vote in the negative and thus created a tie. He then announced that the bill had failed of passage.[44] After adjournment some one picked it up from the table where it was lying, and carried it to the Chief.[45] McCurtain then requested an opinion from National Attorney C. S. Vinson regarding the constitutional right of the Speaker to vote on a bill before the House; he was told that such a vote was legal only to prevent a tie. He then approved the bill.[46]

In its protection of Indian rights this bill presents a striking contrast to the Missouri, Kansas, and Texas grant. While the charter to the earlier road had carried a conditional land grant that encouraged it to intrigue for the extinction of Indian titles, this bill contained the express provision that an attempt to change the Indian tenure of land would work forfeiture. Instead of the complete immunity from taxation enjoyed by the Missouri, Kansas, and Texas this bill provided a yearly payment of two thousand dollars to the Choctaw and Chickasaw governments. To prevent the discriminatory tariffs levied by the Missouri, Kansas, and Texas there was a provision that freight and passenger rates should be kept at the level of the lowest charges in Arkansas or Texas. The railroad was forbidden to take building material from the

[42]*Ibid.*, p. 4.
[43]*Ibid.*, pp. 5-11.
[44]*Ibid.*, pp. 11-14.
[45]Union Agency Files, Choctaw—Railroads, MS record of testimony before a congressional committee.
[46]*Senate Exec. Docs.*, 47 Cong., 1 Sess., No. 15, pp. 14-15. Smallwood was the chairman of a committee that drew up the rules adopted by the House of Representatives in 1878. These rules gave the Speaker only a casting vote in case of a tie. (Union Agency Files, Choctaw—National Council.)

Nation except under contract with the Choctaw and Chickasaw governments. Finally, the civil jurisdiction of the Federal court of the Western District of Arkansas was extended to cover all cases of controversy between the Indians and the railroad. After its passage by the Choctaw legislature the bill was to be presented for ratification to the Congress of the United States.[47]

When the bill was presented to the board of directors of the railroad company, they accepted the terms by a unanimous vote.[48] The Chickasaws, however, passed a resolution protesting against the grant. They believed that the consideration was inadequate, and they objected to the independent action of the Choctaws involving property in which they held a joint interest. They authorized Governor Overton to proceed to Washington and protest against ratification by Congress.[49]

B. F. Smallwood, Isham Walker, and Joseph P. Folsom of the Choctaw House of Representatives also came to Washington to protest against alleged irregularities in the passage of the bill through their Council. Folsom objected to Baxter's right to serve on a committee of the Choctaw Council; Smallwood still claimed his right to vote as the member from Atoka County; and Walker, as Journalist of the House, brought along his minutes to show that the measure had been lost through a tie vote. The force of their protest was lost on the committee of Congress before whom they appeared when by the vagueness of their answers, Folsom and Walker created the impression that their expenses had been paid by a competing railroad.[50]

The bill passed Congress August 2, 1882. It reduced the width of the right of way as granted by the Choctaw Council, and as a result of Governor Overton's protest the yearly payment was raised from two to three thousand dollars, to be divided between the two nations according to the customary ratio of three to one, and provision was made for settlement by arbitration provided this sum were not acceptable. In other respects it was substantially the same as the original bill passed by the Choctaw legislature.[51]

[47]*Senate Exec. Docs.*, 47 Cong., 1 Sess., No. 15, pp. 16-18, text of bill, approved November 10, 1881.

[48]*Ibid.*, p. 22, December 6, 1881.

[49]*House Exec. Docs.*, 47 Cong., 1 Sess., No. 36; Union Agency Files, Choctaw—Railroads, *op. cit.* The Chickasaws passed their resolution of protest on December 17.

[50]Union Agency Files, Choctaw—Railroads, *op. cit.*

[51]*U. S. Statutes at Large*, XXII, 181; Kappler, *Laws and Treaties*, I, 206-9; *House Reports*, 47 Cong., 1 Sess., No. 934.

The railroad constructed under this grant connected Fort Smith, Arkansas, with Paris, Texas, cutting across the Nation from northeast to south. It was completed in 1887.[52]

The next company that built a railroad into the Nation brought almost as much trouble to the Choctaws as the Missouri, Kansas, and Texas had, because of its attempt to secure coal lands and speculate in townsites. It began first as a mining company, and became interested in railroad building in order to open up its coal leases.

The Choctaw Coal and Mining Company was one of the first companies to engage in mining operations in the Choctaw Nation.[53] In 1888, as the Choctaw Coal and Railway Company, it secured a charter from Congress to build a railroad across the country, with branches to its extensive coal lands.[54] Construction of the road began at Wister Junction on the St. Louis and San Francisco, and progressed west to effect a junction with the Missouri, Kansas, and Texas near McAlester. About eighty miles of track was completed in 1890.[55]

Although the charter had granted a right of way of one hundred feet with the same forfeiture provisions against the attempt to secure additional Indian land that were contained in the St. Louis and San Francisco charter, the company immediately began to fence a strip of one hundred feet on each side of the track and to speculate in town lots, selling them to Indians and to whites in violation of Choctaw law. It also attempted by similar methods to obtain possession of Choctaw coal lands,[56] and in this it was partly successful.[57]

The General Council passed a resolution requesting the Secretary of the Interior to revoke the charter, which the company had certainly forfeited by its attempt to secure Indian land. It also instructed the Principal Chief to have the houses which the company had erected in its townsite speculation advertised for sale.[58] Agent Bennett also made

[52]*Report Commissioner of Indian Affairs*, 1886, p. 269; 1887, p. 119; James L. Allhands, "History of the Construction of the Frisco Railway Lines in Oklahoma," *Chronicles of Oklahoma*, III (1925), 232.

[53]Acts of the Choctaw Nation, November 1, 1880. At that time the company was operating a mine near Savanna.

[54]*U. S. Statutes at Large*, XXV, 39; Kappler, *Laws and Treaties*, I, 256-60, February 18, 1888.

[55]*Report Commissioner of Indian Affairs*, 1889, p. 208; 1890, p. 96; Acts of the Choctaw Nation, November 14, 1890.

[56]*Report Commissioner of Indian Affairs*, 1890, pp. 96-98; Acts of the Choctaw Nation, November 11, 1890.

[57]*See infra*, p. 135.

[58]Acts of the Choctaw Nation, November 14, 1890.

Courtesy Oklahoma Historical Society

GEORGE HUDSON, PRINCIPAL CHIEF, 1860–62

ALLEN WRIGHT, PRINCIPAL CHIEF, 1866–70

vigorous protests to the Indian Office against the encroachments of the company.

Apparently, the company had overreached itself in speculating in lands and leases to which it could not secure a clear title. At least it was to this circumstance that Bennett attributed its financial difficulties when it became insolvent in 1891.[59] Its property was thereupon taken over by the Choctaw, Oklahoma, and Gulf Railroad to which it was transferred by act of Congress in 1896.[60] The line now extended from Wister Junction to El Reno, Oklahoma.[61] In 1902 it was taken over by the Rock Island system, and a branch was constructed running southwest to Ardmore in the Chickasaw Nation.[62]

Several railroads were built in the Choctaw Nation toward the close of the tribal period. The Arkansas and Choctaw secured a charter from Congress in 1899 to build an east-west line across the Nation a few miles north of the Red River. In 1902, it was purchased by the St. Louis and San Francisco.[63] The Fort Smith and Western Coal, later known as the Fort Smith and Western, received its first charter in 1896. It crossed the northern part of the Nation, through Skullyville, San Bois, Gaines, and Tobucksy counties, and entered the Creek Nation a few miles west of its junction with the Missouri, Kansas, and Texas at South Canadian.[64] The Denison and Washita Valley, operated by the Missouri, Kansas, and Texas; the Kansas City Southern; and the Midland Valley also ran for a short distance into the Choctaw country. In 1902 the Nation had a total of 780 miles of railway — the greatest mileage of any nation in the Indian Territory.[65]

The Choctaw Nation itself granted franchises to citizens, usually good for ten years, to build and operate short spurs of railroad leading from the main lines to their coal fields.[66] Such franchises were granted also to mining companies with the provision that the land should revert to the Nation when no longer used for coal shipments.[67] The punishment for any citizen who would sell a right of way to a railroad

[59]Report Commissioner of Indian Affairs, 1891, I, 251.

[60]Kappler, Laws and Treaties, I, 595-96, April 24, 1896. See also act, August 24, 1894, authorizing sale—Kappler, I, 547-55.

[61]Indian Citizen, September 26, 1895; Union Agency Files, Choctaw—Railroads, pass for 1895 to National Treasurer W. W. Wilson.

[62]Report Commissioner of Indian Affairs, 1902, p. 209; 1905, p. 453.

[63]Ibid., 1899, pp. 487-90; 1902, p. 209.

[64]Ibid., 1896, pp. 421-23; 1899, pp. 514-17.

[65]Commission to the Five Civilized Tribes, Annual Report, 1902, p. 48.

[66]Acts of the Choctaw Nation, 1883-1884.

[67]Ibid., November 7, 1888.

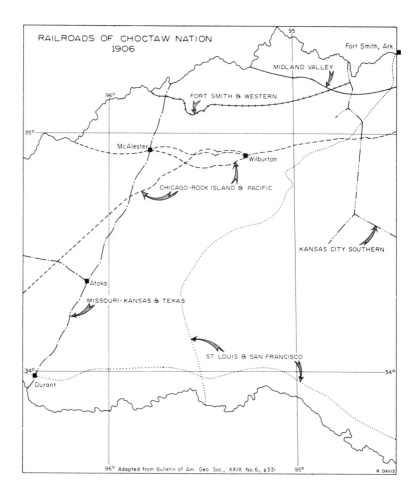

RAILROADS OF CHOCTAW NATION
1906

Fort Smith, Ark.

MIDLAND VALLEY

FORT SMITH & WESTERN

95

96°

35°

McAlester

Wilburton

CHICAGO-ROCK ISLAND & PACIFIC

KANSAS CITY SOUTHERN

Atoka

MISSOURI-KANSAS & TEXAS

ST LOUIS & SAN FRANCISCO

34°

34°

Durant

96° Adapted from Bulletin of Am. Geo. Soc., XXIX No.6, p331   95°   R. DAVIS

126

was a fine and two hundred lashes "during two days well laid on the bare back."[68]

In the early Nineties a corporation known as the Choctaw and Chickasaw National Railway Company sought to secure valuable coal lands under the provisions of the Treaty of 1866 by which the Choctaws might purchase railway stock in exchange for land. The project failed to pass the regular session of the Council in 1893, but at a called session early in 1894 the company secured its charter — by wholesale bribery of the legislators, it was afterwards charged. The granting of the franchise was equivalent to a gift of several millions of dollars, for the projected road was to run through the richest coal fields of the Nation, and the company was to pay only $1.50 an acre for every alternate section in a six-mile strip on each side of the right of way.[69]

This action of the Council aroused great indignation among the Choctaw people, and a determined attempt was made to defeat the scheme. National Attorney C. E. Nelson declared the charter invalid on the ground that the section of the Treaty of 1866 under which the grant was made had never been ratified by the Choctaw Nation.[70] Green McCurtain, Jacob B. Jackson, and Nelson also made strenuous efforts to persuade the Secretary of the Interior to withhold his consent because of the manner in which the law had passed the Council. A strong attempt was made to secure a repeal at another called session of the Council, but it was not successful. The matter was finally settled by the adverse decision of the Secretary of the Interior,[71] and the refusal of the Chickasaw legislature to approve the measure.[72] The new Choctaw Council which convened in the Fall after the election of 1894 then repealed the grant.[73]

Two years later, through the report of Captain McKennon of the Dawes Commission, a public statement was made naming prominent Choctaw citizens as agents of the company in negotiating the alleged bribery, and a list was published citing twenty-three of the thirty-two members of the Council as having received amounts ranging from twenty to one thousand dollars, according to the value or the bargaining power of the legislator.[74]

[68]*Ibid.*, November 2, 1874.
[69]*Ibid.*, January 27, 1894; Charles F. Meserve, *The Dawes Commission and the Five Civilized Tribes of Indian Territory* (Philadelphia, 1896), pp. 17-18.
[70]*Indian Citizen*, February 15, 1894.
[71]*Ibid.*, February 22, March 8, March 15, April 12, April 26, 1894.
[72]*Ibid.*, September 27, 1894.
[73]Acts of the Choctaw Nation, October 8, 1894.
[74]*Indian Citizen*, April 2, April 16, April 30, May 21, 1896.

All of this railroad promotion was closely linked with the development of the coal fields that constituted so large a share of the national wealth. Although a small amount of coal had been dug and used in the blacksmith shops and for other local needs before the Civil War, it did not become accessible for commercial development until the coming of the railroads.

J. J. McAlester in later years claimed the credit of being the one who first realized the possibilities of developing the coal fields. He said that he was living at Fort Smith in 1865, when he happened to see the memorandum book of a geologist who had been a member of a government exploring party that traversed the Indian Territory many years before the Civil War. According to this book the best coal was to be found at the "Cross Roads" where the Texas Trail from Springfield, Missouri, to Preston and Dallas crossed the California Trail from Fort Smith to Albuquerque. Acting upon this knowledge he went to the "Cross Roads" where he established a store and soon became the owner of a flourishing business. By his subsequent marriage to a Chickasaw girl he became entitled to citizenship in the Choctaw Nation. When the Missouri, Kansas, and Texas reached the "Cross Roads" in 1872 the station was named McAlester.[75]

As soon as the coming of the railroad made the coal of commercial value, McAlester and other Choctaw citizens formed a company and began to develop the mines in that region under a provision of the Choctaw constitution that granted to a citizen who should discover any mineral the exclusive right to own and work the mine for the distance of a mile in every direction.[76] McAlester and his associates leased their mine to operators from whom they received a royalty. The Nation laid claim to this royalty, but the owners established their rights through a decision of the Choctaw courts. Chief Coleman Cole, however, was so opposed to the mining operations that he ordered the execution of McAlester and three of his associates. But the lighthorse captain, himself a white man, who was guarding the prisoners allowed them to escape. A compromise was then effected by which half of the royalty was paid to the Nation and half to the owner of the mine, and all contracts were to be approved by the Secretary of the Interior.[77]

[75]Now North McAlester.
[76]Art. VII, Sec. 18.
[77]Thoburn and Wright, *Oklahoma*, II, 879-80, McAlester's account; *Report Senate Committee on Indian Affairs*, IX, 266-70, sworn testimony of McAlester before the committee; Acts of the Choctaw Nation, October 24, 1873. There is every reason to believe that McAlester's story is substantially correct.

128

The importance of the mining operations increased very rapidly with the building of new railroads and the discovery and opening of new mines. In 1887 — fifteen years from the opening of the first commercial mine — the output of Choctaw coal was estimated at over five hundred thousand tons.[78]

In the late Eighties a strong movement developed, apparently under the leadership of Green McCurtain, in favor of having the ownership of the mines revert to the Nation.[79] A proposed amendment to the constitution in 1888 provided that Section 18 of Article VII, which granted the ownership to the discoverer, be stricken out and a section substituted to the effect that mines, minerals, and mineral waters should be the common property of the Nation and subject to the control of the General Council.[80] The amendment was not referred for approval to Chief Smallwood, who was known to be strongly opposed to the change. Smallwood then asked the advice of National Attorney C. E. Nelson, who informed him that the act was not valid without his signature.[81]

In 1895 a bill was again before the Council for the national ownership of the coal mines,[82] but it failed of passage. The next year a law was passed, which, after stating in the preamble that the "search for minerals has been retarded by this uncertainty" over the question of ownership, to the great detriment of the national income from royalties, specifically reënacted previous laws granting ownership of mines to the discoverer, and made it the duty of the National Agent to assist citizens in the search.[83] There was loud talking to the effect that bribery had been resorted to in the passage of this law,[84] but the mines remained under private ownership.[85]

The Choctaws did not work in the mines, although they delivered the ties and props used in mining operations. The development of the coal fields caused the growth of a number of alien settlements; characteristic mining camps sprang up around the "Twin Cities" of Mc-

[78]*Report Commissioner of Indian Affairs*, 1887, p. 119.

[79]O'Beirne, *Leaders and Leading Men*, I, 25.

[80]Acts of the Choctaw Nation, November 5, 1888.

[81]*Indian Citizen*, February 16, April 13, 1889, Nelson's opinion.

[82]*Indian Citizen*, October 24, 1895.

[83]Acts of the Choctaw Nation, September 18, 1896. For duties of the National Agent *see infra*, pp. 132, 143.

[84]Acts of the Choctaw Nation, October 28, 1896.

[85]The county court records in the Union Agency Files show numerous entries of the discovery and claiming of coal mines by various citizens. *See* for example records of Cedar County, 1890-1891.

Alester and Krebs, and around Lehigh and Coalgate. The miners were citizens of the United States and foreigners of various nationalities — Italians, English, Swedes, with some Germans and Belgians, and a few Frenchmen. In 1889 the average number of laborers employed was estimated at 1,873. The most important mining companies were the Osage Coal and Mining Company, the Atoka Mining Company, and the Choctaw Coal and Railway Company.[86]

Sporadic strikes sometimes occurred, but they were usually of short duration.[87] A serious labor outbreak began in the Spring of 1894, when the operators declared a 25 per cent wage reduction. An attempt to work the mines with "scabs" was met by violence on the part of the strikers. At Krebs a mob of about six hundred miners, preceded by about fifty women, drove small parties of workers from the "strip pits" and assaulted the bookkeeper of the Osage Coal and Mining Company. At Alderson and Lehigh the threat of violence was sufficient to drive off the strike breakers.

When the mines became idle, the Choctaws were greatly exasperated at the loss of tribal revenues, and Chief Jones sent a list of two hundred names of striking miners to Agent Wisdom with the request that they be expelled as intruders. Wisdom, who also was very unsympathetic toward the strikers, called in Federal troops who escorted the most active agitators across the national boundary. This action broke the strike, and by Fall the mines were running smoothly, and royalties were coming regularly into the Choctaw treasury.[88]

While the output of the coal mines was becoming increasingly important, there was some attempt made to develop the petroleum industry. Indications of the presence of oil date back to the period before the Civil War; as early as 1844, people resorted to Oil Springs, where miraculous cures of various diseases were reported.[89] In 1883 the Council authorized the National Agent to contract with any operator who would agree to develop the petroleum or salt industry for a royalty of twenty-five cents a barrel.[90] The following year a company of Choctaw

[86]*Extra Census Bulletin*, pp. 11, 60; *Report Senate Committee on Indian Affairs*, IX, 267, testimony of McAlester; *Report Commissioner of Indian Affairs*, 1894, p. 143; Laracy, "Sacred Heart Mission," p. 239.

[87]*Indian Citizen*, May 18, June 1, 1889.

[88]*Report Commissioner of Indian Affairs*, 1894, pp. 74-78, 143-45. Also *see* contemporary numbers of the *Indian Citizen*, especially May 31 and June 21.

[89]E. J. Stanley, *Life of Reverend L. B. Stateler* (Nashville, Tennessee, 1916), pp. 117-18.

[90]Acts of the Choctaw Nation, November 6, 1883.

citizens — J. F. McCurtain, E. N. Wright, A. R. Durant, and Allen Wright — was incorporated under the name of the Choctaw Oil and Refining Company. It was to pay the Nation a royalty of 5 per cent, and was granted a monopoly of petroleum production for twenty years, except that it should not deprive the people of the free use of "natural tar or oil springs."[91] Dr. H. W. Faucett, who was employed by this company, began drilling on the Boggy River about twelve miles from Atoka. When the well had reached a depth of 1,400 feet, a showing of oil and gas was reported, but the death of Faucett caused the enterprise to be abandoned.[92]

But, although the petroleum industry was not to be developed during the tribal period, the economic changes that had taken place were far-reaching in their influence. The evolution of a tenant system of agriculture, the construction of the railroads, the opening of the mines, and the influx of a large non-citizen population brought about a complex economic order very different from the simple agricultural society that had existed before the Civil War. Because of the system of communal ownership these economic changes also brought many problems into the administration of public finance.

[91]Acts of the Choctaw Nation, October 23, 1884.
[92]Muriel H. Wright, "First Oklahoma Oil Was Produced in 1859," *Chronicles of Oklahoma,* IV (December, 1926), 327-28.

THE ADMINISTRATION OF
PUBLIC FINANCE

6

FINANCIAL administration with the Choctaws went beyond the support of governmental and other public functions. The primitive laws of property by which every member of the tribe enjoyed the right to hunt, or to plant a patch of corn in any portion of the land occupied by his people, were extended to comprise the management of a vast common estate possessing great mineral and agricultural wealth and requiring technical skill and capital in its development. The increasing diversity of economic interests, therefore, brought increasing complexity into the financial administration.

The original source of the tribal income was the interest on various sums of money acquired through the treaties by which the Choctaws had sold portions of their lands to the United States. This money was invested in bonds or held by the United States in trust funds, and the income was paid out in the form of annuities. Early in their constitutional development, the Choctaws began to appropriate this income for the support of their schools and tribal government.

The Treaty of 1805, by which the Choctaws relinquished the southern portion of their territory, carried a permanent annuity of $3,000.[1] The Treaty of Doak's Stand, by which they sold a large portion of their Mississippi lands and purchased their territory in the West, carried annuities of $600 for the employment of blacksmiths to assist them in their new agricultural pursuits, and $600 for lighthorsemen to maintain the authority of their rudimentary government.[2] The supplemental Treaty of 1825, by which they surrendered the eastern portion of their

[1]Kappler, *Laws and Treaties*, II, 87-88.
[2]*Ibid.*, II, 192, 193-94, Arts. 6 and 13.

new territory in the West, provided for a permanent annuity of $6,000 and an additional sum of $320 for iron and steel used by the blacksmiths.[3] This gave them a total income from their annuities of $10,520, which the Treaty of 1855 provided should be spent for their benefit or turned over to the General Council to be applied to "objects of general utility."[4]

At the close of the Civil War the trust funds and bonds returned to the Choctaws consisted of $121,000 from the sale of school land set aside for them in the tract they ceded by the Treaty of Doak's Stand,[5] $454,000 of the payment they received when the Chickasaws purchased an interest in their lands,[6] and $500,000 which was invested from their share of the sum paid by the United States for the occupation of the Leased District by other Indians.[7] The interest on these investments in 1866 was $59,500, which with the annuities brought their total income up to $70,020.[8]

It has been pointed out that the payment of the indemnity to the "loyal Choctaws" reduced the $500,000 trust fund to $390,257.92. When the Heald and Wright claims of $90,000 were paid, part of the money was taken out of the current income, certain bonds were sold at a premium, and the school fund was reduced from $121,000 to $52,427.20. These two reductions brought the annual income down to $60,418.52.[9]

This income varied somewhat from year to year. As bonds matured, others were purchased at a premium, or bearing a lower interest rate, or the money was left in the United States Treasury to bear interest.[10] When the Choctaws adopted their freedmen, their general fund was increased by $52,125, which remained as their share of the purchase price of the Leased District taken over by the United States by the Treaty of 1866; but this sum was reduced by $8,300 when eighty-three of their freedmen elected to remove and accept the per caput payment provided by the treaty.[11] These and a few other changes in the principal brought their interest on invested funds to $48,762.94 in 1894, which with the permanent annuities gave them a total income of $59,282.94.[12]

[3] *Ibid.*, II, 212, 213, Arts. 2 and 9.
[4] *Ibid.*, II, 709-10, Art. 13.
[5] *Ibid.*, II, 193, Art. 7.
[6] *Ibid.*, II, 487, Art. 3, Treaty of 1837.
[7] *Ibid.*, II, 709-10, Art. 13, Treaty of 1855.
[8] *Report Commissioner of Indian Affairs,* 1866, tables, pp. 327, 333. There are occasional errors in these tables which must be guarded against.
[9] *Ibid.*, 1869, tables, pp. 482-84, 496.
[10] *Ibid.*, 1873, tables, pp. 349, 376; 1881, table, p. 245, for example.
[11] *Ibid.*, 1885, tables, pp. 288-89; 1888, tables, pp. 352-53.
[12] *Ibid.*, 1894, p. 476.

Shortly after the Civil War the Choctaws began to supplement this income by royalties from the utilization of their natural resources. This practice began with the sale of construction materials to the Missouri, Kansas, and Texas Railroad.

Before the advent of the railroad there had been only a local market for the fine timber that covered so much of the Choctaw country, and its sale was left to private initiative. A citizen could secure a franchise from the Council, which granted him the right to set up a sawmill and monopolize the product of a certain pinery,[13] but it was unlawful for a citizen to lease land to a non-citizen for lumbering operations.[14] The Choctaws realized that the coming of the railroad would create a market for their timber, and before construction reached the borders of their country they placed the sale of timber and stone under national control. A new office was created, that of National Agent, to be filled by appointment of the Principal Chief. It was the duty of this officer to make all contracts between Choctaw citizens and railroad contractors for the sale and delivery of timber and stone used in construction. The Nation was to receive five cents each for railroad ties, and the price of stone was to be fixed at the usual rates in the "States" according to the judgment of the Agent. All contracts between private citizens and the railroad were declared void, and a fine of $1,000 was established as the penalty for private sale.[15]

The railroad ignored this law, and purchased materials from white contractors who bought from individual Choctaws. T. D. Griffith, the United States agent for the Choctaws and Chickasaws, approved these contracts and endorsed the receipts given when the contractors paid the Indians.[16] This was according to the method specified in the bond under which the road was operating.[17]

The Choctaw government seems to have permitted this violation of its law so far as the construction in the Nation was concerned, but after the railroad company had completed its track across the Choctaw country it continued to ship out material for its building operations in Texas. Chief William Bryant then protested to the Secretary of the Interior, and six months later the Indian Office ordered the railroad to stop shipping out timber.[18] R. S. Stevens, the General Manager of the

[13]Acts of the Choctaw Nation, November 1, 1870.
[14]*Ibid.*, April 8, 1870.
[15]*Ibid.*, November 1, 1871.
[16]Indian Office Files, Special Case No. 136, affidavit of S. W. Marston.
[17]*Ibid.*, bond of the M. K. & T., dated August 6, 1870.
[18]Indian Office Files, Choctaw, 1873, B501, D8. Chief Bryant's protest was dated December 21, 1872.

Missouri, Kansas, and Texas, promised to comply with this order, but he expressed his disgust that the Department should prohibit Choctaw citizens "from trading and trafficking, running their mills, disposing of their lumber, and gradually adopting the habits of civilization."[19] In the meantime, Agent Griffith and his successor, Parsons, continued to approve contracts of sale made by individual Choctaws. On August 1, 1873, Chief Bryant presented a bill to the railroad, and Agent Parsons effected a settlement for $1,505, which was paid in the presence of the General Council. The Nation thus established its contention that the sale of construction material was a national rather than an individual matter, but it was commonly charged that the railroad continued to buy timber illegally and ship it out.[20] The Nation kept on presenting claims for this timber, which were soon complicated by other grievances.

An act passed by the Council in 1873 increasing and defining the powers of the National Agent made it his duty to press the claims of individual citizens for injured live stock,[21] and a large number of these claims soon accumulated. The Choctaw government next advanced the claim that the Nation was entitled to compensation for the right of way; individual citizens had been paid for damages to their improvements, but the Nation had received no payment for the land.

Finally, in 1876, President Grant issued an order permitting the Choctaws, with the Chickasaws, to bring suit against the railroad before Agent Marston for the settlement of these claims.[22] After protracted hearings Marston ruled that since, by the Treaty of 1866, the Indians had *granted* the right of way to railroads they were not entitled to compensation; and that by payments to individual citizens the railroad had settled for the purchase of construction material; but that individual claims to the extent of $1,092.42 should be allowed for injured stock and other damages.[23] Both parties appealed from this decision, and after several more years of tedious and expensive litigation the Secretary of the Interior sustained the contention of the railroad on every count, and ruled that neither the Choctaw and Chickasaw nations, nor indi-

[19]*Ibid.*, Choctaw, 1873, S452.
[20]Indian Office Files, Special Case No. 136; *Report Commissioner of Indian Affairs,* 1873, p. 209.
[21]Acts of the Choctaw Nation, October 24, 1873.
[22]Indian Office Files, Union, 1887, I337.
[23]Indian Office Files, Special Case No. 136, report of Agent Marston to Commissioner Hayt, January 3, 1878, executive order of President Arthur, January 24, 1882.

135

vidual citizens were entitled to damages on any of the claims presented.[24]

The Choctaws had other grievances against the railroad that were not included in this suit. An act of the Council in 1876 levied a tax of 1½ per cent upon the property of the railroad, telegraph, and express companies within the limits of the Nation.[25] The railroad attorney then wrote a peremptory letter to the Secretary of the Interior demanding that he suspend the offending law. Secretary Chandler replied that since such legislation was illegal an order for its suspension was superfluous.[26] As a result the railroad continued to operate until the end of the tribal period without paying a tax of any kind.

Although the Choctaws lost their suit and failed in their attempt to tax the railroad, they did establish the principle that the sale of timber was under tribal control, and the royalty law of 1871 became the basis of all later legislation pertaining to natural resources. In 1873 it was provided that the money realized from such sale should be divided equally between the Nation and the citizen in possession of the land, and the prices of the various kinds of timber and lumber were fixed by this and subsequent acts.[27]

With the improved transportation facilities offered by the railroads, sawmills became numerous and lumbering became important. In addition to the ties and timbers used in railroad construction, large quantities of *bois d'arc* posts were shipped out, and millions of feet of pine and walnut lumber were marketed. Stringtown, on the Missouri, Kansas, and Texas, became the most important shipping point.[28]

It became a habit with some of the timber exporters to avoid the payment of royalty by giving a small sum of money to some Indian for silence and protection.[29] Congress finally passed a law against this practice, in 1888, and the Indian agent then secured the conviction of

[24]Indian Office Files, Correspondence Land Division, Vol. 52, Letter Book, 103, Commissioner Price to Secretary of Interior, November 15, 1882; Department of Interior —Letters, Indian Affairs, Secretary's Letter Book, October 11, 1883—January 19, 1884, pp. 448-57, Secretary Teller to Commissioner of Indian Affairs, December 3, 1883.

[25]Acts of the Choctaw Nation, March 9, 1876.

[26]Indian Office Files, Choctaw, 1876, I445, S369, U76.

[27]Acts of the Choctaw Nation, October 24, 1873; November 8, 1878; November 2, 1897; Indian Office Files, Union, 1880, B221.

[28]*Indian Champion*, August 2, 1884; *Atoka Independent*, August 30, 1887; *Reports Commissioner of Indian Affairs*, statistical tables.

[29]*Report Commissioner of Indian Affairs*, 1881, p. 104; 1883, pp. 88, 90; 1887, p. 116.

some of the offenders in United States courts.[30] This lessened, but did not entirely prevent, the depredations of the timber thieves.

Even more important than the timber royalty as a source of tribal income was the royalty on coal. The right of the Nation to control mining contracts, which had been so stubbornly contested by McAlester and his associates, was upheld by the Secretary of the Interior in 1875, when he ruled that all contracts made by individual citizens for the sale of coal were null and void. The royalty to the Nation was fixed by the Council at one-half cent a bushel, and all leases were made by the National Agent and were to run for six years.[31]

In 1890 the Choctaw Coal and Railway Company made an attempt to override these laws and secure valuable coal lands by illegal leases. Certain ignorant Choctaws were induced to sign agreements which were to run for ninety-nine years and pay one-fourth cent royalty to the owner of the mine and nothing to the Nation. The company then began active lobbying to secure the approval of the leases by Congress. The Choctaws protested vigorously, and their delegate, J. S. Standley, exerted his utmost efforts to prevent the passage of the legislation ratifying the leases. Bennett, the United States agent, was greatly aroused by the scheme and made a trip to Washington to defeat it.[32] Congress finally amended the leases to run thirty instead of ninety-nine years and to conform to the Choctaw royalty law. In this form they were approved in spite of the bitter protests of the Choctaw government.[33]

Another export from the Choctaw country was prairie hay, but the government never adopted a consistent policy regarding its sale. In 1880 it was made unlawful to ship it from the Nation; in 1882 both citizens and non-citizens were allowed to ship it upon payment of a royalty of fifty cents a ton; in 1887 non-citizens were prohibited from shipping or even buying it except for their own use; and in 1890 the royalty upon all prairie hay cut for sale was fixed at one dollar a ton, of which 10 per cent was retained by the sheriff who made the collection, and the remainder was paid into the country treasury.[34] The

[30]*Ibid.*, 1888, pp. 326-27; 1889, p. 212.

[31]*The Vindicator*, December 29, 1875—this ruling applied to the sale of timber also; Acts of the Choctaw Nation, October 24, 1873; November 5, 1880.

[32]*Report Commissioner of Indian Affairs*, 1890, pp. 96-98; *Extra Census Bulletin*, p. 34n; Acts of the Choctaw Nation, November 14, 1890.

[33]*Report Commissioner of Indian Affairs*, 1890, pp. 407-9, text of law, approved October 1, 1890; *Indian Citizen*, September 13, September 27, November 15, November 22, 1890.

[34]Acts of the Choctaw Nation, October 28, 1880; November 1, 1882; November 10, 1887; October 30, 1890.

amount of hay cut in the Nation was usually estimated at about fifty thousand tons annually,[35] but the payment of royalty on hay sold to non-citizens was usually neglected.[36]

It became an established custom that the Choctaws should collect three-fourths and the Chickasaws one-fourth of the royalties assessed by the authorities of either nation. The Treaty of 1855, by which the United States secured the use of the Leased District, and the Treaty of 1866, which provided for its sale, had divided both the rental and purchase price in this ratio. This principle of distribution was based upon the comparative population of the two tribes, and therefore represented the share to which each was entitled in their joint domain.

The division of the royalties in the same ratio represented a gradual development of Choctaw law and a clarification of the understanding between the two nations. The first Choctaw laws for the collection of royalty on timber and coal were declared unconstitutional by the Choctaw Supreme Court in 1875 because they had not been approved by the Chickasaws.[37] The Nation was thus left without protection, and the Indian Office at the request of Chief Cole ordered that lumbering and mining operations should cease until the two tribes should reach an understanding.[38] Several conferences then took place between representatives of the two nations,[39] and the principle was recognized in the Choctaw law of 1880 that the Chickasaws were entitled to collect one-fourth of the royalty.[40]

The passage of this law did not prevent occasional friction between the nations regarding the division of the revenues from their common property. In 1885 the Choctaws attempted to collect all the royalty, but the Chickasaws appealed to the Secretary of the Interior, who upheld their contention and directed the mining companies to continue apportioning their payments between the tribes.[41] Shortly after this the Chickasaws denied the right of the Choctaws to collect three-fourths of the royalty paid in their nation, and the Choctaws in turn appealed

[35]*Reports Commissioner of Indian Affairs*, statistical tables.
[36]*Indian Citizen*, June 13, 1895, notice by Judge J. L. Ward of Atoka County. *See* also *ibid.*, March 15, 1894; June 20, 1895.
[37]Union Agency Files, Letters of Chiefs, pp. 161-63, Chief Cole to Secretary of the Interior, October 27, 1875; Acts of the Choctaw Nation, October 26, 1875; *Vindicator*, November 3, 1875.
[38]Union Agency Files, Letters of Chiefs, pp. 202-3, Agent Ingalls to Cole, December 17, 1875.
[39]Acts of the Choctaw Nation, March 8, 1876; October 24, 1877.
[40]*Ibid.*, November 5, 1880.
[41]*Ibid.*, November 3, 1885; *Misc. Docs. Relating to Indian Affairs*, XV, 11729-46.

to the Interior Department.[42] But in spite of occasional attempts on the part of each tribe to monopolize the collections made within its own limits, and a certain amount of friction in the administration of royalty laws, the principle was generally observed that each had the right to legislate exclusively for its own district, but must recognize the right of the other to collect its share of the revenue.[43]

All this development of natural resources brought many white persons to the Choctaw country. The Choctaws had control of immigration by the treaties of 1855 and 1866 that provided that no white persons should enter the Nation but travelers, Federal employees, and employees of internal improvement corporations, except such as were authorized by the tribe.[44]

The whole Choctaw immigration policy was based on the permit law of 1867. It set forth in detail how traders should present to the Principal Chief an application, endorsed by ten respectable citizens, for a permit to remain in the country. They were required to furnish a bond of $1,000, and pay a yearly tax of 1.5 per cent of the value of all goods brought in during the year. Carpenters, shoemakers, wheelwrights, and other skilled workers were granted a permit upon presentation of a similar application endorsed by three citizens, and the payment of an annual fee of twenty-five dollars, and two dollars additional to the sheriff. Citizens were required to pay a yearly permit tax of five dollars for every laborer or farmer in their employ. The sheriffs received 5 per cent of this tax as their payment for collecting it, and the remainder was divided equally between the county and the central government.[45]

The principles embodied in this law became fixed only after a period of experimentation on the part of the Choctaw government. In 1870, when citizens of Skullyville County petitioned the Council for additional legislation against intruders who were "geting too numerous & uncontrolable," the Council decided that the Choctaw laws and the intercourse laws of the United States offered sufficient protection, and recommended strict enforcement on the part of the District Chief and the sheriffs.[46] The next year, however, the Council passed a law revoking all trading permits upon the expiration of the ones already granted,

[42]*Misc. Docs., loc. cit.*

[43]Acts of the Choctaw Nation, November 4, 1896.

[44]Kappler, *Laws and Treaties,* II, 708, 929, Art. 7, Treaty of 1855, and Art. 43, Treaty of 1866.

[45]Folsom, *Digest of Choctaw Law,* pp. 595-96, law enacted November 20, 1867.

[46]Union Agency Files, Choctaw—Intruders, report of committee of Council, October 19, 1870.

but the time was extended at a special session the following March, and in the regular session the Council returned to the policy adopted in 1867.[47]

The Nation established its right to tax non-citizens only after a controversy as bitter as the contest with the railroad over the royalties on construction materials, and with the McAlester group over the mining laws. The Missouri, Kansas, and Texas Railway had barely been completed across the Choctaw country when Manager R. S. Stevens sent an indignant complaint to the Indian Office regarding the "blackmail" levied upon the employees of the Osage Coal and Mining Company. He demanded to know if such a tax was valid.[48]

The Interior Department itself was uncertain as to the legality of the permit laws, and as a result the Choctaws became engaged in a controversy with the Federal Government. A law passed in 1875 increased the tax on licensed traders to 2 per cent; provided that skilled laborers, renters, and professional men should pay the twenty-five-dollar tax as before, but should furnish a bond of five hundred dollars; and raised the fee for unskilled laborers from five to six dollars and required a hundred-dollar bond.[49] Agent Marston characterized this tax as "not moderate or reasonable,"[50] and engaged in a spirited correspondence with Chief Cole, in which he denied the right of the Choctaws to levy a tax of any kind upon United States citizens.[51] In the meantime, the Council, over the veto of the doughty old Chief, repealed the law and adopted rates similar to those established in 1867.[52]

Marston also incurred the displeasure of Cole by declaring a Chickasaw permit law null and void because it had not been approved by him. Cole declared that this was a dangerous precedent, and wrote to Secretary Schurz requesting Marston's removal. Schurz, after advice from the Commissioner of Indian Affairs, apparently sustained Cole in his contention, but he explained to the irate Chief that he could not remove the agent for what was no worse than an error in judgment.[53] Schurz soon concluded that Marston had been correct, basing his opinion on the decision of his predecessor regarding the illegality of the

[47]Acts of the Choctaw Nation, October 28, 1871; November 7, 1872.
[48]Indian Office Files, Choctaw, 1873, S493, Stevens to Commissioner of Indian Affairs, February 12, 1873.
[49]Acts of the Choctaw Nation, November 11, 1875.
[50]Indian Office Files, Union, 1876, M631.
[51]Union Agency Files, Letters of Chiefs, pp. 182-84.
[52]Acts of the Choctaw Nation, October 30, 1876.
[53]Indian Office Files, Union, 1877, I310; 1878, P59.

Courtesy Oklahoma Historical Society

JACKSON McCURTAIN, PRINCIPAL CHIEF, 1880–84

B. F. SMALLWOOD, PRINCIPAL CHIEF, 1888–90

Choctaw attempt to tax the Missouri, Kansas, and Texas Railroad. The Choctaws had been very grateful to Schurz because of the vigor which he had put into the administration of the Indian Office, and the energy with which he had removed intruders, but now the Council authorized the Chief to use his utmost efforts to secure the reversal of this decision. Cole wrote to President Hayes citing the provisions of the Treaty of 1866, and reminding him that "The Treaties are as Sacred to us, as your Constitution is to your people."[54] Cole also obtained a list from the county lighthorsemen giving the names of the intruders in the various counties. A formidable number were reported, many of whom were operating sawmills in defiance of Choctaw royalty laws.[55]

The Council then passed the law making it illegal for citizens to lease any part of the public domain to non-citizens. Another law enacted the same day directed the sheriffs to sell the improvements of such intruders as had not disposed of them by a certain date. As a result of this legislation many applications for permits came in from men engaged in almost every kind of business — general merchandise dealers, druggists, lumber dealers, and cattle and hog buyers[56]— but because of the disapproval of Secretary Schurz the Choctaw government suspended the collection of the tax until the next meeting of the Council.[57]

This Council reënacted the legislation of the preceding year authorizing the sale of intruders' improvements. The time during which they might dispose of their property was extended to the last of January, 1879, after which it would be sold to Choctaw citizens.[58] When the sheriffs began to enforce this law, a flood of indignant complaints poured into the Indian Office. An angry farmer employing two hired hands and two boys, and with one hundred acres of corn and cotton in the Canadian Valley region wrote that he had been cultivating Indian land for six years, and now the Indians informed him he must pay for a permit or be expelled.[59] Others who were engaged in various business enterprises in buildings erected on the coal leases protested that "no one had a thoat that thay wold be a intruder if they bilt on the coal cumpany leas," and complained that their buildings had been confiscated.[60]

[54]Ibid., Union, 1878, P59. This correspondence took place during the Fall of 1877.
[55]Union Agency Files, Choctaw—Intruders. This list was compiled in May, 1877.
[56]Union Agency Files, Choctaw—Traders.
[57]Indian Office Files, Union, 1879, G216.
[58]Acts of the Choctaw Nation, November 7, 1878.
[59]Indian Office Files, Union, 1879, W1136, May 16, 1879.
[60]Ibid., Union, 1879, H388, H557, L143. These complaints came in early in 1879.

The Indian Office replied by withholding the payment of the annuities which were due in January of 1879.[61] Commissioner Hayt then notified Isaac Garvin, who had succeeded Cole as Principal Chief, that no payments would be made until assurance should be given that the laws would be suspended until the next meeting of the Council.[62] Garvin expressed strong convictions as to the legality of the permit laws, but he gave the required promise.[63] Just at that time the "Boomers" began a concerted agitation for the opening of the unoccupied lands of the Indian Territory for homestead entry, and the Choctaws were so grateful for the firm stand taken by the Federal Government against the invaders that they were willing to allow the matter to rest temporarily.

The question was finally settled in 1881 by an opinion of Acting Attorney-General S. F. Phillips, which sustained the Choctaws on every point. Phillips upheld the validity of the permit laws, saying that aside from the temporary sojourners and the internal improvement and federal employees excepted by the treaties of 1855 and 1866 all other non-citizens were subject to the conditions of admission and residence prescribed by the tribal authorities; and he ruled that all who did not conform to those conditions were intruders, and that it was the express duty of the United States to remove them. The Secretary of the Interior adopted this ruling as the decision of the Department and Agent Tufts was instructed to give thirty days' notice to non-citizens to secure permits under the Choctaw laws and to use military force in removing those who did not comply.[64] A resolution of the Council then expressed "profound gratitude and universal joy for the prompt and efficient manner in which the intruders were expelled from the Moshulatubbee District and along the line of the M.K. & T. Railway."[65] It was indeed a victory for the Choctaws when the Federal Government accepted the interpretation of the treaties which their leaders had upheld with such able arguments.

Although the Choctaws had established their right to regulate the conditions under which United States citizens might remain in their country, from this time on they showed more of a tendency to confer

[61]*Ibid.*, 1879, G59, G175, G216, G219, G508, W633.

[62]Union Agency Files, Letters of Chiefs, pp. 239-40.

[63]*Ibid.*, Choctaw—Federal Relations, Garvin to Schurz, May, 1879.

[64]Union Agency Files, Choctaw—Intruders, opinion of Phillips, dated June 25, 1881, and Commissioner Price to Chief McCurtain, July 6, 1881. These documents with some others were published in a pamphlet, apparently by the Choctaw government.

[65]Acts of the Choctaw Nation, October 19, 1881; *Report Commissioner of Indian Affairs*, 1881, p. 104.

with the Federal authorities and to secure their approval of the permit laws.[66] The Federal authorities on their part were more helpful in assisting the Choctaws to control their immigration.[67] The following procedure was eventually adopted: the Choctaw sheriffs made sworn statements regarding any non-citizens failing to secure permits or to leave the Nation when notified; these statements were sent to the Principal Chief, who reported the names of the intruders to the Indian agent with a request for their expulsion; the agent then expelled them by means of the Indian police or Federal troops, and the Choctaw government paid the expense of the removal.[68]

New permit laws were passed from time to time until the system constituted a comprehensive code applying to every vocation carried on within the Nation.[69] The "traders," a term elastic enough to include every kind of business man, paid 1.5 per cent tax on their goods, or a special fee depending upon the nature of the business. Professional men and skilled artisans paid for their own permits, while the fees for tenants and laborers were paid by their employers.[70]

The laws were not uniformly enforced, and especially Choctaws who employed labor violated them with impunity. But if one is to judge by the great stacks of permits in the files of the Union Agency one must conclude that before 1900 at least, a large number of citizens and non-citizens did not evade their payment. When the end of the tribal government was in sight, there was a concerted effort on the part of the white residents to resist the permit laws, and the Choctaws were unable to enforce them.[71]

The Choctaws had also to contend with "intruder cattle," although their troubles in this respect were less serious than those of some other tribes. Their first attempt to tax the cattle droves that passed across their country immediately after the Civil War met with outraged protest from the cattlemen.[72] But the Indian Office upheld the Choctaws, and a law passed in 1870 placed a tax of fifty cents a head on all droves

[66]Acts of the Choctaw Nation, November 2, 1882.

[67]For example see Report Commissioner of Indian Affairs, 1886, p. 158.

[68]Acts of the Choctaw Nation, October 15, October 18, 1886; November 1, 1887; October 7, 1888; October 29, 1895; Report Commissioner of Indian Affairs, 1887, pp. 115-16.

[69]Acts of the Choctaw Nation, November 2, 1882; November 4, 1890; April 6, April 8, 1891; January 26, 1894; November 2, 1897.

[70]Union Agency Files, Choctaw—Permits; Choctaw—Non-Citizens; Choctaw—Traders.

[71]Commission to the Five Civilized Tribes, Annual Report, 1900, pp. 93-95, 123-24.

[72]Indian Office Files, Choctaw, 1868, C868; 1869, O71.

of cattle, horses, or mules passing through the Nation. In 1882, this tax was decreased to ten cents a head, with an additional charge for wintering stock or loitering on the trail, and an exemption was made in the case of emigrant families crossing the Nation with less than twenty head. The tax was collected by the sheriffs, who retained 10 per cent for their services, and turned the remainder over to the central government.[73] The important trails from Texas passed west of the Choctaw country, but a small amount of revenue was realized from this tax.[74]

Numerous Choctaw laws aimed to prevent the occupation of the country by cattlemen. In 1870 it was made illegal for a citizen to lease any portion of the public domain to a non-citizen for grazing purposes,[75] and in 1880 non-citizens who were living in the Nation were forbidden to "own, control, or hold" any kind of stock except a limited number under permit for use and home consumption. Fine and whipping was the punishment for any citizen who would shield intruder cattle by a false claim of ownership, and where the value of the stock was greater than fifty dollars no sale or conveyance from a non-citizen to a citizen was valid unless recorded by county officers.[76] In 1888 it was made unlawful to rent a pasture for grazing purposes, and at the same time even the citizens were forbidden to introduce "steer cattle" into the Nation except in November and December, but this act was repealed the following year.[77]

In spite of these laws the country, especially after 1885, was occupied to a certain extent by intruder cattle. Political campaigns were filled with recriminations, as opponents blamed each other for the presence of the long-horned intruders that were infecting the Choctaw cattle with Texas fever.[78] The laws against false claims of ownership were frequently evaded by recording fictitious bills of sale in the county books. It is said that the fullbloods in such cases seldom or never betrayed the actual owners of the cattle, but that mixed bloods occasionally claimed the privileges of ownership.[79]

The intruder cattlemen increased in number and boldness during

[73]Acts of the Choctaw Nation, October 27, 1870; November 2, 1882.

[74]Union Agency Files, Choctaw—Cattle, reports from sheriffs regarding collections, and receipts for money turned over to the Nation.

[75]Acts of the Choctaw Nation, April 8, 1870.

[76]*Ibid.*, November 5, 1880; November 2, 1882.

[77]*Ibid.*, October 26, October 30, 1888; November 13, 1889.

[78]*Indian Champion*, April 18, 1885; *Indian Citizen*, June 16, June 30, August 5, 1892; *Report Commissioner of Indian Affairs*, 1887, p. 115.

[79]Acts of the Choctaw Nation, November 14, 1889; Carter, *McCurtain County and Southeast Oklahoma*, p. 99.

the remainder of the tribal period, but when the Choctaw government was passing out of existence a determined effort was made to expel them. Under a law passed by the Council in 1901 a number of removals were effected by the Indian police, and the Nation seems to have been cleared of intruder cattle.[80] The collection of a cattle tax was then placed in the hands of the United States agent.[81]

The enforcement of such a comprehensive plan of taxation as was embodied in all these royalty and permit laws necessitated a complicated system of revenue collectors. The National Agent, first appointed under the law of 1871 to make contracts and collect royalties for the construction materials used by the proposed railroad, was two years later placed in charge of the mining leases and the collection of the coal royalty.[82] After a certain period of experimentation[83] provision was made for the appointment of district collectors to collect timber royalties and taxes on traders, weighers to check the output and collect the royalty at each mine, and inspectors to work along the railroads and collect the royalty on timber and stone; and all these officers were placed under the supervision of the National Agent. The sheriffs continued to collect the taxes on hay and cattle, and to assist in the collection of permit fees. The revenue officials, in most cases, were to retain a percentage of their collections as compensation for their services.[84]

Although there were irregularities in the collection of these revenues, the income from such sources was considerable. In 1885 the National Treasurer's report showed that it amounted to $54,611.52 for the fiscal year; the next year it rose to $61,350.17; and in 1890 it had increased to $91,794.22.[85] An analysis of Green McCurtain's report as National Treasurer shows the returns from the following sources of income in 1890:

Coal royalties	$57,839.49
Turned in by district collectors	7,285.88
Turned in by inspectors on railroads	22,011.21
Railroad right of way	4,601.20
Royalty on gravel	56.44

[80] Union Agency Files, Choctaw—Cattle.
[81] Acts of the Choctaw Nation, October 23, 1903.
[82] Ibid., November 1, 1871; October 24, 1873.
[83] Ibid., November 11, 1875; October 23, 1878; November 5, 1880.
[84] Ibid., November 1, 1882; November 6, 1883; November 4, 1884; October 22, 1886; November 9, 1895; Union Agency Files, Choctaw—Minerals, Choctaw—Permits, Choctaw—Non-Citizens, Choctaw—Traders, reports from revenue collectors.
[85] Acts of the Choctaw Nation, October 23, 1885; October 27, 1886; November 14, 1890.

The Choctaws also received $61,362.63 from the Federal Government in 1890 in annuities and interest on invested funds, making a total income of $153,267.75. McCurtain's books at the close of the year showed a balance in the treasury of $120,116.45.[86] In 1897 — the last year in which tax collection was entirely under tribal control — the total revenues were reported as follows:[87]

Collected from coal companies	$ 79,146.05
From annuities and trust funds	59,282.95
Turned in by collectors and inspectors	31,118.34
From other sources	12,199.13
TOTAL	$181,756.47

Under the constitutional provision that no money should be paid out except through appropriations of the General Council[88] a great many special acts and one main appropriation law were passed at each regular session. The regular appropriation act for 1895 embraced the following items:[89]

Principal Chief	$ 2,000.00
National Treasurer, National Auditor, National Secretary	1,800.00
National Agent	800.00
National Attorney	400.00
Private secretary for Principal Chief	500.00
National lighthorsemen	2,450.00
Supreme Judges (three)	1,200.00
Circuit Judges (three)	1,500.00
County Judges (seventeen)	4,250.00
District Chiefs (three)	150.00
District Attorneys (three)	1,500.00
District lighthorsemen (three)	150.00
Election judges and clerks	680.00
Grand and petit jurors	14,900.00
Witness fees for attending circuit court	6,000.00
Superintendent and trustees of schools	1,800.00

[86]McCurtain reported a balance of $142,554.92, but $22,438.47 of this amount was the remainder of an appropriation made by the United States to pay the Net Proceeds claim.

[87]Union Agency Files, Choctaw—Principal Chief, annual message of Chief McCurtain, 1897.

[88]Constitution, Art. VII.

[89]Acts of the Choctaw Nation, November 12, 1895.

Contingent fund of Principal Chief	400.00
Contingent fund of superintendent of schools	450.00
Contingent fund of district trustees (three)	225.00
Contingent fund of National Auditor	400.00
Contingent fund of National Treasurer	400.00
Contingent fund of National Secretary	400.00
Publication fund	350.00
Clerk of Supreme Court	100.00
Clerks of county courts (seventeen)	1,700.00
Clerks of circuit courts (three)	900.00
Sheriffs (seventeen)	5,100.00
County rangers (seventeen)	850.00
Sheriffs and deputies attending circuit court	1,850.00
Deputy sheriffs	6,800.00
Sheriffs attending Supreme Court	50.00
Sheriffs for executing prisoners	50.00
General Council, lighthorsemen, and clerks of committee on citizenship	10,000.00
Students in the "States"	12,600.00
Neighborhood schools	35,000.00
Boarding schools (seven)	74,950.00
Delegate to United States	5,000.00
Attorney of delegate	2,000.00
Special for relief of Spencer Academy	558.00
TOTAL	$200,213.00

In spite of their great ability in other fields, the Choctaws were almost unbelievably careless and incompetent in their financial administration. The statement sometimes made by travelers[90] that the Choctaws were the best business men of the five tribes must have applied only to their private business, or it indicated a very low business ability on the part of their neighbors.

The Council received yearly reports from the National Auditor, the National Treasurer, the school officials, and the revenue collectors. These reports were examined by a joint Finance Committee and approved or rejected by the Council. The Finance Committee and the Council alike were usually satisfied with an account that seemed approximately correct. If they discovered a deficit they requested the

90Henry King, "The Indian Country," *Century Magazine*, XXX (August, 1885), 602; W. D. Crawford, "Oklahoma and the Indian Territory," *New England Magazine*, II (June, 1890), 456.

official to make good the amount;[91] if the error was of the opposite kind they directed the National Treasurer to issue a warrant to the official.[92] Once they approved the report of the National Agent with the naïve comment that his account was correct and his "money satisfactorily accounted for, in fact he holds receipts from the National Treasurer" for $2,660.76 "in excess of amount reported by the Treasurer."[93] Occasionally they showed some annoyance: they approved a National Treasurer's report as "substantially correct" although "mistakes have been made which should not occur in official business," and they recommended that he should be more careful the next year; they said of a railroad inspector that "his report is in such shape that it is impossible to understand it," and directed him to make good a deficit of $497.57 and submit a "full, complete and intelligent report" to the next meeting of the Council; they recommended that one of the school trustees be suspended from office because he had failed to make a report for two years in succession.[94] When the deficit was sufficiently large they accused the officer of defaulting and directed the district attorney to enter suit to recover on his bond.[95]

Although some of the Choctaw leaders were incorruptible, the government as a whole was permeated with peculation and bribery, which frequently involved the Principal Chiefs and other high officials. Great indignation was aroused upon the exposure of official misconduct, but it was rarely sustained for a period sufficient to impair the political fortunes of the principals; charges of malfeasance in office were brought as a matter of course against the opposing party and as lightly dismissed when the rapid shifting of Choctaw politics brought opponents into temporary alliance. Since the Choctaw government administered the communal estate, these corrupt manipulations often involved interests of great magnitude to the Choctaw people — for example, the division of the attorneys' fees in 1866, which might easily have endangered the peace negotiations, or the scheme to despoil the Nation of its coal lands in 1894.

Little attempt was made to punish official corruption. The embezzlement of public money was made a felony in 1880, and the offender

[91]Acts of the Choctaw Nation, October 27, November 5, 1879; November 7, 1881, for example.
[92]Ibid., October 21, 1886; October 23, 1888; December 12, 1891.
[93]Ibid., November 11, 1885.
[94]Ibid., November 7, 1881; November 10, 1887; October 30, 1879.
[95]Ibid., November 4, 1882; October 27, 1885. Recovery was made at least part of the time, for forfeited bonds occasionally appear among the receipts in the National Treasurer's reports.

148

was subject to a penalty of one hundred lashes, but apparently none of the Choctaw leaders ever suffered this humiliation. There seems to have been no law to punish bribery until 1890, when it also was made a felony; the punishment was a fine of one hundred to five hundred dollars, or whipping for those who refused to pay the fine, but this law, too, was allowed to lapse.[96]

Nepotism also was rampant, but it was the naïve unconscious nepotism of a natural aristocracy. Certain prominent families were expected to occupy positions of leadership, and their younger members accepted appointment as an inherited prerogative. Nearly all these families were distinguished by great ability, and some of them were actuated by a high sense of public duty. Upon the whole the nepotism practiced by the Choctaws does not seem to have been the corrupting influence that it might have been in a more populous society. Indeed, in a republic as small as the Choctaw Nation with its interlocking system of family relationships the appointment of relatives was almost unavoidable.

But in spite of chaotic bookkeeping and peculation, and official favoritism, the national finances during most of the period were in excellent condition. The enormous debt contracted during the Civil War was paid during the Seventies, and the National Treasurer's report for 1884 showed a balance of $38,938.62 at the end of the year.[97] In spite of an increased outlay for education in general and the necessity of establishing an extra system of schools for the newly adopted freedmen, and the construction of a new capitol, the balance in the treasury continued to increase. Choctaw warrants were at par, and the revenues were sufficient for all national needs.

In 1894 the Nation for the first time since the reconstruction period was short of funds. A serious election disturbance during 1892-1893 had caused an extraordinary outlay of at least $28,600,[98] the coal strike during the Spring and Summer for a time completely stopped the payment of coal royalties, and in addition there seems to have been deliberate dishonesty on the part of certain school officials.[99] As a result of this financial stringency the schools were in session about three or four months only, and the young people at college in the "States" were

[96]*Ibid.*, November 3, 1880; November 3, 1890.

[97]*Ibid.*, October 23, 1885.

[98]*Ibid.*, October 26, 1892; July 1, July 3, 1893. For militia, $23,000; for a special delegation to go to Washington to explain the riot, $3,100; and for special counsel, $2,500.

[99]*Ibid., November* 4, 1896; *Indian Citizen,* January 14, 1897.

149

brought home.[100] The school warrants were not paid promptly, and by 1896 they were discounted from 15 to 25 per cent.[101]

A number of laws were passed in 1896 to improve the financial administration and to correct irregularities in school expenditures,[102] but conditions did not improve. In 1897 the Chief and the National Treasurer were authorized to borrow $150,000 "to meet the Nation's present needs," for not less than a year at interest not to exceed 9 per cent, and to pledge the income from royalties and invested funds.[103]

These last years did not represent a normal period in Choctaw finance, for by this time the Nation was engaged in the negotiations that led to the surrender of tribal government, and there were numerous expenses incident to the change. As the Choctaws entered this period of transition, the United States gradually took over the management of the tribal finances.

The financial administration of the Choctaws had expanded very rapidly in the course of the generation following the Civil War. The permit law of 1867, the timber law of 1871, and the coal law of 1873 had each been the occasion of bitter controversy; but the Choctaws had established their right to enact such legislation and it formed the basis of a comprehensive code that regulated the development of a complex industrial civilization. During this generation the political system designed for an isolated agricultural community had expanded its functions to include the management of complicated economic interests and the regulation of a large non-citizen population. The increasing problems and responsibilities of managing the tribal estate were therefore closely connected with the political history and the evolution of governmental machinery.

100Acts of the Choctaw Nation, October 25, October 26, 1894; *Indian Citizen*, November 1, 1894; April 9, 1896.
101Acts of the Choctaw Nation, October 29, 1901; *Indian Citizen*, January 30, August 27, 1896.
102Acts of the Choctaw Nation, October 15, October 30, November 4, 1896.
103*Ibid*, November 10, 1897; Union Agency Files, Choctaw—Principal Chief, annual message of Chief McCurtain.

THE POLITICAL HISTORY OF
THE CHOCTAW NATION

7

THE government of the Choctaw Nation was based upon the constitution adopted at Doaksville, January 11, 1860. This document separated the governmental functions into legislative, executive, and judicial departments, and specified the powers and duties of each; it included a bill of rights inspired by Anglo-American political experience, and stating such principles as the equality of man, the compact theory of government, the sovereignty of the people, and such guarantees of personal freedom as trial by jury, the right of assembly, and religious liberty; and it provided for amendment by a majority of the Council and a majority of the qualified voters at a general election.

This constitution represented a compromise between the three-fold tribal division of primitive times, and the centralizing tendencies of the rejected Skullyville constitution. The old divisions were preserved in the Moshulatubbee, Pushmataha, and Apukshunnubbee districts named for the three great District Chiefs who had signed the Treaty of Doak's Stand, but they existed mainly as convenient administrative units—for school and judicial districts, for the collection of revenue, for the apportionment of Senators, and for the distribution of members on committees and delegations. At the head of each district was a District Chief, elected by the voters, who held office for two years and served as a subordinate local administrator under the direction of the Principal Chief.[1]

The importance of the district gradually declined as the memory of

[1]Constitution, Art. V; Union Agency Files, Letters of Chiefs, p. 35, circular letter from Chief Wright to District Chiefs, April 25, 1867, asking information regarding schools and other local affairs, and directing them to require the county judges to enforce the laws relating to road work.

151

the old tribal divisions faded out, and the duties of the District Chief almost disappeared. A constitutional amendment to abolish the office passed the Council in 1880, but it did not secure the approval of the voters.[2] In 1885 the salary was reduced from $150 to $50 a year,[3] but the office in an attenuated form continued to exist until the end of the tribal period.

At first the districts were divided into counties as follows: Moshulatubbee District — Sugarloaf, Skullyville, San Bois, Gaines, and Tobucksy; Pushmataha District — Kiamitia, Blue, Atoka, and Jack's Fork; and Apukshunnubbee District — Towson, Cedar, Wade, Red River, Boktucklo, Eagle, and Nashoba.[4] In 1886 a new county—Jackson —was created out of land formerly belonging to Kiamitia, Blue, and Atoka counties.[5] Changes were occasionally made in county boundaries by special acts of the legislature.[6]

The county constituted an election district for members of the Council, and served as a unit of local administration. The county officers, who were elected by the voters for a two-year term, consisted of a judge, who in addition to certain judicial powers, had control of the disbursement of local funds and the control of local concerns and improvements;[7] a sheriff, who attended to the collection of certain taxes, the reporting of intruders, the taking of the census, and the execution of judicial decrees;[8] and the ranger, who attended to the advertising and sale of strayed live stock.[9] The county judge appointed an officer who served as clerk and treasurer,[10] and the sheriff was authorized to appoint deputies.[11]

The district and county officers received their commissions from the

[2]Acts of the Choctaw Nation, October 22, October 29. 1880; November 12, 1881.
[3]Ibid., August 1, 1886.
[4]Report Commissioner of Indian Affairs, 1887, p. 98.
[5]Acts of the Choctaw Nation, October 21, 1886.
[6]The following is typical of the complicated descriptions tracing these lines: "the Northeastern boundary line of Cedar County shall commence at a point on Little River at the mouth of Wm. Wards creck, thence up said creek to its source, then on a strait line to the top of the Kiamishi Mountains, then running westward to a spring at Okchayas old place on the road leading from Doaksville to Fort Smith, when it intersects the old line between Wade and Cedar Counties." (Acts of the Choctaw Nation, October 25, 1873.)
[7]Constitution, Art. IV.
[8]Ibid., Art. V. Acts of the Council often stipulated that the provisions should be carried out by the sheriff.
[9]Acts and Resolutions of the General Council, 1852-1857, pp. 194-96, November 3, 1857; Acts of the Choctaw Nation, November 5, 1886; November 14, 1890.
[10]Acts and Resolutions of the General Council, 1860-1861, pp. 58, 63-66.
[11]Ibid., p. 66.

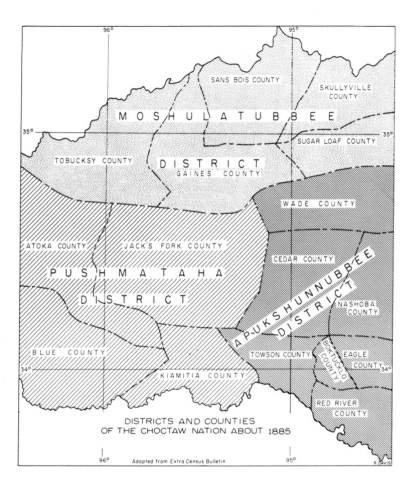

DISTRICTS AND COUNTIES
OF THE CHOCTAW NATION ABOUT 1885

Adapted from Extra Census Bulletin

153

Principal Chief, who was the head of the national administration. The executive authority of this officer was very great, partly through his constitutional powers, and partly through the powers entrusted to him by legislative enactment.

The Principal Chief was elected by the people for a two-year term under a provision that disqualified him from serving more than two terms in succession. He had to be a free male citizen at least thirty years old, a lineal descendant of the Choctaw or Chickasaw race, and a resident of the Nation for at least five years preceding his election. He had the power to enforce the laws, command the militia, convene special sessions of the Council, and fill all vacancies in elective offices by temporary appointments that remained in force until the next general election. In the event of his death he was succeeded by the President of the Senate, who also carried on his duties in case of his absence or temporary disability.[12]

It was customary for the Council to entrust the Chief with immense discretionary power in the expenditure of contingent funds; in appointments, which, however, were often made subject to the approval of the Senate; and in the employment of counsel to represent the Nation in lawsuits, and the conduct of relations with the United States. Through his messages to the Council he also exerted great power over law-making. He was at first paid an annual salary of one thousand dollars, which was increased in 1883 to two thousand.[13] In 1881 he was given a private secretary, who in time came to carry on much of the routine work of the administration.[14]

The Choctaws never worried about what to do with their former Principal Chiefs. As soon as a man had served his constitutional limit of two terms in succession it was common for him to enter the Council, where the prestige and experience he had acquired as chief executive made him a leading member. Moreover, it was customary to seek election for a third term as soon as the constitutional disability had expired. In one way or another the former Principal Chiefs usually remained in active politics the rest of their lives.

The Principal Chief was generally designated unofficially as the "governor"; newspapers almost invariably used the title, and even acts of the Council occasionally showed erasures where the commonly ac-

12Constitution, Arts. V, VII, VIII.
13Acts of the Choctaw Nation, October 30, 1869, appropriations for 1869; *ibid.*, November 5, 1883.
14 *Ibid.*, November 11, 1881. In time the secretary even signed the bills approved by the Chief.

cepted term had been used by mistake, and then changed to the official title.[15] The expression was favored by that party among the Choctaws who wished to abolish the tribal divisions and centralize the government in imitation of the American states; and both the Skullyville constitution and the proposed constitutional amendment abolishing the office of District Chief carried the new title. But these innovations were defeated by the voters, and the term "Principal Chief" continued to be the official designation of the chief executive.

The other executive officials of the central government, the National Secretary, National Treasurer, National Auditor, and National Attorney, were often referred to as the "governor's cabinet." Strictly speaking they did not constitute a cabinet, for they were elected by the people for two-year terms on the years between the gubernatorial elections;[16] but they were subject to removal by the Council, and the Chief's power of appointment where vacancies occurred in elective offices put them somewhat under his control.[17]

The National Secretary was entrusted with the great seal and the public documents of the tribe. The National Treasurer had control of the disbursement of funds, which he paid out on tribal warrants. The National Attorney was expected to give legal advice to the Principal Chief and other officers of the government.[18] The National Auditor was originally intended to head the financial administration, and present financial plans and advice to the General Council, but the importance of his office declined until he became little more than an accountant.[19]

The legislative department of the Choctaw government was vested in a General Council of two houses — a Senate and a House of Representatives.

[15]Sometimes the correction was not made and the unofficial title was allowed to stand. *See* Acts of the Choctaw Nation, November 7, 1884; October 22, 1897.

[16]Constitution, Amendments, Section I. Adopted, August 16, 1862. It will be remembered that the office of National Agent was appointive.

[17]Acts of the Choctaw Nation, October 25, 1873.

[18]Acts and Resolutions of the General Council, 1860-1861, pp. 29-34, October 16, October 24, October 26, October 29, 1860; Acts of the Choctaw Nation, October 25, 1873; October 7, 1881.

[19]Union Agency Files, Choctaw—Auditor. William Robuck's report to Council, October, 1871, wherein he advises the legislators to waste less time in passing laws, abolish the office of District Chief, and place taxes on sawmills and salt-licks in order to balance the budget,—also a letter to Chief Bryant in which he speaks of the Council as a "body of illiterate men" too ignorant to read his report, and advises the Chief to embody it in his message in order to call it to their attention—*see* also the report of the National Auditor to Chief McKinney; Acts of the Choctaw Nation, reports of the National Auditor as accepted by the Council.

The Senate consisted of twelve members — four from each district — so apportioned that the most populous counties elected one Senator each, while those with fewer inhabitants were joined together for election purposes. The Senators were elected for a two-year term, and the election took place during the even years. To be eligible for the Senate one had to be a male citizen of Choctaw or Chickasaw descent, at least thirty years old, a citizen of the Nation for at least one year, and a resident of the district for at least six months. The Senate had the power to try impeachments and to confirm a large number of the appointments made by the Principal Chief. It elected its President from its own membership.[20]

The House of Representatives consisted of about eighteen or twenty members,[21] elected for a term of one year. They were elected by counties according to population, one for approximately one thousand inhabitants. They were required to be male citizens of Choctaw or Chickasaw descent, at least twenty-one years old, and inhabitants of their county for at least six months preceding their election. The House of Representatives had the power of impeachment. Its presiding officer was a Speaker elected from its own membership.[22]

Laws were commonly enacted by a majority vote of both houses and the approval of the Principal Chief. An executive veto might be overridden by a two-thirds vote. If the Chief failed to take action upon a bill presented during the session, it became a law upon the expiration of three days, unless it was presented the day before adjournment, when it became law unless specifically vetoed. A declaration of war could be made only by a two-thirds vote of the Council and the approval of the Chief.[23]

Regular sessions of the Council began the first Monday in October, and usually lasted about thirty days. As soon as the two houses organized, they met in joint session to listen to the Chief's message. In the case of a newly elected Chief this was on the order of an inaugural address; at other times it was a sort of summary of the year's events. Sometimes it was packed with specific recommendations, but often it

[20]Constitution, Arts. III, VII. For impeachment procedure see ibid., Art. VI, and Acts of the Choctaw Nation, November 8, 1887.

[21]There were eighteen members in the House when Speaker Smallwood attempted to defeat the St. Louis and San Francisco charter. During the latter part of the tribal period there were twenty members. See testimony of National Treasurer Geo. W. Scott (Report Select Committee, II, 926).

[22]Constitution, Arts. III, VII.

[23]Loc. cit.

WILLIAM BRYANT, PRINCIPAL CHIEF, 1870–74

COLEMAN COLE, PRINCIPAL CHIEF, 1874–78

was of a more general nature, and definite advice was given to the legislators in later messages.

Every communication from the executive was referred to a standing joint Committee on the Chief's Message, which reported to the Council recommending the manner in which it should be referred by subject matter to the appropriate committees. When the Council accepted this report, the committees began working on sections of the message as referred to them, and submitted reports to which bills were usually appended embodying their recommendations. The law in its final form often included the committee report with the bill; in fact much of Choctaw legislation was in the form of a report accepted by the Council and approved by the Chief. The principal committees were those on the Chief's Message, Reports, Schools, Finance, Citizenship, Judiciary, and Relations with the United States. Apparently they were all joint committees with an equal representation from each house or with a larger membership from the House of Representatives.

The Council was very strongly influenced in legislation by the recommendations of the Principal Chief. When he made a specific recommendation on one subject, his message, the favorable report of the committee, the acceptance by both houses, and his official approval were often recorded on the same sheet of paper, and the law was filed away in that form by the National Secretary. Occasionally, however, the Council adopted an independent policy; the Committee on the Chief's Message in 1877, for instance, was very free in recommending that certain suggestions of Governor Cole should not be acted upon.[24] Cole on his part, was capable of vigorous veto messages; on one occasion he referred the lawmakers to a certain article of the constitution with the advice, "you will please read it and interpreted and get the understanding."[25]

The deliberations were carried on in Choctaw and interpreted into English. The text of the bills was usually in English, but occasional bills, particularly acts of special legislation, were written in Choctaw. They were endorsed with the formula, "Read and interpreted and taken up by the Senate," and "Read and interpreted and taken up by the House." Each house was entitled to elect an official interpreter, who

[24]Union Agency Files, Choctaw—National Council—these documents contain minutes of the legislative committees; Acts of the Choctaw Nation,—these original MS acts of the Council are endorsed by the presiding officer of each house, approved by the Chief, and filed by the National Secretary, and they also contain many committee reports accepted by the Council.
[25]Union Agency Files, Letters of Chiefs, p. 159.

157

received the same pay as the members, and who was required to be on hand at all sessions.[26] An interpreter was occasionally employed to assist a committee in its work.[27] The laws were published in both languages.[28]

Each day's business began by roll call, after which prayer was offered "by some pious member." The journal of the previous day was next read and interpreted. The presiding officer then called up any bill on the table, giving preference to committee reports and bills from the other house. After a bill had passed both houses, it was carried to the Chief by the sergeant-at-arms or doorkeeper.[29]

The Choctaws enjoyed the proceedings of deliberative assemblies, and many of them attended the Council as visitors. The delivery of the Principal Chief's annual message was an especially interesting occasion. The capital swarmed with lobbyists also.[30] White visitors were invariably impressed even in the earliest period of Choctaw constitutional development, by the gravity of the deliberations and the eloquence of the orators.

The capital of the Choctaw Nation remained for twenty years at the old Armstrong Academy, where it had been established in the Fall of 1863. It was usually known by the official name of Chahta Tamaha, but was occasionally referred to by the English equivalent as Choctaw City.[31] An attempt made in 1876 to remove it to the growing town of Atoka, on the Missouri, Kansas, and Texas Railroad, was defeated by the veto of Governor Cole, although some uncertainty existed as to the Chief's right to veto a constitutional amendment.[32]

An amendment proposed by the Council in 1882 and ratified by the people the following year, provided for the permanent location of the capital. The site selected lay in a beautiful prairie valley with mountains in the background, about two and a half miles east of

[26]O'Beirne and O'Beirne, *The Indian Territory*, p. 50; Acts of the Choctaw Nation, October 30, 1869; October 26, 1888.
[27]Acts of the Choctaw Nation, November 3, 1896.
[28]*Ibid.*, October 31, 1890; October 27, 1893, for example.
[29]Acts of the Choctaw Nation, December 27, 1899; Union Agency Files, Choctaw—National Council,—these papers contain fragments of journals kept by the two houses and the rules adopted by the House of Representatives in 1878 and 1901; *see* also Choctaw—Railroads, for the journal carried to Washington by Isham Walker, and the testimony of Smallwood in regard to legislative procedure.
[30]*See* any contemporary newspaper account of a session of the Council for the names of visitors at the capital, for example, the *Vindicator*, October 11, 1876.
[31]*See* especially the auditor's warrants in the Union Agency Files for use of the name Choctaw City.
[32]*Vindicator*, March 15, April 19, 1876.

Nanih Waya, where a big log council house had been built by the Choctaws soon after they settled in their western home. The name given the new seat of government was Tuskahoma, meaning Red Warriors.[33]

A commodious capitol was erected and occupied in the Fall of 1884. A large two-story brick building with a garret under the mansard roof, it was hailed as the finest building in the Indian Territory. It provided large rooms for the Senate, the House of Representatives, and the Supreme Court; a spacious executive office; five smaller rooms for national officers;[34] and five committee rooms. It was heated by wood fires in numerous fireplaces, and the water supply was drawn by buckets from a well dug on the grounds.[35]

When the General Council convened in its new quarters, a busy town sprang up at Tuskahoma. Several hotels and stores were erected, a barber shop, blacksmith shop, and photograph tent did a flourishing business, and a number of private residences were built.[36] But when the St. Louis and San Francisco Railroad came through, it missed the town by about two miles; the business houses moved to the new location, and the old site was deserted except during the Council sessions.

Although the constitution required that the Principal Chief and the National Secretary, National Treasurer, National Attorney, and National Auditor should "reside at or near the seat of government,"[37] this provision was disregarded. When the Council met for the first session in the new capitol, the retiring Chief, J. F. McCurtain, recommended in his farewell address that five dwelling houses should be erected at the new site for the use of the national officers,[38] but no action was taken. Even the Principal Chief continued to live in his own home except during the Council session and to date his official correspondence from his private office. Isham Walker violated no precedent when he carried the House Journal to Washington with him in his attempt to defeat the St. Louis and San Francisco charter, and when the fire that destroyed the residence of National Auditor S. H. Woods burned up

[33]Acts of the Choctaw Nation, October 20, 1882; January 1, 1884. Variants are "Tuskahomma," "Tushka Homma," and "Tushka Humma."

[34]That is, the National Secretary, National Treasurer, National Auditor, National Attorney, and National Agent.

[35]Acts of the Choctaw Nation, October 25, November 6, 1883; September 15, November 6, 1884; October 25, 1892; October 19, 1893.

[36]*Indian Champion*, November 1, 1884.

[37]Constitution, Art. V, Section 15.

[38]*Indian Champion*, October 25, 1884, retiring address of Governor McCurtain, October 9, 1884.

at the same time about $150 worth of his contingent fund and all the books and records of his office, the Council simply made an appropriation for new office supplies.[39]

Elections were held every year in the Choctaw Nation on the first Wednesday in August. The most important elections occurred on the even years when the Principal and District Chiefs, the entire membership of the Council, the judicial officers, and the county officers were chosen. On the odd years occurred the election of the "governor's cabinet" and the members of the House of Representatives. All males over eighteen years of age who had been citizens for at least six months were qualified to vote.[40]

Election precincts were established, and constantly changed, by special acts of the Council. They varied in voting population from ten to over a hundred. It was the duty of the county judge to appoint three judges of the election for each precinct, but if this measure had been neglected the voters were authorized to select their own judges after they had assembled.

All elections were by ballot, but the voter's choice was a matter of public record. The name of the candidate was written on one side of a scrap of paper; on the other side was the name of the voter and a number showing the order in which he voted. The votes were recorded in "poll books," which were sheets of paper ruled by hand. In the left hand column the names of the voters were recorded and numbered consecutively as they voted, to correspond with the names and numbers on the ballots. At the top were the names of the candidates. The sheets were ruled in squares and a check was made opposite the name of the voter and under the name of the candidate for whom he voted. The returns were made out in the form of tally sheets showing the total for each candidate. Only the names of candidates were recorded; no party designation appeared on the ballot, the poll book, or the return sheet. After 1889, it became increasingly common to use printed forms for the poll books, and to omit recording the voters' choice on those sheets.[41]

The returns for the office of Principal Chief were counted at the beginning of the regular session of the Council in the presence of both

[39]Acts of the Choctaw Nation, November 1, 1900.
[40]Constitution, Arts. IV-VII, Amendments, Sec. 1.
[41]Acts and Resolutions of the General Council, 1860-1861, pp. 79-82, election law adopted, October 30, 1860; Acts of the Choctaw Nation, October 30, 1888; Union Agency Files, Choctaw—Elections,—there are large bundles of ballots, poll books, and return sheets in these papers.

houses, and the successful candidate was formally notified, and entered immediately upon his duties. The Supreme Judge for each district received the returns for district and county offices, and certified the result of the election to the National Secretary. The Principal Chief then issued commissions to the successful candidates.[42]

Party machinery in the Choctaw Nation was not very well developed, and nominations were made in various ways. The favorite method of selecting a candidate for Principal Chief was by a meeting of both houses of the Council and other officers and prominent citizens in the Representative Hall of the capitol at some time during the session. Although other candidates entered the field, so great was the prestige of the Council nomination that the one who received it almost invariably won the election.[43]

The nomination of Thompson McKinney in the Fall of 1885 is typical of the procedure usually followed in such a meeting. When the nomination was made, it was seconded by Edmund McCurtain, who was at that time Principal Chief, and a number of government officials and other prominent citizens subscribed their names to a pledge to support his candidacy. The nominee thanked them and promised to perform his duties faithfully if elected.[44]

The other candidates were selected by private initiative. A group of citizens would choose a candidate, and then publish in a newspaper a formal request over their signatures asking him to accept the nomination. The candidate would signify his acceptance through the same medium.[45] Nominations for the lesser offices were made still more informally. Some citizen would publish a newspaper communication naming a certain man as a promising candidate.[46] Others would announce their own candidacy.[47] After nominations had been made by political parties, it was very common for other candidates to run independently.[48]

[42]Constitution, Art V; Acts of the Choctaw Nation, November 13, 1890; Union Agency Files, Court Records.

[43]Atoka Independent, May 12, 1888; Indian Citizen, January 18, 1894.

[44]Indian Champion, October 24, 1885. See also nomination of Benjamin Smallwood, Indian Citizen, November 30, 1889

[45]Vindicator, May 17, May 24, 1874; June 14, 1876.

[46]Indian Citizen, April 26, 1890. The writer of this notice learns with regret that the county judge and the sheriff of his county are not candidates for reëlection; and so, he nominates them for the House and Senate.

[47]Vindicator, June 21, 1873, announcement for National Secretary; ibid., May 17, 1876, announcement for District Chief.

[48]For example see Indian Citizen, July 11, July 18, 1891.

About 1890 the Choctaws began to develop a convention system of nomination, but there was always a tendency to revert to the old method of selecting candidates at the Council or by irregular and independent action. Leaders of both parties met at the capital before the Council adjourned that year and made plans for the election of the following August. The Progressive Party, to which the governor belonged, followed the usual method and made nominations for the four national offices, but their opponents, the National Party, met only to arrange for a convention at which all the counties of the Nation would be represented.[49] This convention met at Antlers, January 7-8, drafted a platform, and made nominations.[50] County conventions of the National Party also convened later and nominated candidates for the House of Representatives.[51] In addition to the party nominees there were a number of independents in the field, who announced their candidacy through the press.[52] It will be remembered that this was the odd-year election at which only the four national officers and the lower house of the Council were elected.

At the main election of the following year both parties used the convention method. County conventions made nominations for county officers, and elected delegates to district and national conventions.[53] Two years later the National Party attempted to return to the old method, and nominated Jefferson Gardner as Principal Chief at a meeting held during the Council session;[54] but numerous county conventions repudiated this action, which they characterized as undemocratic, and elected delegates to a national convention instructing them to support the nomination of Jacob Jackson.[55] The national convention accordingly met and nominated Jackson. The Progressives then held a national convention and nominated Gardner as their candidate.[56]

The acceptance of Gardner by the Progressives after the attempt to make him the National nominee illustrates the irregular nature of party alignments in the Choctaw Nation. Although the Nationals made of their party a sort of lodge with initiation ceremonies and pledges,[57] they were not able to maintain its unity. Parties were made

[49]*Indian Citizen*, November 22, 1890.
[50]*Ibid.*, January 17, 1891.
[51]*Ibid.*, May 9, 1891.
[52]*Ibid.*, July 11, July 18, 1891.
[53]*Ibid.*, January 28, February 11, March 10, March 24, 1892.
[54]*Ibid.*, November 2, 1893.
[55]*Ibid.*, January 18, March 1, May 17, 1894. This convention met February 24.
[56]*Ibid.*, April 26, 1894.
[57]*Ibid.*, May 17, 1894.

up mainly of personal followings or temporary groupings which changed with kaleidoscopic frequency.[58] Personalities and issues always entered into a campaign more than party regularity, and independent action frequently manifested itself through mass meetings of voters.[59]

Notwithstanding the informal character of party organization and the lack of party discipline, the conventions were models of parliamentary smoothness. The work of the national committee, the examination of credentials, the election of the permanent chairman, the drafting of the platform, the balloting for nominations all proceeded with the skill and dispatch which the Choctaws showed to such an unusual degree in all their deliberative assemblies.[60] Sometimes a leader of the opposition would be present, and would engage in a formal debate with the party nominee.[61]

The Choctaws enjoyed political activity. They entered into the public life of their tiny republic as ardently as their untutored ancestors had once joined in primitive councils. They were constantly holding mass meetings, where they could make speeches and pass resolutions. They gathered at church grounds and courthouses to listen to candidates, who canvassed the country making addresses in English and Choctaw.[62] Individually or in groups they sent frequent communications to the newspapers supporting the candidacy of certain individuals. It was the fullblood element that entered most heartily into politics. The intermarried citizens and mixed bloods usually devoted themselves to money-making, though they sometimes sought to manipulate the elections from the background.[63]

The consecutive story of Choctaw administrations presents a record of active political life, and reveals the influence of many able personalities. These administrations began with the adoption of the constitution of 1860, which created the central executive.

The first three administrations covered the Civil War period — George Hudson, 1860-1862; Samuel Garland, 1862-1864; and Peter P.

[58]The editors of the *Indian Citizen*, for instance, supported Jackson and attacked the McCurtains with great bitterness in 1892, only to support the McCurtains and attack Jackson with equal bitterness in 1896. Their championship of Dukes in 1900 was changed to abusive opposition in 1902.

[59]For example *see Indian Citizen*, May 24, 1894.

[60]For proceedings of conventions *see* for example, the *Indian Citizen*, February 11, 1892; December 13, 1893; May 21, 1896; May 5, 1898.

[61]*Ibid.*, March 10, 1892.

[62]*Vindicator*, January 21, July 19, 1876; *Indian Citizen*, July 2, July 16, 1896.

[63]Benson, *Life among the Choctaw Indians*, pp. 101-5.

Pitchlynn, 1864-1866. It was Pitchlynn who signed the armistice and assisted in the negotiation of the Peace Treaty.

Allen Wright was elected as Principal Chief in 1866. He was a full-blood, brilliantly educated, who had been active in public life and had taken part in negotiating the alliance with the Confederacy and the Treaty of 1866. At the time of his election he was serving his third term as National Treasurer. It is said that he was nominated by the Council while he was in Washington as a member of the treaty delegation and elected without his consent.[64]

He took office under "the depressing influences which have surrounded us since those bloody years" of war,[65] and his administration was a struggle with public debt, moral and educational collapse, the freedman problem, the depredations of cattle thieves, the breakdown of law enforcement, and other reconstruction problems that seemed insurmountable. He was an able executive, but his leadership was hampered by his connection with the unsavory financial transaction that occurred during the treaty negotiations. The Council failed to endorse his candidacy for reëlection and he won his second term after a bitter campaign in which the anti-treaty party accused him of misapplying the national funds.[66]

William Bryant, who owed his nomination to the favor of the Council, was elected in 1870. He was a man of limited education, but of considerable intelligence. In 1872 his reëlection was opposed by the Progressive Party, which was organized that year by Wright and other prominent men at New Boggy, upon a platform of sane progress, the integrity of the Treaty of 1866, and opposition to the railroad schemes for territorial government. His opponent was T. B. Turnbull, who had served as District Chief of Pushmataha District and President of the Senate. Bryant won the election.[67] The most important event of his administration was the coming of the Missouri, Kansas, and Texas Railroad, and his fight to establish the principle of national control of rock and timber sales.

In 1874 Joel Everidge, C. E. Nelson, and Coleman Cole were candi-

[64]*Indian Champion*, April 11, 1885, "Biography of Rev. Allen Wright"; *Atoka Independent*, May 12, 1888.
[65]Union Agency Files, Letters of Chiefs, pp. 11-12, Thanksgiving proclamation of Governor Wright, November 22, 1866.
[66]*Ibid.*, pp. 77-79, special message to Council, November 14, 1867; *Indian Champion, loc. cit.; Atoka Independent, loc. cit.*
[67]*Atoka Independent, loc. cit.; Vindicator*, June 14, 1876; Acts of the Choctaw Nation, October 21, 1870.

dates. The election went to Cole, the most conservative of the three,[68] and the most picturesque Principal Chief that ever presided over the Choctaw administration. He was almost without formal education, but had a vast fund of native shrewdness. He was a strong supporter of the schools, favored the adoption of the freedmen, opposed white immigration, and fought for the right of the Nation to collect royalty on timber and coal. He had been defrauded of his land when he elected to remain in Mississippi at the time of the removals, and his favorite project was the creation of machinery to take care of the Net Proceeds payment, which he believed to be delayed only through the intrigues of Pitchlynn, whom he distrusted and hated. With the fullblood's implicit trust in the President of the United States, he wrote long letters to Grant and Hayes in his labored penmanship and broken sentences trying to explain a point of view that was often statesmanlike in its grasp of principles.[69] He was very outspoken in his opposition to men and measures that he opposed, and was constantly involved in controversy with the Indian Office, the railroad, the Council, or the Net Proceeds delegation. He once voiced the opinion that since all the land had formerly belonged to the Indians it was only just that the United States should pay them "as a tribute, annual stated sums of moneys."[70]

Upon the expiration of his first term he was opposed for reëlection by the two former Chiefs, Wright of the Progressive Party, and William Bryant. The old treaty story came up again to Wright's discredit, and Cole was overwhelmingly elected.[71]

Cole became engaged in a stormy controversy with the last regular Council that met during his administration. His annual message recommended the extension of the machinery for distributing the Net Proceeds money, and the appointment of a new delegation, on the ground that the existing one was responsible for the delay in payment.[72] The Committee on the Chief's Message, contrary to the usual custom, adopted a very independent policy; they advised the Council that it was "impolitic improper and illegal to attempt to supplant the old Delegation," and recommended that other suggestions of the Chief

[68]*Oklahoma Star*, June 5, July 24, 1874.
[69]Indian Office Files, Choctaw, P180, example of his letters to Grant; *Vindicator,* October 13, 1875, annual message to Council; Union Agency Files, Letters of Chiefs, pp. 191-92, education message.
[70]*Atoka Independent*, March 8, 1878.
[71]*Vindicator,* May 17, June 14, August 9, October 11, 1876; *Oklahoma Star,* June 22, 1876; Union Agency Files, Choctaw—Elections. The official returns showed that Cole received 1,286 votes; Bryant, 672; and Wright, 406.
[72]Union Agency Files, Letters of Chiefs, pp. 187-88.

should be disregarded.[73] The Council then approved Pitchlynn's report of his handling of the Net Proceeds matter, and Cole vetoed the resolution. The House of Representatives thereupon impeached the Chief, but the Senate by a vote of six to four failed to convict.[74]

The same Council by a unanimous vote nominated Judge Garvin as the next candidate for the governorship. He was elected by a vote of 1,852 to 683 for his opponent, A. R. Durant.[75] Garvin was a man of superior education and unusual intellectual gifts. His administration was occupied mainly with the attempt to uphold the integrity of the Choctaw government and land title against the activities of the "Boomers" and threatened action by Congress. He died before the expiration of his term of office, and was succeeded, February 20, 1880, by Jackson F. McCurtain, the President of the Senate.[76]

McCurtain was descended from a famous fullblood family long prominent in Choctaw history. He was a son of Cornelius McCurtain, who had been Chief of Moshulatubbee District before the constitution of 1860 had created a central administration. He, himself, had had a distinguished career as an officer in the Civil War and a member of the Senate. His accidental elevation to the governorship was the beginning of an administration that is generally conceded to have been the greatest in Choctaw annals.[77]

In the election following the death of Garvin, the candidates were McCurtain, Cole, and Durant. McCurtain was victorious, with 1,541 votes, to 974 cast for Cole, and 192 for Durant.[78] He was again elected in 1882, thus serving two full terms in addition to filling out Garvin's unexpired term. During his administration the Council passed the act adopting the freedmen, the charter was granted to the St. Louis and San Francisco Railroad, and the constitution was amended to provide for the removal of the capital to Tuskahoma.

In the election of 1884 the candidates were Edmund McCurtain, a younger brother of Jackson McCurtain, who had been active in the Council and was at that time Superintendent of Schools; and Joseph P. Folsom, who had compiled an official digest of all Choctaw legislation

[73] Acts of the Choctaw Nation, October 19, 1877.
[74] *Atoka Independent*, October 26, 1877.
[75] *Loc. cit.;* Union Agency Files, Senate Records, Choctaw Nation, 1878, p. 58.
[76] Union Agency Files, Letters of Chiefs, pp. 231-36, Garvin's inaugural, October 8, 1878; *Indian Champion,* October 25, 1884, retiring address of Chief McCurtain.
[77] Acts of the Choctaw Nation, December 19, 1902,—this resolution characterized him as "the most celebrated chief in the history of the Choctaw people"; O'Beirne, *Leaders and Leading Men,* I, 140-41.
[78] Union Agency Files, Senate Records, p. 148.

enacted before 1869, and as a member of the Council, had opposed the grant of the St. Louis and San Francisco charter. McCurtain was elected by 1,578 votes to Folsom's 1,044,[79] and began his administration in the new capitol. Although he was a capable official, his public career is somewhat overshadowed by the greater statesmanship of his more distinguished brother.

At the expiration of his term of office he was not a candidate for re-election, but he used his influence in securing the nomination of Thompson McKinney. During their long control of the administration, the McCurtains had built up a powerful personal following in the Progressive Party, and McKinney received this support. The candidate of the opposition or National Party was Benjamin F. Smallwood, a well educated and popular man, who had had a long and distinguished career in the House of Representatives.[80] McKinney with the McCurtain support won the election and served for one term — from 1886 to 1888.

In the next election Wilson N. Jones was the Progressive candidate. He was a man almost devoid of education — his opponents even claimed that he was unable to speak English — but his extraordinary business ability had enabled him to rise from poverty to the possession of ranching, mining, and commercial interests that made him the wealthiest man in the Choctaw Nation. He was not without political experience for he had served as district school trustee and as National Treasurer.[81] Benjamin Smallwood was again the candidate of the National Party, and A. R. Durant and C. E. Nelson also entered the race.[82]

The real contest centered in the rivalry between the Jones and Smallwood factions, and the campaign was very bitter. The United States had finally decided to pay the Net Proceeds claim, which by that time had become so complicated that opposing opinions were held as to the proper disposition of the money, and both parties fought for the privilege of paying it out.

Although the Progressives had secured a majority in both houses, the Council declared Smallwood elected, but feeling ran so high that

[79]*Indian Champion*, August 23, November 8, 1884; *Indian Citizen*, November 8, 1890; O'Beirne, *Leaders and Leading Men*, I, 178-79; Union Agency Files, Choctaw—Elections.

[80]O'Beirne, *Leaders and Leading Men*, I, 50-51. *See* Acts of the Choctaw Nation for his career in the House, where he spent forty years of almost continuous service, and was several times elected Speaker.

[81]*Atoka Independent*, May 19, 1889; O'Beirne, *Leaders and Leading Men*, I, 28-29.
[82]Union Agency Files, Choctaw—Elections.

he took the oath of office at the Robuck hotel in Tuskahoma to avoid a fight with the McCurtain faction in the capitol.[83] He had considerable difficulty with a hostile Council during his administration, but the national officers elected in the middle of his term, with the exception of National Treasurer Green McCurtain, all belonged to his party.[84] It will be remembered that the fight between the Chief and the Council over the ownership of the coal lands occurred during his administration.

In 1890 Smallwood was a candidate for reëlection, and Jones was again his opponent.[85] This campaign also excited intense feeling; Jones, in fact, characterized it as the bitterest and most hotly contested election he had ever known.[86] The Council was rather evenly divided between the two parties, and Jones was elected by a majority of about two hundred.[87]

The election of 1892 was the occasion of the most serious disorder that ever occurred in the Choctaw Nation. Jones was again the candidate of the Progressive Party, and the Nationals nominated Jacob B. Jackson, a fullblood who had attended college in the "States," had served in the Senate, and was at that time National Secretary.[88]

It is difficult to account for the bitterness of the campaign. The desire to control the expenditure of a large sum of money which the United States had recently voted as payment for the Leased District seemed to intensify the bad feeling between the two parties. Part of the fight centered around the conduct of the National Agent's office by the Progressive, Dr. E. N. Wright, who was accused by the Nationals of showing favoritism in awarding contracts, and who was defended by the Progressives as the victim of a plot on the part of the white element to defeat the Nation in its collection of revenue. Enmity between the two factions was undoubtedly aggravated by inflammatory articles published in the *Indian Citizen,* which supported Jackson, and the *Choctaw Herald,* the organ of the Progressives; in fact, when the contest had approached the dimensions of civil war there were observers who attributed the whole difficulty to the machinations of newspapers and white citizens who, for their own ends, aroused the Indians,

[83]*Indian Citizen,* July 26, 1890, "A Smallwood Man"; *Report Commissioner of Indian Affairs,* 1888, p. 127.
[84]*Indian Citizen,* June 14, November 22, 1890.
[85]Union Agency Files, Choctaw—Elections.
[86]*Indian Citizen,* October 18, 1890, "Gov. Jones' Message."
[87]*Ibid.,* August 18, 1890.
[88]*Indian Citizen,* July 7, 1892, "Sketch of the Hon. J. B. Jacksons Career."

and thus loosed forces which they could not control.[89] The violence was probably heightened by the abundance of "Choctaw beer" which was sold by non-citizens in defiance of Choctaw enforcement officers, under recent rulings of United States courts upholding the legality of the traffic.[90]

As the campaign progressed, the Choctaws expressed their feelings through angry communications to the newspapers, and the holding of mass meetings where abusive speeches were made and acrimonious resolutions adopted. The Nationals were soon known as "Buzzards," and their opponents as "Bald Eagles" or "Pole Cats." Each side charged the other with a plot to murder its opponents and thus secure control of the government.[91]

The election was very close. Each side claimed the victory and accused its opponents of allowing non-citizens to vote, and of manipulating the returns. Conventions were held by both parties, and excited plans were made to defeat the nefarious schemes of the opposition.[92]

On September 11, a party of Nationals in Gaines County assassinated four officials who belonged to the Progressive Party, and then proceeded to McAlester where they planned to kill more. Governor Jones, who was afraid to leave his home at Caddo, telegraphed for help to Bennett, the United States agent, who was stationed at Muskogee in the Creek Nation. Bennett arrived at McAlester where he found the people greatly excited and a large body of the Nationals camped about two miles west of town. Jones with his adherents then took up his station at South McAlester. Bennett arranged a conference between the leaders of both factions, and persuaded them to sign an agreement on September 15. The Nationals were to surrender the murderers to a sheriff of their own party, all armed bodies congregating throughout the Nation were to disband, and Bennett was to be present with Indian police and soldiers when the Council should convene, to prevent the attendance of non-citizens. The leaders of both factions pledged themselves to use their influence for peace.[93]

The Nationals then surrendered to Bennett seventeen men said to

[89]Union Agency Files, Choctaw—Elections, letter of W. L. Austin from South McAlester, September 22, 1892; *Indian Citizen*, September 22, 1892, text of agreement signed at McAlester, September 15, 1892.

[90]*Indian Citizen*, June 23, June 30, 1892.

[91]*Ibid.*, May 5, 1892; *Report Commissioner of Indian Affairs*, 1892, p. 260.

[92]*Report Commissioner of Indian Affairs*, 1892, *loc. cit. See* also any contemporary issue of the *Indian Citizen*.

[93]*Indian Citizen*, September 22, 1892, text of agreement.

be implicated in the murders, and their party disbanded. Jones, however, maintained a large number of armed men at South McAlester under the command of Green McCurtain. They demanded the custody of the prisoners, and threatened to attack the camp where twenty Indian police were guarding them; but Bennett ordered his men to defend themselves, and no clash occurred. Bennett then turned them over to Sheriff Perry of Gaines County, and the Progressive forces also dispersed.[94]

While these events were taking place in the vicinity of McAlester, armed bands were collecting in other parts of the Nation. A telegram came to Bennett on September 14 that thirty armed men were surrounding the home of Sheriff Perry twelve miles east of Hartshorne, and he immediately dispatched a runner on horseback to inform them that the leaders at McAlester were negotiating an agreement. The streets of Antlers were thronged with armed Nationals, but Jackson, and Judge C. S. Vinson, a prominent Progressive, managed to persuade them to disarm and gather in the schoolhouse where both men addressed them, advising them to let the law take its course.[95]

Chief Jones showed a tendency, perhaps justifiable in view of the assassinations that had already occurred, to treat the armed groups of Nationals as rioters, and to call out similar groups of his own supporters through his constitutional power of calling out the militia.[96] Members of both parties were in great fear of secret assassination, and collected in armed bands for protection.[97] There seemed to be no disposition to engage in open warfare.

On September 22 Jackson made a proposition to Jones that all contests in counting the election returns should be referred to Bennett for settlement, but Jones postponed his decision until the Council would convene on October 3.[98] As that time approached, it was reported that armed bands of Nationals were marching on the capitol from all directions. Jones sent out a party of lighthorsemen who arrested one party of forty-eight during the night of October 2, and locked them in the

[94]*Ibid.*, September 15, 1892; *Report Commissioner of Indian Affairs*, 1892, pp. 260-62;Union Agency Files, Choctaw—Elections, Austin's letter.

[95]*Report Commissioner of Indian Affairs*, 1892, p. 263; 1893, p. 83; *Indian Citizen*, September 22, 1892.

[96]Acts of the Choctaw Nation, October 26, 1892; July 1, 1893—these appropriations show that Jones' supporters at South McAlester were militia; *Indian Citizen*, September 22, 1892, text of proclamation of Chief Jones against the assembling of political conventions on the ground that they furnished incentives for murder.

[97]*Report Commissioner of Indian Affairs*, 1892, p. 263.

[98]*Loc. cit.*

170

garret of the capitol. He then placed a strong guard around the building.[99]

On the morning of October 3, hundreds of Indians from all parts of the Nation were assembled in Tuskahoma. An observer reported that not a drunken man was in the crowd, and that all were strongly impressed with the gravity of the situation. Bennett, in response to the request of both parties, was present with United States cavalry — a circumstance new in Choctaw history. The members of the Council were sworn in, and both houses were seen to be overwhelmingly Progressive. C. S. Vinson was chosen as President of the Senate, and Wesley Anderson was unanimously elected as Speaker of the House. In the afternoon there was a conference of the two leaders and their advisers, at which Bennett was present, and Jones definitely rejected Jackson's offer to refer disputed points to Bennett for arbitration.[100]

Two days later the Council passed an act providing that only members of the Council and the officers connected therewith should be present while the election returns were being canvassed, and that Bennett with his soldiers should be requested to coöperate with the lighthorsemen in guarding the entrances. It is typical of the intense personal interests that formed the background of the official transactions of this little republic that this act was approved by Jones in his official capacity as Principal Chief and attested by Jackson as National Secretary.[101]

A joint session of the Council the following day declared that 1,705 votes had been cast for Jones and 1,697 for Jackson. The Nationals believed that they had been cheated out of the election, but they were inclined to accept the result. One prominent Choctaw was heard to say, "Life is too short and Indians are too few for them to kill each other." Bennett remained at the capital until October 12, and the troops stayed two weeks longer.[102]

Jones's inaugural message was not conciliatory. He thanked the people for his reëlection, and spoke of the acts of the opposition as an attempt to assassinate the Chief and other officers, and destroy the government. He warned the Council that such outbreaks were very

[99]*Indian Citizen*, October 6, 1892; Peter J. Hudson, personal interview. Hudson's brother was captain of the lighthorse that made the arrests.

[100]*Indian Citizen*, October 6, 1892; *Report Commissioner of Indian Affairs*, 1893, p. 85.

[101]Acts of the Choctaw Nation, October 5, 1892.

[102]*Report Commissioner of Indian Affairs*, 1893, p. 85; *Indian Citizen*, October 13, 1892.

likely to occur again, and advised the passage of laws to suppress them.[103] The Council responded by strengthening the militia.[104]

The trouble broke out again in December when a lighthorseman under the Chief's orders arrested Willis Jones for participation in the murders. Jones was rescued by Albert Jackson and others, and taken to the home of V. M. Locke, an intermarried citizen. A large party of Nationals then collected at the home of Locke and prepared to protect Jones and Jackson. Chief Jones then called out the militia to arrest the men and all others interfering with the officers. The militia assembled at Antlers, and, as Locke's supporters continued to increase, a battle seemed imminent.[105]

The clash occurred toward the end of March. Apparently a group of the militia under irresponsible private leadership became intoxicated, and began to "shoot up" the town of Antlers. Citizens took refuge in their homes while bullets lodged in the Methodist church, the railway station, and the Masonic hall. A battle then took place between the militia and the Nationals who were barricaded in Locke's home, and several on each side were wounded. Agent Bennett hastened to the scene of the disturbance, a temporary truce was arranged, and the armed forces began to disband.[106]

Bennett was deeply concerned over this second outbreak. He said that a feeling of dread and uncertainty existed and that no compromise was apparently possible. He blamed the militia as the aggressors, and said that it would be committing judicial murder to permit them to make arrests. He advised that the Nation be put under martial law.[107]

Captain Guthrie with forty-one men was accordingly dispatched by the War Department and arrived at Antlers on April 11. Special Agent Faison was sent to take charge, and both Guthrie and Bennett were under his orders. Faison ordered the arrest of Willis Jones and Albert Jackson, and placed them in jail at Hartshorne. The opposing forces signed an agreement early in May, but the soldiers remained in the Choctaw country until after the regular meeting of the Council.[108]

The Choctaw leaders were very much concerned for fear this dis-

103*Indian Citizen*, October 13, 1892, text of message.
104Acts of the Choctaw Nation, October 26, October 28, 1892.
105*Indian Citizen*, March 30, 1893; *Report Commissioner of Indian Affairs*, 1893, pp. 87-88.
106*Indian Citizen*, April 6, 1893; *Report Commissioner of Indian Affairs*, 1893, p. 86-87. This disturbance is still known by Choctaws as the "Locke War."
107*Report Commissioner of Indian Affairs*, 1893, pp. 88-89.
108*Loc. cit.; Indian Citizen*, May 4, May 11, May 18, June 29, October 5, 1893.

CAPITOL OF THE CHOCTAW NATION AT TUSKAHOMA, BUILT IN 1884

Courtesy Oklahoma Historical Society

SAMUEL GARLAND, PRINCIPAL CHIEF, 1862–64

turbance would bring about the loss of their national autonomy. It did, in fact, create a bad impression at Washington, and it strengthened the sentiment in favor of the law recently passed by Congress looking to the ultimate extinction of the tribal governments.[109] Green McCurtain, Joe Everidge, C. S. Vinson, and Dr. Wright were accordingly dispatched to the Federal capital to explain the riot at Antlers, and J. W. Ownby of Paris, Texas, was employed as counsel to represent the Nation before the United States.[110]

A special session of the Council convened in June and made appropriations to defray the expenses incurred during the insurrection. Although the odd-year election seldom occasioned much interest in the Choctaw Nation, the one that took place that Summer was even more quiet than usual. The four national officers were elected from the National Party, and the Progressives again secured a majority in the House of Representatives.[111] An appalling number of political assassinations occurred among the partisans of both sides during September and October,[112] but no armed demonstration resulted. When the Council met, Captain Guthrie with twenty soldiers camped near the capitol. Locke was present and was reported as smiling and greeting his former enemies. Everything was outwardly calm, but both sides were tense and watchful. An amnesty bill introduced in the Council failed of passage.[113]

The men who had surrendered to Bennett were tried at Wilburton by Judge Holson of the Choctaw criminal court, under the protection of United States troops stationed there, and nine of them were sentenced to be shot.[114] The Department of the Interior intervened, and asked the Chief if he had the pardoning power. He replied in the negative, but at the request of Colonel Faison he ordered the sentence to be suspended, at the same time making a strong protest against the interference of the United States in the execution of the tribal laws.[115] After subsequent delays and reprieves at the request of the United States,[116] one of the men, Silan Lewis, was finally executed, November 5, 1894. He was a fullblood about fifty-four years old who had once

109*Indian Citizen*, April 13, 1893. The law creating the Dawes Commission was passed March 3 of that year.
110Acts of the Choctaw Nation, July 1, July 3, 1893; *Indian Citizen*, April 27, 1893.
111*Indian Citizen*, August 10, October 12, 1893.
112*Ibid.*, September 28, October 19, 1893.
113*Ibid.*, October 5, October 19, 1893.
114*Ibid.*, June 29, July 13, 1893; *Report Commissioner of Indian Affairs*, 1893, p. 90.
115*Indian Citizen*, July 20, 1893.
116*Ibid.*, September 7, September 14, 1893; May 10, October 4, October 11, 1894.

been sheriff of his county. He met death like an old-time Choctaw, refusing to take advantage of the comparative freedom that was allowed him, and walking in from the woods in time for his execution. A threatened uprising in his behalf did not materialize, probably because he did not encourage it.[117] His eight companions were dismissed and allowed to leave for the Chickasaw Nation.[118] This ended the most serious political disturbance in the history of the Choctaw people.

The election of 1894 was very quiet. It will be remembered that the Nationals at this time repudiated the nomination of Jefferson Gardner at the Council and again chose Jackson as their leader, while the Progressives made Gardner their candidate. Political alignments were consequently confused, and Gardner won the election. The Nationals, however, secured a majority in the Council and elected V. M. Locke as Superintendent of Schools.[119]

The new Chief was a successful farmer and stockraiser, and managed a store and postoffice at Eagletown. He had served as Senator, National Treasurer, and Supreme Judge for his district. His administration as Principal Chief was inharmonious, for the National majority in the Council subjected the reports of the appointive officers, who of course were Progressives, to hostile scrutiny, and the Senate refused to confirm his nominations.[120] Gardner's enemies claimed that he had not enough decision and firmness of character to make him a capable executive.

The election of 1895 was quiet and orderly. The National Party had split in two factions over the nomination of Gardner, and several independent candidates were in the field. A reminder of the stirring events of 1892 was seen in the nomination of Locke by the Nationals for National Treasurer, but he was defeated by W. W. Wilson, an Independent National. J. B. Jackson was again elected as National Secretary.[121]

This was the last election that took place under the old tribal régime. Although the government existed for some time longer, subsequent elections were concerned with the manner of dissolution, and properly belong to a consideration of that period.

[117]Ibid., November 8, 1894; Oklahoma City Times, March 11, 1932, "Whipping Post is Favored by Indian Peace Officer," reminiscences of Lyman Pusley.

[118]Indian Citizen, November 15, 1894.

[119]Ibid., October 18, October 25, 1894. See also communications from correspondents during the summer.

[120]Ibid., October 25, 1894; O'Beirne, Leaders and Leading Men, I, 174-77.

[121]Indian Citizen, July 18, October 10, 1895.

CRIME AND THE ADMINIS-
TRATION OF JUSTICE

8

THE lowest Choctaw court was the county court, which convened on the first Monday in each month. It kept a record of marriage licenses, the discovery of minerals, and the sale of improvements on land. It had charge of probate matters, and the power to examine criminal cases and commit them to a higher court. The judge might call a jury of seven men.[1]

Above the county courts came the district courts. The Nation was divided into three judicial districts which coincided with the political divisions: Moshulatubbee, constituting the first judicial district; Apukshunnubbee, the second; and Pushmataha, the third. The voters of each district elected the judge and district attorney. These courts had original jurisdiction over all criminal cases and civil cases involving property worth more than fifty dollars, and appellate jurisdiction over cases arising in the county courts. Trials were by jury and a unanimous verdict was required to convict.[2]

The court act of 1860 provided that the district judge should hold court in each county, but this practice was not altogether satisfactory because the number of citizens in some counties was so small that it was difficult to secure enough competent jurors. In his inaugural message in 1878, Chief Garvin recommended a change, but it was not

[1]Constitution, Art. IV; *Indian Champion,* October 17, 1885; *Report Senate Committee on Indian Affairs,* IX, 224-25, 396-97, testimony of Napoleon B. Ainsworth and Robert J. Wood before the committee; Union Agency Files, Choctaw—Estates, County Court Records; Acts of the Choctaw Nation, October 26, 1871.

[2]Constitution, Art. IV; A. R. Durant, *Constitution and Laws of the Choctaw Nation together with the Treaties of 1837, 1855, 1865, and 1866* (Dallas, 1894), pp. 129-43.

until 1883 that a law was enacted providing that court should be held at only one place in the district.[3]

Indictments were presented by a grand jury of six or seven with at least five required to return a true bill. The jury might indict upon the testimony of its own members, and it was the duty of each juror to inform the district attorney if he knew of any violation of law. The jurors regulated their own hours of meeting and adjournment, and selected one of their number to keep a record of their proceedings and of the testimony they took.[4]

The highest Choctaw court was the Supreme Court, which had only appellate jurisdiction. It had three judges, one from each district, elected for four-year terms by a joint vote of both houses of the Council. It held its sittings at the capital in April and October.[5] This court had the power to pass on the constitutionality of laws. It not only set aside certain Choctaw laws as unconstitutional when cases were brought before it, but at the request of the Chief it gave opinions upon points of law not raised by inferior courts.[6]

Each Choctaw county was required to provide its own courthouse and jail. Most courthouses were mere boarded-up shanties located in isolated places, standing closed all of the time when the court was not sitting.[7] Jails were very inadequate, and prisoners were often held by guarding them or by chaining them to trees or to each other; as a result they were likely to be rescued by friends or mobbed by enemies. It was common to release on bail even criminals under sentence of death.[8] After the court law of 1883 abolished the sittings of the district

[3]*Report Senate Committee on Indian Affairs, loc. cit.; Atoka Independent,* October 17, 1885; Union Agency Files, Letters of Chiefs, pp. 231-33, Garvin's inaugural; Acts of the Choctaw Nation, November 3, 1883; *Indian Champion,* October 25, 1884, retiring address of Chief J. F. McCurtain, October 9, 1884.

[4]*Vindicator,* December 29, 1875, charge of Judge Ward to grand jury.

[5]Constitution, Art. IV; *Indian Champion,* October 17, 1885; *Report Senate Committee on Indian Affairs,* IX, *loc. cit.;* Union Agency Files, Choctaw—Courts, Supreme. *See* also court records for examples of appeals. Appeals were granted on grounds of evidence and technicalities.

[6]*Vindicator,* October 11, 1876, text of opinion setting aside a law giving extra pay to Council members—opinion requested by Chief Cole; *Indian Citizen,* April 8, 1897, text of opinion setting aside coal law of 1896—in this case the Chief first secured an opinion of the National Attorney, which he submitted to the court and the court concurred in the opinion.

[7]*Extra Census Bulletin,* p. 57; Carter, *McCurtain County and Southeast Oklahoma,* p. 32, excellent photograph of old Choctaw courthouse at Eagletown.

[8]*Indian Champion,* October 17, 1885; Union Agency Files, Choctaw—Courts, Second District, 1859-1899 inc., bonds for $500, $600, and $800 for men charged with murder,—also writs to sheriff to bring in men to defend forfeited bonds.

court in each county, the central government undertook to build one substantial jail in each district;[9] but the Choctaws always depended largely upon guarding their prisoners or keeping them in the informal custody of a friendly deputy sheriff. Although Choctaw criminals under sentence could no longer be trusted to present themselves on the day of their execution as they had done in earlier times, very few of them made a determined effort to escape.[10]

Choctaw law prescribed the death penalty for murder, rape (second offense), robbing with dangerous weapons, and treason. As an indication of the developing civilization of the Choctaws it is significant that in 1834 murder was specifically made to include the killing of a witch or wizard, and in 1850 the killing of a murderer in custody. Treason was defined in 1839 as the act of a chief, captain, or citizen in signing a sale of Choctaw land.[11] Among other crimes were theft, arson, selling intoxicating liquor, perjury, forgery, polygamy, adultery, gambling or bringing in cards or any gambling device, disturbing religious services, bribery, carrying pistols, skinning dead animals on the range, disturbing the peace, and defacing public buildings.[12]

The Choctaws punished crime by fine, whipping, or death by shooting, never by prison sentence. In cases of whipping, the sheriff was assisted by several deputies. The accused was stripped to the waist and two men grasped his hands and held him with his breast against a tree, while several others took turns in administering the prescribed number of lashes.[13] Several deputies also assisted the sheriff when a capital sentence was inflicted. The breast of the accused was bared and a mark drawn over his heart; he was then seated on a blanket facing his executioner while a man on each side drew his arms apart and held them extended while the fatal shot was fired.[14] The columns of contemporary newspapers and the court records indicate that executions were very frequent.

[9]Acts of the Choctaw Nation, November 4, 1886; November 2, 1887; October 21, 1890.

[10]*See* contemporary newspaper accounts. For instance, *Indian Champion*, October 24, 1885, "The Assassination of a Choctaw Prisoner."

[11]Folsom, *Digest of Choctaw Law*, pp. 485, 487, 493, 501.

[12]*Ibid.*, 485-528; Acts of the Choctaw Nation, October 23, 1869; October 24, 1879; October 28, 1880; November 1, 1883; November 10, 1887.

[13]J. Y. Bryce, "Perryville at one Time Regular Military Post," *Chronicles of Oklahoma*, IV (June, 1926), 184-91; Czarina C. Conlan, "Chickasaw Courts," *Chronicles of Oklahoma*, V (December, 1927), 400-4.

[14]Folsom, *Digest of Choctaw Law*, pp. 593-94; James, *My Experience with Indians*, pp. 70-71; *Indian Citizen*, May 7, 1896; *Oklahoma City Times*, March 11, 1932.

In addition to the sheriffs the Choctaws had a special group of enforcement officers known as lighthorsemen. The Principal Chief had six — later increased to nine — whom he appointed, and who served as his special agents in carrying messages, making arrests, keeping liquor at a distance during the Council sessions, and assisting the United States Indian agent in the enforcement of the laws.[15] At first there were county lighthorsemen also, but in 1878 the office was abolished and each District Chief was authorized to appoint a district lighthorseman, who served under his orders as a peace officer and messenger.[16] A law passed in 1888 provided for the appointment of two additional lighthorsemen as a bodyguard for the National Treasurer.[17]

When the regular enforcement officers were not sufficient, the Chief called out the militia to suppress disorders. In the early Eighties a feud that originated in the southeastern part of the Nation over the "spilling" of a jug of whiskey became so serious that a law was passed providing for the enlistment of three regular companies of fifty men each, who should serve under the orders of the Chief, and assist the sheriffs in arresting criminals, guarding prisoners, suppressing riots, and "spilling" whiskey. The regular officers finally succeeded in establishing order, and the act providing for the organization of the militia was repealed;[18] but although there was no permanent organization after this, the militia was called every few years, sometimes in large numbers, into the service of the Nation.[19]

All this complex system of law and law enforcement applied only to those who were under the jurisdiction of the Choctaw government. Under the Treaty of 1866 all Choctaw citizens, whether native born, intermarried, or adopted, were subject to the tribal law.[20] The Chickasaws who were living in the Nation were under the same authority by the dual citizenship arrangement of the treaty of separation.[21] Citizens of the Cherokee, Creek, and Seminole nations also came under the

[15]Folsom, *Digest of Choctaw Law,* pp. 561-62, act of October 29, 1860; Acts of the Choctaw Nation, November 7, 1889.

[16]Acts of the Choctaw Nation, November 9, 1887; October 16, 1888.

[17]*Ibid.,* November 9, 1887; October 16, 1888.

[18]*Indian Champion,* May 10, 1884; Acts of the Choctaw Nation, November 1, 1883; November 6, 1884; November 7, 1888.

[19]Acts of the Choctaw Nation, November 11, 1881; October 25, 1883; November 6, 1883; November 5, 1884; October 19, 1887. These laws all appropriate sums of money varying from $50 to $8,400 for payment of militia called out on several occasions during the Eighties.

[20]Kappler, *Laws and Treaties,* II, 928, Art. 38.

[21]*Ibid.,* II, 707-8, Art. 5, Treaty of 1855.

jurisdiction of Choctaw courts by the compact signed at North Fork Village in 1859.[22] The decision of the highest Choctaw court was final; it was a complete departure from precedent when the Department of the Interior intervened to delay the execution of Silan Lewis and his associates.[23]

Extradition of criminals between the Choctaws and Chickasaws was provided by the treaty of separation.[24] A similar arrangement was made with the other three tribes by the North Fork compact.[25] The treaties of 1855 and 1866 provided that Choctaws should deliver criminals demanded by state and federal authorities,[26] but the obligation was not reciprocal. The Choctaws, however, sometimes offered rewards for the return of their fugitives from justice, who would then be captured and delivered by peace officers of neighboring states.[27]

Since the jurisdiction of Choctaw law rested entirely upon citizenship, the laws regulating admission into the tribe were of great importance. Before the Civil War it had been the custom to admit intermarried whites to membership in the Nation,[28] but the number of these adopted citizens had been small. When with the increasing development of natural resources Choctaw citizenship came to mean an economic privilege that entitled the holder to an equal partnership in the public domain it was greatly sought after by many whites. To protect their daughters against unprincipled individuals of this class the Choctaws enacted the oft-quoted marriage law of 1875.

This act provided that no white man should marry into the Nation except under a license secured from a county official upon the payment

[22]Union Agency Files, Letters of Chiefs, p. 89, letter of Chief Wright to Chief Downing of the Cherokee Nation, January 22, 1868, making requisition for Cherokee citizens accused of stealing horses in the Choctaw Nation; Folsom, *Digest of Choctaw Law*, p. 589, law of October 19, 1865, extending Choctaw jurisdiction over war refugees. It is possible that the North Fork agreement was not ratified, but it was frequently referred to, and whether ratified or not it was observed as a custom that had the binding force of law.

[23]*Commission to the Five Civilized Tribes, Annual Report*, 1899, appendix, p. 161, decision of the United States Supreme Court in a citizenship case, May 15, 1899.

[24]Kappler, *Laws and Treaties*, II, 708, Art. 6, Treaty of 1855.

[25]Examples of requisition may be found in Union Agency Files, Creek—Foreign Relations; Creek—Choctaw; Choctaw—Foreign Relations; Chickasaw Nation—Foreign Relations. A lighthorseman was usually sent by the Chief to make the arrest or to receive the fugitive.

[26]Kappler, *Laws and Treaties*, II, 710, 929, Art. 15, Treaty of 1855, and Art. 42, Treaty of 1866. For example of arrest and delivery of a criminal upon requisition from the governor of Texas *see* Acts of the Choctaw Nation, October 22, 1888.

[27]Acts of the Choctaw Nation, October 13, 1887.

[28]Folsom, *Digest of Choctaw Law*, p. 488, act passed October, 1840.

179

of a twenty-five-dollar fee and a certificate of good moral character signed by at least ten "respectable Choctaw citizens" who had known him for at least twelve months immediately preceding his application. He was then required to take the following oath:

"I do solemnly swear that I will honor, defend, and submit to the constitution and laws of the Choctaw Nation, and will neither claim nor seek from the United States government or from the Judicial tribunals, thereof any protection privilige or redress incompatibable with the same, as guaranteed to the Choctaw Nation by the treaty stipulations entered into between them so help me God."

It was further provided that an intermarried citizen who would abandon his wife should forfeit his citizenship, but that the death of the Choctaw spouse should not work forfeiture except in the event of his subsequent marriage to a non-citizen.[29] In 1887 the license fee was increased to one hundred dollars.[30] It was possible to evade these laws by a marriage in a neighboring state, but in such cases although the marriage was legal and the children legitimate, and although the husband could cultivate his wife's land, he could not claim for himself the political or economic privileges of Choctaw citizenship.[31]

No special restrictions were placed upon the intermarriage of white women. Any white woman legally married to a Choctaw man was recognized as a citizen, but her citizenship was subject to the same conditions of forfeiture that applied to the intermarried man.[32]

An increasing number of claimants came to the Nation, and established their right to citizenship by proof of Choctaw descent. J. S. Standley, for example, lived in Mississippi as a white man until 1873 when he came to the Choctaw country and was admitted to citizenship in the tribe.[33] These claimants, however, became too numerous, and a law was enacted in 1886 providing that such applicants must have at

[29] Acts of the Choctaw Nation, November 9, 1875.

[30] *Ibid.,* November 10, 1887; Union Agency Files, Choctaw—Marriage License. These licenses are signed by ten or eleven character witnesses, often very prominent Choctaws. Some are made out in the form of a recommendation by the character witnesses; others are in the form of a petition on the part of the applicant. They are written with pen and ink on ordinary paper.

[31] *Report Commissioner of Indian Affairs,* 1898, pp. 467-71, decision of Judge Clayton in case of *W. R. Senter* v. *the Choctaw Nation.*

[32] Acts of the Choctaw Nation, October 30, 1896, instructions to commission making citizenship roll.

[33] *Ibid.,* November 2, 1874, law conferring citizenship on the Standley family. This act was vetoed by Chief Cole, but was passed over his veto.

180

least one-eighth of Choctaw blood, and that the admixture must be white and Indian. Persons convicted of felony were also excluded. The act set forth the principle that such recognition of citizenship was a matter "of *Grace* on the part of the Nation rather than rights demandable of the Choctaw Nation and enforceable by the government of the United States."[34]

Although the Choctaws were not willing to grant citizenship to all persons who could claim remote descent from a Choctaw ancestor, they welcomed the immigration of such of their own people as had remained in Mississippi. In 1889, apparently through the influence of Standley they became especially interested in the condition of these people, who, as they said, were denied the rights of citizenship in Mississippi and Louisiana and were too poor to emigrate; and the Council memorialized Congress to appropriate money for their removal.[35] Although Congress failed to act, a large number were persuaded to come during 1890. Numerous acts of the Council granted citizenship to these new arrivals, often designated as fullbloods, and money was frequently appropriated to support them until they should be able to raise a crop.[36] In 1891 the Council appropriated $1,792.50 to pay the expenses of removal and provided for the appointment of two commissioners to go to Mississippi "to collect up the Choctaws and bring them to this Nation."[37] Solomon Hotema and Robert Benton, who were entrusted with this mission, returned with eighty new citizens, and many more were admitted before the end of the year.[38] As late as 1895 frequent grants of citizenship and money were made to fresh recruits from Mississippi and Louisiana.[39]

As Choctaw citizenship continued to advance in economic value the Nation was forced to deal with an increasing number of claimants. In 1872, the year of the coming of the first railroad, the judges of the Supreme Court were given the power to decide cases of disputed citizenship, and the rejected claimants were then to be reported to the United States agent for removal as intruders.[40] The next year the

[34]*Ibid.*, November 5, 1886.
[35]*Indian Citizen*, November 9, 1889; Acts of the Choctaw Nation, December 24, 1889.
[36]Acts of the Choctaw Nation, October 29, October 30, October 31, November 13, November 14, 1890; April 4, April 9, 1891, ff.
[37]*Ibid.*, October 20, 1891.
[38]*Indian Citizen*, December 12, 1891; Acts of the Choctaw Nation, December 8, 1891, ff.
[39]Acts of the Choctaw Nation, October 28, 1895, for example.
[40]*Ibid.*, March 20, 1872.

Nation adopted the custom, which was followed during all the rest of its history, of referring such cases to the General Council, which investigated them through a special committee and legalized the citizenship of successful claimants by legislative enactment.[41]

At first the Choctaws did not recognize any right of appeal from their decision, but that fact did not deter rejected claimants from presenting their grievances to the Interior Department.[42] To prevent these annoyances the Council in 1882 requested that contested cases be referred to the decision of the United States agent, and agreed to abide by his decision provided the Nation should receive proper notification and should be privileged to employ counsel for its defense.[43] The Indian Office accepted this arrangement, but Acting Commissioner Brooks ruled that claimants could not be removed as intruders. As he neglected to set a time limit within which they should present their claims, they remained in the Nation through the simple process of neglecting to bring their applications before the Council.[44] When the Choctaws protested, the Indian Office notified the claimants to appear before the Council at the next session, and an agreement was made between the federal officials and the Choctaws by which appeals from the agent's decision might be made to the Department.[45]

About three hundred claimants accordingly presented their applications to the Council in the Fall of 1884. Chief Edmund McCurtain reminded the legislators that every fraudulent claim allowed represented a loss to the Choctaw people of $2,000, and he recommended that counsel be employed to represent the Nation before the Citizenship Committee.[46] The Council accepted the suggestion and Campbell LeFlore was appointed.[47] A large number of claims was rejected, and the claimants thereupon appealed to the agent. The pressure of other agency business delayed the hearing of the appeals for two years, but in the Fall of 1886 Agent Robert L. Owen went to Tuskahoma where he took additional testimony and gave his decision.[48]

41*Ibid.*, October 25, 1873. For example of special law recognizing the citizenship of certain individuals *see ibid.*, October 26, 1886. *See* Union Agency Files, Choctaw—Citizenship, for examples of petitions to the Supreme Court and the Council.

42Indian Office Files, Union, 1880, T65.

43Acts of the Choctaw Nation, October 21, 1882.

44*Indian Champion*, March 29, 1884, Delegates Campbell LeFlore and J. S. Standley to Commissioner Price, January 23, 1884.

45*Ibid.*, April 5, 1884, letter of Secretary Teller to Commissioner of Indian Affairs.

46*Ibid.*, October 25, 1884.

47Acts of the Choctaw Nation, October 19, 1884; *Indian Champion*, November 1, 1884.

48*Report Commissioner of Indian Affairs*, 1886, p. 155.

The claimants contended that intermarried citizenship was permanent, and could not be forfeited by marriage to a non-citizen after the death of the Choctaw spouse. A white man, for instance, claimed citizenship through his wife, the daughter of a white woman and a white man who had once been married to a Choctaw wife.[49] The Department of Justice eventually sustained the Choctaw law.[50]

The claimants also denied the principle that Choctaw blood did not of itself confer citizenship. The most persistent were the members of the Glenn-Tucker family, descended from a woman born in 1760, alleged to be half Choctaw. She had left the Nation in her infancy and neither she nor any of her descendants had ever been enrolled or recognized as members of the tribe. They had been living in various parts of Arkansas, Texas, Louisiana, Mississippi, and California, but for some years they had been collecting in the Nation demanding citizenship, and 236 who had been rejected by the Council now appeared before the agent.[51]

Owen decided against their claims, and they appealed to the Department. The Secretary of the Interior upon the advice of the Attorney General also decided adversely, and in 1890 ordered their removal as intruders. But they managed to have the case reopened, and the General Council appropriated $5,000 to fight them. By this time they numbered about five hundred.[52] In 1895 the Secretary of the Interior again rejected their claims and ordered their removal. Chief Gardner then served notice that such as had not left the Nation by January 31, 1896, would be reported as intruders.[53] This ended a troublesome contest that had involved the Nation in eleven years of litigation.

The Choctaws were strongly opposed to any grant of United States citizenship that would break down their tribal jurisdiction. As early as 1877, with the Chickasaws, they protested against such a bill before the United States Senate on the ground that if dual citizenship were permitted it would create a large class of people in their country not subject to the jurisdiction of their laws.[54]

[49]*Ibid.*, 1887, p. 114.

[50]Indian Office Library, *Misc. Docs.* XXV, 21841, A. H. Garland to Secretary of Interior, March 1, 1888.

[51]Indian Office Files, Union, 1880, T65; *Indian Champion*, November 1, 1884, "Notes from the Council"; *Report Commissioner of Indian Affairs*, 1887, p. 114.

[52]*Indian Citizen*, July 12, 1890, "Our Washington Letter"; *Report Commissioner of Indian Affairs*, 1890, p. 103; 1891, I, 251; Acts of the Choctaw Nation, April 9, 1891.

[53]*Indian Citizen*, March 28, December 12, 1895; January 23, 1896.

[54]*Senate Misc. Docs.*, 45 Cong., 2 Sess., No. 8.

Congress finally passed such a law as a part of the Organic Act of 1890 creating a territorial government for Oklahoma. It provided that Indians might apply to the newly created Federal Court of the Indian Territory for United States citizenship without forfeiting any of their tribal rights or privileges.[55]

The Choctaws were greatly aroused over this attempt to undermine their government, and strong efforts were made to prevent their citizens from taking the oath of allegiance to the United States.[56] When the Council met, a law was passed disqualifying such apostates from voting, holding office, or serving on the jury.[57] The United States had expected that large numbers would apply for citizenship, but almost the only applications came from a few who had violated Choctaw law and wished to escape the jurisdiction of the tribal courts.[58]

This law did have the effect of creating a court for citizenship claimants. These people had formerly been outside the protection of any law; they could not sue in Choctaw courts because they were not recognized by the Choctaw government, and they were not willing to apply to United States courts because such action would be an admission that they were not citizens of the Choctaw Nation. Now they could take out United States citizenship without imperiling their claims, and enjoy the protection of United States law.[59]

United States citizens living in the Nation enjoyed extra-territorial privileges. By the Treaty of 1866 the Choctaws had consented to the establishment of Federal courts within their country so long as they did not interfere with the tribal judiciary,[60] but Congress was very slow in providing them.

At first there was no court with civil jurisdiction. In business transactions in which one or both parties were United States citizens there was no legal method of enforcing the payment of debts or the fulfilment of contracts. It was unsafe for wholesale dealers to extend credit to Indian Territory merchants, because there was no possibility of collecting payment from the dishonest. People from the "States" who

[55]Report Commissioner of Indian Affairs, 1890, p. 384, text of law, enacted May 2, 1890.

[56]Indian Citizen, August 9, 1890.

[57]Acts of the Choctaw Nation, October 25, 1890.

[58]Indian Citizen, September 19, 1895, "Important Decision," statement by Judge Parker; Report Commissioner of Indian Affairs, 1890, p. 103, Edmund McCurtain to Agent Bennett, August 25, 1890.

[59]Report Commissioner of Indian Affairs, 1894, p. 142.

[60]Kappler, Laws and Treaties, II, 922, Art. 8.

wished to defraud their creditors often took refuge in the Indian Territory, but in this case there was some slight redress, for the Indian agent was likely to convey the defaulter with his property to the border, and thus place him again within civil jurisdiction.[61]

Criminal cases involving a United States citizen were under the jurisdiction of the Federal court for the Western District of Arkansas at Fort Smith. Judge Isaac C. Parker, who presided over this court from 1875 to 1896, established an unusual record as a firm dispenser of justice.[62]

The location of this court was very inconvenient for the Choctaws. Part of the time there were no United States commissioners in the Indian Territory and preliminary examinations had to be held at Fort Smith. Moreover, the docket was so crowded that the trial was often postponed for a year. A witness summoned from the southern part of the Choctaw Nation was often obliged to make three or four trips on horseback covering a total distance of more than a thousand miles. The people preferred to suffer almost any crime without complaint rather than be subjected to the penalty of bearing testimony. In 1885 the Choctaw government requested the United States to establish courts for the southern part of their Nation at Denison and Paris, Texas, but no immediate action was taken.[63]

Arrests were usually made by United States marshals who traveled over the Territory collecting prisoners, whom they conveyed in a wagon by day and guarded in a tent at night. The Indian police also arrested criminals and turned them over to the marshals. Minor offenders were disregarded, and arrests were seldom made even for serious crimes except where the guilt was evident. The prisoner often traveled thirty or forty days in the custody of the marshal before he arrived at Fort Smith, where he was sometimes confined for a year before his case came up for trial. The jail was a place of horror beyond description, with the prisoners all huddled together in two filthy underground rooms and given food reeking with vermin. A decent jail was built in 1887 but it was always overcrowded.[64]

In 1886 a United States commissioner was located at Muskogee in

[61]Report Commissioner of Indian Affairs, 1877, pp. 107-8; 1885, p. 106; 1886, p. 157.

[62]Ibid., 1885, p. 106; 1886, p. 156; 1887, p. 115.

[63]Ibid., 1877, p. 108; 1886, p. 157; Report Senate Committee on Indian Affairs, VIII, xxii, IX, 215, 222-23.

[64]S. W. Harmon, Hell on the Border (Fort Smith, 1898), pp. 24-25; Report Senate Committee on Indian Affairs, VIII, xxiii; IX, 214-15.

the Creek Nation, but the office was soon abolished.[65] In 1889 the southern and western part of the Choctaw Nation was taken from the jurisdiction of the Fort Smith court and placed, so far as major criminal cases were concerned, under the Federal court for the Eastern District of Texas, sitting at Paris. The same act established a Federal court at Muskogee with jurisdiction over minor criminal cases and civil suits involving more than one hundred dollars. For the first time United States citizens in the Choctaw Nation were under civil jurisdiction. The new court was immediately deluged with lawsuits, and Agent Bennett pronounced it a decided success in substituting a legal remedy for the former custom of "shooting out" private differences.[66] The Choctaws, however, resented the establishment of a Federal court within the Indian Territory.[67]

The following year the Organic Act of Oklahoma created three divisions of this court. The Choctaw Nation constituted the second division with court sitting at South McAlester. The law provided for the appointment of not more than three commissioners for each division, who should conduct preliminary examinations and have justice-of-the-peace authority in cases involving less than one hundred dollars, with provision for appeal to the higher court. It will be remembered that this law sought to remove Indians from tribal control by granting them the opportunity to acquire United States citizenship, but it specifically reaffirmed the exclusive jurisdiction of the tribal courts where United States citizens were not involved.[68]

The United States next planned to extend the jurisdiction of this court to include the criminal cases then under the jurisdiction of the Federal courts at Fort Smith and Paris. An attempt was made to secure an expression from the Choctaw people at a public meeting called by the Chief at Tuskahoma, during a special session of the Council. The sentiment of the meeting was overwhelmingly opposed to the change, and the Council passed a resolution against the multiplication of Federal courts in the Indian Territory and the extension of their authority, on the ground that since the criminals were United States citizens they should be removed and tried among their own people.[69]

[65]Report Commissioner of Indian Affairs, 1886, p. 157; 1888, p. 136.
[66]Ibid., 1889, pp. 203, 442-45.
[67]Acts of the Choctaw Nation, December 20, 1889.
[68]Report Commissioner of Indian Affairs, 1890, pp. 380-84, text of law, adopted May 2, 1890.
[69]Indian Citizen, December 12, 1891; Acts of the Choctaw Nation, December 5, 1891.

The Indian agents, however, believed the Indian Territory court should have full jurisdiction. They said that conflicting opinions of the Federal courts at Fort Smith and Paris and Muskogee often worked injury and hindered law enforcement, and that people on trial in the border towns encountered a certain amount of suspicion and prejudice.[70]

Such legislation was enacted in 1895. Three judicial districts were created in the Indian Territory, of which the Choctaw Nation comprised the Central District with court meeting at South McAlester, Atoka, Antlers, and Cameron. These courts were given original jurisdiction over all cases involving United States citizens, and the three judges together constituted a court of appeal sitting at South McAlester.[71]

Soon after this the Choctaws entered into the negotiations with the United States that terminated their national existence, and their courts were restricted in authority and eventually abolished. This was the end of the Choctaw system of jurisprudence that had grown in less than a century from the first rudimentary conceptions of public justice to a highly developed and distinctive legal code.

During all the time that United States citizens and Choctaws were living side by side under separate systems of law there were constant conflicts of jurisdiction that increased with the growing power of the Federal courts and ended only with the abolition of the tribal judiciary. United States citizens while peddling whiskey or resisting arrest, were sometimes killed by Choctaw enforcement officers, and the Council thereupon found it necessary to appropriate money to enable their sheriffs or lighthorsemen to defend themselves against murder charges in Federal courts.[72] The Council also offered rewards for the arrest and delivery to the Federal court of white criminals who had murdered Choctaw peace officers.[73] Sometimes cases in which all the parties were Choctaw citizens would be brought before the United States courts, and the Nation would protest to the Indian Office or employ counsel to defend its jurisdiction.[74] Occasionally the Nation interested itself in a citizen whose sentence imposed by a Federal court seemed too se-

[70]*Report Commissioner of Indian Affairs*, 1888, pp. 135-36; 1892, p. 249; 1893, pp. 149-50.

[71]*Ibid.*, 1895, pp. 445-50; 1896, p. 151.

[72]Acts of the Choctaw Nation, October 20, October 26, 1877; November 2, 1886; October 13, November 6, 1888; November 8, 1889.

[73]*Ibid.*, October 20, 1881.

[74]*Ibid.*, November 4, 1882; November 10, 14, 1889; *Indian Citizen*, June 28, 1890.

vere, and assisted him to secure a pardon from the President.[75] The Choctaws usually won these cases, but the conflicts were inconvenient. As soon as the court was established at Muskogee with civil jurisdiction, the conflicts increased. When sheriffs of the Nation "spilled" liquor owned by non-citizens or sold the houses of intruders, they were subjected to suits for damages.[76] The Nation eventually won the right to sell buildings illegally erected by non-citizens, but only after expensive litigation.[77] A resolution of the Council, adopted soon after this court was established, is representative of Choctaw feeling — "said Court hesitates not to exceed its legitimate authority and jurisdiction, and continues its encroachments on Choctaw rights with a confident assurance that Congress will relieve it of its embarrassment to the extent of its assumption: and . . . . said Court has congregated around it a class of persons whose sole object is to manufacture litigatioñ and multiply its causes."[78]

During this whole period a third system of jurisdiction was represented by the authority of the Indian agent. Before any federal civil jurisdiction was established, disputes involving United States citizens were often arbitrated by the agent under a voluntary agreement of both parties. In some of these cases important interests were at stake; one instance is given in which store privileges in connection with the Lehigh coal mines were involved, amounting to $75,000. Attention has already been given to the complicated disputes between the Choctaw Nation and the Missouri, Kansas, and Texas Railroad, which were settled by the agent, and the contested citizenship cases, which were referred to the same tribunal. An appeal was always allowed from the agent's decision to the Commissioner of Indian Affairs.[79]

In addition to his quasi-judicial duties the agent also had a great deal of police power. At first he had to send to Fort Smith for a United States marshal to carry out his orders, but in 1878 a force of Indian police was created to serve under his direction.[80] These men were citizens of the Indian nations, and were selected by the agent on the basis

[75]Acts of the Choctaw Nation, November 5, 1884; April 8, 1891; *Branding Iron,* March 15, 1884; *Indian Champion,* February 7, 1885. This was the case of a Choctaw who killed a white man in self defense and was given a prison sentence by Judge Parker. He was pardoned by the President at the request of the Council.

[76]Acts of the Choctaw Nation, November 14, 1889; October 30, November 8, 1895.

[77]*Ibid.,* October 30, 1895; *Indian Citizen,* October 18, October 25, 1894; May 30, June 6, 1895.

[78]Acts of the Choctaw Nation, December 20, 1889.

[79]*Report Commissioner of Indian Affairs,* 1880, p. 94; 1888, p. 135; 1892, p. 248.

[80]Indian Office Files, Choctaw, 1873, P112; *ibid.,* Union, 1880, T1385, T1463.

188

Courtesy Oklahoma Historical Society

Courtesy Oklahoma Historical Society

Thompson McKinney, Principal Chief, 1886–88

WILSON JONES, PRINCIPAL CHIEF, 1890–94

of local recommendation. They were a hard-riding, straight-shooting, resourceful group of men who rendered invaluable service in keeping order in the Indian country. Usually about nine of them were assigned to the Choctaw Nation.[81]

The Indian police were completely under the orders of the agent. They occasionally assisted in the enforcement of tribal laws as they did in the riot of 1892, but they dealt mainly with United States citizens. They arrested criminals, whom they turned over to the United States marshals, and removed the intruders who had been reported to the agent by the Principal Chief. They arrested fugitives from justice and turned them over to the officers of neighboring states when the governors made requisition upon the agent, as they sometimes did, instead of upon the Principal Chief. Above all they tried to carry out the Federal laws against introducing liquor into the Indian country. They were paid a salary ranging from five to fifteen dollars a month by the United States, and received additional payments from the Choctaw Nation for special services in removing intruders and for their presence at the Council on certain occasions when a disturbance was anticipated.[82]

The Indian police experienced great difficulty in keeping liquor out of the Nation, especially after the coming of the Missouri, Kansas, and Texas Railroad. Certain wholesale merchants of St. Louis disguised shipments of liquor in almost every package. The officials of the Pacific Express Company, which operated along the railroad, at first questioned the right of the Indian police to inspect their shipments; but when the Indian agent convinced them of his authority they coöperated loyally and ordered their agents in the states not to accept liquor shipments to points in the Indian Territory. As a result the introduction of liquor through express shipments almost ceased. The same coöperative spirit was not shown by the officials of the Missouri, Kansas, and Texas Railroad. Upon advice from their legal representatives they shipped in whiskey as freight, and instructed their station agents to resist inspection.[83]

A great increase of drunkenness arose in the Nineties from the manufacture and sale of the so-called "Choctaw beer," a synthetic drink

[81]*Report Commissioner of Indian Affairs*, 1887, pp. xxxvi-xxxvii; *Report Senate Committee on Indian Affairs*, IX, p. 212.

[82]*Report Commissioner of Indian Affairs*, 1897, p. 531; *Report Senate Committee on Indian Affairs*, IX, pp. 211-23; Acts of the Choctaw Nation, November 9, 1895; November 4, 1896; *Indian Citizen*, October 15, 1896.

[83]*Report Commissioner of Indian Affairs*, 1889, p. 210; 1890, pp. 92-93; 1891, p. 249.

made of barley, hops, tobacco, fishberries, and a small amount of alcohol, which was sold principally in the mining towns. The Choctaw prohibitory law was strengthened in 1886 to include this new beverage,[84] and for a time the United States agent interpreted the Federal laws to exclude it as well as distilled liquor.[85] But in 1891 Judge Bryant of the Federal court at Paris ruled that it was not illegal to ship malt liquor into the Indian country. The result was the immediate opening of beer saloons in his district, which included the southern and western part of the Choctaw Nation. Agent Bennett under his authority to regulate trading in the Indian country ordered his police to close the saloons, seize the intoxicants, and put the dealers out of the country, but when they placed the property in the custody of the United States marshal none of it was libeled and nobody was convicted. Breweries were established, saloons were operated openly, and drunkenness became so prevalent that it was reported by Agent Bennett to be unsafe for a woman to walk on the streets. Judge Parker ruled that the sale of beer was illegal, and his decision enabled the police to restrict the traffic within his jurisdiction, which, however, did not include the larger towns or the mining camps. The Choctaw enforcement officers were helpless, because the sales were carried on by United States citizens; some of them did "spill" stocks of the liquor at Lehigh and Coalgate, and suit was immediately brought against them by the owners in the new Federal court at Muskogee.[86]

In 1892 Congress attempted to remedy the situation by amending the law to prohibit the introduction of ardent spirits, ale, beer, wine, or intoxicating liquors of any kind.[87] This closed the saloons until somebody discovered that the prohibition against the "introduction" of intoxicating liquor did not extend to its manufacture or sale. The saloons then reopened and carried on a flourishing business, especially in Coalgate, Lehigh, Alderson, Hartshorne, and Krebs, where thousands of miners were employed. Women, especially, were engaged in the manufacture, a circumstance that the agent found very embarrassing in his attempts at enforcement. Clifford L. Jackson, United States attorney for the Federal court at Muskogee, refused to prosecute the

[84]Acts of the Choctaw Nation, October 18, 1886.
[85]*Indian Citizen,* July 6, July 13, 1889.
[86]*Report Commissioner of Indian Affairs,* 1891, pp. 248-49; 1892, pp. 258-60; *Indian Citizen,* May 12, June 2, 1892; Acts of the Choctaw Nation, November 8, 1895.
[87]*Report Commissioner of Indian Affairs,* 1892, p. 722, text of law, passed July 23, 1892.

liquor dealers, on the ground that the law against "introducing" did not apply.[88]

Congress then passed a law forbidding anyone to "manufacture, sell, give away, or in any manner, or by any means furnish to anyone, either for himself or another, any vinous, malt, or fermented drinks of any kind whatsoever, whether medicated or not, or who shall carry, or in any manner have carried, into said Territory any such liquors or drinks."[89] This law was sufficiently comprehensive, and the agent was able to close the saloons.

The Choctaw beer episode illustrates the confused administration of justice between tribal jurisdiction, the conflicting decisions of three federal courts, and the police power of the Indian agent.

It was partly because of this three-fold system of law enforcement that crime flourished in the Choctaw country. Although the bulk of the white population consisted of industrious and orderly people who adapted their business relations and social intercourse to the extra-legal situation in which they found themselves, and lived at peace with citizen and non-citizen, there was a large number of white criminals who made the country their rendezvous. The death sentences pronounced by Judge Parker during his twenty-one years of dispensing border justice reached the shocking total of 172, with eighty-eight actual executions; and sixty-five deputy marshals of his court were slain during the same period. Nearly all of the malefactors he sentenced were Indian Territory criminals, of which the Choctaw Nation because of its greater economic development and the consequent influx of white population contributed more than its proportion.[90]

Judge Parker always maintained that the Indians were law-abiding, and that the crime in their country was due largely to a class of criminal intruders who were fugitives from justice in the "States,"[91] but one is forced to admit that even Judge Parker was mistaken and that the amount of crime among the Choctaws themselves was abnormally high. An analysis of Judge Parker's own cases, though presenting numbers too small to be conclusive, is at least indicative of this condition. Of the eighty-eight criminals hanged at Fort Smith by his sentence, twenty-nine at least were executed for crimes committed in the Choctaw country. Of this number there were nine whites, nine Negroes,

[88]Ibid., 1894, p. 143; 1895, pp. 58-59.
[89]Ibid., 1895, pp. 448-49, text of law, enacted March 1, 1895.
[90]Harmon, Hell on the Border, pp. 84-89.
[91]Ibid., p. 412; Indian Citizen, March 15, 1894.

and eleven Indians, of which at least two were classed as fullbloods.[92] When one is reminded that all Indians were under tribal jurisdiction except where a United States citizen was involved, the comparison is all the more surprising. Moreover, the white population in the Choctaw country by the end of Judge Parker's régime outnumbered the Choctaws three to one.

It is impossible to convey an adequate picture of the frequency with which Choctaw murders were reported by contemporary newspapers. Some newspapers published few murder stories or any other local news, and others, notably the *Oklahoma Star,* exaggerated and capitalized the crime in the interest of their campaign for the abolition of tribal government, but such periodicals as the *Indian Champion* and the *Indian Citizen* recorded murders with an unconcern and frequency that is almost incredible. It was said by a somewhat hostile critic that in one year toward the close of the tribal government there were one hundred murders committed in the Choctaw Nation, and that in one cemetery there were thirty-one Indians and whites that had "died with their boots on."[93]

These murders seem in some cases to have been caused by obscure feuds, and in others simply by a wanton desire to kill. The defense in the case of Eli Lucas, a young fullblood Choctaw who was sentenced by Judge Parker for the murder of a half-witted Negro, is significant. He had boasted to friends that he had followed the Negro from a ball game and shot him, because he was staying at the home of an Indian in the community and becoming a pest. His defense was, that the story he had told his friends was not to be taken seriously; it was told "in a joking manner, often assumed by young fellows who wish to gain the reputation of being 'killers.' The defense also proved that the firing of guns was of frequent occurrence in the neighborhood, where the negro was killed; that during the day of the ball game, there were numerous shots fired, in the direction of where the dead body was afterwards found and that the killing was as likely to have been done by some other as by Lucus."[94]

There was also a great deal of horse and cattle stealing carried on by organized gangs. One formed during the Winter of 1872-1873 became so troublesome that Chief Bryant ordered one of the District

[92]Harmon, *Hell on the Border,* tables, pp. 158, 171-80, 312.
[93]Meserve, *The Dawes Commission,* p. 21.
[94]Harmon, *Hell on the Border,* pp. 179, 364; *see* also Carter, *McCurtain County and Southeast Oklahoma,* p. 132, and *Indian Citizen,* July 13, 1889, "Caddo Notes."

Chiefs to destroy it. About forty members of the gang were arrested, of whom fifteen were immediately tried and shot.[95] In 1884 a gang operating in San Bois County said to have a hundred members, committed so many depredations that Chief J. F. McCurtain called out the militia to assist the civil officers in making the arrests.[96] During the Nineties the Carpenter gang stole from small farmers and stockmen all along the Red River and the valleys of the Kiamichi, Little, Boggies and Blue and with the help of confederates, who were never suspected, operated well defined "Thief Runs" through the southern counties to the Washita River and then north to Kansas and New Mexico. This gang was finally hemmed in by United States deputy marshals on one of the Boggies and several of its members were killed, and the rest disbanded.[97]

It is impossible to say to what extent the Choctaws might have succeeded in the enforcement of their laws if it had not been for the presence of a large alien population. The commission of wanton crimes by people outside Choctaw jurisdiction, the wholesale flouting of tribal laws by intruders and liquor dealers, and the embarrassment to which their enforcement officers were often subjected by the United States courts may have weakened the influence of the law upon their own people. Whatever its cause lawlessness was so serious that it furnished one of the arguments for those who sought to destroy the tribal government.

[95]Indian Office Files, Choctaw, 1873, P112, monthly report of Agent Parsons, May 17, 1873.

[96]*Indian Champion,* June 21, 1884. *See* also any issue of the *Indian Champion* for advertising of the Protective and Detective Association of Dallas, which had a branch at Atoka.

[97]Carter, *McCurtain County and Southeast Oklahoma,* p. 89; *Indian Citizen,* August 22, 1895, ff.

RELATIONS WITH THE UNITED STATES

9

In the background of Choctaw control of government, courts, and finance, was the supervising authority of the United States. The relationship was that of a protectorate, and was based upon the complicated system of treaties, which the Choctaws learned to quote so fluently, modified by the sovereign authority which the United States was likely to exert in dealing with the weaker people. The main events in the relationship were: the collection of several long-standing claims against the United States; and the struggles by which the Choctaws averted for a generation the dissolution of their national government and the division of their tribal estate.

The Indian agent was the official representative of the United States in dealing with the Choctaws. The Treaty of Doak's Stand, by which they secured their lands in the West, established an agency in the new location; and later treaties confirmed the provision.[1] When the separation of the Choctaws and Chickasaws was effected, the two tribes were placed under the supervision of the same agent.[2] The agency during the post-war period was at New Boggy Depot until 1874, when the agencies for the Five Civilized Tribes were consolidated in the Union agent with headquarters at Muskogee in the Creek Nation.[3]

The Choctaws sometimes attempted to influence the government in the selection of the agent. The Treaty of Dancing Rabbit Creek had stated the principle that Choctaw opinion was entitled to respect in the matter of appointment and that the agent would be removed on

[1]Kappler, *Laws and Treaties*, II, 192, 213, 312-13, Treaties of 1820, 1825, 1830.
[2]*Ibid.*, II, 710, Art. 21, Treaty of 1855.
[3]*Report Commissioner of Indian Affairs*, 1874, p. 71.

petition of the Choctaws provided the President was satisfied with the cause shown.[4] In 1870, when a new agent was to be appointed, a resolution introduced by J. P. Folsom passed the House of Representatives requesting the United States to select a man "of temperate and strictly moral habits as well as having legal qualifications therefor" who had never served before as agent for the Choctaws and Chickasaws nor been employed in any capacity about the agency.[5] It has been pointed out in another connection that Chief Cole requested the removal of Marston for his unsympathetic attitude toward the permit tax. When Robert L. Owen, who was a citizen of the Cherokee Nation, was serving as agent, the Council passed a resolution characterizing his appointment as "a handsome recognition of the Indian Territory, a just appreciation of the advancement and progress of the five civilized tribes, and a precedent practical and worthy of continuance by the U. S. Government."[6] When Owen's removal was anticipated because of the Republican victory of 1888, the Council memorialized President-elect Harrison to appoint Dr. Leo E. Bennett, who had been on the editorial staff of the Muskogee *Phoenix*.[7] Whether this request carried any influence or not, Bennett received the appointment.

The agents usually supported measures of the Indian Office bitterly opposed by the Choctaws, such as the allotment of land, the extension of United States courts, and the development of a territorial government; but they were nearly always sympathetic toward the Indians, and tried to influence governmental policy in their behalf. The only conspicuous exception was Albert Parsons, the last tribal agent before the consolidation at Muskogee; he seemed to hate the Choctaws, and filled his reports with sarcastic references to the ulterior motives of "these noble red men," who preferred their own government to the beneficent rule of the United States.[8]

The Choctaws usually found it to their interest to maintain representatives at Washington. The Net Proceeds delegates appointed in 1853 attended to other tribal interests as long as they lived; after that, Campbell LeFlore and J. S. Standley served as delegates. They were expected to work against hostile legislation and to push Choctaw claims, and were paid by a percentage of the money they recovered.

[4]Kappler, *Laws and Treaties*, II, 312-13.
[5]Union Agency Files, Choctaw—Federal Relations.
[6]Acts of the Choctaw Nation, October 30, 1886.
[7]*Ibid.*, January 17, 1889; *Indian Citizen*, April 27, 1889.
[8]Indian Office Files, Choctaw, 1874, P100.

In addition to these standing delegations, special commissions were created for specific occasions and paid by the General Council.

The Choctaws found that it paid to be vigilant when supposedly permanent annuities were dropped out of the appropriation bill, or lands were sold to which they could claim title. In 1886 the Supreme Court awarded them $59,449.32 for annuities unpaid since the Civil War;[9] in the Eighties and Nineties they secured sums varying from $482.88 to $20,406.25 from the sale of land set aside in Mississippi for the benefit of their orphan children;[10] in 1890 they recovered $15,000 taken out of their orphan fund during the Civil War and diverted to the support of loyal Cherokee refugees;[11] and in 1893 they secured $3,000 for back annuities that had been omitted from the appropriation bills from 1886 to 1890.[12] But the most protracted and most complicated negotiations which the Choctaws conducted with the Federal Government were the claims arising out of the eastern boundary, the Leased District, and the Net Proceeds.

Because of the smaller value of the claim, the eastern boundary was the least important of the three. It will be remembered that the Choctaws had retroceded a large tract of their western land to the United States in 1825, when it was found to be already occupied by white settlers. The eastern boundary was at that time established on a line beginning on the Arkansas River one hundred paces east of old Fort Smith and running due south to the Red River.[13] When this boundary was surveyed, the Choctaws believed that the line was inaccurate and diverged to the west, thus depriving them of a triangular tract of territory on their eastern border. It will also be remembered that the Treaty of 1855 contained a provision for a new survey; and one was attempted the next year, but it was abandoned at the request of the Indian Office.[14] The Nation frequently instructed its delegates to push this claim,[15] and it was settled in 1886 by a decision of the Supreme Court of the United States which awarded the Choctaws $68,102.[16] The

[9]*U. S. Reports*, CXIX, 41.

[10]*Indian Champion*, April 26, May 3, May 10, May 17, 1884; Acts of the Choctaw Nation, January 26, 1894.

[11]*Indian Citizen*, August 2, 1890.

[12]*Ibid.*, April 11, 1891; Acts of the Choctaw Nation, April 9, 1891; October 19, 1893.

[13]Kappler, *Laws and Treaties*, II, 211-12, Art. 1, Treaty of 1825.

[14]*House Exec. Docs.*, 40 Cong., 2 Sess., No. 133; *Senate Reports*, 45 Cong., 3 Sess. No. 714, Vol. II.

[15]*Acts and Resolutions of the General Council*, 1858, p. 72; *ibid.*, 1860-61, pp. 92-93; Acts of the Choctaw Nation, February 3, 1874; November 11, 1881.

[16]*U. S. Reports*, CXIX, 41.

Chickasaws laid claim to one-fourth of this amount, which after protracted negotiation was paid to them by the Choctaws in 1905.[17]

A larger tract of land was involved in the controversy over the Leased District. It will be remembered that this tract lying west of the Chickasaw district was leased to the United States for the use of Indian tribes by the Treaty of 1855, and ceded by the Treaty of 1866. It was commonly understood by the Choctaws that it was ceded for the settlement of Indians and the colonization of freedmen; that purpose was generally expressed during the negotiations, and both the preliminary treaty of Fort Smith, and the draft treaty submitted to the Choctaw and Chickasaw delegates at the same time, stated that the settlement of Indians was the object of the cession. The Treaty of 1866, however, simply used the word "cede" with no statement of purpose.

The Federal Government established reservations in the Leased District for the Kiowas, Comanches, and Apaches in 1867, for the Wichitas and affiliated bands in 1868, and for the Cheyennes and Arapahoes in 1869. In 1869 Chief Bryant asked the Secretary of the Interior if it was still open to settlement by the Choctaws and Chickasaws as it had been under the Treaty of 1855. Commissioner Hayt replied that since, by the Treaty of 1866, the Choctaws and Chickasaws had ceded the lands for the use of other Indian tribes they had "ceded unconditionally said lands to the United States, and there is now no law which would authorize the citizens of either of the said Nations to settle within said 'Leased District.' "[18]

In 1885 the Federal Government decided that such of the lands ceded in 1866 as had not been utilized for the location of Indians should be thrown open to white settlement. By an act of March 1, 1889, Congress made an appropriation to pay the Creeks and Seminoles for their unassigned lands,[19] and, on the following day, authorized the President to appoint commissioners to negotiate with Indian Territory tribes owning lands west of the meridian of 96°.[20]

When the General Council met the following Fall, Chief Smallwood reported that A. M. Wilson, who was at the head of this commission, had expressed a desire to negotiate with the Choctaws; and he recommended the creation of a delegation for that purpose.[21] The Council then passed a law declaring willingness to conform to the

[17]Acts of the Choctaw Nation, October 28, 1903; November 16, 1905.
[18]Indian Office Files, Union, 1879, G279.
[19]*Report Commissioner of Indian Affairs*, 1889, pp. 438-41, text of law.
[20]*Ibid.*, 1889, p. 462.
[21]*Indian Citizen*, November 2, 1889, text of message, October 29, 1889.

needs of the United States to use the Leased District for a purpose different from the terms of the cession of 1866, and providing for the appointment of three commissioners to negotiate an absolute cession. Chickasaw coöperation was invited, and the commissioners were instructed "to actively and strenuously oppose and resist" any attempt to include the lands within the proposed Oklahoma Territory until the rights of the two tribes were secured. Each commissioner was to receive six dollars a day and a travel allowance of ten cents a mile.[22]

The Chief appointed Robert J. Ward, Henry C. Harris, and J. S. Standley to carry on the negotiations.[23] The Chickasaws also appointed a commission which came to Atoka to confer with the Choctaw commission.[24] In response to unofficial notification that the two nations were ready to treat, the Federal commissioners replied that the United States already owned the Leased District, but would negotiate with regard to the purchase of that portion of the Chickasaw Nation that lay between the Leased District and the ninety-sixth meridian.[25]

The Chief then called a special session of the Council, which met December 16 and drew up a memorial to the United States Government protesting against the failure of the United States to give the Choctaws and Chickasaws the same consideration as the other tribes in the purchase of the Oklahoma lands from the Creeks and Seminoles and the proposed purchase of the Outlet from the Cherokees.[26] The next day legislation was enacted renewing the authority of the commission and providing a contingent fee of 25 per cent instead of the salary provided by the previous law.[27]

The United States Government meanwhile had induced the Cheyennes and Arapahoes to accept allotments of one hundred and sixty acres for each citizen in their section of the Leased District, and prepared to throw the rest of the land open for white settlement. In 1891 the Choctaw-Chickasaw delegation secured an appropriation of $1.25 an acre, or $2,991,450, for their title to this land to be divided between the two tribes in the usual three to one ratio.[28]

Governor Jones then convened the Council on April 1, and legislation was enacted authorizing the officials of the Nation to make

[22]Acts of the Choctaw Nation, November 5, 1889.
[23]*Indian Citizen*, November 16, 1889.
[24]*Ibid.*, November 23, 1889.
[25]*Ibid.*, November 30, 1889, text of letter from United States Commissioners.
[26]*Ibid.*, December 28, 1889; Acts of the Choctaw Nation, December 17, December 23, 1889.
[27]Acts of the Choctaw Nation, December 24, 1889.
[28]Kappler, *Laws and Treaties*, I, 418, March 3, 1891.

requisition on the United States for the money and to sign the necessary papers for the release of the land.[29] It was provided that the delegation should receive their 25 per cent, that $25,000 should be deducted for the necessary expenses in procuring and distributing the money, and that the remainder should be paid out on a per caput basis to Choctaw citizens by blood.[30]

When, however, the representatives of the Nation appeared at Washington to make requisition for the money they were put off on various pretexts. At first they believed that the delay was due to a desire on the part of the government officials to show a balance in the treasury at the end of the fiscal year, and that payment would be made after June 30, but as time passed they began to realize that President Harrison and Secretary Noble were opposed to the payment.[31]

While the delegates waited at Washington with increasing impatience, the Indian Office was investigating charges against the Choctaws from two different sources. R. J. Ward, a member of the delegation created in 1889, signed a statement before Agent Bennett that he had given notes to five Choctaw Senators in the name of the delegation for amounts ranging from $2,500 to $15,000 to secure confirmation of the appointment.[32] A. D. Chase, an intermarried citizen who had acquired United States citizenship under the Federal court act of 1889, also came to Bennett complaining against the proposed distribution to citizens by blood only. Secretary Noble submitted this complaint to the President with a copy of the Choctaw law disfranchising their citizens who should take out United States citizenship, and advised that the payment be withheld.[33]

When the Council met in October, the belief was prevalent that the enormous fees to the delegates provided by the legislation of 1889 was the reason for Federal disapproval. A law was accordingly enacted canceling their contracts on the ground that they had failed in their mission and authorizing a new commission to receive the money and sign the conveyance;[34] but the National Attorney declared this law unconstitutional because it impaired the obligation of contracts, and

[29]Acts of the Choctaw Nation, April 9, April 13, 1891; *Indian Citizen*, April 11, 1891.
[30]Acts of the Choctaw Nation, April 10, April 11, 1891.
[31]*See Indian Citizen* through Summer of 1891.
[32]*Indian Citizen*, March 3, 1892, statement signed before Bennett, April 4, 1891.
[33]*Ibid.*, November 14, 1891, text of all the documents in the case.
[34]Acts of the Choctaw Nation, October 19, 1891.

because of a technical irregularity in its passage.[35] The new delegation however, proceeded to Washington where it was no more successful than its predecessor.

A special session of the Council then reaffirmed the claims of the old delegation, and created a new one with authority to employ attorneys at a 5 per cent contingent fee to institute suit against the United States.[36] Harris and Standley also made sworn statements that they had not known of the notes made out in their names to members of the Senate at the time of their appointment. Ward stated that he was the only one who took part in the transaction, and that the bribery was used only to secure his confirmation and not to influence the granting of the 25 per cent fee.[37]

The President then sent a message to Congress explaining his failure to carry out the appropriation. He said that he would have vetoed it at the time of its passage if he could have done so without obstructing other appropriations. He believed that Congress should protect the wards of the nation against the extortion represented by the 25 per cent fee, especially after Ward's confession of bribery of Choctaw Senators. He believed that the discrimination against other than citizens by blood in the Choctaw plan of distribution was unjust, especially to the freedmen. Finally he was convinced that the cession in 1866 had been absolute and that payment for the Cheyenne and Arapaho lands would set a precedent for other parts of the Leased District. The entire document revealed a vagueness regarding the treaties that presents a sharp contrast to the fluency with which the Choctaws were accustomed to quote them in all their controversies with the United States.[38]

J. S. Standley, the chairman of the first delegation, presented a very able memorial in answer to this message. He defended the excessive fees on the ground that at first only a very moderate salary had been provided for the delegation, and that the refusal of the United States commissioners to treat had made the ultimate payment so uncertain that the Nation could not finance the contest, especially in view of the fact that the Net Proceeds claims had run for fifty-eight years before settlement was finally made. He said that Ward's confession exoner-

[35]*Indian Citizen*, November 7, 1891, text of opinion, given October 30; Constitution, Art. II, Section 21.
[36]Acts of the Choctaw Nation, December 12, 1891.
[37]*Indian Citizen*, March 10, May 12, 1892. Standley was part owner of this newspaper, but the charges were made so publicly that it was compelled to publish the documents in the case.
[38]*Ibid.*, February 25, 1892, text of message.

ated the other members of the delegation, and that an entirely new Council had reaffirmed the contract in April and again in December of 1891. As to the argument that Congress should protect the Indians against extortion he replied that the loss of one-fourth of their money was not so serious as the policy that would deprive them of the entire amount. Regarding the exclusion of the freedmen he pointed out the undeniable fact that by the Treaty of 1866 and the act of adoption their rights were specifically limited to forty acres of the public domain in the event of allotment. As to the discrimination against white citizens, he quoted the opinion of Attorney-General W. H. H. Miller that Congress had appropriated the money to be paid over to the two nations and that the Secretary of the Interior had no authority over the distribution.[39]

When the Cheyenne and Arapaho lands were thrown open for white settlement, April 19, 1892, the matter was still pending. In May the Senate by a vote of forty-three to thirteen passed a resolution that "there is no sufficient reason for interference in the due execution" of the law making the appropriation to the Choctaws and Chickasaws,[40] and in December the House took similar action. Congress then passed a law, which was fully approved by the Choctaws, providing that $48,800 of the original appropriation should be converted back into the treasury to allow for 244 additional Cheyenne and Arapaho allotments. It was also provided that the payment should not be construed as a precedent obligating the United States to pay for the remainder of the Leased District.[41]

A special session of the Council was then called in February of 1893, which changed the instructions of the delegates to accord with the change in the amount of the appropriation to be requisitioned and the number of acres to be conveyed.[42] The releases were signed on February 23, but President Harrison, on the pretext that he had no time to examine them, went out of office without authorizing the payment.[43] President Cleveland approved the papers on May 24, and the money was paid to the Choctaw delegates on June 6.[44] It was this

[39]*Ibid.*, March 31-April 21, 1892, "Choctaws Memorial." *See ibid.*, April 21, April 28, for memorial by the new delegation.
[40]*Indian Citizen*, May 10, 1892. *See* also *Senate Exec. Docs.*, 51 Cong., 1 Sess., No. 78, and *Senate Reports*, 52 Cong., 1 Sess., No. 552.
[41]*Indian Citizen*, December 22, 1892; January 12, 1893; *U. S. Statutes at Large*, XXVII, 753; Kappler, *Laws and Treaties*, I, 504.
[42]*Indian Citizen*, February 16, 1893; Acts of the Choctaw Nation, February 17, 1893.
[43]*Indian Citizen*, March 2, March 9, 1893.
[44]*Ibid.*, June 1, June 6, 1893.

complicated negotiation that intensified the bitter feelings of the campaign of 1892, with the assassinations and riots that followed.

The Council met in June and provided additional machinery for distributing the money.[45] After the 25 per cent and 5 per cent fees and other expenses were subtracted each Choctaw by blood received $103. The payments began at Talihina in July, and continued during the Summer. A few claimants that were overlooked at that time received their share as late as 1906.[46]

The Choctaws and Chickasaws never received payment for the lands opened to white settlement in the remainder of the Leased District — a tract which comprised the surplus from the allotments of the Wichita and affiliated bands; the Kiowa, Comanche, and Apache lands; and Greer County, which was awarded to the United States by a Supreme Court decision defining the northern boundary of Texas. Their title to the Wichita reservation was referred to the Court of Claims, which decided in their favor in 1899; but the case was appealed to the Supreme Court, which ruled that the cession of 1866 had been absolute and that if the treaty had done the Indians an injustice the remedy lay with Congress.[47] The Choctaws then memorialized Congress not to "take advantage of the language in which the treaty was drafted, but, in the exercise of sovereign power, according to conscience, grant us justice."[48] When Congress failed to take action, the Choctaws authorized the Chief to employ counsel to present their claims, but by that time the acts of the Council were subject to Federal approval, and President Roosevelt vetoed the bill on the advice of Commissioner Leupp, who held that since the Supreme Court had passed on the case the claim should be abandoned.[49] The Choctaws, however, have continued their efforts to secure recognition of their title[50] in spite of the disapproval of the Indian Office. The difficulty of collecting the appropriation made in 1891 and the failure to secure payment for the rest

[45]Acts of the Choctaw Nation, June 29, July 1, 1893.
[46]*Indian Citizen*, July 27, 1893; Union Agency Files, Choctaw—Per Capita Payments; Acts of the Choctaw Nation, October 30, November 29, 1905.
[47]*Report Commissioner of Indian Affairs*, 1895, pp. 458-59; 1896, pp. 470-71; *House Reports*, 71 Cong., 2 Sess., No. 1693, pp. 16-17.
[48]Acts of the Choctaw Nation, January 7, 1901.
[49]*Ibid.*, November 22, 1905, vetoed December 20, 1905, Leupp to Secretary of Interior, December 13, 1905.
[50]*House Reports*, 71 Cong., 2 Sess., No. 1693; Chief Ben Dwight to Angie Debo, November 29, 1933.

of the Leased District furnishes the best justification for the size of the contingent fee voted to the delegates in 1889.[51]

The Net Proceeds claim was the subject of even more protracted negotiation with the Federal Government, and still more complicated tribal politics. It has been pointed out that in 1859 the United States Senate made an award of $2,981,247.30, of which $250,000 was paid upon the eve of the Civil War and an equal amount in bonds was confiscated when the Choctaws joined the Confederacy.

The original delegation appointed in 1853 to push this claim consisted of Peter P. Pitchlynn, Israel Folsom, Dixon W. Lewis, and Samuel Garland. It was they who negotiated the Treaty of 1855 referring the question to the United States Senate, and who secured the appropriation of 1861. They were to pay their own expenses, and to receive a contingent fee of 20 per cent.[52]

The delegates employed Albert Pike as attorney, with an additional fee of 25 per cent, but in 1855 they revoked this contract and employed John T. Cochrane for a 30 per cent fee. It was afterwards charged by National Attorney Sampson Folsom that the change had been made because of an agreement with Cochrane that he would give one-third of his fee to the delegates.[53] In 1866 the treaty delegation employed Latrobe, who was associated with Cochrane and Douglas H. Cooper, to negotiate the treaty, and Allen Wright who became Principal Chief shortly after was determined that Latrobe should handle the Net Proceeds matter also. It will be remembered that Pitchlynn as Principal Chief also entered into the negotiations with Latrobe and shared the treaty fee that was to be the occasion of so much scandal.

In the meantime, Cochrane had died, but he had willed his interest to Luke Lea. A quarrel then arose between the "old delegation," who wished to employ Lea, and Wright, who contended that the Nation was bound by the Latrobe contract and that the "old delegation" was pushing the Net Proceeds claim to the exclusion of others because of the personal interest involved in its recovery. Finally in May, 1867,

[51]Many documents bearing on this case have been collected in *Choctaws et al. vs. United States et al.*, Vols. I-VII, Phillips Collection, University of Oklahoma.

[52]*Acts and Resolutions of the General Council, 1852-1857 inc.*, pp. 54, 55, 56, November 9, 1853; *Court of Claims Reports*, LIV, 56; Kappler, *Laws and Treaties*, II, 707.

[53]*Senate Reports*, 49 Cong., 2 Sess., No. 1978; Acts of the Choctaw Nation, 1869, report of Sampson Folsom to Allen Wright, September 30, 1869; Folsom, *Digest of Choctaw Law*, pp. 592-93.

Wright revoked the commissions of Pitchlynn and Folsom, the most active members of the delegation.[54]

When the Council convened, Wright reported these matters and recommended a new delegation consisting of one member from the "old delegation," one from the treaty delegation, and one from the Nation at large, or else that the whole negotiation be entrusted to the Principal Chief.[55] It is evident that either one of these plans would have furnished Wright an opportunity to confirm the Latrobe contract.

A bitter fight then took place in the Council. The same party that had opposed the ratification of the treaty the previous year now opposed the Latrobe contract.[56] Finally a law was passed confirming the authority of the "old delegation" with the substitution of Peter Folsom's name for that of Lewis, who had died, and providing that no money should be paid to the delegates or their attorneys until investigation by the National Attorney and action by the Council.[57] Wright approved this bill, but he sent a message to the legislature stating that he regarded it as unconstitutional and had signed it only because his opinion was not sustained by the National Attorney.[58]

When the Council met a year later, Wright again recommended his plan for a new delegation. He said that the legislation of the previous Council providing for an audit was in effect a repudiation of former contracts, and had so impaired confidence in the national pledges that it had destroyed the influence of the attorneys.[59] A year later the Council did repeal this provision of the law.[60]

By 1870, Israel Folsom and Garland had died, leaving only Pitchlynn of the original delegation. He and Peter Folsom then employed James G. Blunt and Henry E. McKee. These new attorneys were to receive the 30 per cent contingent fee, and assume an obligation to Mrs. Cochrane of 5 per cent, and adjust the claims of all other parties

[54]Union Agency Files, Letters of Chiefs, pp. 30-39, 47-49, Wright to Pitchlynn and Folsom, Latrobe, and the Commissioner of Indian Affairs, and the counsel of the Cochrane estate.

[55]Ibid., pp. 66-72.

[56]Ibid., pp. 83-85, Wright to Latrobe, November 21, 1867.

[57]Folsom, Digest of Choctaw Law, pp. 592-93, enacted November 18, 1867; Union Agency Files, Choctaw—Federal Relations, opinion of National Attorney C. E. Nelson to Chief McKinney, July 25, 1887.

[58]Union Agency Files, Letters of Chiefs, p. 80, special message, November 18, 1867. Apparently his contention was based on the argument that the bill would curtail the appointing power of the executive. See ibid., pp. 81-82.

[59]Ibid., p. 115, message, October 7, 1868.

[60]Acts of the Choctaw Nation, October 26, 1869.

Courtesy Oklahoma Historical Society

EDMUND McCURTAIN, PRINCIPAL CHIEF, 1884–86

ISAAC GARVIN, PRINCIPAL CHIEF, 1878–80

who had rendered service in prosecuting the claim.[61] Latrobe protested to the Secretary of the Treasury against this arrangement, saying his appointment by the treaty delegation had been confirmed by the Chief and ratified by the Council, and that his contract had never been revoked so far as the recovery of the bonds was concerned.[62] He also informed Bryant, who was by that time Principal Chief, that Pitchlynn and others were scheming for the delivery of the bonds so that they might cheat the Nation out of the premium and accrued interest.[63] Bryant did not continue Wright's championship of Latrobe. He informed Pitchlynn and Folsom that they were the only authorized delegation, and that the act of the Council in ratifying the peace treaty did not constitute recognition of the Latrobe contract.[64]

While this controversy was in progress, Congress, on March 3, 1871, again provided for the delivery of the bonds. Latrobe and the Pitchlynn group both claimed the right to represent the Nation. Moreover, the assignees of a certain Lehman and Company brought suit in the Federal courts for the bonds on a requisition claimed to have been made by Pitchlynn and the Folsoms, April 27, 1861.[65] A special session of the Council thereupon repudiated the Latrobe contract, denied the rendering of any services by Lehman and Company, and acknowledged no attorneys' fees except under the Cochrane contract. Under an act passed in 1859, a court of claims was now created, consisting of one member from each district, which should pay out the money to individual claimants and audit the claims of delegates and attorneys.[66] This measure met with some opposition, on the ground that private claims were not sufficiently protected; and Agent Griffith was requested by numerous citizens to forward protests to the Indian Office and the Secretary of the Treasury against the delivery of the bonds on those terms.[67] At the next regular session of the Council a law was passed designating the National Treasurer as the proper person to receive

[61]Opinion of C. E. Nelson; Acts of the Choctaw Nation, February 25, 1888. Blunt and McKee were employed July 16, 1870.

[62]Union Agency Files, Letters of Chiefs, pp. 148-49, Latrobe to Secretary of Treasury, January 10, 1871.

[63]*Ibid.*, pp. 149-51, Latrobe to Bryant, January 30, 1871.

[64]*Ibid.*, pp. 138-39, Bryant to Pitchlynn and Folsom, March __, 1871. It will be remembered that the treaty was ratified by a resolution approving the report of the delegates. It was upon this action that Latrobe based his claim that the Council had approved the contract.

[65]*Vindicator*, August 24, 1872; Acts of the Choctaw Nation, October 30, 1872.

[66]Acts of the Choctaw Nation, March 18, 1872.

[67]Indian Office Files, Choctaw, 1872, G349, Griffith to the Commissioner of Indian Affairs, March 18, April 1, 1872.

the bonds.[68] Congress then voted to suspend the payment, and provided that the Secretary of the Treasury should investigate the liabilities of the Choctaw Nation to individuals and present a report showing how much money should be subtracted from the final settlement to satisfy these claims.[69] Secretary Bristow made a full report, Pitchlynn continued to besiege Congress with petitions, and many committees recommended settlement, but the matter was allowed to lapse.[70]

During 1873 the Choctaw Nation continued to pass laws for distributing the expected appropriation. A list of the claimants of 1830 was secured from the Indian Office, and the cost of collection was limited to the 30 per cent due under the Cochrane contract and the 20 per cent due the delegates.[71]

At a special session called in January of 1874 Chief Bryant advised the Council to investigate the validity of the Cochrane contract; he was inclined to believe that the death of Cochrane had relieved the Nation from any obligation except as to the service he had actually rendered, and there was a possibility also that the agreement had not been approved by the Chief and was therefore void.[72] A legislative committee, of which Coleman Cole was chairman, then reported a bill revoking this contract and all other contracts made by the Choctaw delegates with claim agents. This bill became law on February 3.[73]

Cole was elected as Chief the following Summer. He believed that the Nation should adjudicate all the claims, and that the United States Government should ignore the delegates and make the payments directly to the claimants. He sent frequent memorials to Congress, the President, and other Government officials, in his picturesque English, describing "Speculators Standing at the doors of Congress Stretching forth their hands crying and howling. and saying give me. the whole of that Indian money. for I am their king and ruler of the Nation. to receive their moneys." He explained that the contracts had been repudiated and that the whole sum could go directly to the claimants.[74]

[68]Acts of the Choctaw Nation, October 30, 1872.
[69]U. S. Statutes at Large, XVII, 462, February 14, 1873; ibid., XVIII, Part 3, 230, June 23, 1874.
[70]House Exec. Docs., 43 Cong., 2 Sess., No. 47, Bristow's report; House Misc. Docs., 42 Cong., 3 Sess., No. 94, February 13, 1873; House Misc. Docs., 44 Cong., 1 Sess., No. 40, and Senate Misc. Docs., 44 Cong., 1 Sess., No. 34, January 13, 1876; House Misc. Docs., 45 Cong., 1 Sess., No. 14, November 10, 1877; Senate Misc. Docs., 45 Cong., 2 Sess., No. 59, May 1, 1878.
[71]Acts of the Choctaw Nation, October 23, October 30, 1873; October 18, 1877.
[72]Indian Office Files, Choctaw, 1874, P94, message January 20, 1874.
[73]Acts of the Choctaw Nation, February 3, 1874.
[74]Indian Office Files, Choctaw, 1875, C1528, C1580, T917; 1876, C329.

Under Cole's vigorous leadership the individual claims were carefully adjudicated during 1875 and 1876. A court of claims for each district held sessions at convenient places and listed the claims under three heads: under *lost property* was live stock, sometimes in considerable numbers, left in Mississippi or lost on the journey, growing crops, and such household conveniences as iron pots; under *self-emigration* was a charge of $46.50 for each slave and member of the family, and twenty-five dollars for the rifle promised by the treaty to every Indian man; under *land* was a list copied from the roll made by the captains and their claimants in 1850 showing the members of the tribe electing to remain in Mississippi, who failed to receive their allotments through the hostility and neglect of Agent Ward.[75] As more than forty years had elapsed since the losses had occurred the heirs of the claimants had to be identified and listed.

When the courts had completed their findings, Cole notified President Grant that he was ready for the distribution; he sent complete copies of the lists with the request that a detachment of soldiers should be sent along as a guard when the money was paid out to the claimants. When this payment was not immediately forthcoming, the trusting old Chief addressed a perplexed letter to Commissioner Smith to inquire if President Grant had received the express package containing the list of claimants.[76]

All this time the Council had followed Cole's leadership, but his failure to secure the money seems to have impaired his influence with the legislators. It was at the next session that they refused to extend the authority of his courts of claims, approved Pitchlynn's report, and brought articles of impeachment against the Chief.[77]

Pitchlynn now became convinced that Congress would never take action. Fourteen committees had reported at various times, and every report had recommended immediate redress of the Choctaw grievances; but the prospect of settlement seemed more remote than ever.[78] Pitchlynn therefore appealed to Congress in 1878 asking that the case be

[75]Acts of the Choctaw Nation, March 4, March 8, November 1, 1876; *Vindicator,* July 31, 1875; August 2, 1876; Union Agency Files, Letters of Chiefs, p. 164, reports of commissioners of the courts of claims, Fall of 1875; Union Agency Files, lists of claims.

[76]Indian Office Files, Union, 1877, C631. The totals were as follows: Moshulatubbee District, $359,659.10; Apukshunnubbee District, $226,356.00; Pushmataha District, $313,548.80; Total, $899,563.90.

[77]*Supra,* pp. 164-65.

[78]For example of committee reports *see House Reports,* 45 Cong., 2 Sess., No. 251, and *House Reports,* 52 Cong., 2 Sess., No. 2544. The last mentioned report was made by I. C. Parker, who afterward became so famous as the dispenser of Federal justice at Fort Smith.

referred to the courts. He said that the Choctaws would prefer a Senate investigation to any other, but the experience of more than twenty years had convinced him that the Senate was too busy with lawmaking to give time to the investigation of claims.[79] Ex-Chief Cole wrote one of his characteristic letters to Commissioner Towbridge to protest against this action. He said the "pretended" delegates had no right to settle for individuals. He, for instance, had owned a farm in Mississippi, and the United States had sold it "from under my foot." It was natural then that the United States should pay *him*. He had never delegated his rights to Pitchlynn.[80]

In 1881 Pitchlynn secured legislation by Congress referring the case to the Court of Claims.[81] He died the same year, the last survivor of the original delegation, after devoting twenty-eight years of his life to prosecuting the claim.[82] Blunt also had died, and at the request of McKee, John B. Luce was chosen to assist in the suit, under a contract by which he was to receive 5 per cent of the original contingent fee.[83]

The Court of Claims awarded the Choctaws $408,120.32 for the delayed annuities, the eastern boundary, and the Net Proceeds. Both parties appealed to the Supreme Court, which in 1886 reversed the judgment, and confirmed the Senate award of 1859.[84]

Before the award was made, Peter Folsom also had died, and Campbell LeFlore was appointed as the Choctaw delegate.[85] LeFlore, at the request of McKee, asked Chief McKinney to secure an opinion as to the validity of the law of 1874 revoking the Cochrane contract. National Attorney C. E. Nelson pronounced it unconstitutional on the ground that it impaired the obligation of contracts.[86] LeFlore then advised the Council to instruct him to make requisition for the money; he drafted a resolution which he said "is a complete answer to Coleman Cole's old memorials which might otherwise be resurrected and used to our injury and delay as they were before." A fight took place in the Council, but the resolution in a changed form was finally adopted.[87]

[79]*Senate Misc. Docs.*, 45 Cong., 2 Sess., No. 59.
[80]Indian Office Files, Union, 1880, C610, April 6, 1880.
[81]*U. S. Statutes at Large*, XXI, 504, March 3, 1881.
[82]Acts of the Choctaw Nation, October 13, 1881.
[83]*Ibid.*, November 11, 1881; November 1, 1884; February 25, 1888; Union Agency Files, Choctaw—Attorneys, report of Luce to Peter Folsom, July 1, 1884.
[84]*U. S. Reports*, CXIX, 2, 41.
[85]*Court of Claims Reports*, LIV, 60-61; Acts of the Choctaw Nation, May 23, 1883.
[86]Nelson's opinion, July 25, 1887.
[87]Acts of the Choctaw Nation, November 10, 1887.

Congress made the appropriation in 1888. The sum was $2,731,-247.30, the amount of the Senate award of 1859 less the $250,000 paid in 1861. Interest was also to be paid for the time that had elapsed between the Supreme Court decision in 1886 and the date of the appropriation.[88] Before the appropriation was made, a called session of the Council met in February to make arrangements for receiving and disbursing the money. Edmund McCurtain was appointed as a special delegate to assist LeFlore, and the 20 per cent voted to the original delegation was to be placed in their hands for distribution. The 30 per cent due under the Cochrane contract was entrusted to McKee, with the exception of the 5 per cent voted to Luce. Provision was made for deducting from the shares of delegates and attorneys certain advances made from time to time, and the payments made from the sum distributed in 1861.[89]

McKee as the recipient of the attorneys' fees undertook to pay all claims under the Cochrane contract, but they had reached a state of almost inextricable confusion, and a complicated series of suits between various groups of attorneys was instituted in the Federal courts.[90] After Albert Pike died, his heirs brought suit against the Choctaw Nation in the Court of Claims for $200,000, and at the same time sought a Congressional appropriation of $100,000 for his services before the delegates entered into the agreement with Cochrane. The Nation compromised this claim in 1896 by a payment of $75,000, which it was hoped would secure friends for the recognition of the Leased District title.[91]

It was the duty of LeFlore and McCurtain, as the successors of the original delegation, to pay the heirs of the deceased delegates. These claims also were greatly complicated: advances and loans had been made by the Council from time to time which were to be deducted from the payment; they had received part of the appropriation made in 1861; and Pitchlynn, the most active delegate, had never satisfactorily accounted for part of the Nation's money placed in his hands in 1861, and had benefitted from the division of the Latrobe fee during the treaty negotiations. LeFlore and McCurtain evaluated these transactions, and divided the money among the claimants. They then rendered

<hr/>

[88]Kappler, *Laws and Treaties*, I, 285-86, June 30, 1888.

[89]Acts of the Choctaw Nation, February 25, 1888; Union Agency Files, Choctaw—Federal Relations, appointment of McCurtain.

[90]*Indian Citizen*, March 21, 1895.

[91]*Court of Claims*, XLV, 156-59; Acts of the Choctaw Nation, October 26, 1892; September 18, 1896.

their account to the Nation in the form of a published report showing how they had distributed this payment. They paid out $145,450.15 as the liabilities of the original delegation. They distributed $85,020 to sixteen persons, whose services were entered in the report under the euphemism, "on promises made at Tushkahoma"; Chief Smallwood received $5,500 of this sum as his reward for calling the special session of the Council to authorize distribution of the money without an audit by the Net Proceeds Commission, and all the other beneficiaries were men of almost equal prominence. They apportioned the rest of the money among the heirs of the delegates. The Pitchlynn heirs, who received $107,311.29, refused to receipt in full, and carried their claims to the United States Supreme Court, which in 1927 after an involved computation of the legitimate and illegitimate advances made to Pitchlynn awarded them $3,113.92. The Garland heirs, who received $43,-943.20, also refused to accept the settlement. They carried their claims to the Council, which in 1897 voted them $117,576.83, but the appropriation was vetoed by Chief Green McCurtain on the ground that the account had not been thoroughly investigated. They then brought suit in the Federal courts, and the Supreme Court on the same day that it made the Pitchlynn award decided that they were entitled to no further compensation.[92]

When it came to paying out the 50 per cent remaining after the fees has been subtracted, the Choctaws had occasion to be grateful to Coleman Cole. The simple-minded old Chief had shown no conception of the binding force of the obligations assumed by the Nation in employing counsel, and he had undervalued the services of the delegates and attorneys, but he had understood the importance of determining the amount of individual claims. When the appropriation was made, the Council created a commission which issued certificates to the claimants according to the findings of the court of claims he had set up in 1875 and 1876. Provision was made for examining any claims that had been overlooked, and in numerous cases it was necessary to determine the heirs of the claimants listed in the records; but the work had been done thoroughly, and the distribution was mainly a matter of routine.[93] Robert L. Owen was employed as the fiscal agent

[92]*Indian Citizen,* November 11, 1897; Union Agency Files, House Records of the Choctaw Nation, 1897, pp. 173-76; *Court of Claims Records,* LIV, 55-70; LIX, 768-813; *U. S. Reports,* CCLXXII, 728-31.

[93]*A Complete Roll of all Choctaw Claimants and their Heirs* (St. Louis, 1889). The notations opposite the names in this book indicate the pages in the original court of claims record from which they were copied. A copy of the book may be found in the Union Agency Files.

of the Nation; he was put under bond for a million dollars, and was authorized to make requisition on the United States treasury for the money to be distributed. Payment began at McAlester in March, 1889, and continued during the Summer and Fall.[94]

A special committee of the Council appointed to audit the books of the commission and the fiscal agent requested to be discharged on the ground that the records "are in such a state of inextricable confusion and irregularity: and . . . . the most important witnesses whom the Special Committee desired to use appear to have skipped the country: and . . . . it appears there are already certificates outstanding and unpaid by the Fiscal Agent sufficient to consume the balance reported on hand by the Fiscal Agent: and . . . . there are others who may be more competent to bring order out of chaos." The Council did not agree with this report except to the extent of relieving the committee; a resolution passed the same day commended Owen for the "accuracy and care exhibited in his accounting," reported a distribution of $1,436,000, and voted that a fee amounting to 3.5 per cent of his disbursements should be paid him from the balance in his possession, and that the remainder — a sum of $22,423.47 — should be turned over to the National Treasurer.[95] This balance with a slight reduction remained in the treasury until 1897, when a new commission was appointed to search out and pay all unpaid claims from the distribution of 1889.[96] With the exception of the Pitchlynn and Garland claims, which were not settled for thirty years, this ended the most famous case in the history of the Nation — a contest that had corrupted Choctaw politics for two generations, and brought strife to the grandchildren of those who had lost home and goods in 1830.

During the same period that the Choctaws were contending for the settlement of these claims they were engaged in a constant struggle with the United States to preserve their system of common ownership of land and the integrity of their tribal government.

It has been pointed out that the Treaty of 1866 contained optional provisions calculated to induce the Choctaws and Chickasaws to accept lands in severalty,[97] and a few of their leaders were at first inclined to favor the plan. A pamphlet circulated by Chief Pitchlynn and Governor Colbert of the Chickasaw Nation in the Summer of 1866 recom-

[94]Acts of the Choctaw Nation, November 6, 1888; January 18, October 14, 1889; *Indian Citizen*, March 9, March 30, May 4, 1889.
[95]Acts of the Choctaw Nation, November 2, December 24, 1889.
[96]*Ibid.*, April 2, 1894; November 10, 1897.
[97]Kappler, *Laws and Treaties*, II, 923-27, Arts. 11-33.

mended allotment on the ground that it was the system of common ownership that had put their lands in jeopardy as a result of the war.[98]

The Chickasaw legislature thereupon voted for allotment,[99] but when the Choctaw Council ratified the treaty, the decision of the allotment question, as has been pointed out, was postponed until it could be referred to the people. Since the Council had provided no machinery for a referendum, Chief Wright wrote to the District Chiefs the following June directing them to present the matter to their people who might then petition the Council to provide for the submission of the question to the voters.[100]

Wright brought up the matter in his annual message to the Council. He said he realized that bitter prejudice existed against allotment, but that in his opinion it was inevitable. Since the treaty provided that the land should be surveyed at Federal expense, he favored the acceptance of the offer. He believed that the American Republic was drifting rapidly toward anarchy or monarchy and that it would be the part of wisdom for the Choctaws to safeguard their landed interests before the change.[101] The Council, however, took no action regarding allotment, but authorized the National Attorney to go to Washington to delay the creation of a territorial government; the United States was to understand that the "habits and customs of Indian nation cannot be easily changed, whether for weal or woe, without their consent."[102]

When the Choctaws seemed satisfied to delay the allotment question indefinitely, Agent Olmstead made a strong effort to influence them in its favor; but the utmost he was able to accomplish was its submission to the voters, where it was overwhelmingly defeated at a special election held July 4-5, 1870.[103] The Federal Government then prepared to survey the Chickasaw district. Delegate Pitchlynn protested, but Secretary Cox decided that since the contracts had already been made with the surveyors the work should continue. He professed to be greatly surprised at the Choctaw opposition, saying that the Treaty of 1866 was certainly an authoritative expression of opinion on the part of the two nations, and that the survey was a free gift from the United

[98]Union Agency Files, Choctaw—Federal Relations.
[99]Indian Office Files, Choctaw, 1873, P310, November 9, 1866.
[100]Union Agency Files, Letters of Chiefs, pp. 45-46, letter dated June 17, 1867.
[101]*Ibid.*, pp. 53-63, message, October 8, 1867. Wright at this time often spoke of the probable downfall of the Federal Government.
[102]Folsom, *Digest of Choctaw Law*, pp. 594-95.
[103]*Report Commissioner of Indian Affairs*, 1870, p. 291; Indian Office Files, Choctaw, 1870, O107.

States.[104] The Council then protested to Governor Brown of the Chickasaw Nation on the grounds of the joint ownership of the tribal land, saying that the recent Choctaw election had shown such an overwhelming vote against the measure that if all the Chickasaws favored it they were still in the minority.[105]

The survey was begun during the Winter of 1870-1871, and continued until 1872. The only satisfaction that Pitchlynn received from the Federal Government in answer to his constant protests was the assurance that the question would be referred to the Attorney-General before the land should be actually allotted.[106] As soon as the survey was started, homeseekers began to inquire of the Indian Office as to how they could secure land: two men from Kansas asked to know when the lands would be open for settlement as "we see the surveyors ar at work South of Kansas"; another man from the same state had read that the Choctaw-Chickasaw lands were being surveyed and wanted "to Know all a Bought the way they ware to be Disposed of"; a man in Minnesota inquired if the Choctaw country was open for homestead entry "& if not please state when it will be."[107]

But in spite of the consent of the Chickasaws the Choctaws managed to thwart the purpose of the Federal Government to allot their lands. In 1872 the Chickasaw legislature requested the United States to proceed with the allotment, but Secretary Delano ruled that it could not be done in the absence of Choctaw consent. Commissioner Smith met a committee of the Council at Boggy Depot in the Fall of 1873 and tried to bully them into sectionalizing, but without result.[108]

The treaty plan of course did not contemplate the confiscation of the lands remaining after the allotments were made, but bills sponsored by the railroads were constantly introduced in Congress providing that the surplus lands should become part of the public domain of the United States. In 1872 Pitchlynn protested vigorously against such a bill.[109]

The establishment of a territorial government was so closely joined

[104]Union Agency Files, Choctaw—Federal Relations. This correspondence between Pitchlynn and Cox took place during August of 1870.

[105]Acts of the Choctaw Nation, October 14, 1870.

[106]Indian Office Files, Choctaw, 1871, L38, L54, L82, L163, P54.

[107]Ibid., Choctaw, 1871, B28, K4; 1873, B18.

[108]Indian Office Files, Choctaw, 1873, P310, P433; 1874, D276, P94, P167; Acts of the Choctaw Nation, October 11, 1873; February 3, November 3, 1874—see also copy of letter of Chief Bryant to William Robuck, July 22, 1873, in Acts of the Choctaw Nation; Vindicator, November 23, 1872.

[109]Senate Misc. Docs., 42 Cong., 2 Sess., No. 53, Vol. I.

with the allotment project not only in the desires of the Federal authorities but in the opposition of the Choctaws that the two questions can hardly be considered separately. As it has been pointed out, the creation of an Indian territory or state had long been contemplated by the United States, and the treaties of 1866 had provided for a council of the Indian Territory tribes which should legislate on matters of intertribal interest. The Federal Government undertook to pay the delegates, and the Superintendent of Indian Affairs was to act as presiding officer under the title of "Governor of Oklahoma."[110]

Although the Federal Government was especially interested in this plan of union,[111] the inter-tribal council was not convened until 1870. It met at Okmulgee, the capital of the Creek Nation, in the latter part of September. Neither the Choctaws nor Chickasaws attended this meeting, although Chief Wright sent a message that he had been unable to choose delegates in the absence of any legislation authorizing their selection. The council adjourned to meet in December, after adopting a resolution that since the machinery of union had been created by the treaties of 1866 all the signatories whether present or not were bound by its acts.[112]

This threat had the desired effect. Chief Bryant presented an invitation from the Okmulgee Council to the Choctaw legislature, and provision was made for the appointment of five delegates from each dis-

[110]Kappler, *Laws and Treaties*, II, 921-22, Art. 8. *Oklahoma* is a Choctaw expression meaning "Red People." It was in common use among the Choctaws. One of the leaders mentioned in the Treaty of Dancing Rabbit Creek was named Oaklahoma (Kappler, *Laws and Treaties*, II, 317), and one of the original Net Proceeds claimants was called Ok lah o mah (Union Agency Files, list prepared by the Indian Office, claimant No. 62). The Treaty of Dancing Rabbit Creek constantly referred to the Choctaws as "the Choctaw Nation of Red People," which would be "Oklahoma" in the Choctaw version. During the treaty negotiations in 1866 Allen Wright suggested the name for the proposed territory; he was a scholar who translated a number of books into the Choctaw language, and his mind had naturally been called to the name by his reading of the earlier treaties. From 1866 on, it was common in the Choctaw country to refer to the Indian Territory as Oklahoma (for instance, "Atoka is the best town in Oklahoma"— *Vindicator*, February 16, 1876), and all bills for establishing a territorial government were known as "Oklahoma bills." There was a store and postoffice called Oklahoma in San Bois County during the Eighties (Acts of the Choctaw Nation, October 12, 1883), but the name was changed after the founding of Oklahoma City. During the agitation for the opening of the "unassigned lands" ceded by the Creeks and Seminoles the name became restricted to that section, and thus became the name of the territory settled by homesteaders.

[111]*Report Commissioner of Indian Affairs*, 1866, pp. 9-10, 283-86; 1867, p. 317; 1868, pp. 276-79; 1869, pp. 8-9, 401-2.

[112]Union Agency Files, Choctaw—Foreign Relations, notification to Chief Wright from Agent Olmstead, September 17, 1870; *Chronicles of Oklahoma*, III (June, 1925), 42-43, journal of the Council.

trict. From the communications that passed between the Chief and the General Council it is evident that the reluctance of the Choctaws to participate in this inter-tribal action was due to their determination not to accept lands in severalty and their unwillingness to join in a union with the tribes that had adopted their freedmen.[113]

Among the Choctaw delegates were Coleman Cole, A. R. Durant, Campbell LeFlore, and Joseph P. Folsom. They entered actively into the proceedings of the Okmulgee Council, for they had decided that if its action would bind all the signatories to the treaties they could best safeguard the interests of their Nation by joining in the writing of a constitution defining its powers and procedure.[114] A constitution was adopted December 20. It provided for a General Assembly, elected by the different tribes according to population, which could legislate only upon matters of inter-tribal concern; a Governor elected by the whole people; and a system of courts having jurisdiction over cases of trade and intercourse between the various nations, and cases arising under acts of the General Assembly.[115] The Choctaws ratified it by a unanimous vote of both houses of the Council at the regular session in the Fall of 1871, but it never went into effect because it never received the approval of all the tribes.[116] The Okmulgee Council, however, continued for some years to meet annually under the provisions of the treaties.

An interesting view of the Choctaw attitude toward this inter-tribal project is revealed by Chief Bryant's instructions to the delegates shortly after the General Council had ratified the constitution. They were to confine themselves strictly to the subjects of legislation enumerated in the Treaty of 1866. If they were requested to take an oath of allegiance to the United States they were to refuse; the Chief suspected that such an oath would make the Choctaw freedmen citizens of the Nation, and he believed that the Negro question should be settled by a Choctaw-Chickasaw agreement without the advice of the tribes that had already adopted their freedmen. He expected the question of sectionalization to be taken up; in that case they were to confer with

[113]Union Agency Files, Choctaw—Foreign Relations; Acts of the Choctaw Nation, October 31, 1870.

[114]Union Agency Files, Letters of Chiefs, pp. 146-47, report of delegates to Chief Bryant, dated Okmulgee, December 20, 1870.

[115]This constitution may be found in *Chronicles of Oklahoma*, III, (September, 1925), 218-28, and the *Vindicator*, June 21, 1873.

[116]Acts of the Choctaw Nation, October 18, 1871. The Chickasaws rejected it overwhelmingly at a popular referendum; they especially opposed the proportionate representation in the Assembly. *Report Commissioner of Indian Affairs*, 1871, p. 571; 1872, p. 237.

the Chickasaw delegates and make a solemn protest against the sectionalizing of the Chickasaw district. If the question of drafting a constitution for a territorial government should arise, they were to invite the Chickasaws to join them and withdraw from the Council.[117]

The Chief, however, had nothing to fear from the attitude of the Okmulgee Council, for at the next meeting a resolution was unanimously adopted to memorialize President Grant against changing their governments and land tenure in favor of the railroads and other interests.[118] The next year an even more solemn protest was drawn up by a committee, of which Joseph P. Folsom was chairman, and adopted by the Okmulgee Council. It reviewed the Indians' titles to their lands as guaranteed by the treaties, and showed how the provisional grants in the railroad charters had created such powerful inducements to break them down. It pointed out the danger to the Indians if "the faith of the U. S. Govt. should prove weak enough to give way before these attacks," and closed with this appeal — "in full view of these above stated facts, and the fate of all Indians who have lost their lands and their homes,— of the pauperism, the degradation and ruin to our people which must follow such a disaster, [we] appeal to your sense of honor as our defense and only hope in this extremity, to repeal" the contingent grants to the railroads, and enact legislation to protect the Indian titles.[119]

In 1874 and 1875 the Okmulgee Council sent similar memorials to the Federal Government.[120] A few attempts were made to secure ratification of the constitution adopted in 1870 or to draw up a new one, but nothing was accomplished.[121] It must have been evident by this time that a united Indian state owning lands in severalty would never develop from the Okmulgee Council, and early in 1876 the executives of the various tribes were notified by the Indian Office that it would not convene again until further notice.[122] It had made no progress in the

[117]Union Agency Files, Letters of Chiefs, p. 135, November 23, 1871.

[118]*Journal of the Third Annual Session of the General Council of the Indian Territory* (Lawrence, Kansas, 1872).

[119]Acts of the Choctaw Nation, 1875. Also printed as *House Misc. Docs.,* 43 Cong., 1 Sess., No. 88. The Missouri, Kansas, and Texas was the only railroad operating under such a grant that crossed the Choctaw Nation; it was recognized as the north-south road of the treaties. The franchise for the east-west road was secured by the Atlantic and Pacific, which did not enter the Choctaw country.

[120]Acts of the Choctaw Nation, *loc. cit.; Vindicator,* September 18, 1875.

[121]*Vindicator,* June 21, 1873, "Okmulgee Constitution"; *Journal of the Adjourned Session of the Sixth Annual General Council of the Indian Territory* (Lawrence, Kansas, 1875), pp. 8-20, 29.

[122]*Vindicator,* April 26, 1876.

direction of the territorial government so greatly desired by the United States, but it had served as a convenient agency for voicing the protests of the Indians against the territorial bills sponsored by the railroads and landseekers.

Other protests against these "Oklahoma bills" were presented to Congress by the delegates of the various tribes at Washington. Pitchlynn, who represented the Choctaws, sometimes joined the others and sometimes presented memorials of his own.[123]

The Choctaw Council was also busy with memorials. The one adopted in 1875 is typical in its solemnity of expression and its able presentation of Choctaw rights under the treaties. It asserted that the Choctaw people formed a distinct political community with rights of self-government that could be destroyed only by superior force or by their voluntary consent. "Among the rights inuring to them as such are the right of self-government; the right to decide for themselves the character of government under which they wish to live; the right to determine the status of citizenship among themselves; the right to acquire lands, and to determine how they shall be held, used, and disposed of, none of which rights have ever been abridged by any of their treaties with the United States, and which as a free people they are bound to assert."[124]

The Choctaws were very anxious to make a favorable impression upon the Committee on Territories of the United States Senate, which planned to visit them in 1875. Chief Cole invited the committee to attend the meeting of the Council in October, and discover the sentiments of the people with regard to sectionalization and territorial government. "How much glad that I would be to Show you my people. My Sons and my Daughters. O how deplorable and harmless they are."[125] He was officially notified that the visitors would arrive during the middle of September and made his plans for a hospitable reception, but only the chairman of the committee came, late in November, and made a superficial inspection before hurrying back to Washington

[123]*Senate Misc. Docs.*, 41 Cong., 2 Sess., No. 143, May 23, 1870—this protest is plainly under Cherokee influence; *House Misc. Docs.*, 42 Cong., 2 Sess., No. 51, January 24, 1872, also under Cherokee influence; *Senate Misc. Docs.*, 42 Cong., 2 Sess., No. 53, Vol. I, Choctaw protest by Pitchlynn; Indian Office Files, 1878, P462, joint protest forwarded to the President by Pitchlynn, February 15, 1878; *House Misc. Docs.*, 46 Cong., 1 Sess., No. 13, joint protest, April 22, 1878, Vol. I; Indian Office Files, Union, 1880, A58, joint protest to Congress, January 21, 1880.

[124]Acts of the Choctaw Nation, October 29, 1875. *See* also *ibid.*, April 5, 1870; February 3, 1874.

[125]Union Agency Files, Choctaw—Federal Relations, letter dated July 5, 1875.

to be present at the opening of Congress. The Choctaws were acutely disappointed; they said that the visitor had interviewed only freedmen and white people and that the representatives of the Nation had been given no opportunity to be heard.[126]

In 1878 the United States Senate voted to investigate the expediency of territorial government; to find out if it were possible to allot the Indian lands without confirming the railroad grants; and to discover how much money the Indians had spent during the preceding five years in maintaining delegates at Washington to oppose territorial government, whether it came from the school fund, and, if so, what laws were necessary to prevent such misappropriation. When the Council met that Fall, Chief Garvin presented a very strong and able message against allotment. He said that only the tribal governments and common ownership of land had saved the Five Civilized Tribes from the ruin that had overtaken other Indians, and that no nation had greater cause to dread allotment than the Choctaws with their experience in Mississippi, and the wrongs that had since gone unredressed for more than a generation.[127] The Council then informed the Senate that $4,500 had been spent to pay the expenses of a special delegation that had been sent to Washington the previous year to urge settlement of the eastern boundary question and protest against territorial government, and that none of the money had been taken from the school fund; so far as the expediency of territorial government was concerned, the Council, speaking for the Nation, was unanimously opposed to it, and life and property was as safe under the jurisdiction of Choctaw courts as in either of the adjoining states; the matter of allotment had already been settled when the people overwhelmingly rejected the plan in 1870, and had never shown the slightest desire to reopen the question; and that the Senate should secure its information from the Choctaws and not from unauthorized and irresponsible people who were not citizens of the Nation.[128]

The following year the "Boomers" began to agitate for the opening of the lands ceded by the Creeks and Seminoles in 1866 and never assigned to other Indian tribes. Although President Hayes made a proclamation on April 26 against the attempts of "certain evil-disposed

[126]*Ibid.*, memorial to Congress by Chief Garvin, December 24, 1878.
[127]Union Agency Files, Letters of Chiefs, pp. 231-36, October 8, 1878.
[128]Acts of the Choctaw Nation, October 15, November 5, 1878; Union Agency Files, Choctaw—Federal Relations—these documents were printed as *Senate Misc. Docs.*, 45 Cong., 3 Sess., No. 52.

persons" who were trying to settle on Indian lands,[129] colonies of home-steaders gathered on the border and began to invade the Indian country.[130]

An attempt was made to carry on "Boomer" propaganda from Caddo, where the Ceded Land Colonization Society was organized during the Summer of 1879, with the declared purpose of securing an opinion from the Attorney-General as to whether the lands were open to homestead entry, and if so to induce the settlers to pass through Caddo on their way to the new land. The president was Israel W. Stone, a United States citizen who held three Federal appointments: postmaster, employee of the quartermaster's department, and commis-sioner of Judge Parker's court. He was also the owner of the Caddo *Free Press,* which published "Boomer" propaganda, under the editor-ship of one Neely Thompson. Chief Garvin complained of Stone's activities, with the result that he was suspended from his offices of quartermaster and postmaster at the request of the Secretary of the Interior, who also requested the War Department to remove him as an intruder. Stone became alarmed and explained that only one meet-ing of the society had been held before it voted to disband, and that before Garvin had complained he had discharged Thompson for the offending articles. He also forwarded a statement from Judge Parker, in which Parker commended him for his fearless administration of jus-tice, which had aroused enemies who were intriguing for his removal. He found a champion in Senator Ingalls of Kansas, whose sympathies he enlisted by showing that he was a good Republican who had sacri-ficed a leg in the war, and that his loyal Union sentiments made him offensive to the "rebel" Indians. The Interior Department still held him under suspicion, however, and Chief Garvin continued to request his removal; but after Garvin's death, Chief McCurtain wrote to the Com-missioner of Indian Affairs that since the real author of the offending articles had left the country, and since the society had ceased to exist, he was satisfied to drop the matter.[131]

The Choctaws also joined in inter-tribal action against the "Boom-ers." They took part in conferences which passed resolutions of grati-tude to the Federal Government in removing the invaders, and they

[129]James D. Richardson, *Messages and Papers of the Presidents* (Washington, 1898), VII, 548.

[130]For examples of "Boomer" literature *see* Library of Congress, MS division, *Official Papers Civil Service and Interior Department,* handbills, etc., from "Boomer" colonies in Kansas towns, Summer of 1879.

[131]Indian Office Files, Union, 1879, S1277, W2003, W2376, W2560; 1880, M1051.

appropriated $1,540 to assist in the prosecution of the "Boomer" agitator, David L. Payne, at Fort Smith.[132] When Congress began to contemplate the purchase of the Creek, Seminole, and Cherokee interests in the lands not occupied by Indian tribes, and to induce the western tribes to accept allotments, the Choctaws joined in meetings of protest.[133]

But in spite of their disapproval, the western half of the Indian country was opened for settlement and became the Territory of Oklahoma. The creation of this new frontier community upon their borders increased the pressure upon the Indian nations that culminated in the appointment of the Dawes Commission. By their remarkable ability as diplomats and constitutional lawyers the Choctaws had fought off for a generation the intrigues of the railroads, the greed of the settlers, and the benevolent intentions of the Federal Government, all of which sought to destroy their institutions; but during the Nineties the pressure became too strong, and the dissolution of their tribal government was in sight. But before taking up this phase of their history it is necessary to devote some time to the life and social institutions of the Choctaw Nation during the tribal period.

[132]Acts of the Choctaw Nation, October 15, November 4, November 5, 1880; Indian Office Files, Union, 1880, M781; Union Agency Files, Choctaw—Intruders.

[133]Acts of the Choctaw Nation, October 22, 1885; *Report Commissioner of Indian Affairs*, 1886, pp. 158-59; 1887, pp. iv-xiv, 116-18; 1888, pp. 124-27.

SOCIETY IN THE CHOCTAW
NATION

ANY attempt to understand the life of the Choctaw Nation during the period from the close of the Civil War to the end of the tribal government will have to take into account the fact that there were two distinct races occupying the country, meeting frequently in friendly intercourse, but almost completely separated as far as fundamental social institutions were concerned. The isolation that had enabled the Choctaws to develop an independent society in the generation before the Civil War was now broken down through white immigration until they were overwhelmingly outnumbered by an alien population.

Every few years the Choctaws instructed their sheriffs to take a careful census. The population was listed by name and classified according to age, sex, race (whether Indian, Negro, or white), and tenure of occupancy. Economic statistics were collected regarding the acreage of each crop, the yield an acre, and the numbers of live stock of all kinds.[1]

In 1860 a census of non-citizens showed only forty-six heads of families, mostly living in the vicinity of Doaksville. From the close of the Civil War on, the Choctaw population remained stationary at about 13,000. The census taken in 1867 placed the population of the Nation, exclusive of San Bois County, at 13,161 Choctaws, 1,732 Choctaw freedmen, and 249 freedmen from other nations and neighboring states.[2] The census taken in 1885, the year citizenship was granted to the freedmen, listed 12,816 Indians, 427 intermarried whites, and 38 Negroes, making a total of 13,281 citizens. These numbers seem fairly

[1] For a typical census law *see* Acts of the Choctaw Nation, November 6, 1884.
[2] Union Agency Files, Choctaw—Census.

accurate except that in 1885 the freedmen were evidently not all enumerated.[3]

No Federal census was taken in the Choctaw Nation until 1890. At that time J. M. Lane, the special census enumerator, was assisted by Peter J. Hudson, Jefferson Gardner, and other Choctaws, and every effort was made to allay the suspicion of the Indians who feared a new scheme to despoil them of their possessions. According to the findings of this commission the population consisted of 10,017 Choctaw Indians, 4,406 Negroes including Choctaw citizens and claimants to citizenship, and 28,345 whites including citizens and claimants. Lane believed the total was correct, but he admitted that it was very difficult in some cases to distinguish between Indians and whites, and that he probably listed some people in the wrong column. This census also listed 1,040 Indians of other tribes living in the Nation, and 1,017 Choctaw citizens — 760 Indians, 230 white citizens, and 27 Choctaw freedmen — living in the Chickasaw district. The Choctaws, according to these figures, constituted only about one-fourth of the population of their Nation, a smaller proportion than that of any other Indian tribe except the Chickasaws, who made up only 9 per cent of the inhabitants of their country.[4] The white immigration increased even more rapidly after 1890.

The presence of the whites and the economic development which they carried on was responsible for the growth of towns. The Choctaws were essentially an agricultural people, and their towns had consisted of a blacksmith shop, a store and possibly a postoffice, and two or three residences. The stores were usually owned by Choctaws, but some belonged to intermarried citizens or licensed traders. The goods was freighted by oxen or mules from Texas or Arkansas. Considerable business was carried on — for besides the emigrant trains and stages that passed through the country on the Texas and California highways the Choctaws themselves had needs similar to those of other frontier people of their day — but there was a complete absence of civic spirit. Such towns continued to exist in places remote from the railroads during the whole tribal period.[5]

The coming of the railroads and the consequent development of

[3]*Extra Census Bulletin*, p. 56.

[4]*Ibid.*, pp. 3-5; *Indian Citizen*, July 26, 1890.

[5]*Atoka Independent*, July 27, 1877, description of Little Boggy, before the coming of the railroad; J. Y. Bryce, "Some Notes of Interest Concerning Early Day Operations in Indian Territory by the Methodist Church South," *Chronicles of Oklahoma*, IV (September, 1926), 233-41, description of Stringtown; Carter, *McCurtain County and Southeast Oklahoma*, pp. 121, 125, description of towns in that region; *Vindicator*, 1872, advertisements of goods sold at New Boggy.

222

the mines caused towns to spring up which were essentially alien in population and culture. Atoka, which grew up at the site of Little Boggy, on the Missouri, Kansas, and Texas, became the social and educational center of this non-citizen life. The "Twin Cities" of McAlester and Krebs were thriving business centers populated mostly by miners. Lehigh, though smaller than the "Twin Cities," was the business center of the mining area to the southwest, and Alderson, Savanna, Hartshorne, and Coalgate were mining camps. South McAlester,[6] the headquarters of the Choctaw Coal and Railway Company, was becoming an industrial center with the railroad roundhouse and a planing mill. Caddo, the largest agricultural town of the Nation, shipped much cotton from the rich lands of the Red River region. South Canadian, with its three cotton gins was the center of the farming section of the north. The population of the towns as given in the census of 1890 was as follows: McAlester and Krebs, 3,000 each; Caddo, 2,170; Lehigh, 1,600; Hartshorne, 939; Coalgate, 818; and Atoka, 800. The twenty postoffices named in the *Vindicator* in 1875 had increased to seventy-three by 1890.[7]

The volume of business carried on by these towns was far greater than would be indicated by their population and appearance, for permanent growth was discouraged by the extra-legal status of the white residents of the Choctaw country. The buildings were erected upon land to which it was impossible to secure title. The taxes went to the support of the Choctaw government and schools. There was no provision for incorporation; consequently, there was no paving, no city water and sewers, no police and fire protection. The people of Krebs and Lehigh petitioned Agent Owen in 1888 for the right to incorporate, but when the question was referred to Chief Smallwood he refused his permission.[8] In several of the towns, however, a sort of unofficial government was formed, backed only by public opinion; an informal organization of the leading residents functioned as a regular municipality through its standing committees on such subjects as finance, streets, and sanitation.[9]

[6]In 1907 the names of South McAlester and McAlester were changed to McAlester and North McAlester respectively.

[7]*Vindicator*, March 27, 1875; *Atoka Independent*, July 27, 1877; O'Beirne, *Leaders and Leading Men*, I, 167-68; *Extra Census Bulletin*, pp. 10, 60; R. J. Hinton, "The Indian Territory, its Status, Development, and Future," *American Review of Reviews*, XXIII (April, 1901), 455.

[8]*Report Commissioner of Indian Affairs*, 1888, pp. 128, 135; *Indian Citizen*, August 3, 1889; June 7, 1890.

[9]*Indian Citizen*, June 7, 1890, proceedings of the Lehigh Board of Control; *ibid.*, February 24, 1898, "Town Meeting," example of the Atoka system.

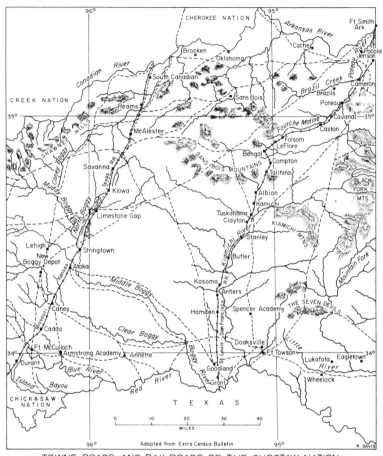

TOWNS, ROADS, AND RAILROADS OF THE CHOCTAW NATION
ABOUT 1887

The social activities of these towns were similar to those of other white communities of the time. Along with the church activities went such affiliated organizations as the Christian Endeavor, the Epworth League, and the Woman's Christian Temperance Union. Debating societies, dances, and picnics furnished recreation. An elaborate Fourth of July observance at Atoka in 1875 caused a Choctaw to inquire if his people were commemorating their deliverance from British rule, but Chief Cole and former Chief Wright both made speeches felicitating their white brethren upon their national holiday, and both races participated in a typical frontier celebration of the day. Farmers' Alliances and Agricultural Wheels became very active in the late Eighties, and coöperative stores and gins and grist mills were started at Caddo and Canadian. A Masonic lodge, of which part of the members were Choctaws, existed at New Boggy as early as 1872, and others were soon founded at Caddo and McAlester; the Odd Fellows began their work at about the same time; a chapter of the Eastern Star seems to have been organized at Atoka in 1879; and in the Nineties the Knights of Pythias became influential at Atoka and in the mining towns. When Federal patronage became important in the Nineties, with the establishment of United States courts and the increasing amount of post-office business, Democratic and Republican conventions and mass meetings were held, which agitated for the abolition of tribal government, endorsed applicants for Federal appointments, and in some cases complicated the issues of tribal elections. All of these activities were so inherently foreign to their own social institutions that with the exception of their presence at picnics and the Masonic affiliations of some of their leaders the Choctaws did not participate in them.[10]

[10]Of the many social activities recorded by the local newspapers the following will serve as examples:

Religious activities—*Vindicator*, 1872; *Indian Citizen*, August 23, 1890; October 24, 1891; March 14, 1895.

Lodges—*Vindicator*, July 11, 1872; *Atoka Independent*, December 14, 1877; *Oklahoma Star*, January 18, 1876; *Indian Citizen*, May 10, 1894; "Notes for a Talk to Kiowa Chapter No. 650 E. S. by Mrs. Mary M. Rogers, Past Grand Matron of Atoka, Oklahoma," *Chronicles of Oklahoma*, IV (September, 1926), 298.

Farmers' Alliances and Agricultural Wheels—*Indian Citizen*, May 18, June 8, 1889; August 16, 1890.

Dances, picnics, etc.—*Vindicator*, April 26, 1876; *Atoka Independent*, May 10, 1878; Carter, *McCurtain County and Southeast Oklahoma*, pp. 93-94.

Fourth of July celebrations—*Vindicator*, June 21, July 10, 1875; *Indian Citizen*, June 28, July 4, 1890.

Republican and Democratic political activity—*Indian Citizen*, May 26, June 9, 1892; March 4, 1897; August 14, 1902.

The activities of the white population were recorded in newspapers that for the most part were also of alien management and interests, although they usually carried Choctaw columns for the convenience of their Indian readers. The first newspaper published in the Choctaw Nation after the Civil War was the *Vindicator*, which was first printed at New Boggy in 1872. It led an irregular existence moving back and forth from New Boggy to Atoka, suspended publication for a short interval, and finally consolidated with the *Oklahoma Star* in 1877. It favored sectionalization on the ground that the Choctaws would be more prosperous under individual ownership, but it opposed the "Oklahoma bills" and the opening of the country to white settlement.[11]

The *Vindicator* had an opponent in the *Oklahoma Star*, which started at Caddo in 1874. It was a "Boomer" sheet defending the "Oklahoma bills," capitalizing all the murders to prove that the Choctaw government should be overthrown in the interest of law enforcement, attacking Chief Cole with all the virulence of a personal enmity, and stating frequently and offensively that the white race was destined to own every foot of land on the American continent. In 1876 it removed to McAlester, where, a year later, it consolidated with the *Vindicator*, and continued its existence for a short time as the *Star-Vindicator*.[12] Soon after the consolidation Chief Cole complained that one of the editors was abusing the permission he had secured from the War Department to sell liquor in his drug store for medicinal purposes, and the Federal Government revoked his permit.[13]

The *Atoka Independent* began in 1877. It contained little news at first, but continued to improve, and to become more identified with Choctaw interests until it was purchased by the *Indian Citizen* in 1889. The *Caddo Free Press* had a brief existence as a "Boomer" paper; it will be remembered that its editor left the Indian country because he had incurred the hostility of the Choctaw government by his activities in 1879. The *Indian Missionary*, a Baptist paper edited by J. S. Murrow, was published at South Canadian and Atoka during the Eighties and Nineties. The *Lehigh News*, a publication devoted mainly to mining interests, was published in 1888, and continued until its purchase by the *Indian Citizen* in 1889.[14]

[11]*Vindicator*, February 28, November 23, December 21, 1872; December 8, 1875.
[12]*Oklahoma Star*, March 20, 1874; June 13, 1876; January 13, 1877.
[13]Indian Office Files, Union, 1878, W431, W454.
[14]*Atoka Independent*, July 27, 1877; May 19, 1888; *Report Commissioner of Indian Affairs*, 1886, p. 154; 1887, pp. 617, 650; 1888, p. 123; 1890, p. 100.

Perhaps it was the foreign and sometimes hostile character of their press that determined the Choctaws to publish a national newspaper that would be the official organ of the government in publishing the acts of the Council, the Federal laws and rulings relating to the tribe, and all other state papers of interest to the citizens. An appropriation was made by the Council, and the publication began at Atoka, February 23, 1884. L. H. and R. M. Roberts, the proprietors of the *Indian Journal* at Muskogee, were employed to manage it and the Choctaw section was edited by Allen Wright. It was known at first as the *Branding Iron,* but the name was soon changed to the *Indian Champion.* The Nation withdrew its support in the Fall of 1885, and the paper seems to have suspended publication about the same time.[15]

The most important newspaper ever published in the Choctaw Nation was the *Indian Citizen,* which was owned and operated by Choctaw citizens, and devoted exclusively to Choctaw interests. It purchased the *Atoka Independent* and *Lehigh News* and began publication at Atoka in 1889 as the only newspaper published in the Nation. It was edited by J. S. Standley, and his son-in-law, Butler S. Smiser, a white man who had come from Kentucky to take charge of the Atoka Baptist Academy, and had become a Choctaw citizen through his marriage to Norma Standley. As Standley's duties as Choctaw delegate kept him in Washington most of the time, he confined himself to reporting the Washington news, and Smiser and his wife took over the active editorship.[16]

The *Indian Citizen* was an excellent country newspaper, with its correspondents recording the local happenings and personal gossip of both whites and Choctaws for the entire Nation. It gave a complete and accurate summary of all the Washington news affecting the Choctaws, and the official acts of the Choctaw government with the texts of the laws, proclamations, and court decisions affecting Choctaw interests. It entered violently into the political campaigns, joining in all the temporary personal alliances and enmities so characteristic of Choctaw politics. It was generally read by the Choctaws and furnished an open forum for the expression of Choctaw opinion. At first it was bitterly opposed to allotment but as the non-citizen population grew more numerous and more vociferous it came to advocate a voluntary division

[15]Acts of the Choctaw Nation, November 6, 1883; October 30, 1885; The *Branding Iron,* February 23, 1884; *Indian Champion,* March 22, 1884.

[16]*Indian Citizen,* March 2, May 4, May 11, 1889; March 28, 1891; O'Beirne, *Leaders and Leading Men,* I, 117.

of the tribal estate as a defense against forced sectionalization by the Federal Government.[17]

Although the *Indian Citizen* began as the only newspaper published in the Nation it was joined before the year was over by the *Twin City Topics* of McAlester and Krebs, and by many others during the Nineties. These new publications nearly always belonged to the "Boomer" element, and some of them became very bitter and defiant in their attacks upon the Choctaw government. Their activities properly belong to the period of white settlement following the tribal period.[18]

One receives the impression from reading these newspapers that aside from certain inconveniences in the way of land ownership, the absence of law, and the denial of political rights, the life and institutions of the non-citizen element differed little from that of any other frontier region. There were the towns, with their feverish "booster" spirit and their striving for the culture and niceties of an older society, and a rural population made up of the tenants on the Choctaw farms, an untutored people vastly interested in the all-day picnics and the rough-and-ready games of a frontier community.

In the midst of this foreign population the Choctaw people existed almost as a separate society with their own customs and institutions. Their favorite sport was still the native ball play, into which they entered with the zest of primitive days.[19] They also enjoyed fishing, often making it the occasion of a neighborhood gathering. They would purchase fish berries at a store, load their light canoes into wagons and gather in large numbers at the appointed place. The men sowed the berries on the surface of the water while the women and children prepared a large brush fire. When the fish became drugged and rose to the surface, the men would dart to them in the canoes, seize them, and throw them on the shore. The women would then place them alive on the coals, and when they were sufficiently roasted, the skin and scales would be removed and the offal thrown aside, and the whole party would enjoy a feast on the meat. The Choctaw country with its clear mountain streams and remote lakes was a fisherman's paradise.[20] The men engaged in bear hunts also, in which a captain

[17]*Indian Citizen*, February 25, 1892.

[18]*Indian Citizen*, December 28, 1889; November 28, 1891; February 14, 1895; July 14, 1898; *Antlers Democrat*, November 2, 1901.

[19]Carter, *McCurtain County and Southeast Oklahoma*, pp. 85-87; *Indian Citizen*, September 11, 1902.

[20]James *My Experience with Indians*, pp. 55-57; O'Beirne and O'Beirne, *The Indian Territory*, pp. 66-67, 485.

and other officers were elected, and the rules of the camp and hunt were carefully drawn up. The Choctaws were very careful not to kill game wantonly, and bear, deer, and wild turkey were very plentiful.[21]

Another Choctaw gathering was the "funeral cry," an ancient cere-monial greatly modified by Christian conceptions. Few tears were shed at the time of a death, and the burial took place very quietly and simply. The bereaved family then sent invitations to the relatives and friends, who assembled on the day appointed for the "cry." A feast was pre-pared in the open. Religious services were held in a church or brush arbor, and a prominent man delivered a eulogy of the deceased. The congregation then retired to the grave and formed a kneeling circle around it, wailing and shedding tears freely. The alternate wailing and feasting sometimes continued for two or three days.[22]

The Choctaws liked to assemble in brush arbors or groves for camp meetings, Sunday School conventions, and other religious gatherings, which usually lasted for several days. They would sit flat on the ground about a rude pulpit, joining in songs and prayers, and listening to speeches and sermons by their pastors and leading men. They feasted on stewed meats cooked in large pots, and the ever-present "tofulla," and drank great quantities of coffee. At night they camped in the circle of woods surrounding the place of meeting.[23]

In remote places along the streams and in the groves were the log churches where the Choctaws gathered for worship. Nearly all of their preachers were Choctaws, many of them highly educated, but a few missionaries continued to work among them.[24]

The Choctaws always had the most profound respect for legitimate missionary enterprise, but with the coming of intruders they found it necessary to protect themselves against white encroachments in the guise of religious work. The Treaty of 1866 had provided that in the event of allotment, missionaries who had served in the Nation a speci-fied number of years before the Civil War should be entitled to home-steads.[25] Certain persons professing to be missionaries and ministers

[21]O'Beirne and O'Beirne, *op. cit.,* pp. 52, 65-66.

[22]James, *My Experience with Indians,* p. 109; Carter, *McCurtain County and South-east Oklahoma,* pp. 127-28; J. J. Methvin, "Reminiscences of Life among the Indians," *Chronicles of Oklahoma,* V (June, 1927), 166-79; Emma Ervin Christian, "Memories of My Childhood Days," *Chronicles of Oklahoma,* IX (June, 1931), pp. 162-63.

[23]James, *My Experience with Indians,* pp. 71-76; *Atoka Independent,* August 23, 1878, "A Choctaw Camp Meeting"; *Indian Citizen,* August 9, 1890, "Children's Day at Many Springs"; *Report Select Committee,* I, 925.

[24]*Report Commissioner of Indian Affairs,* 1871, p. 571; 1876, p. 64; 1889, p. 207.

[25]Kappler, *Laws and Treaties,* II, 925, Art. 17.

then settled upon Choctaw land claiming that this provision exempted them from the operation of the permit laws. The law of 1876 that attempted to tax the Missouri, Kansas, and Texas Railroad also provided for the removal of these intruders, with this qualification,

"Be it further enacted, that no part of this act is intended to prevent or restrain or discourage the dissemination of the refining influences of Christianity, but to declare to the world that if the Choctaw Nation should throw open her doors and set apart a reservation or claim with all the rights and privileges of occupying such as are enjoyed by Choctaw citizens to every individual who might presume to be a Minister of the Gospel or Missionary, said Nation would soon be flooded with a most demoralizing population."[26]

Revenue Collector J. S. Standley then served notice that missionaries who were engaged solely in religious work would not be disturbed, but that those taking part in other enterprises would be expected to conform to the permit law. Some Choctaws strongly disapproved of this policy fearing that it was anti-religious legislation, but the Nation continued to enforce it.[27] It will be remembered that a controversy arose at this time with Secretary Schurz over the sale of the intruders' improvements, and one of the complaints that reached the Indian office came from a certain S. P. Hicks, who protested that "the undersigned is a misionary lawfuley Sent in hear by the Church hold my credentles and continue to preach and instruct."[28]

As soon as the dispute with the Interior Department was settled, a law was passed in 1881 that missionaries who could produce credentials from some board or church, and recommendations from the missionaries already working in the Nation might receive permits by special act of the Council "only so long as they shall confine themselves to the sacred office of ministers." Under this system the Choctaws continued to admit missionaries to the Nation, but their laws specifically stated that the allotment plan of the Treaty of 1866 had been rejected, and consequently "missionaries have no rights thereunder."[29]

[26]Acts of the Choctaw Nation, March 9, 1876.
[27]*Vindicator*, March 29, April 5, 1876.
[28]Indian Office Files, Union, 1879, H352, March 8, 1879.
[29]Acts of the Choctaw Nation, November 12, 1881; November 10, 1885; November 9, 1887, laws regulating rights of missionaries; *ibid.*, October 13, 1883; November 12, 1889; October 24, 1895, special laws admitting missionaries; *Indian Champion*, October 24, 1885, message of Chief Edmund McCurtain advising Council to define rights of missionaries, on the ground that some were engaging in secular pursuits.

The Choctaws had very strict ideas regarding Sunday observance. In 1853 ball plays and horse racing for bets were forbidden on Sunday, a law of 1873 provided that business houses should be closed, and in 1883 it was made unlawful to hunt with dog or gun.[30] The Choctaws were annoyed at the laxness of the miners in this respect, and Chief Cole complained to Agent Marston, who requested them to refrain from desecrating the day, and so far as practicable to attend church and observe the "laws of both God and man."[31]

The Choctaws were never troubled by the fear of any undue ecclesiastical influence in their government. A large number of their officials — members of the Council, national officers, and one Chief, Allen Wright — were Presbyterian or Methodist ministers, and part of the time their boarding schools were under denominational control. In 1900 the Council made an appropriation for a more accurate translation of the New Testament into Choctaw — "to bring it up to date and make it more perfect for the use of our people."[32] Although their bill of rights provided that no religious test should ever be required as a qualification for office, another section of their constitution prohibited any person who denied the existence of a God or a future state of rewards and punishments from holding office or from taking a valid oath.[33]

Most of the Choctaws at first were Presbyterians or Methodists, according to the denominational affiliations of their earliest missionaries. The Baptists, however, came in 1858, and carried on their work with great success; their leader, Rev. J. S. Murrow, was the most active missionary of the post-war period. Father Robot established the first Catholic church, in 1875, at Atoka, and congregations were soon formed at McAlester, Savanna, Lehigh, and Krebs; but the influence of this church was stronger among the non-citizens, especially the miners, than among the Choctaws.[34]

As the statistics kept by the religious bodies do not show the racial composition of their membership it seems impossible to discover what

[30]Folsom, *Digest of Choctaw Law*, p. 504; Acts of the Choctaw Nation, October 23, 1873; October 17, 1883.
[31]Union Agency Files, Letters of Chiefs, p. 180, Marston to Cole, February 10, 1877.
[32]Acts of the Choctaw Nation, October 26, 1900.
[33]Constitution, Arts. I, VII.
[34]*Report Commissioner of Indian Affairs*, 1876, p. 64; 1871, p. 571; 1889, pp. 206-7; *Vindicator*, October 13, December 8, 1875; January 19, April 19, 1876; Laracy "Sacred Heart Mission and Abbey"; W. H. Underwood, "Rev. Dr. Joseph Samuel Murrow," *Chronicles of Oklahoma*, VII (December, 1929), 487-89.

proportion of the Choctaws were members of churches. One observer, who was probably unduly optimistic, estimated that 75 per cent were professed Christians.[35] The census figures for Eagle County in 1878 showing 105 Christians in a Choctaw population of 795 are probably more indicative of the proportion in the Nation as a whole.[36] The religious statistics obtained in the Federal census of 1890 for the entire population were as follows:[37]

	NO. OF ORGANIZATIONS	NO. OF MEMBERS
Southern Baptists	56	2,388
Roman Catholic	7	735
Church of God	1	50
Congregational	4	90
Disciples of Christ	27	512
African Methodist Episcopal	6	320
Colored Methodist Episcopal	13	291
Methodist Episcopal	6	125
Methodist Episcopal South	97	2,312
Methodist Protestant	6	110
Cumberland Presbyterian	27	597
Southern Presbyterian	11	454
Northern Presbyterian	28	548
TOTAL	289	8,532

Observers of the Choctaws in primitive times had described them as a chaste people whose family life was pure; and this characteristic, to a certain extent at least, seems to have persisted. Adultery did occur, however, and divorces were fairly common. The equality of the husband and wife was recognized by the marriage laws of a very early period. A law of 1852 provided that in cases of separation the property accumulated during the period of wedlock should be divided equally, and that the custody of the children should be decided by seven disinterested persons. Later laws placed divorce matters under the jurisdiction of the circuit courts. The legal grounds for divorce were

[35]James, *My Experience with Indians*, p. 71.
[36]Union Agency Files, Principal Chief. The returns of the other counties for the census of 1878 seem to have been lost.
[37]*Extra Census Bulletin*, pp. 16-19

232

impotence at the time of marriage, adultery subsequent to the marriage, and inhumane treatment endangering the life of the spouse.[38]

The Choctaw children were usually born under the trees without much ceremony, and when a few hours old they were carried into the house by the mother. The birth rate was high but the infant mortality was appalling, and accounts to a certain extent for the stationary character of the population.[39]

There seems to have been a great deal of illness among the adult Choctaws. The country was infested with malaria, and diarrhoea and dysentery were almost as common. Most serious of all was a marked susceptibility to tuberculosis, which sometimes claimed every adult member of a Choctaw family. The indolence which was admitted by friendly observers as a racial characteristic was possibly due in part to physical weakness.[40]

Sickness was still treated to some extent even among the educated Choctaws by the old "medicine." The "doctors" were frequently women, and their ministrations consisted of ceremonial feasting, wierd music and dancing, and steaming with magic herbs.[41]

The Choctaws had excellent physicians, however, who had been educated, sometimes at public expense, in the foremost medical colleges in the United States. But the Nation had serious trouble with non-citizen quacks who refused to conform to their medical requirements and were very difficult to expel. As an example of the educational attainments of this class, a letter written by one J. B. Kilgo to Secretary Carl Schurz during the permit controversy seems fairly typical—"I Have Bin Living in the Chocktaw Nation 3 years & Bin doing a Successful practice of medicin all the time."[42]

In 1884 the Council provided for the appointment of a Medical Board of three Choctaw citizens, graduates of medical colleges, which

[38]James, My Experience with Indians, pp. 61-64, 93; Acts and Resolutions of the General Council, 1852-1857, inc., p. 49; ibid., 1860-1861, pp. 107-8; Acts of the Choctaw Nation, November 6, 1885; Union Agency Files, Choctaw—Divorce, these are divorce petitions before the circuit courts—the grounds specified are usually adultery, desertion, and cruelty.

[39]James, My Experience with Indians, p. 80; O'Beirne, Leaders and Leading Men, I, 70, 80, 90, 107, 110, for examples.

[40]For the prevalence of tuberculosis see obituaries in the Indian Citizen—for instance, November 10, 1902, "At rest." See also O'Beirne, Leaders and Leading Men, I, 25, and Indian Citizen, December 25, 1902, "To the real Indian." For the prevalence of malaria and dysentery see nostrums advertised in the Indian Citizen.

[41]Christian, "Memories of My Childhood Days," pp. 161-62; Swanton, Choctaw Social and Ceremonial Life, p. 232.

[42]Indian Office Files, Union, 1880, K1324.

should have charge of the examination and licensing of non-citizens.[43] This law had the desired effect; Agent Owen reported that it brought about the discontinuance of quack practice and "an addition to the farming class of about sixty persons."[44] Later it was allowed to fall into disuse, but in 1895 a determined effort was again made to enforce it. Dr. G. W. Harkins, the secretary of the Board, reported at that time that of 275 men practicing medicine in the Choctaw Nation only nine had obeyed the notice to appear for examination.[45] When the delinquents remained obdurate the Council appropriated money for their removal and Chief Green McCurtain secured the half-hearted coöperation of the Indian agent.[46] Some of them were expelled as intruders by the Indian police and the law was not so flagrantly violated again, but as the tribal government soon began to surrender its powers to the United States the non-citizen physicians became especially defiant in resisting its authority.[47] In 1904 a law of Congress placed the licensing of physicians in the hands of a district board of examiners appointed by the United States district judge.[48]

The efficiency of the Choctaw physicians was demonstrated in the serious smallpox epidemic of 1899-1900. The disease seems to have started in June at Hartshorne, and spread from there to Atoka and other towns. Most of the cases were among the mining population, which was even more heterogeneous than usual because of a strike that had caused the introduction of strike breakers, many of whom were ignorant Negroes. On October 12, Chief McCurtain requested the medical board to take charge of the situation so far as the protection of Choctaws was concerned, and Agent Shoenfelt at the same time requested them to take similar action with regard to United States

[43]Acts of the Choctaw Nation, October 29, 1884.
[44]*Report Commissioner of Indian Affairs*, 1887, p. 102; 1888, p. 132.
[45]*Indian Citizen*, January 24, July 11, August 22, 1895.
[46]*Ibid.*, May 6, 1897, notice of Medical Board to intruder physicians, also letter from Agent Wisdom to Green McCurtain.
[47]Union Agency Files, Choctaw—Intruders—among these papers is the record of an involved correspondence that took place in 1899-1900 between Agent Shoenfelt and the Choctaw officials regarding the removal of Dr. R. H. Lipscombe who frankly stated that he did not intend to apply for a license—the agent delayed action on various pretexts until Lipscombe finally left the country of his own accord; *ibid.*, Choctaw—Doctors and Vaccination, report of Dr. LeRoy Long, President Choctaw Board of Health, to Council October 25, 1900; *Report Commissioner of Indian Affairs*, 1899, p. 119; *ibid.*, 1900, p. 95—Indian Inspector Wright reported that sixty physicians who had failed to pass or had refused to take the examination required in the Choctaw Nation had removed during the year to avoid expulsion.
[48]*Report Commissioner of Indian Affairs*, 1904, pp. 493-95, text of law, enacted April 23, 1904.

citizens. They began work at Atoka where they at first attempted to stamp out the contagion by such radical measures as burning houses and destroying property, but when they realized the widespread character of the epidemic they began to build detention camps. The Council strengthened their authority by reorganizing them as a Board of Health and giving them complete control over sanitary and quarantine measures, and appropriated $10,000 to defray their expenses. At the same time the Council requested the United States Government to take similar measures for the protection of its citizens.[49]

The Board of Health ruled that all citizens should be vaccinated, and employed physicians to enforce this regulation. As a result few cases developed among the Indians, and not a single death occurred. The members of the Board regretted their inability to force the vaccination of United States citizens, but feared to take strong measures because of the danger of lawsuits in Federal courts. They did, however, with the coöperation of the Indian agent take complete charge of the quarantine regulations among the miners. They established about twenty-nine pest camps, where 844 cases of smallpox were treated. They secured physicians and nurses, and employed a number of cooks and laborers. They purchased the necessary supplies — tents, fixtures, and food — with great difficulty, on credit, because the Federal Government did not make an appropriation to care for its citizens until the epidemic was over. They employed guards to enforce the quarantine regulations; at one place it required the services of thirty guards to quarantine an entire mining settlement with a population of several thousand Negroes. They had the situation under control by the Spring of 1900, and the last of the camps was closed in May. The death rate during the course of the epidemic was about 2.5 per cent of those affected.[50]

The skill shown by the Board of Health in dealing with this emergency seems characteristic of the professional ability of the educated Choctaws. Their superior intellectual attainments were the result of the comprehensive educational system that had been established before the Civil War.

[49]Acts of the Choctaw Nation, October 31, November 1, 1899. At that time acts of the Council required the approval of the President, and Roosevelt did not approve the law creating the Board of Health until April 18, 1900, but the Board worked under the direction of the Chief, and the approval of the Indian agent.

[50]Report Commissioner of Indian Affairs, 1900, pp. 102, 136-37; 1901, p. 230; Union Agency Files, Choctaw—Doctors and Vaccination, report of Dr. Long; Acts of the Choctaw Nation, October 26, October 31, November 1, 1900; November 6, 1901; November 1, 1904.

No discussion of Choctaw institutions would be complete without a description of the tribal schools. The belief in education was universal; the Choctaws were proud of their civilization which they regarded as the product of their educational institutions, and they believed that their racial existence was dependent upon their ability to continue their cultural development. The Chiefs unfailingly and earnestly upheld the schools whether their sentiments were expressed in the halting English of Coleman Cole or the polished language of Wright or Garvin, and no other public policy ever received such careful direction or such consistent support at the hands of the Council.

The entire educational system was under the control of a board of trustees consisting of a superintendent and three district trustees, elected for a term of two years by a joint ballot of both houses of the Council. This board exercised a supervisory control over the neighborhood schools and boarding schools, and selected the students who were to be maintained in boarding school or college at public expense. They met at the capital while the Council was in session, and submitted to it their accounts and reports. In 1890 the board of trustees was reorganized, the Principal Chief was made a member, and the name was changed to Board of Education of the Choctaw Nation.[51]

Each district trustee established neighborhood schools in his district at the request of the local community, which was supposed to provide the building and equipment. He appointed three substantial citizens, who served as local trustees. It was their duty to select the teacher, who was then sent to the district trustee for examination; and to visit the school, reinforce the teacher's authority, and encourage the attendance of the children. In 1882 the number of local trustees was reduced to one, and a salary of two dollars a month was provided.[52]

Nominally the neighborhood schools ran for nine or ten months, but they were frequently closed at the end of half that period because the funds were exhausted.[53] A compulsory attendance law was passed in 1884 penalizing the parents by a fine of ten cents a day for the absence of each child between the ages of seven and eighteen that could

[51]Acts of the Choctaw Nation, October 31, 1872; November 7, 1879; October 31, 1890; December 12, 1891.
[52]*Report Commissioner of Indian Affairs*, 1870, p. 294, report of Superintendent LeFlore, August 29, 1870; Acts of the Choctaw Nation, November 7, 1879; November 9, 1881; November 1, 1882.
[53]*Vindicator*, March 16, 1872; July 3, 1875; *Indian Champion*, August 30, 1884; *Indian Citizen*, October 11, 1890.

NEW HOPE SEMINARY, ESTABLISHED IN 1845

JEFFERSON GARDNER, PRINCIPAL CHIEF, 1894–96

not be excused through bad weather, high water, or sickness.[54] Free text books adopted by the Council — later by the Board of Education — were furnished the children, and the course of study was similar to that of the neighboring states even to the inclusion of United States history. The instruction was carried on in English, and, as many of the children spoke only Choctaw, the *Choctaw Definer* was a necessary part of the school's equipment.[55]

Some of the teachers were white, but most of them were Choctaws who had been educated in the tribal schools. They were examined in the Choctaw constitution and the common school subjects including United States history and government. They received a salary of two dollars a month for each child.[56] They attended frequent teachers' meetings and institutes and summer normals, and at one time published a professional magazine called the *Choctaw School Journal*.[57]

Although the neighborhood schools were apparently as good as those of the surrounding states, they formed the weakest part of the Choctaw educational system; they received nothing like a proportionate share of legislative appropriations, and they were often badly taught and irregularly attended. The boarding schools on the other hand maintained scholastic standards that would be a credit to any school system.

It has already been stated that the boys' school at Spencer and the girls' school at New Hope were the first boarding schools to be opened after the Civil War. In the Fall of 1870 the Council authorized the board of trustees to contract with Methodist, Presbyterian, or Baptist mission boards to conduct these schools. A contract was accordingly made with the Methodist Episcopal Church South, by which for $5,000 annually the church agreed to take charge of New Hope, furnish the superintendent and teachers, and board, clothe, and instruct fifty girls.[58] A similar contract was made with the Presbyterian church regarding Spencer, and both schools were opened for the term of 1871–1872.[59]

[54]Acts of the Choctaw Nation, November 6, 1884; November 5, 1886.

[55]*Ibid.*, November 10, 1881; Allen Wright, *Chahta Leksikon* (St. Louis, 1880).

[56]Acts of the Choctaw Nation, October 31, 1890; *Report Commissioner of Indian Affairs*, 1870, p. 295, report of Superintendent LeFlore.

[57]*Vindicator*, April 24, 1875; *Indian Citizen*, August 23, 1890; September 5, 1891; July 26, 1894.

[58]Union Agency Files, Choctaw—Schools, contract between Superintendent LeFlore and the Methodist Church, July 25, 1871.

[59]Acts of the Choctaw Nation, November 2, 1870; November 1, 1872; October 23, 1876; *Report Commissioner of Indian Affairs*, 1871, p. 618.

These two schools were the leading educational institutions of the Choctaws until the close of the tribal period. The old Fort Coffee property was soon turned over to New Hope,[60] and in 1882 a substantial building was erected for the boys in Kiamitia County and Spencer was removed to the new location.[61] Other improvements were made from time to time and the capacity of each school was increased to one hundred — thirty-three from each district, and one from the Choctaw population living among the Chickasaws.[62] The quota from each district was distributed among the various counties according to their population in order to give equal privileges to all communities.[63] In 1896 Spencer was destroyed by a fire in which four boys lost their lives, and New Hope was burned down a few months later. The Nation made an attempt to rebuild Spencer, but by that time the educational system was passing out of tribal control and the importance of the two historic schools was ended.[64]

The children who attended these boarding schools were selected by the trustee of their district until 1890, after which they were selected by the county judge. The appointment was made upon the basis of their "promptness in attendance and their capacity to learn fast." They were held responsible for regular attendance at classes and progress in their studies, and not more than one was to be selected from any family. The ages were at first from ten to sixteen for girls and twelve to eighteen for the boys, and they had to be able to read in the *Third Reader* before entering.[65]

In 1885 the Council became dissatisfied with the mission management, and after a period of experimentation the two schools were placed under the control of the board of trustees. The teachers' qualifications as specified in the school law of 1890 were, for the men, graduation from a standard college and the ability to teach Greek, Latin, French, and German; and, for the women, graduation from a college or normal school and ability to teach two modern languages

[60]Acts of the Choctaw Nation, October 22, 1873; October 28, 1876; October 16, 1880.

[61]*Ibid.*, November 5, November 9, 1881; October 29, 1884.

[62]*Ibid.*, November 7, 1879; October 22, 1883; December 7, 1887; November 3, 1890.

[63]Peter J. Hudson to Grant Foreman, September 6, 1932.

[64]*Indian Citizen*, October 8, 1896; Acts of the Choctaw Nation, November 11, 1897; March 25, November 1, 1899; November 6, 1901; *Report Commissioner of Indian Affairs*, 1897, p. 144.

[65]Acts of the Choctaw Nation, November 7, 1879; November 5, 1880; October 19, 1883; December 20, 1889; October 31, 1890.

besides English. The salaries were $1,200 a year for the superintendents, and $750 to $1,200 for the teachers. The faculties usually included both white and Choctaw teachers.[66]

As the national revenues increased from the royalties and taxes, other boarding schools were established. When Spencer was removed to the new location, an orphans' home for both boys and girls was established temporarily in the old buildings. As soon as the old Armstrong Academy building was vacated by the removal of the capital to Tuskahoma, the boys' orphan school was located there. At the same time the old Wheelock buildings were repaired and a school was established at that place for the orphan girls.[67]

Children from six to twelve years of age who had lost one or both of their parents were placed in these schools, where they might remain both Summer and Winter until the girls were sixteen and the boys eighteen years old. They were selected by the county judges, who, it will be remembered, had charge of probate matters. They were chosen upon the basis of their needs, and the rule that limited one pupil to a family was set aside. In addition to the academic subjects the boys received agricultural and manual training, and the girls were instructed in home economics.[68]

Governor Smallwood believed that additional provision should be made for those children who were growing up in ignorance because they lived in places too remote for attendance upon the neighborhood schools. He recommended the establishment of numerous small boarding schools in which the pupils should be selected exclusively from this class of children.[69] The Council did not act on this recommendation, but three new boarding schools were established during the next administration — Jones Academy, near Hartshorne, for boys; Tuskahoma, near the capital, for girls; and Tushka Lusa, "Black Warriors," for the freedmen. These schools were opened in the Fall of 1892 under Choctaw principals, Peter J. Hudson at Tuskahoma, S. T. Dwight at Jones, and Henry Nail, a Choctaw freedman, at Tushka Lusa.[70]

[66]*Ibid.*, November 5, 1880; October 28, November 10, 1885; November 5, 1886; October 31, 1890; *Report Commissioner of Indian Affairs*, 1887, p. 106; 1892, p. 255.

[67]Acts of the Choctaw Nation, November 11, 1881; November 3, 1882; October 22, October 25, 1883.

[68]*Ibid.*, November 11, 1881; November 2, 1883.

[69]*Indian Citizen*, October 12, 1889; October 11, 1890, annual messages of Chief Smallwood.

[70]Acts of the Choctaw Nation, November 14, 1890; April 4, December 5, December 10, 1891; *Report Commissioner of Indian Affairs*, 1892, p. 255.

The Choctaws received their higher education at colleges in the "States." Well-to-do parents often sent their children away to complete their education, and it will be remembered that soon after the Civil War the Nation resumed the practice of maintaining a selected group of students in college at public expense. It was the duty of the district trustees to be present at the closing exercises of the boarding schools in their respective districts, and at that time upon the recommendation of the superintendent and teachers they chose the young people who were to be sent to college by the Nation. Both young men and young women were chosen, upon the basis of their promise, and they were allowed to continue in college until they had completed graduate and professional courses.[71] Allen Wright, Jacob B. Jackson, and Napoleon B. Ainsworth were among the Choctaw leaders who received both their undergraduate and professional training in this way.

Afflicted children were also supported in special schools by the Nation. Several deaf children were sent to a school in Illinois, and blind children were cared for in schools where they received special training.[72] The children who were selected for the boarding schools, however, were required to pass a physical examination, and were to be removed unless their health was such that they could continue their course with profit to themselves and promise to the Nation.[73]

A few statistics will indicate the progress of the Choctaw schools during the period under consideration. For the school year of 1868-1869, before the reopening of the boarding schools, Superintendent Forbis LeFlore submitted the following report:[74]

NEIGHBORHOOD SCHOOLS	NO. OF SCHOOLS	PUPILS	COST
Pushmataha District	27	718	$7,028.45
Apukshunnubbee District	23	618	6,312.87
Moshulatubbee District	19	511	6,027.72
TOTAL	69	1,847	$19,369.04
At colleges in the "States"		22	7,600.00
TOTAL		1,869	$26,969.04

[71] *Report Commissioner of Indian Affairs,* 1869, p. 410, report of Superintendent LeFlore, September 6, 1869; Acts of the Choctaw Nation, October 30, 1876; October 9, 1877; November 7, 1879; November 11, 1881; Peter J. Hudson to Grant Foreman, September 7, 1932.

[72] Acts of the Choctaw Nation, October 27, 1893; October 26, 1894; October 26, 1895; November 4, 1896; October 26, 1900.

[73] *Ibid.,* October 11, 1877.

[74] *Report Commissioner of Indian Affairs,* 1869, pp. 409-10.

When the boarding schools were opened, the expense of the neighborhood schools was curtailed and the number of students in the "States" was reduced. The following enrollment was reported by Superintendent Bond for 1874-1875:[75]

Number enrolled in 50 neighborhood schools	1,118
Number enrolled in Spencer	60
Number enrolled in New Hope	50
Number enrolled in the "States"	10
TOTAL	1,238

The reports of the district trustees for 1885-1886, the year schools were established for the freedmen, give the following information regarding the neighborhood schools:[76]

	NO. OF SCHOOLS			NO. OF PUPILS		
	Choc.	Freed.	Total	Choc.	Freed.	Total
Moshulatubbee District	39	3	42	721	34	755
Apukshunnubbee District	35	10	45	744	263	1,007
Pushmataha District	60	21	81	1,200	550	1,750
TOTAL	134	34	168	2,665	847	3,512

When the orphan schools were established and functioning normally, the enrollment and attendance at the different schools for the year 1887-1888 were reported as follows:[77]

BOARDING SCHOOLS	ENROLLMENT	AVERAGE ATTENDANCE
Spencer	100	78
New Hope	108	97
Wheelock	58	56
Armstrong	52	48
TOTAL	318	279

NEIGHBORHOOD SCHOOLS	NO. OF SCHOOLS	ENROLLMENT	AV. ATTEND.
Moshulatubbee District	48	693	470
Apukshunnubbee District	48	1,046	791
Pushmataha District	64	1,370	1,208
TOTAL	160	3,109	2,469

[75]*Vindicator*, July 3, 1875.
[76]Acts of the Choctaw Nation, October 30, 1886.
[77]*Report Commissioner of Indian Affairs*, 1888, pp. 120-21. The authority is not given for these statistics, but they appear to be substantially correct.

The enrollment for 1892-1893, the year of the opening of the new boarding schools, was reported by J. B. Jeter as follows:[78]

NEIGHBORHOOD SCHOOLS	NO. OF SCHOOLS	ENROLLMENT
Moshulatubbee District	53	742
Apukshunnubbee District	57	892
Pushmataha District	79	2,185
TOTAL	189	3,819
Boarding schools	7	490
Students in "States"		40
TOTAL ENROLLMENT		4,349

This entire school system was supported by the annuities, the income from invested funds, the royalties, and the permit taxes. The Choctaw people never paid school taxes except in the sense that they voted at a very early period to apply to the support of education the annuities that had formerly been paid out per caput to the citizens. When Edmund McCurtain was trustee of Moshulatubbee District in 1874, he persuaded the voters of his district to sign a petition requesting the Council to lay a property tax on live stock for the support of the schools. He urged the other districts to take similar action but they failed to do so, and although McCurtain used all his influence with the Council, the petition died in the committee room.[79] This seems to have been the only tax measure ever attempted in the Choctaw Nation, unless the use of the income from the tribal estate for school and governmental purposes may be classed as a tax which bore equally upon all citizens.

As a result of its excellent public-school system the Choctaw Nation had a much higher proportion of educated people than any of the neighboring states; the number of college graduates one encounters in any contemporary record is surprising, and the quality of written English used by the Choctaws both in their official and private correspondence is distinctly superior to that of the white people surrounding them. Education, however, was not universal. A large number of the depositions before the courts of claims in 1875 and 1876 were made out by apparently illiterate people, but this may be accounted for to a certain extent by the fact that the older people had grown up before the development of the public schools, and that one group of young

78*Ibid.*, 1893, p. 146.
79*Vindicator*, May 8, 1875.

242

people had been deprived of educational opportunities when the schools closed for five years during the Civil War period. All of the newspapers except those entirely hostile to Indian interests carried columns and communications in Choctaw; the *Indian Citizen* in fact published in that language the complete text of treaties and Federal laws and court decisions. Apparently many Choctaws who were unable to read English easily, subscribed to a newspaper and kept themselves informed on public questions, and were able to understand the most technical documents when written in their native tongue. In the absence of any literacy statistics as the basis of accurate judgment one may only conclude in general that the educational development of the people as a whole did not correspond with the superior cultural achievements of the leaders.[80]

While the Choctaws were providing at least the rudiments of an education for the entire people, and superior training for the few, the children of the non-citizen population were growing up almost completely ignorant of books. Some irregular provision was made for their education — schools were maintained by subscription in some of the towns; some white children attended the Choctaw neighborhood schools by the payment of tuition; and schools were established by the churches in all the larger towns, especially by the Presbyterians at McAlester, the Baptists at Atoka, and the Roman Catholics at McAlester, Atoka, and Lehigh — but, except where the parents were unusually progressive the schooling of the white children was entirely neglected.[81]

Such was the life in the Choctaw Nation during the generation following the Civil War. It is very difficult to present a generalized description of this society because of the great diversity of racial and cultural types. Of the various non-citizen elements there were the intruders, assertive, defiant, and often criminal; the white tenant farmers, usually kindly and intelligent but ignorant and shiftless; the miners, usually Negroes or aliens, living a life apart in their crowded camps; and the professional and business classes in the towns, working consciously or unconsciously for the extinction of tribal institutions and the "development of the country." Entirely apart from these groups and greatly outnumbered by them were the owners and rulers of the land — a people strangely gifted in thought and speech but slow in action and practical judgment, deeply susceptible to religious feeling

[80]Union Agency Files, court of claims records.
[81]*Report Commissioner of Indian Affairs*, 1887, p. 111; 1889, p. 205; 1890, p. 93; 1892, p. 256; 1897, p. 144; *Vindicator*, November 15, 1876.

but inclined to violent deeds, withdrawing to themselves in clannish reserve and yet kindly and friendly to other races, loving their country but condoning official corruption, receptive to new ideas but clinging to their institutions with desperate tenacity — a people who were being submerged but not absorbed in the waves of white immigration that were flooding their country. Sharing their citizenship was a small group of intermarried whites, most of them completely identified with tribal interests but with a disturbing minority who sympathized with the intruder element and brought pressure upon the Choctaw institutions from within. The Choctaw freedmen formed still another citizen group — a people generally more thrifty and self-assertive than most members of their race, cultivating farms of their own or working as laborers, living apart from whites and Choctaws but to a certain extent holding themselves superior to Negro immigrants from the "States."[82] It was the increasing difficulty of this racial situation along with the legal and political complications that accompanied it that brought the United States to the decision to end the tribal government.

[82]A cross section of life in the Choctaw Nation in 1885 may be found in the testimony before the Senate Committee on Indian Affairs. *See Report, IX, passim.*

THE SURRENDER TO THE
UNITED STATES

II

ALTHOUGH the Five Civilized Tribes of the Indian Territory had successfully resisted for a number of years all attempts to change their institutions, the great influx of white immigration, especially in the Choctaw and Chickasaw nations, and the difficulty of maintaining a minority government made it increasingly apparent by 1890 that the United States would soon terminate their political and economic control.

The United States agents with the single exception of Robert L. Owen condemned the Indian system of landholding. The Commissioner of Indian Affairs in 1886 declared that the treaties should be disregarded if necessary to bring about a change —"the treaties never contemplated the un-American and absurd idea of a separate nationality in our midst. . . . . These Indians have no right to obstruct civilization and commerce and set up an exclusive claim to self-government, establishing a government within a government, and then expect and claim that the United States shall protect them from all harm, while insisting that it shall not be the ultimate judge as to what is best to be done for them in a political point of view." He recommended the forcible allotment of the land in quarter section tracts and the purchase of the remainder for homestead entry.[1] The *Special Census Bulletin* of 1890 expressed great concern for the investments made by United States citizens in town property to which they could secure no title, and recommended a similar policy of allotment and forced sale with the Federal Government determining questions of citizenship.[2]

[1]*Report Commissioner of Indian Affairs*, 1886, pp. v, viii, x-xii. *See ibid.*, 1888, p. 134, for Owen's defense of the land system.
[2]*Special Census Bulletin*, pp. 23-24, 32-33. *See* also *Report Commissioner of Indian Affairs*, 1892, p. 251, for Agent Bennett's opinion regarding needs of towns.

With the first opening of Oklahoma in 1889 it became necessary to create a territorial government for the new community. The needs of this new settlement thus furnished the occasion for introducing bills in Congress for the extinction of the Indian titles and the dissolution of the tribal governments. The apprehension with which the Choctaws viewed these proposals is reflected in the *Indian Citizen,* which began early in 1892 to advocate voluntary division of the tribal estate as the only protection against unfriendly legislation.[3] At the same time it became a favorite calumny of Choctaw politics to charge political opponents with favoring allotment.[4]

When the bill creating the Dawes Commission was before Congress in February of 1893 a circular letter was sent to the executives of the five nations by their delegates at Washington warning them against the proposed legislation. The Choctaw members of this group were J. S. Standley, H. C. Harris, Green McCurtain, D. W. Hodges, Thomas Ainsworth, and Jacob B. Jackson, most of whom were in Washington at that time to sign the necessary papers for the release of the Choctaw claim to the Cheyenne and Arapaho lands.[5] They warned their constituents that the United States no longer considered the treaties binding, but recommended no specific policy to "meet the danger that threatens."[6]

The law was enacted on March 3. It authorized the President to appoint three commissioners to negotiate with the Five Civilized Tribes to effect the extinction of their titles to the land, either by cession to the United States, allotment, or any other method, with the ultimate purpose of creating a state, or states, of the Union. It was expected that quarter-section allotments would be made and the remainder of the land purchased by the United States, but the commissioners were given great discretionary powers in negotiating a settlement.[7] The President accordingly appointed Henry L. Dawes of Massachusetts, Meredith H. Kidd of Indiana, and Archibald S. McKennon of Arkansas, of whom the last named became the most active in the negotiations and the most popular with the Choctaws.[8]

[3]*See* for example *Indian Citizen,* January 4, 1890, and February 25, 1892. In 1893 the editors of this paper became convinced for a time that the Federal Government would not use force, and that tribal action could be safely postponed—*ibid.,* October 5, 1893.

[4]*Ibid.,* July 4, August 2, October 9, 1890, for example.

[5]Acts of the Choctaw Nation, December 11, December 12, 1891; February 17, 1893.

[6]*Indian Citizen,* October 7, 1895, text of letter.

[7]*Report Commissioner of Indian Affairs,* 1893, pp. 512-14, text of law.

[8]*Ibid.,* 1894, p. 27; Acts of the Choctaw Nation, October 20, 1897.

This Commission to the Five Civilized Tribes, or, as it was usually designated, the Dawes Commission, held a meeting in Washington on December 8, and proceeded to the Indian Territory where it established its headquarters at Muskogee. On December 12 Governor Jones issued a proclamation requesting the people of each county to meet in their respective courthouses the second Monday in January, and draw up instructions to their Senators and Representatives so they would be prepared to act according to the wishes of their constituents at a special session of the General Council soon to be convened.[9]

At these meetings, which took place on January 8, the Choctaw people expressed themselves as overwhelmingly opposed to change.[10] The called session of the Council then convened January 22. Kidd and McKennon were both present and spoke to the legislators, but a law was enacted providing for the appointment of a commission to attend an inter-tribal council and protest "against any dissolution of our present tribal relations or tenure of our lands." The commission was also to meet the Dawes Commission and receive any propositions they might present.[11]

Delegate Standley in the meantime was writing from Washington advising the Choctaws to negotiate in order to avoid compulsion. He was reported to have admitted to a committee of Congress that a large majority of the leading men of the Nation realized that the treaties were no longer binding and that a change was inevitable.[12]

On February 23 the Dawes Commission presented a tentative plan to the Choctaw commission. All the land except the mineral land and townsites, which would be subject to special agreement, would be allotted among the citizens with the provision that a quarter section of each allotment would be inalienable; and a territorial government would be established with the Nation retaining control over its tribal funds and property and with the voting during the territorial period confined to citizens. The Choctaws protested against any attempt to change their institutions and returned home.[13]

The Dawes Commission removed in March to South McAlester, where it met all the tribes except the Seminoles in an international

[9]*Indian Citizen*, December 14, 1893.

[10]*Ibid.*, January 18, 1894.

[11]*Ibid.*, January 25, February 1, 1894; *Commission to the Five Civilized Tribes, Annual Report*, 1894, pp. 7-11; Acts of the Choctaw Nation, January 26, 1894.

[12]*Indian Citizen*, February 22, 1894; Acts of the Choctaw Nation,—the date appears to be April 4, 1894.

[13]*Indian Citizen*, March 1, 1894, "The Dawes Plan."

council which lasted three days. Resolutions were adopted at this meeting advising all the tribes to resist any change.[14]

The Choctaw Council was then convened in another special session on March 28. It directed the Chief to notify the Commission that the Choctaws would not consent to any change in their land or government. It adopted resolutions repudiating Standley's reported admission that the treaties were outdated, saying:*"We cannot bring ourselves to believe that such a great, grand, and Christian Nation, as the U. S. Government would so stultify itself in the eyes of the civilized world, by disregarding treaties heretofore solemnly entered into, with a weak and dependent people, regardless of justice and equity,— Simply, because, she is numerically able to do so."* It authorized the appointment of three commissioners able to speak both English and Choctaw, who should offer every courtesy to the Dawes Commission in conducting them to various parts of the Nation, urging them to "remain long enough to see practically all the Choctaws," and assisting them to discover by public meetings and private interviews the real sentiments of the people regarding their mission.[15]

The Dawes Commission submitted a new set of proposals to the Choctaws and Chickasaws on April 23. There were the same provisions regarding allotments and mineral lands and townsites, and an additional guarantee that the United States would place each citizen in possession of his allotment without expense to the allottee. All claims against the United States including the Leased District claim would be settled. All invested funds and the proceeds from the sale of minerals and townsites and the money awarded by the settlement of any claim against the United States would be divided per caput. If the Choctaws and Chickasaws should so decide, a territorial government would be established over them and any others of the Five Civilized Tribes that might accept allotment, but the tribal governments would continue until the allotments should be completed and the per caput distribution of tribal funds should be effected.[16]

During the Spring and Summer the members of the Dawes Commission were escorted over the Nation by the committee appointed for their entertainment. Apparently they enjoyed themselves thoroughly, making speeches in the various towns and meeting the people, but it

[14]*Commission to the Five Civilized Tribes, Annual Report*, 1894, pp. 7-11.
[15]*Indian Citizen*, March 29, 1894; Acts of the Choctaw Nation, April 2, April 4, 1894.
[16]*Commission to the Five Civilized Tribes, Annual Report*, 1894, pp. 7-11; *Indian Citizen*, May 10, 1894.

is evident that their contacts were mainly with the non-citizen element.[17] Although they showed tact and patience in dealing with the Indians during the protracted negotiations, their reports indicate that they never at any time appreciated the attachment of the Choctaw people to their institutions. They believed that the Indian governments were corrupt and inefficient, and that only a scheming set of place-holders sought to continue them, from motives of personal profit. They were convinced that the communal ownership of land enabled the aristocratic and wealthy leaders of the tribe to enjoy more than their share, and that consequently only this class was opposed to division. They never realized the universal character of the Choctaw resistance.

Apparently they tried at one time to deliver an ultimatum to the Indians. A conference was held at Atoka on June 28. The Choctaws were represented by nine men from each district appointed by Governor Jones, and a delegation from the Chickasaw Nation was also present. The Indians became greatly displeased at what they regarded as an overbearing attitude on the part of the Commission and nothing was accomplished.[18]

A convention of the Choctaw Colored Citizens' Association took place at Goodland, and prepared a statement of principles which was presented to the Commission in August. The freedmen complained of inadequate school privileges and bad treatment at the hands of the Choctaws, citing their exclusion from the distribution of the Leased District payment the preceding year. They protested the injustice of the limited citizenship provided in the Treaty of 1866, and requested equal division of all tribal property. The whole purpose of the petition was to secure for the Negroes an equal share of the Choctaw estate, but it made an impression upon the members of the Commission, who did not seem to understand that by no possible interpretation were the freedmen entitled to share in the Leased District payment, and that the Choctaws had provided educational facilities beyond the obligations assumed in the act of adoption by opening a boarding school for them the year before.[19]

The question of negotiating with the Dawes Commission entered very little, if at all, into the tribal election that took place in 1894. When the Council met for the regular session, the new Chief, Jefferson Gardner, advised his people to resist all change.[20] Green McCurtain,

[17]*See* any contemporary number of the *Indian Citizen* for accounts of these meetings.
[18]*Indian Citizen,* June 21, July 5, 1894.
[19]*Commission to the Five Civilized Tribes, Annual Report,* 1894, pp. 19, 24-32.
[20]*Indian Citizen,* October 11, 1894, text of Chief Gardner's annual message.

however, who had been representing the Choctaw Nation at Washington under a law enacted the year before, presented a report to the Council which seems to have been the first official presentation of any counter-proposals looking to a settlement with the Dawes Commission. He advised against the establishment of a territorial government, but advocated the division of the land with the title to remain in the Nation for twenty-five years. He recommended that the freedmen should each receive forty acres in the division, but did not express a definite opinion regarding the share of the intermarried whites. He believed that the United States should appropriate $100,000 annually for the support of Choctaw schools, and that the Choctaws should surrender their claim to the remainder of the Leased District.[21] The Council refused to follow McCurtain's recommendations, but his report did have the effect of alarming the intermarried citizens, who began to hold meetings and organize societies and pass resolutions against being left out of any plan of division.[22]

During the Winter of 1894-1895 the Choctaws were conscious that their opponents were becoming more determined to break down their opposition. The press of the neighboring states was clamoring for a change, various associations were formed having the same purpose, and numerous bills were introduced in Congress expressly abrogating the treaties and placing the whole country under Federal control.[23] The only action taken by Congress, however, was an appropriation for a survey of the Indian Territory and the enlargement of the Dawes Commission by two additional members.[24]

The reorganized Commission returned to the Indian Territory and addressed very conciliatory letters to Governor Gardner, who remained at his home at Eagletown and showed a tendency to ignore the communications.[25] Surveying parties worked in the Choctaw Nation during the Summer laying off quarter sections and townships.[26] The Indians watched them with apprehension but made no attempt to interfere.

A few Choctaw leaders at this time began to work actively for

[21]Acts of the Choctaw Nation, October 19, 1893, October 5, 1894; *Indian Citizen*, October 25, 1894.

[22]*Indian Citizen*, November 8, 1894, "Organization Effected."

[23]For the apprehension with which the Choctaws watched these movements *see* the *Indian Citizen*, December 6-27, 1894; February 14, March 7, March 14, 1895.

[24]*Commission to the Five Civilized Tribes, Annual Report*, 1900, p. 58, text of law, enacted March 2, 1895; *Indian Citizen*, March 14, 1895.

[25]*Indian Citizen*, May 30, 1895; *Commission to the Five Civilized Tribes, Annual Report*, 1895, pp. 62-63.

[26]*Indian Citizen*, June 27, 1895.

negotiation with the Dawes Commission. In July a mass meeting of citizens at Hartshorne adopted resolutions requesting the Council to treat. Green McCurtain was one of the leaders at this gathering; he warned his countrymen that the Choctaws were already losing their independence and being crowded out by a population which they could no longer control, and he advised negotiating before it should be too late. Captain McKennon was also present and made a very conciliatory speech.[27] Dr. E. N. Wright, who was elected that Summer as a member of the House of Representatives from Atoka County, also favored allotment. He was one of the leaders at a convention held at Atoka early in September. At this meeting a call was issued to the citizens to hold conventions at their county court grounds to adopt resolutions and elect delegates to a convention which should meet at Hartshorne shortly before the Council convened. When the convention met, however, Wright and two others from Atoka County and one delegate from Blue County seem to have made up the entire attendance.[28] An additional influence in favor of negotiation was the *Indian Citizen,* which carried on an active campaign during the entire Summer.

The opponents of allotment were also active, and much more numerous. Chief Gardner, Jacob B. Jackson, and J. C. Folsom were among the leaders. Jackson and Folsom, in fact, were unofficial delegates at an inter-tribal council which met at Eufaula in the Creek Nation to plan a united resistance to the Dawes Commission.[29]

The Chief's message to the Council that Fall was tragically solemn in tone. He admonished the legislators to "make plain paths which will lead our people safely through the darkest problems of their situation as a nation," and recommended the appointment of a special committee of the Council to confer with the Dawes Commission and report back before adjournment.[30] A bill was introduced giving the Chief power to appoint such a committee, but an amendment in the Senate placed the appointment in the hands of the presiding officers, and it passed in that form.[31] J. P. Folsom, the President of the Senate, then refused to appoint the members of the committee from that body.[32]

The members from the House were appointed, however, and an informal conference took place with the Dawes Commission at Tuska-

[27]*Ibid.,* July 18, July 25, 1895.
[28]*Ibid.,* August 29, September 12, September 26, 1895.
[29]*Ibid.,* July 4, July 11, 1895.
[30]*Ibid.,* October 24, 1895, text of Gardner's message.
[31]Acts of the Choctaw Nation, October 21, 1895.
[32]*Indian Citizen,* October 31, 1895.

homa. The members of the Commission said that they had no intention of taking the Indians' land but desired only to negotiate regarding some plan of division. They said they were willing to accept any reasonable proposition, but if they failed to make some settlement Congress would force allotment without the Indians' consent. The committee answered that neither they nor their constituents were in favor of change, and that they relied on their treaties which they did not believe the United States would repudiate.[33] They again secured formal propositions from the Dawes Commission, and after conference with a Chickasaw committee they reported to the Council advising rejection.[34] The Council then passed the following resolution: "We ask the honorable Dawes Commission to make their report to the Congress of the United States favoring the extension of justice to us and our peaceful homes and ask to be permitted without molestation to possess that which is ours and only ours."[35]

During the same session Folsom introduced a bill in the Senate providing that any citizen who should attempt to overthrow the Choctaw government or system of landholding or to convey any Choctaw lands to non-citizens "or attempt to betray said land and Choctaw country into the hands of a foreign power" should be guilty of treason and subject to a jail sentence and fine for the first offense and death for the second. This bill passed the Senate with only the dissenting vote of Joe Everidge, but failed to pass the House.[36]

The Dawes Commission then returned to Washington and reported its failure. It painted a very gloomy picture of conditions in the Indian Territory, and recommended that the treaties should not be permitted to stand in the way of their correction.[37] President Cleveland, however, was very considerate of the Indians; he desired the liquidation of tribal affairs, but he hoped to effect his purpose by patient negotiation.[38] There was no mistaking the temper of Congress. As soon as it convened, a number of hostile bills were introduced, of which the one proposed by Delegate Flynn of Oklahoma Territory will serve as an

[33]*Ibid.*, November 7, 1895.

[34]*Ibid.*, November 12, 1895.

[35]Acts of the Choctaw Nation, November 12, 1895.

[36]*Indian Citizen*, November 7, "Choctaw Council"; *Commission to the Five Civilized Tribes, Annual Report*, 1895, p. 67. The jail sentence would have been an innovation in Choctaw law, which punished only by fines, whipping, or death.

[37]*Commission to the Five Civilized Tribes, Annual Report*, 1895, pp. 75-79.

[38]For example *see Indian Citizen*, December 5, 1895, "Dawes Commission."

Courtesy Oklahoma Historical Society

GREEN McCURTAIN, PRINCIPAL CHIEF, 1896–1900 AND 1902–10

GILBERT W. DUKES, PRINCIPAL CHIEF, 1900–1902

example; his plan was to compel the Indians to accept allotments and throw the rest of the land open for homestead entry.[39]

Standley wrote from Washington that such legislation was almost certain to be enacted, and Green McCurtain decided to defeat it by convincing his people that their only hope lay in submission. He believed that Gardner's policy of passive resistance was extremely dangerous, and he wrote to W. W. Wilson, who had great influence with the Chief, urging him to persuade Gardner to go to Washington to "stave off" hostile legislation. He also wrote letters to leading Choctaws inviting them to a convention which he called at Tuskahoma to formulate measures of defense, and to petition Gardner to go to Washington and to support him "in any thing he may see fit to do while there, for the public good."[40]

The convention met at Tuskahoma on January 23, 1896. There were thirty present from the northern and western counties; Moshulatubbee, McCurtain's own district, had a full representation, and only Blue County was missing in the delegation from Pushmataha, but Apukshunnubbee was represented by Wade County only. Among the leaders were Green McCurtain, E. N. Wright, A. R. Durant, Wilson N. Jones, Peter J. Hudson, Wesley Anderson, and S. E. Hotema. After a discussion which lasted through the afternoon and extended into the night they drew up a memorial, which only five of their number failed to sign, requesting Congress if changes were felt to be imperative to change only their tribal judiciary and postpone other changes for twelve months during which they would use their utmost efforts to convince their people to make an agreement with the United States. They selected Judge Durant and Dr. Wright to go to Washington, and with Captain Standley to present this petition to the Government officials. They also organized as a political party and drafted a platform advocating equal division of the land and opposition to Federal legislation affecting their land and government.[41]

This action certainly influenced Congress to give the Indians another chance, and no legislation was enacted to destroy the tribal governments or titles, although an appropriation was made for continuing the survey of the Indian Territory and the powers of the Dawes Commission were extended. It was declared to be the duty of the United

[39]For the vigilance with which the Choctaw leaders watched these proposals, *see*, for example, *Indian Citizen*, December 5, 1895.

[40]Union Agency Files, Choctaw—Federal Relations, McCurtain to Wilson, January 9, 1896.

[41]*Ibid.*, McCurtain to Wilson, January 23, 1896; *Indian Citizen*, January 30, 1896.

States to establish a government in the Indian Territory which would "rectify the many inequalities and discriminations now existing in said Territory, and afford needful protection to the lives and property of all citizens and residents thereof." The Dawes Commission was required to investigate and present a full report to Congress regarding tribal and individual leases, and authorized to make complete citizenship rolls of the various tribes. The existing tribal rolls were confirmed, but claimants whose names were not on the rolls were given the privilege of a hearing before the Commission with the right of appeal to the United States district court.[42]

An attempt was also made at this time to enforce the provisions of the Treaty of 1866 by which the Choctaws and Chickasaws consented to the settlement of a limited number of Kansas Indians within their borders. In the Fall of 1895 the Absentee Wyandottes had appeared before the Choctaw Council with a request for permission to settle in the country, but their petition had been refused, although it seems to have been supported by Jacob B. Jackson and J. C. Folsom, who hoped to fill the country with Indians until there would be no opportunity for white encroachments. Congress now appropriated $21,686.80 to be divided between the Choctaws and Chickasaws in the usual three to one ratio and directed the Secretary of the Interior to settle the Wyandottes in their territory.The project was not carried out, however, and the next year the act was repealed.[43]

When Wright and Durant returned from Washington after presenting their petition to the Federal authorities they tried to induce Governor Gardner to call an extra session of the Council to authorize negotiations with the Dawes Commission, but he refused to take any action.[44] The members of the Commission returned to the Indian Territory in the Summer after their work with Congress was completed, and began to hear citizenship claimants at Vinita in the Cherokee Nation. During July and August they wrote several letters to Chief Gardner explaining the new law, and requesting with increasing impatience that he supply them with the tribal rolls and the necessary data about leases. Gardner at first replied that he was unable to act until the Council should convene, but he ignored part of their letters,

[42]*Report Commissioner of Indian Affairs*, 1896, pp. 446-47, 449, text of law, enacted June 10, 1896.

[43]Kappler, *Laws and Treaties*, II, 927-28, arts. 30, 31, 37, Treaty of 1866; *ibid.*, I, 600, 621-22, laws enacted June 10, 1896, and June 7, 1897; *Indian Citizen*, June 18, 1896.

[44]*Indian Citizen*, February 27, March 26, 1896.

and when they notified him that they would be at the capital on July 27 he failed to appear.[45]

In the meantime an international convention met at Eufaula and passed resolutions recommending the various executives to appoint commissions to treat with the Dawes Commission. The Choctaws were not officially represented, but Green McCurtain requested some members of his party to be present. They were not admitted to seats in the convention, but they passed resolutions of their own of similar purport.[46]

The election in the Choctaw Nation that Summer was very bitter. There were four candidates for Principal Chief. The National Party, which had split in two factions over the nomination of Jefferson Gardner two years before, was still divided; during the regular Council session in the Fall of 1895 the Independent Nationals nominated Gardner, while the more conservative faction — the so-called "fullblood Nationals"— held a convention at Atoka early in February and again nominated Jacob B. Jackson. The new party organized by those who favored making an agreement with the Dawes Commission took the name of the Tuskahoma party; they held another convention in May and nominated Green McCurtain upon a platform of equal division of the land among the white and Indian citizens and allotments of forty acres to the freedmen. The remnants of the old Progressive Party met at Talihina in March and nominated Gilbert W. Dukes.[47]

Dr. Wright, who was McCurtain's campaign manager, arranged the free barbecues and the mass meetings with speaking in English and Choctaw that added such zest to tribal campaigns. A strong attempt was made to enlist the support of the freedmen, but as usual they voted almost solidly against the McCurtain group. The Intermarried White Citizens' Association on the other hand came out with an official endorsement of the Tuskahoma platform.[48]

The result of the election was widely heralded as a decisive victory for allotment, but if the opponents of allotment had not divided their vote among three candidates McCurtain would have been defeated by a majority of almost two to one. The official count was as follows:[49] McCurtain, 1,405; Jackson, 1,195; Dukes, 613; and Gardner, 596.

[45]*Commission to the Five Civilized Tribes, Annual Report,* 1896, pp. 93-96.
[46]*Indian Citizen,* August 6, 1896.
[47]*Ibid.,* November 21, 1895; February 13, March 26, May 21, 1896.
[48]*Ibid.,* June 11, July 16, July 30, September 3, October 8, 1896.
[49]*Ibid.,* October 8, 1896, "Council Notes."

Shortly after the election, Chief Gardner issued a proclamation calling the Council to meet September 8 to arrange for taking a census to supply the Dawes Commission with a citizenship roll. The Council accordingly passed a census law, and authorized the appointment of two commissioners to visit the capitals and principal cities of the northern and eastern states to present the cause of the Indians to state legislatures and commercial clubs and thus arouse public sentiment against the evident purpose of the Federal Government to destroy their institutions.[50]

The next month the new administration came into office, and for the first time the Choctaw government was committed to a policy of dividing the land and negotiating with the Dawes Commission. The Tuskahoma party secured control of both houses of the Council and was thus enabled to elect from its supporters the judges of the Supreme Court and the school superintendent and trustees.[51] The new Chief, a younger brother of Jackson and Edmund McCurtain, had already had a distinguished career as Speaker of the House, District School Trustee, District Attorney, National Treasurer, and Delegate to the United States. His only formal education had been secured in the neighborhood schools before the Civil War, but he had a penetrating intellect and a statesmanlike grasp of the problems confronting his people. His opponents sometimes found him stubborn and domineering, but so great was his ability and patriotism that his countrymen upon the whole were glad to trust his judgment, and follow his leadership. It is doubtful whether any other citizen of the Choctaw Nation could have carried through the unpopular policy of relinquishing the tribal institutions.[52]

There is reason to suspect that the Tuskahoma Party secured the united support necessary to carry out its program through high-handed dealings with its political opponents. A committee of the Council appointed to investigate the official acts of National Secretary Jacob B. Jackson brought specific charges of negligence in caring for the national archives, and failure to publish official notices and to provide public officials with copies of the laws. Jackson's testimony before the committee revealed an almost unbelievable carelessness and forgetfulness in carrying out the duties of his office, but no intentional miscon-

[50]Ibid., August 27, October 1, 1896; Acts of the Choctaw Nation, September 18, 1896.
[51]Indian Citizen, October 8, October 22, 1896.
[52]For biographies of Green McCurtain see Indian Citizen, October 23, 1902, and Report Commissioner of Indian Affairs, 1900, p. 148.

duct. He resigned his position, however, and McCurtain appointed Solomon J. Homer, who had been secretary of the investigating committee, to take his place. It is fairly evident that Jackson's removal was due to political expediency.[53]

McCurtain's annual message recommended a friendly and conciliatory policy toward the United States. He advised that the land be divided by either of the following methods: to list all the land in three classes — bottom, upland, and mountain — and let each citizen take his share of each; or to appraise the land, and let each select an amount equal to a specified monetary value. He was inclined to favor the latter plan, which, it should be noted, was eventually adopted by the Dawes Commission. He did not advocate an immediate change in the government, believing that the United States would grant a delay in that respect, once the Choctaws had adopted an allotment policy. He advised the Council to appoint a commission to treat with the Dawes Commission.[54]

These recommendations were embodied in legislation enacted October 22. The law provided for the appointment of a commission of nine members including the Chief, which was authorized to negotiate with regard to the division of the land and mineral interests, the perpetuation of the present form of government for as long as possible, the right of the Nation to decide citizenship cases, the settlement of Choctaw claims growing out of treaty stipulations, and the preservation of the tribal patent inviolate.[55]

McCurtain then called an international conference to meet at South McAlester on November 11. He notified the Dawes Commission of this meeting, and expressed the willingness of the Choctaws to begin negotiations at Fort Smith, November 16.[56]

Representatives of all the civilized tribes attended the conference at South McAlester. The Choctaw Nation was represented by the delegation appointed to treat with the Dawes Commission — Green McCurtain, J. S. Standley, N. B. Ainsworth, Amos Henry, A. S. Williams, Wesley Anderson, D. C. Garland, E. N. Wright, and Ben Hampton. J. S. Standley was elected president of the meeting, and Robert L.

[53]Union Agency Files, Choctaw—National Secretary, report of committee, also bond given by Homer; *Indian Citizen*, October 31, 1895—this paper carries the official notice that Jackson was charged with failure to publish—he had evidently published it and forgotten the incident.

[54]*Indian Citizen*, October 8, 1896.

[55]Acts of the Choctaw Nation, October 22, 1896.

[56]*Commission to the Five Civilized Tribes, Annual Report*, 1896, pp. 97-98.

Owen of the Cherokee Nation was chosen as secretary. Resolutions were unanimously adopted recommending the opening of negotiations with the Dawes Commission upon the following principles: the division of the land, with the reservation of certain portions for school purposes; the payment of five hundred dollars to each citizen as compensation for the surrender of tribal citizenship, and such inconveniences as the necessity of constructing new improvements and laying out new roads; the admission of Indian Territory to statehood with no territorial stage, and no union with Oklahoma, and with absolute prohibition of the liquor traffic; and the continuance of tribal government until the preceding conditions should be carried out — a suggested period of twenty-five years. The resolutions closed with the following declaration:

"We represent sixty-five thousand of sober, industrious, self-supporting and God-fearing people; owners of the entire soil of Indian Territory by solemn treaty and patented titles; people who came to a wilderness, driven by force, and made it a cultivated land: people who have erected schools, churches and courts of justice and governments under which they have found safety and happiness. We rely on the justice of our cause and the guidance of Divine Providence and we appeal to the moral sentiment of a great and magnanimous nation, in whose hands is our ultimate destiny and in whose honorable national life and history we have earned a decent and honorable place."[57]

After this inter-tribal council closed, the Choctaw delegates went to Fort Smith where they had daily conferences with the Dawes Commission from November 16 to December 12. They then adjourned to Muskogee, hoping representatives from the Chickasaws would meet them there, but the Chickasaws were not yet prepared to treat. During these negotiations the Dawes Commission again submitted their proposals, which the Choctaws accepted wholly or in part. The Choctaws made the following additional proposals: the continuance of the tribal government until the land should be divided, payment for the remainder of the Leased District, compensation for the surrender of tribal citizenship, and a stipulation that the land should be inalienable and nontaxable for a specified period.[58] While these negotiations were in progress, members of the old Progressive and National parties met in

[57]*Indian Citizen*, November 12, November 19, 1896.
[58]*Commission to the Five Civilized Tribes, Annual Report*, 1896, p. 99. For negotiations with the Chickasaws *see ibid.*, pp. 109-22.

convention at Antlers — always a conservative stronghold — and passed resolutions against any agreement with the Dawes Commission or any change in the government and land tenure.[59]

An agreement was signed at Muskogee on December 18. It provided that the Chief should deed to the United States the entire tribal domain, which should then be divided equally among the citizens except that each of the freedmen should receive only forty acres. The allotments were to remain inalienable and non-taxable for twenty-five years, except that provision was made for the sale of certain portions at stated intervals. The townsites, public buildings, and mineral lands were to be reserved from allotment; the proceeds from the sale of town lots were to be distributed equally among all the citizens except the freedmen; and the mineral revenues were to be used by the United States Government for the support of education. The tribal governments should continue until March 4, 1905, but acts of the Council would be subject to the approval of the President of the United States. All outstanding claims between the Choctaw and Chickasaw nations and the Federal Government would be arbitrated by the United States Senate. The trust funds held by the United States would be capitalized and paid out per caput. Finally the agreement was to be valid when ratified by the Congress of the United States and by the Choctaw and Chickasaw nations.[60] Thus after three years of persuasion backed up by the threat of hostile legislation the Dawes Commission succeeded in making an agreement with the representatives of the first of the Five Civilized Tribes to consent to negotiation.

As soon as the agreement was signed, the members of the Dawes Commission went to Washington to present it to Congress. At the same time Anderson, Ainsworth, and Standley were sent by the Choctaw government to assist them in securing its ratification.[61] On the other hand a number of influences sought to bring about its defeat. E. N. Wright, the only member of the Choctaw commission who had refused to sign it, worked actively against it among his own people.[62] A Chickasaw delegation went to Washington to protest; the Chickasaws were opposed to the sale of town lots, and they especially objected to the trust plan of conveyance, insisting that the title to allotments

[59]*Indian Citizen*, December 3, December 10, 1896.

[60]*Indian Citizen*, December 31, 1896; January 7, 1897; *Commission to the Five Civilized Tribes, Annual Report*, 1896, pp. 100-6.

[61]Union Agency Files, Choctaw—Principal Chief, annual message of McCurtain, 1897.

[62]*Indian Citizen*, December 31, 1896.

should be made by the executives of the two tribes rather than the United States.[63] It was mainly because of the Chickasaw protests that Congress did not ratify the agreement.

Congress then sought to terminate the tribal governments by compulsory legislation applying to all five tribes. Official delegations from the Cherokee, Chickasaw, Creek, and Seminole nations drew up a protest in which J. B. Jackson, G. W. Dukes, E. N. Wright, and D. M. Hailey joined, saying that the first declaration of a definite policy on the part of the Federal Government was embodied in the legislation of June 10, 1896, and that the members of the Dawes Commission had then become so engrossed with citizenship cases that the only opportunity given the Indians to treat had been the interval between December 14 and their departure for Washington on December 19. They therefore, requested an opportunity to enter into a voluntary agreement before they should be subject to drastic legislation without their consent.[64] As the Dawes Commission had spent three years in trying to negotiate with the Indians, this argument could not have been very convincing, and the bill passed Congress and was defeated only by the "pocket veto" of President Cleveland.[65]

The Chickasaw Nation now appointed a commission with power to treat, Governor McCurtain removed Wright from the Choctaw commission, and the two groups met at Atoka and came to an understanding with each other. They then opened negotiations with the Dawes Commission on the first day of April,[66] and the Atoka Agreement, as it soon came to be called, was signed on April 23. The terms of this important document were similar to those of the unratified Muskogee agreement in the allotment provisions, the reservation of mineral lands and townsites, the capitalization and distribution of treaty funds, the limited continuance of tribal government, and the method of ratification, although there were some differences of detail, and the Chickasaw objection to the trust plan of conveyance was met by the provision that the executives of the two tribes should execute the patents to the allottees.[67]

---

[63]Ibid., January 14, February 4-18, 1897, "Washington Letter." There was a danger that the trust plan of conveyance would automatically ratify the contingent grants to the railroads.

[64]Ibid., February 18, February 25, 1897; Congressional Record, 54 Cong., 2 Sess., XXIX, Part 2, 1917-1918. This protest was presented to the Senate, February 17, 1897.

[65]Indian Citizen, March 11, 1897.

[66]Ibid., March 11, March 25, April 1, 1897.

[67]Report Commissioner of Indian Affairs, 1897, pp. 409-15. It will be necessary to refer to the terms of this settlement in more detail from time to time.

The election of 1897 was the occasion of more interest than usually marked the odd-year elections. The Union Party was formed by the opponents of the Atoka Agreement, while the Tuskahoma Party carried on an educational campaign explaining its provisions and pointing out its advantages. When the Council convened, the political complexion of the new House of Representatives was still in doubt and twenty-four claimants appeared for the twenty seats. After the contests were settled and one or two appointments had been made by the Chief because of a tie, the Tuskahoma Party was in control with eleven members to nine of the opposition.[68]

Governor McCurtain delivered his annual message in words of deep solemnity. He described the evident determination of the Federal Government to force a change, and reminded his hearers that the United States "is much more powerful than we are, and is able to enforce these demands should we refuse to accede to them"; he warned the legislators to be careful in their deliberations and to "Contend for every thing that is justly due your people; but be cautious that these contentions are not made recklessly, but intelligently, and on reasonable grounds"; he explained that the tribal authority rested on minority control and was therefore doomed, although he could conceive of no greater sacrifice than to surrender the government "to which we have become attached from long and fond associations"; and he pointed out the expediency of compliance in order to save at least the tribal property before it should be too late. He reported the result of the negotiations — the agreement signed in December, and the failure of Congress to ratify it because of the opposition of the Chickasaws, and the Atoka Agreement, which he believed represented the utmost concessions that could have been obtained — but he advised the Council that it would not "be prudent nor wise" to act on it before its ratification by Congress.[69]

McCurtain became convinced later in the session that ratification by the Council would create a good impression, and so advised the legislators.[70] The Council then ratified it by a vote of thirteen to six in the House, and six to four in the Senate, and requested Congress to adopt it and carry it out in good faith.[71] The Chickasaws, however, rejected it at a popular election which was held in December.

[68]*Indian Citizen*, July 22, August 26, October 7, 1897.

[69]Union Agency Files, Choctaw—Principal Chief, text of message.

[70]*Indian Citizen*, November 4, 1897, special message, October 27.

[71]Acts of the Choctaw Nation, November 4, 1897; *Indian Citizen*, November 4, 1897.

Wesley Anderson was again sent to Washington to secure ratifica-tion by Congress,[72] and the agreement, with some amendments, was finally embodied in the Curtis Act which became law on June 28, 1898. This law provided for allotting the land and terminating the govern-ments of the Five Civilized Tribes, but specified that the provisions should not apply to the Choctaw and Chickasaw nations if they would ratify the amended Atoka Agreement at a joint election before Decem-ber 1. Although some of these amendments were concerned only with the modification of details in the interest of more efficient administra-tion, several important changes were introduced. The original agree-ment had made no provision for the Chickasaw freedmen, who it will be remembered had never been adopted by that tribe; it was now stipu-lated that they should be provided for, the same as their brethren of the Choctaw Nation. The royalty had been fixed on coal and asphalt with the provision that it might be reduced by the tribal legislatures; the power to reduce or advance it was now placed under the control of the Secretary of the Interior. Instead of referring the Leased District claim to the arbitration of the Senate it was provided that the decision pending in the Federal courts regarding the Wichita lands should be made the basis of settlement for the remainder of the tract.[73]

The Curtis Act prescribed the manner in which the Atoka Agree-ment should be ratified by the Choctaws and Chickasaws. Ratification was to depend upon the result of a joint election rather than separate action by the two nations. Voting was to be restricted to those who were qualified to vote under the tribal laws, and citizenship claimants were excluded. A returning board, consisting of the two chief execu-tives, the national secretaries, and a member of the Dawes Commission, was to meet at Atoka and canvass the votes. Chief McCurtain instructed the election judges to forbid the voting of freedmen, since the election concerned the disposal of Choctaw property in which they owned no share, but the Department of the Interior decided against this ruling, and he recalled his instructions. The election was held on August 24, and the agreement carried by a vote of 2,164 to 1,366. The ratification was officially proclaimed on August 30.[74]

The Atoka Agreement was also the main issue in the regular Choctaw election in the Summer of 1898. The Tuskahoma Party

[72]Acts of the Choctaw Nation, October 25, 1898.
[73]Report Commissioner of Indian Affairs, 1898, pp. 425-48, especially pp. 434-43, text of Curtis Act with the Atoka Agreement as amended by Congress.
[74]Report Commissioner of Indian Affairs, 1898, p. 435; Indian Citizen, July 21, August 12-25, September 1, 1898.

again nominated McCurtain as its candidate for Principal Chief, upon a platform supporting the agreement. The Union Party, composed of all the opposition groups, nominated Wilson N. Jones; this party no longer opposed negotiation, but contended that better terms should have been secured. It is characteristic of the rapid shifting of Choctaw political alignments that Jones who had been the McCurtain candidate in three of the most hotly contested elections ever held in the Nation was now McCurtain's opponent, and that Jones was supported by Jackson, whose opposition had brought the Nation to the verge of civil war six years before, and by Wright who had been McCurtain's campaign manager in 1896.[75] The Tuskahoma Party was victorious; McCurtain was reëlected and his party secured a safe majority in both houses of the Council.[76]

Almost immediately after the ratification of the Atoka Agreement differences of opinion arose as to the disposal of the mineral lands. A great deal of impatience also developed as the allotment of the land was delayed by complicated questions of citizenship. Both of these issues entered into the election of 1900. Three nominations were made for Principal Chief. As McCurtain was disqualified to serve another term, the Tuskahoma Party nominated Gilbert W. Dukes upon a platform of fidelity to the Atoka Agreement, speedy settlement of tribal affairs, and continued leasing of the mineral lands for the support of education. This party occupied a sort of middle position between the extreme conservatives, who again supported Jacob B. Jackson, and the Union Party, which nominated E. N. Wright and adopted a very radical platform condemning the Atoka Agreement as inadequate and slow, and advocating immediate sale of all the mineral lands and division of the proceeds.[77] The Tuskahoma Party elected its candidate for Principal Chief and secured control of the Council,[78] but it soon adopted the policy of the Union Party regarding the sale of the mineral lands.

The main event of Duke's administration was the negotiation of the so-called Supplementary Agreement. This compact was signed at Washington, March 21, 1902, and ratified by Congress on July 1. It contained minute specifications regulating the allotment of land, created a citizenship court, and provided for the sale of the mineral lands

[75]*Indian Citizen*, June 16, 1898.
[76]*Ibid.*, October 6, 1898. The Tuskahoma Party secured twelve out of the twenty seats in the House, and nine out of the twelve in the Senate.
[77]*Ibid.*, May 31, June 21, July 19, July 26, 1900.
[78]*Ibid.*, August 16, October 4, 1900.

within three years from the date of ratification and before the dissolution of the tribal government. It was to be referred to a joint vote of the citizens of the two nations on September 25.[79]

The supporters of the agreement carried on an intensive educational campaign to secure its adoption. During the Summer the *Indian Citizen* printed the text in both English and Choctaw, and carried articles explaining its provisions. A Supplementary Agreement Executive Committee, of which D. C. McCurtain, son of Green McCurtain, was chairman, mailed circular letters and copies of the agreement to the voters, and just before election the leaders of the Tuskahoma Party met at the capital and arranged to send workers into every county of the Nation.[80] This campaign was successful and the agreement was ratified by a vote of 2,140 to 704.[81]

The Supplementary Agreement also entered into the regular election, as the Atoka Agreement had done four years earlier. The campaign was a very bitter one. Although McCurtain had supported Dukes two years before, an open rupture between the two men soon occurred. At the expiration of his term of office as Chief, McCurtain became an active member of the Council and as chairman of the Finance Committee he began in the regular session of 1901 to report fraud and peculation in the conduct of official business, which he charged to the negligence of Dukes.[82] The Tuskahoma Party then nominated McCurtain as its candidate for Principal Chief, and Dukes and his supporters bolted and held another convention. At this meeting Dukes and Thomas W. Hunter were candidates for the nomination, but Hunter was successful because he opposed the Supplementary Agreement, which as an accomplishment of his administration Dukes naturally felt bound to support.[83] The old Union Party held an irregular convention at Antlers, and endorsed the candidacy of Hunter. The issue was now drawn between the Tuskahoma Party supporting the Supplementary Agreement, and the Hunter Party opposing it. Solomon J. Homer, V. M. Locke, and G. W. Dukes were among Hunter's sup-

[79]*Report Commissioner of Indian Affairs*, 1902, pp. 514-29, text of agreement.

[80]Union Agency Files, Choctaw—Federal Relations, letter from Supplementary Agreement Executive Committee, September 9, 1902; *ibid.*, Choctaw—Intruders, letter by Chief Dukes enclosing copy of agreement; *Indian Citizen*, September 11, 1902.

[81]*Indian Citizen*, October 2, 1902, proclamation of the returning board. The original is in the Union Agency Files. The votes were canvassed by a returning board similar to the one that canvassed the results of the election on the Atoka Agreement.

[82]Acts of the Choctaw Nation, November 6, November 14, 1901—these reports were not approved by the Chief; *Indian Citizen*, January 30, 1902.

[83]*Indian Citizen*, June 12, June 19, 1902.

porters, while James S. Standley, Wesley Anderson, and Napoleon B. Ainsworth supported McCurtain.[84]

The election was close and both sides claimed the victory.[85] As trouble was anticipated at the canvassing of the returns, Agent Shoenfelt was at the capital with his Indian police when the Council convened. Marshal Hackett had also been sent there by the Department of Justice. Governor Dukes using tactics similar to those employed by the McCurtain party in 1892 held the capitol with his lighthorsemen and refused to let the McCurtain faction enter. Shoenfelt, whose partisanship of McCurtain is plainly evident in his report, wished to clear the capitol of all armed men including the lighthorsemen. Hackett on the other hand with his deputies supported the lighthorsemen as the lawfully constituted authorities of the Nation. It required all Shoenfelt's persuasion to prevent McCurtain and his supporters from rushing the capitol and taking forcible possession of the government.

The Council attempted to convene on Monday, October 6. The McCurtain faction had a clear majority in the Senate, and the organization was effected without difficulty. There were several contested seats in the House, and while Dukes and his lighthorsemen had control of the building the Hunter members organized with Hodges as Speaker. The votes for Principal Chief could not be counted, however, for the judges of the Supreme Court, who were holding the returns of fifty out of the fifty-one precincts, refused to bring them to the capitol, saying that they would be forcibly taken out of their possession. The McCurtain members of the House, expelled from Representative Hall by their opponents, met separately and organized with Robert J. Ward as their presiding officer.

This deadlock continued until Saturday when in response to a call from Shoenfelt two companies of Negro soldiers under Major Starr arrived from Fort Reno. Starr ordered all armed men to leave the capitol, including Dukes' lighthorsemen and Hackett's deputies, and the McCurtain supporters were now able to enter the building. A quarrel then took place between the two rival groups, each of which claimed to be the regularly organized House of Representatives. "Speaker" Ward asked "Speaker" Hodges to vacate the chair and when Hodges refused he pulled him out and sat down. Hodges then secured a chair and sat down beside him, both clerks called their rolls, and for thirty minutes both Speakers attempted to preside over the

[84]*Ibid.*, July 10, July 17, 1902.
[85]*Ibid.*, August 6 (August 7), August 14, 1902.

deliberations of rival bodies meeting in the same room. They then adjourned to canvass the election returns.

After the troops arrived, Shoenfelt detailed members of his Indian police to escort the Supreme Judges to the capitol. The McCurtain Council then met in the Supreme Court chamber and counted the votes. National Secretary Solomon J. Homer, a Hunter partisan, refused to attend and deliver the votes from the Supreme Judges to the presiding officers of the houses, but the formality was omitted and Ward announced that McCurtain had received 1,645 votes to Hunter's 956. McCurtain, who was at the hotel, was then notified of his election, and he came and took the oath of office.

In the meantime, Hunter was also inducted into office. Chief Dukes, by the exercise of his constitutional power to fill vacancies in elective offices, appointed five Senators, who with the Hunter members of the Council canvassed the returns of the Atoka precinct which they had in their possession and declared Hunter elected. Hunter was then sworn in by a friendly Supreme Judge. When the McCurtain faction secured control of the capitol, this government withdrew, carrying the great seal and the house journals and other official papers which were in the possession of National Secretary Homer.[86]

Shoenfelt, however, refused to recognize Hunter as Chief and McCurtain was left in possession of the government. The whole disturbance was accompanied by intense excitement, but no violence occurred. Many Choctaws even to the present day (1933) believe that Hunter was elected, and that McCurtain owed his position to the determination of the Federal Government to place him in control.

This session of the Council was mainly occupied in consolidating the control of the government by the McCurtain faction. On the Monday following the arrival of the troops and the counting of the votes, McCurtain made eight appointments to fill "vacancies" in the House of Representatives; and these new members constituted the entire representation from Pushmataha District.[87] On the same day an act was passed increasing the number of lighthorsemen under control of the Chief from nine to thirty, but it was later vetoed by President Roosevelt.[88] On the following Friday, Solomon J. Homer was impeached for

[86]Arthur Fairfield Chamberlin, personal interview—Chamberlin, a citizen of the Cherokee Nation, was a member of Shoenfelt's Indian police; *Indian Citizen*, October 9, October 16, October 23, 1902; *Report Commissioner of Indian Affairs*, 1903, pp. 173-74.

[87]Union Agency Files, Choctaw—National Council, certificates of appointment, dated October 13, 1902. The Atoka precinct was in this district.

[88]Acts of the Choctaw Nation, October 13, 1902—vetoed by Roosevelt, January 8, 1903.

neglect of duty in absenting himself from the capitol during the counting of the votes; failure to deliver the journals and other records to the clerks of the two houses; loss or wilful destruction of the report which Green McCurtain had filed when, as National Treasurer, he had distributed the Leased District money; and habitual drunkenness. When the time came for his trial before the Senate, he failed to appear or make any answer to the charges, and by a vote of ten to two he was convicted on every count and removed from office and "disqualified to hold any office of honor or trust or profit under the Choctaw Nation."[89] The Council also made an appropriation of ten dollars to procure an exact duplicate of the great seal that had been "lost, destroyed, or misplaced,"[90] and sent a memorial to the President requesting the removal of Marshal Hackett.[91] An act was also passed vacating all the offices of the Pushmataha District, but McCurtain vetoed it, saying that the trouble had gone far enough.[92] Three years later the impeachment and conviction of Homer was "repealed and held for naught," and the articles were ordered to be expunged from the records.[93]

Although the political opposition to the new order was about silenced from this time on, there was still a great deal of dissatisfaction among the conservative fullblood members of the tribe. When the party favoring negotiation with the Dawes Commission first secured control of the government in 1896, these irreconcilables began to despair of their ability to hold back the changes that were at hand, and when the Atoka Agreement was signed, a considerable movement developed among both Choctaws and Chickasaws to sell the whole country and purchase land in Mexico.[94] A party even visited Mexico during the Winter of 1897-1898 to look at the land.[95] At the time of the Crazy Snake disturbance among the Creeks there was also a Snake Band of Choctaws, who insisted that the Dawes Commission had no lawful authority, elected a chief and council which claimed to exercise functions of government, and sought by intimidation to prevent their

[89]*Ibid.,* October 21, 1902.

[90]*Ibid.,* October 22, 1902.

[91]*Ibid.,* October 24, 1902. Hackett was in fact dismissed from office a year later—S. B. Hackett, personal interview.

[92]*Indian Citizen,* October 23, 1902.

[93]Acts of the Choctaw Nation, October 24, 1905.

[94]*Indian Citizen,* July 22, 1897. A similar movement was especially strong at the same time among the Creeks—*Report Commissioner of Indian Affairs,* 1897, p. 141.

[95]*Indian Citizen,* March 17, 1898.

people from filing on land.[96] Some of them refused to choose allotments, and when the Dawes Commission made arbitrary selections for them they rejected the patents to their land.[97]

When a special committee of the United States Senate visited the Choctaw country in 1906, Jacob B. Jackson, who seemed to be the leader of the movement, explained the dissatisfaction of the conservatives who still hoped to remove to Mexico or even South America as soon as it would be possible to wind up their tribal affairs and sell their property. He said that about two thousand Choctaw and Chickasaw fullbloods had held meetings and had appointed him and J. C. Folsom, S. E. Coe, Saul Folsom, and Willis Jones as a committee to draw up a memorial which he presented. The memorial stated that they had opposed the agreements with the Dawes Commission but allotment had been accepted over their protest. They preferred the old system of land ownership where they could move about, have all the land they wanted, and let their live stock run at large without being hailed into the white man's court to pay damages. Since they had been outnumbered and defeated they asked only the opportunity to continue their institutions in some remote place. "Our educated people tell us that the white man came to this country to avoid conditions which to him were not as bad as the present conditions are to us; that he went across the great ocean and sought new homes in order to avoid things which to him were distasteful and wrong. All we ask is that we may be permitted to exercise the same privilege." The majority of their people might remain and mingle with the whites and lose their racial identity, but they believed that the Great Father of all had created the Indians to fill a proper place in the world with the "right to exist as a race."[98]

But the tract of land in Mexico was never purchased, and the irreconcilables finally accepted allotment with the rest of their people. After the agreement with the United States the only remaining phase of Choctaw tribal history was concerned with the manner of terminating the national government and closing out the common estate.

[96]Acts of the Choctaw Nation, October 22, 1903.
[97]Commissioner to the Five Civilized Tribes, Annual Report, 1908, p. 210.
[98]Report Select Committee, I, 956-61.

THE DISSOLUTION OF TRIBAL
INTERESTS

I 2

The actual work of closing out the tribal estate and terminating the tribal government was carried out by the Dawes Commission partly under the provisions of the Atoka and Supplementary agreements. Congress, however, did not feel bound by the terms of the settlements, that had been the subject of such protracted negotiations, and in several instances passed arbitrary laws setting their provisions aside. As the work went on, it became apparent that both the Indians and the members of the Dawes Commission had underestimated the magnitude of the task, and that it would not be completed within the specified time. As a consequence, the tribal government did not end as contemplated in the Atoka Agreement, but has continued in an attenuated form even to the present (1933). But the main part of the work was accomplished in the decade between 1896 and 1906, and a consideration of that period may be said to close the independent history of the Choctaw Nation.

Since the liquidation of the tribal estate involved the division of the common property, the determination of citizenship was of the first importance. The act of June 10, 1896, which had authorized the Dawes Commission to hear citizenship claimants, had provided that all applications had to·be received within three months from the passage of the act.[1] The Commission accordingly sent out notices from Vinita, inviting claimants to make application.[2] A large number of persons whose claims to citizenship were very remote presented their cases to the Commission, and those who failed to secure recognition appealed to Judge Clayton of the Federal court for the Central District of the

[1]*Report Commissioner of Indian Affairs*, 1896, pp. 446-47.
[2]*Indian Citizen*, July 16, 1896.

269

Indian Territory. A total of 2,175 of these "court citizens" was thus added to the Choctaw roll.[3]

It has been pointed out that Chief Gardner at first followed a policy of passive resistance, and ignored or evaded the requests of the Commission for the tribal rolls, but he finally employed E. B. Stewart as an attorney to represent the Nation before the Commission,[4] and called a special session of the Council to make provision for taking a census. The Council accordingly authorized the appointment of a commission in each county and one in the Chickasaw district to enroll all recognized Choctaw citizens in three classes — freedmen, citizens by blood, and intermarried citizens.[5] This law was supplemented by additional legislation,[6] and the tribal rolls were carefully checked and revised.[7]

The Nation also took steps to protect itself from the "court citizens." In August of 1897 Chief McCurtain published an indignant notice to these people that his time was too precious to spend in acknowledging receipt of their requests for enrollment, and that the Nation denied their citizenship and would appeal, for although the white man was smart enough to manufacture almost anything he could not manufacture Indians.[8] When the Choctaw schools were opened the following month, the newly made citizens demanded school privileges for their children. As the teachers of the neighborhood schools were paid according to the enrollment, the admission of these children would have made a serious drain on Choctaw revenue, and the Chief ordered the schools to be closed on September 24 as a temporary measure of protection.[9] When the Council convened, the Board of Education decided to forbid the attendance of children whose citizenship was not recognized by the Nation, and the schools were reopened.[10]

In his annual message the Chief pointed out the loss to the Nation

[3]*Report Commissioner of Indian Affairs*, 1898, pp. 459-73—this volume gives the text of important decisions each involving the citizenship of a large number of persons; *Commission to the Five Civilized Tribes, Annual Report*, 1900, p. 18; *Indian Citizen*, December, 1896-January, 1897—the names of those admitted to citizenship are printed in these issues.

[4]*Indian Citizen*, August 13, 1896.

[5]Acts of the Choctaw Nation, September 18, 1896.

[6]*Ibid.*, October 30, November 4, 1896; November 4, 1897.

[7]*Indian Citizen*, December 9, 1897, notice of Chief McCurtain.

[8]*Ibid.*, August 19, 1897.

[9]*Ibid.*, September 16, 1897.

[10]Union Agency Files, Choctaw—Principal Chief, annual message of Chief McCurtain, 1897; *Indian Citizen*, November 18, 1897, notice of Butler S. Smiser, District Trustee.

through the admission of these "court citizens," and recommended that the Council bring it to the attention of Congress. The Council authorized the Chief to seek a judgment of the United States Supreme Court against the constitutionality of the law which gave to the Dawes Commission and the Federal courts the power to determine Choctaw citizenship, and directed the attorney employed by the Nation to endeavor to persuade Congress to repeal the law.[11] Congress did pass a law at the next session providing that all cases involving the constitutionality of legislation regarding citizenship or allotment might be appealed from the Federal courts in the Territory directly to the Supreme Court.[12] A test case was then made in the form of an appeal from one of Judge Clayton's decisions, and the Supreme Court upheld the constitutionality of the law and the jurisdiction of the court in citizenship cases.[13]

D. C. McCurtain, who had been appointed Choctaw delegate to Congress under an act of 1899,[14] then reported to Chief Dukes and the Council that most of the "court citizens" had secured their claims through fraud, but that it would involve much expensive and tedious litigation to prove this contention. He therefore advised that the Nation fight its case on the technicality that the judgments were invalid because the appeals from the decision of the Dawes Commission had been taken against either the Choctaw or the Chickasaw Nation according to the alleged citizenship of the claimant instead of against both tribes as should have been done in a case of joint ownership.[15] The Chickasaws, whose experience in the court of the Southern District had been similar to that of the Choctaws, joined with the Choctaws in demanding a special court to pass on citizenship cases, and they managed to secure such a provision in the Supplementary Agreement.[16]

The Citizenship Court set up under the terms of this compact was in existence from 1902 to the end of 1904. It rendered a decision, December 17, 1902, in the case styled *The Choctaw and Chickasaw Nations or Tribes* v. *J. T. Riddle et al.,* that the Federal courts of the

[11]Union Agency Files, Choctaw—Principal Chief, *op. cit.;* Acts of the Choctaw Nation, November 4, 1897.

[12]*Report Commissioner of Indian Affairs,* 1898, text of law enacted July 1, 1898.

[13]*Commission to the Five Civilized Tribes, Annual Report,* 1899, appendix, pp. 160-78, decision rendered May 15, 1899, *Choctaw Nation* v. *F. R. Robinson.* Cases involving the other four nations were decided at the same time.

[14]Acts of the Choctaw Nation, October 19, 1899.

[15]Union Agency Files, Choctaw—Federal Relations, report of McCurtain to Council, 1901.

[16]*Report Commissioner of Indian Affairs,* 1902, pp. 520-21, section of agreement creating citizenship court.

Indian Territory had not followed the correct procedure by allowing suit to be brought against each tribe separately, and by trying the cases *de novo* instead of admitting only the evidence submitted to the Dawes Commission.[17] This ruling gave the Choctaws and Chickasaws the desired opportunity for a rehearing of their cases before the Citizenship Court, and they secured an almost complete reversal; the claims of about 3,403 persons for citizenship in the two tribes were rejected, and only about 156 were sustained.[18] The Choctaws thus secured at the cost of much expensive litigation[19] the results that could have been obtained at the beginning by a law that would have provided proper consideration of citizenship cases.

While the two nations were trying to protect their rolls through court procedure, the members of the Dawes Commission were engaged in the actual enrollment of citizens. They began work in the Chickasaw Nation in the Fall of 1898, and enrolled at the same time the Choctaws who were living in that district.[20] When they entered the Choctaw Nation they were assisted by a citizenship commission created by the Council,[21] consisting of S. E. Lewis, Gilbert W. Dukes, and A. J. Harkins with A. Telle serving as clerk. They began at Alikchi in the Spring of 1899, and spent most of the Summer in field work visiting the most remote parts of the Nation in the attempt to discover every person listed on the tribal rolls or admitted under the act of 1896 by their own ruling or the decision of the court. They failed to locate some of the most conservative fullbloods who stayed away on account of sickness or poverty or disapproval of the whole proceeding, but they made a total enrollment of 16,253 including 1,777 Choctaws previously enrolled in the Chickasaw district. They also enrolled 3,985 Choctaw freedmen, including 468 who were living in the Chickasaw Nation. The work seems to have been carried on with a high degree of efficiency, and the most harmonious relations existed between the members of the Dawes Commission and their Choctaw assistants.[22]

[17]*Report Select Committe*, I, 935-36; *Report Commissioner of Indian Affairs*, 1903, pp. 453-54; *Commission to the Five Civilized Tribes, Annual Report*, 1904, pp. 9-10.
[18]*Court of Claims Reports*, LXII, 501.
[19]For lawyers' contracts, etc., *see* Acts of the Choctaw Nation, March 23, March 25, October 19, 1899, and Union Agency Files, Choctaw—Citizenship, and Choctaw—Attorneys.
[20]*Commission to the Five Civilized Tribes, Annual Report*, 1899, p. 14.
[21]Acts of the Choctaw Nation, March 24, 1899.
[22]Union Agency Files, Choctaw—Citizenship, report of citizenship commission to Council, October, 1899; *Commission to the Five Civilized Tribes, Annual Report*, 1899, pp. 14-15; Acts of the Choctaw Nation, November 1, 1899, approval of report of citizenship commission.

After the Dawes Commission had completed its field work, it referred the names of those who had failed to enroll to the tribal authorities. During 1900 the Choctaw citizenship commission searched out these delinquents and accounted for almost every person listed in the tribal rolls.[23] A few more missing citizens were located afterward, but the work of the citizenship commission was virtually completed, and it was abolished by act of the Council in 1903.[24]

During the enrollment period many applications were presented by people claiming to have Choctaw blood, who had lived outside the Nation and had never been recognized as citizens. The Dawes Commission uniformly decided against these claimants, and Judge Clayton also ruled that since the object of the removal treaties had been to limit the Choctaws to a certain area, and since the title to their lands was to exist only so long as they should live there, Choctaw blood did not of itself confer citizenship. These claimants continued, however, to harass the Dawes Commission until 1900, when Congress settled the matter by a law that no applications should be received from any person who was not a recognized citizen of the Nation.[25]

An exception was made in the case of the Mississippi Choctaws, since the Treaty of Dancing Rabbit Creek, which had given the Choctaws the option of taking allotments in Mississippi, had further provided that "Persons who claim under this article shall not lose the privilege of a Choctaw citizen, but if they ever remove are not to be entitled to any portion of the Choctaw annuity." It will be remembered, moreover, that during the entire course of their national life in the West the Choctaws had encouraged the immigration of their people from Mississippi and had freely admitted them to citizenship.

An act of June 7, 1897, made it the duty of the Dawes Commission to report to Congress whether or not the Mississippi Choctaws were entitled to citizenship privileges. The Commission then made an investigation and reported that to be eligible for enrollment it would be necessary for such Indians to take up a bona fide residence in the Choctaw Nation and establish their identity as the descendants of those

[23]Acts of the Choctaw Nation, October 31, 1900, report of citizenship commission to Council, October, 1900; Commission to the Five Civilized Tribes, Annual Report, 1900, pp. 14-16.

[24]Acts of the Choctaw Nation, October 22, 1900; November 6, 1901; October 22, 1903.

[25]Report Commissioner of Indian Affairs, 1898, pp. 466-67, Judge Clayton's ruling in case of Sidney J. Cundiff v. the Choctaw Nation; ibid., 1900, p. 75, text of law, enacted May 31, 1900; Commission to the Five Civilized Tribes, Annual Report, 1900, pp. 16-17.

who had elected to take allotments under the treaty of Dancing Rabbit Creek. The Curtis Act then made it the duty of the Commission to identify them.[26]

Identification would normally have been established by showing that a request for allotment had been made under the Treaty of Dancing Rabbit Creek, but since Agent Ward had been intemperate and incompetent as well as abusive to the Choctaws he had kept no proper record of these requests. The Dawes Commission therefore assumed that the Choctaws living in Mississippi were the descendants of those who would have made a declaration of their intention to remain if they had been given fair treatment, and that no further identification was necessary.[27] Since this interpretation would have made every person of Choctaw descent in Mississippi eligible to citizenship, the Supplementary Agreement provided that it should apply only to fullbloods, and that mixed bloods must prove that their ancestors had made applications for allotment under the Treaty of Dancing Rabbit Creek. The Supplementary Agreement also stipulated that persons identified as Mississippi Choctaws should not be eligible for enrollment unless they should remove to the Choctaw-Chickasaw country, and that they should receive allotments only after three years' residence.[28]

More than six thousand applications were received by the Dawes Commission at Atoka and Muskogee during 1901 and 1902 by persons, apparently white or with Negro blood, who claimed to be Mississippi Choctaws; but few if any of these claims were allowed. In April of 1901, representatives of the Commission went to Mississippi, where they spent more than a year trying to identify all the fullbloods of that region. There again they were deluged with applications from doubtful claimants, but the real Mississippi Choctaws remained in their remote fastnesses, suspicious and fearful of some new scheme of the white man to tear them from their homes. The workers spent months in the field, camping in the neighborhood of fullblood settlements in Jasper, Newton, Scott, Leake, and Neshoba counties, sent interpreters to the homes, and gradually secured the information necessary for identification.[29]

[26]*Commission to the Five Civilized Tribes, Annual Report*, 1899, pp. 73-77, Appendix, p. 68; *Report Commissioner of Indian Affairs*, 1898, pp. 432-33.

[27]*Commission to the Five Civilized Tribes, Annual Report*, 1899, pp. 77-80.

[28]*Report Commissioner of Indian Affairs*, 1902, pp. 523-24, provisions of Supplementary Agreement.

[29]*Commission to the Five Civilized Tribes, Annual Report*, 1902, pp. 25-30. *See* diagram opposite p. 130 showing specimen of family tree worked out to simplify identification.

In 1903 Congress made an appropriation to aid these fullbloods in removal, and before the year was over about three hundred were brought by train, and assisted to settle in the Choctaw country. Many others were brought by speculators, who hoped in this way to secure a lien on their allotments. They were a primitive people entirely unable to cope with the problems that came to them with their new possessions.[30]

The Choctaw freedmen made up still another group of citizens whose enrollment presented special problems. The Choctaws had never kept a roll of freedmen, and in some cases it was difficult to distinguish the descendants of their former slaves from non-citizen Negroes. The citizenship commission that worked with the Dawes Commission in 1899 enlisted the services of Len Colbert, a Negro, who was able to render them material assistance in the work of identification.[31]

As the Atoka Agreement had followed the provisions of the Treaty of 1866 and the act of adoption in limiting the allotments of the freedmen to forty acres, and had expressly stipulated that they were not to share in any distribution of tribal funds, the Choctaw and Chickasaw Freedmen's Association employed attorneys and attempted to effect the transfer of a large number of names from the freedman rolls to the Choctaw rolls. They claimed that many of their people were illegitimate descendants of Choctaw fathers and Negro mothers and that they were therefore entitled to be classed as Choctaws. Congress attempted to settle the matter in 1906 by providing that illegitimate children should take the status of their mother,[32] but the freedmen continued to agitate for the change. They presented their case to a committee of the United States Senate that visited their country in the Fall of 1906,[33] and early in 1907 their lawyers made a special attempt to secure legislation by Congress providing for the transfer of all freedmen with Choctaw or Chickasaw blood to the tribal rolls. Melven Cornish, who was the attorney for the two nations, pointed out that according to their laws illegitimate children always followed the status of the mother, and that any other rule would lead to impossible complica-

---

[30]*Report Commissioner of Indian Affairs*, 1903, p. 93; 1906, p. 232; *Commission to the Five Civilized Tribes, Annual Report*, 1904, p. 15; *Report Select Committee*, I, 1018, 1118-19; G. E. E. Lindquist, *The Red Man in the United States* (New York, 1923), pp. 112-15, study of the Choctaws who remained in Mississippi.

[31]*Commission to the Five Civilized Tribes, Annual Report*, 1902, p. 16; Union Agency Files, Choctaw—Citizenship, report of citizenship commission to Council, October, 1899.

[32]Kappler, *Laws and Treaties*, III, 170, law enacted April 26, 1906.

[33]*Report Select Committee*, I, 524-45, 938-48, 962-63; II, 1497-1623.

tions.[34] Congress, influenced by these considerations, refused to take action, and the tribal rolls were closed on March 4.

The original roll enumerated all Choctaw citizens who were living on September 25, 1902. To this total were added all children born after that date and living on March 4, 1905, and a later list of "newborns" living on March 4, 1906. The sum of these three rolls, although still cited by the Indian Bureau in population statistics, is obviously larger than the number living at one time. Even so, it has some significance as indicating the relative racial composition of the tribe. The figures are as follows:[35]

Choctaws
    Fullbloods   7,076
    Mixed bloods, three-fourths or more   706
    Mixed bloods, one-half to three-fourths   1,636
    Less than one-half including whites   9,563
            TOTAL   18,981
Freedmen   5,994
Mississippi Choctaws
    Fullbloods   1,344
    Mixed bloods, three-fourths or more   85
    Mixed bloods, one-half to three-fourths   27
    Less than one-half including whites   183
            TOTAL   1,639
           GRAND TOTAL   26,614

Since these rolls were prepared for the sole purpose of determining who was entitled to share in the tribal estate, the division of the common property was the next task of the Dawes Commission. During 1899 and 1900 field parties under the supervision of the Commission worked in the Choctaw Nation appraising the land. They disregarded the value of the improvements and such items as accessibility to markets, and listed the land, according to physical features, in ten different classes, which were further subdivided to make a total of nineteen. They then placed an arbitrary allotment value on each class, which,

[34]*Senate Docs.,* 59 Cong., 2 Sess., No. 257; *Report Commissioner of Indian Affairs,* 1907, pp. 106-7; *Court of Claims Records,* LXII, 458-516.
[35]*Commissioner to the Five Civilized Tribes, Annual Report,* 1908, p. 195.

although expressed in monetary units, represented the comparative value of the various grades of land, and not the real value.[36]

The Atoka Agreement had contemplated the division of all the land except that reserved for townsites, minerals, and public purposes, but the Supplementary Agreement had provided that each Choctaw citizen exclusive of the freedmen should receive an allotment of 320 acres of average land.[37] According to the table of comparative prices fixed for the different grades of land this allotment carried an arbitrary value of $1,041.28, which the allottee might invest as he chose, thus securing an allotment varying in size from 160 to 4,165 acres according to the type of land he selected. By the same computation each freedman was entitled to an allotment value of $130.16 which he might invest in the same way.[38]

The allotments began in the Spring of 1903. The land office for the Choctaw Nation was located at Atoka, and for the Chickasaw at Tishomingo. Owners of improvements were given preferred claim on the land where their improvements were located, but aside from that, every Choctaw and Chickasaw citizen might select freely in compact or widely scattered tracts in either nation or both nations as he should choose. In most cases the entire amount of land was not selected at once, and after a homestead of convenient size was secured, many allottees showed little interest in completing their allotments. In 1909 it was provided by Congress that allottees entitled to remnants of not more than fifty dollars in comparative value should receive a cash payment from tribal funds of double the amount in lieu of allotment.[39]

Just before the allotment began, the Choctaw Nation attempted to create an allotment commission to assist such of its citizens as might require guidance in selecting their land, but the bill was vetoed by President Roosevelt upon the advice of the Department, which held that the Dawes Commission could attend to the matter without assistance. A later attempt to provide such protection met the same fate.[40]

[36]*Commission to the Five Civilized Tribes, Annual Report*, 1899, pp. 24-26, exhibit 21; 1900, pp. 28-30; 1901, p. 32; 1903, pp. 31-32, 53-54; Union Agency Files, Choctaw—Land Division—these papers contain some of the field records of the appraisers.

[37]*Report Commissioner of Indian Affairs*, 1902, p. 515.

[38]*Commission to the Five Civilized Tribes, Annual Report*, 1903, p. 54.

[39]*Report Commissioner of Indian Affairs*, 1903, p. 91; Union Agency Files, Choctaw—Land Division—among these documents are numerous applications for allotments showing locations of various tracts, and the values are added to make the total of $1,041.28; *Commission to the Five Civilized Tribes, Annual Report*, 1903, p. 54; *Commissioner to the Five Civilized Tribes*, 1908, pp. 197-99; Kappler, *Laws and Treaties*, III, 412, law enacted March 3, 1909.

[40]Acts of the Choctaw Nation, December 12, 1902; October 29, 1903.

As a result the more ignorant members of the tribe selected their allotments according to the advice of swindlers who assisted them for a consideration often amounting to almost the entire value of the allotment. Although the Atoka Agreement and subsequent laws of Congress sought to protect the Indians against these exactions, the fullblood usually kept his contract with the sharper to his own hurt.[41]

The Federal Government also experienced some difficulty in carrying out its engagement to put the allottees in possession. White intruders attempted to hold the lands they had illegally acquired, and instituted contests in the courts and before the Indian agent, and tried to influence Congress to legislate in their favor. But these troublesome contests were finally decided, and the intruders were removed by the agent and his Indian police.[42]

After the allotments were made, Congress had difficulty in formulating a policy to protect the Indians against alienation. Both the Atoka and Supplementary agreements had provided for the selection of homesteads which for twenty-one years should be inalienable and nontaxable, and a limited sale of the remainder; but these provisions were never carried out.[43] After a period of experimentation[44] Congress passed a law in 1908 removing all restrictions from the allotments of intermarried whites, freedmen, and mixed bloods who had less than one-half Indian blood, and providing protection for other Indians according to the degree of Indian blood.[45]

The Atoka Agreement had provided that townsites should be withheld from allotment, and that the money realized from the sale of lots should be distributed per caput to all citizens exclusive of freedmen. The platting of townsites and the appraisal and sale of lots was to be under the direction of a townsite commission consisting of one member of the Dawes Commission and one member appointed by the Principal Chief. The improvements were not to be appraised; the owner was given the privilege of purchasing at reduced rates the lots on which his improvements were located, or if he did not take advantage of this opportunity the improvements were to be sold at auction

[41]*Report Commissioner of Indian Affairs*, 1898, p. 410; *Report Select Committee*, I, 896-97, 909-12, 1023-26, 1040, 1111-25.

[42]*Report Commissioner of Indian Affairs*, 1903, pp. 162-63, 172-73; 1904, pp. 195-97, 477.

[43]*Ibid.*, 1897, p. 410; 1902, p. 516.

[44]*Ibid.*, 1904, pp. 206-7, 476; Kappler, Laws and Treaties, III, 176-77; *Report Select Committee*, I, 650-72; II, 1859.

[45]*Report Commissioner of Indian Affairs*, 1908, pp. 101-3; 1909, p. 375.

for his benefit. The unimproved lots were to be sold at the appraised value.[46]

John A. Sterritt of Troy, Ohio, was appointed by the President as the member of the townsite commission representing the Federal Government, and Butler S. Smiser was appointed by Chief McCurtain to represent the Choctaws. On May 31, 1899, they began work at Cale, which now received the name of Sterritt. It was a town of about eight hundred population, on the Missouri, Kansas, and Texas Railroad. Here they platted an area of 480 acres which they sold for $17,780.36. They next platted Atoka, which occupied them from September 1 to November 6. They then proceeded to South McAlester, where they experienced so much difficulty with the irregular topography and heavy timber that it required a year for them to complete the work.[47]

While the townsite commission was working at South McAlester, Congress passed a law providing that the platting should be done under the authority of the Department of the Interior, and that the townsite commission should not begin work until the plat was approved by the Department.[48] The Choctaw government insisted on carrying out the terms of the Atoka Agreement, and when Smiser refused to follow the new ruling he was removed by the Secretary of the Interior. After prolonged controversy over the right of the Department to discharge the Choctaw member of the commission, the matter was finally settled when the law of 1900 was embodied in the Supplementary Agreement, and Smiser was reinstated.[49]

The platting went on rapidly under the new plan, and lot sales were very brisk. Each town carried on an active advertising campaign through local newspapers and commercial clubs, and thousands of inquiries poured into the Indian Office from every state in the Union. New towns were springing up everywhere and the Choctaw Nation

[46]*Ibid.*, 1897, pp. 411-12; 1898, p. 438. The special rate to the owner of improvements was 50 per cent of the appraised value for one residence and one business lot, and 62.5 per cent for the remainder of his improved lots.

[47]*Ibid.*, 1899, pp. 126-27; *Commission to the Five Civilized Tribes, Annual Report,* 1900, pp. 96-97.

[48]*Commission to the Five Civilized Tribes, Annual Report,* 1900, pp. 226-29, text of law enacted May 31, 1900.

[49]*Report Commissioner of Indian Affairs,* 1902, pp. 524-25; *Commission to the Five Civilized Tribes, Annual Report,* 1902, pp. 188-89; 1904, pp. 217-18; Union Agency Files, Choctaw—Federal Relations, report of Delegate D. C. McCurtain to Chief and Council, Fall of 1901; *Indian Citizen,* March 27, October 23, 1902; Acts of the Choctaw Nation, December 13, 1902.

was rapidly filling with new settlers. About ninety towns were platted in the Choctaw Nation by 1907.[50]

These towns immediately established municipal governments and began laying taxes. The Curtis Act had provided that towns with a population of two hundred or more might incorporate, and tax personal property and improvements, and establish schools. The lots also were subject to taxation as soon as the purchasers had secured titles. Bond elections were held under the supervision of the Department of the Interior, and schoolhouses, electric light plants, and water systems were constructed. The towns of the Choctaw Nation began to assume the characteristics of towns in the neighboring states.[51]

The Choctaws were dissatisfied with the slowness of the Federal Government in distributing the proceeds of townsite sales. The Atoka Agreement had provided that distribution should begin one year from the date of ratification, and should be made annually thereafter.[52] In 1902, and again in 1903, the Council requested that the money be paid out so that the poorer members of the tribe would not be tempted to accept the assistance of speculators in settling on their new allotments, but the Secretary of the Interior ruled that the payments should not begin until the tribal affairs were more nearly settled.[53] In 1902 Congress made an appropriation of townsite money, which a Choctaw commission advanced to citizens who were actually destitute;[54] but the per caput payments did not begin until 1904.[55]

The Choctaws were more seriously disappointed by the failure of the United States to carry out the terms of the Supplementary Agreement with regard to the sale of their coal lands and the asphalt deposits of the Chickasaw Nation. The Atoka Agreement had placed the supervision of the mines under two trustees, one from each tribe, nominated by the chief executive and appointed by the President of the United States. The royalties were to be paid into the United States Treasury

[50]*Indian Citizen*, November, 27, 1902, "Facts about Greater Atoka," an example of the advertising carried on in local papers; *Report Commissioner of Indian Affairs*, 1905, p. 207; 1907, pp.334-35; *Commission to the Five Civilized Tribes, Annual Report*, 1904, pp. 201-2.

[51]*Report Commissioner of Indian Affairs*, 1898, pp. 429-30; 1902, p. 525; 1903, p. 90; 1904, p. 111; 1905, p. 133; 1906, p. 140; *Antlers Democrat*, March 29, 1901.

[52]*Report Commissioner of Indian Affairs*, 1897, p. 412.

[53]Acts of the Choctaw Nation, December 18, 1902; October 22, 1903.

[54]Kappler, *Laws and Treaties*, I, 748-49; *U. S. Statutes at Large*, XXXII, 177; Acts of the Choctaw Nation, November 2, 1904.

[55]*Report Commissioner of Indian Affairs*, 1904, pp. 520-21; 1905, pp. 208-9.

and the revenues were to be used to support the schools.[56] Napoleon B. Ainsworth of the Choctaw Nation and Lemuel C. Burris of the Chickasaw Nation were appointed as trustees, and they carried on their work under the regulations of the Interior Department.[57] But the Choctaws became impatient for the complete liquidation of the tribal estate, and the Supplementary Agreement contained elaborate provisions for the segregation and sale of the coal and asphalt lands. They were to be sold at public auction within three years from the date of ratification, by a commission of three appointed by the President, two of whom were to be citizens by blood of the Choctaw and Chickasaw nations respectively, nominated in each case by the chief executive of the tribe. Both the leased and unleased land was to be sold, the leased land being subject to the provisions of the leases.[58]

A study was made by J. A. Taff of the United States Geological Survey, and upon his recommendation 445,052.23 acres in the Choctaw Nation was segregated as coal land. In 1904 Congress repealed the terms of the Supplementary Agreement by providing that this land should be sold in 960-acre tracts by sealed bids, and that the sale should be directed by the Secretary of the Interior with the commission exercising only advisory functions. Certain tracts of unleased land were placed on the market during 1904 and 1905, but the few offers received were so low that the Department felt bound to reject them.[59]

The time limit specified in the Supplementary Agreement expired September 24, 1905. During the regular session of the Council that Fall, Chief McCurtain informed the legislators that there was an unofficial offer of fifteen million dollars for the entire tract, and requested them to draw up recommendations regarding its sale. The Council declared itself in favor of private sale or public auction, rather than sealed bids, with the price subject to the approval of the President. Believing that the offer of only the unleased and undeveloped land had retarded the sale of the more desirable property, it favored the sale of all the land without discrimination. It advised selling in any amount from forty acres up, since the 960-acre tracts had proved too large to attract the small buyer and too small to interest the important capitalist.[60]

[56]*Ibid.*, 1897, pp. 412-13; 1898, p. 440, text of Atoka Agreement, and amendment by the Curtis Act.
[57]*Ibid.*, 1898, pp. 546-51; 1899, pp. 110, 195-96; 1900, pp. 88-89, 208-20.
[58]*Ibid.*, 1902, pp. 526-27, text of Supplementary Agreement.
[59]*Ibid.*, 1903, p. 83; 1904, pp. 108-10, 479, 513-14.
[60]Acts of the Choctaw Nation, November 25, 1905.

These recommendations were submitted to the Federal Government, but in spite of strong efforts on the part of the Choctaws the law passed by Congress in 1906 for the final settlement of tribal affairs provided that none of the land should be sold until all the leases should expire.[61] Since the leases made under the Atoka Agreement were to run for thirty years, the effect of this law would have been to postpone the sale for a generation. Congress also appropriated fifty thousand dollars of tribal funds to test the accuracy of the segregation, by drilling and a study of formations, against the indignant protests of the Choctaws, who pointed out that under the agreements the Federal Government was to bear all the expense of platting and surveys, and that the Indians certainly should not be penalized for its mistakes.[62]

When a special committee of the United' States Senate visited the Indian Territory in 1906, the Choctaw and Chickasaw nations appointed committees which presented the views of the two tribes at a hearing at South McAlester on November 20. They asked that the segregated mineral lands be sold at once and the money distribuated in per caput payments according to the terms of the Supplementary Agreement. They said that they were not concerned about the formation of a possible monopoly, but wished the surface and minerals to be sold together, in tracts of any size, at public auction.[63] At the same time Leupp, the Commissioner of Indian Affairs, recommended the creation of a corporation in which the President of the United States, the Secretary of the Interior, the Commissioner of Indian Affairs, the Secretary of the Treasury, the Secretary of Commerce and Labor, and a representative from each of the two nations should be officers and directors, and the stock should be held by the citizens.[64] A bill embodying these principles was introduced in Congress during the 1906-1907 session, but it failed to pass.[65]

At the same time the Choctaws attempted to sell the mineral lands to the proposed state of Oklahoma to endow the public school system, but they were not successful. In the Fall of 1907 they again memorialized Congress to carry out the terms of the Supplementary Agreement, so that no undivided interest should remain after the dissolution of the

[61]Acts of the Choctaw Nation, February 9, February 15, 1906; Kappler, *Laws and Treaties*, III, 174

[62]Kappler, *Laws and Treaties*, III, 214, law enacted June 21, 1906; Acts of the Choctaw Nation, October 11, 1909.

[63]*Report Select Committee*, I, 885-89, 894-95, 899-901.

[64]*Ibid.*, II, 1649-50.

[65]*Report Commissioner of Indian Affairs*, 1907, pp. 96-99.

282

tribal government.[66] Just at this time, however, the oil development of the Creek and Cherokee nations was becoming important, and within two years the mines began to close down because of the competition of this new fuel.[67] This complication reduced the value of the coal land, and although Congress eventually provided for its sale,[68] a total of 373,922 acres of Choctaw and Chickasaw mineral land still (1933) remains unsold.[69] In no other respect were the terms of the agreements so completely set aside by subsequent legislation.

Next to the minerals, the most important undivided property of the Choctaws and Chickasaws was the unallotted land. The total area of the Choctaw Nation comprised 6,953,048.07 acres. Of this amount, 462,533.06 acres was reserved for public purposes, townsites, and minerals, and 4,299,111.25 acres was allotted, leaving 2,191,403.76 acres to be sold.[70] At one time the Department of the Interior and the Department of Agriculture contemplated setting aside a portion of this land as a forest reserve, but the Choctaws protested, Congress failed to authorize the reservation,[71] and the land was advertised to be sold at auction in 1910, 1911, and 1912. Most of it was sold at that time, but a small portion remained, and as late as 1933 the Choctaw and Chickasaw nations still owned 25,252.09 acres of unallotted land.[72]

While the Dawes Commission was engaged in closing out the tribal estate, the Choctaw government was gradually losing its power. The Atoka Agreement provided that only routine legislation could be enacted by the Council without the approval of the President; it gave the Federal courts of the Territory jurisdiction over an enumerated list of serious crimes without regard to the citizenship of the parties; and it stipulated that the tribal government should continue only until March

[66]*Report Select Committee*, II, 1639-41; Acts of the Choctaw Nation, Otcober 15, 1907.

[67]*Report Commissioner of Indian Affairs*, 1907, pp. 377-79, 383; *Commissioner to the Five Civilized Tribes, Annual Report*, 1909, pp. 400-1.

[68]Kappler, *Laws and Treaties*, III, 513-16; IV, 102, 143-45, 287, laws enacted in 1912, 1917, 1918, 1921.

[69]*Oklahoma City Times*, April 22, 1932, "Hoover Signs Bill to Lease Coal Lands of State Indians"; Chief Ben Dwight to Angie Debo, November 29, 1933.

[70]*Report Commissioner of Indian Affairs*, 1910, p. 167.

[71]*Commission to the Five Civilized Tribes, Annual Report*, 1904, p. 38; *Report Select Committee*, II, 1657-58, 1687-1773; *Report Commissioner of Indian Affairs*, 1910, p. 51; Acts of the Choctaw Nation, February 21, October 15, 1907.

[72]*Report Commissioner of Indian Affairs*, 1910, p. 169; 1911, pp. 385-86, 398-99, 403; 1913, p. 436; Chief Ben Dwight to Angie Debo, September 26, 1932; November 29, 1933.

4, 1906.[73] Congress also embodied similar provisions in the Indian Appropriation Act of June 7, 1897, so that the surrender of the tribal government was not a voluntary action dependent upon ratification of the Atoka Agreement.[74]

' The Nation continued for some time to exercise a limited control over taxation. The management of the mines was taken over by the trustees provided by the Atoka Agreement, and the royalties were collected by Federal officials and paid into the Federal Treasury; in 1903 the Council laid a tax of twenty cents a head upon the cattle of non-citizens, which was collected by the Indian agent; but for a time the tribal officials continued to collect the other taxes except for a short period in 1898 when the Indian agent collected them also.[75] The curtailment of tribal authority encouraged the non-citizens to make a determined effort to resist the payment of permit taxes, but the Department ruled that all tribal laws were in force unless specifically repealed by the Curtis Act. The tribal authorities continued to report delinquents for removal as intruders, until Congress passed a law in 1902 that no person could be removed who was in lawful possession of any townsite land. Some collections were made, however, by tribal officers until Congress provided that all tribal taxes should cease on December 31, 1905.[76]

During this period the Nation exercised a certain independence in the disbursement of all the revenues except the mineral royalties. The Council continued to make appropriations for the regular running expenses of the government, but all extraordinary appropriations were subject to the approval of the President. It has been noticed in another connection that finances became disorganized just before the loss of tribal independence, and that the warrants fell below par. Congress sought to remedy this condition in 1899 by providing that Choctaw warrants to the extent of $75,000 should be paid out of tribal funds in the United States Treasury. This sum with a few special appropria-

[73]Report Commissioner of Indian Affairs, 1897, pp. 413-14; 1898, p. 441, provisions of Atoka Agreement, and amendments embodied in Curtis Act.

[74]Ibid., 1897, pp. 400-1, text of law.

[75]Ibid., 1898, pp. 79, 155; 1899, pp. 112-13, 120; 1904, p. 209; Acts of the Choctaw Nation, October 21, 1898; October 23, 1903.

[76]Ibid., 1899, pp. 113, 148; 1902, p. 491; Commission to the Five Civilized Tribes, Annual Report, 1902, p. 196; Acts of the Choctaw Nation, October 15, October 22, 1903; October 24, November 16, 1905; February 27, March 2, March 3, 1906; Kappler, Laws and Treaties, III, 173.

tions later made from Choctaw funds by Congress was sufficient to balance all outstanding obligations.[77]

When the Choctaws relinquished their control of the mineral royalties, they incidentally lost control of their school system. Since the Atoka Agreement provided that the revenues from the coal and asphalt leases should be paid into the United States Treasury and should be used for education, the Secretary of the Interior ruled that the schools were thereby placed under his control. In 1899 he appointed John D. Benedict of Illinois as superintendent of schools for the Indian Territory, and E. T. McArthur of Minnesota as supervisor of the Choctaw schools. Benedict met with the members of the Choctaw Board of Education in April and found them, he said, very eager to surrender the schools to him. He and McArthur then assumed the management of the schools and held examinations and selected teachers.[78]

Benedict's reports show that he was without tact, and that he failed to appreciate the pride which the Choctaws felt for their most cherished institution. He drew a very dark picture of the incompetence and corruption that characterized the tribal school administration — a description that may have been true in a few instances, but was certainly grossly exaggerated if one is to judge the school system by the results it had accomplished in making the Choctaws a literate people. He condemned the emphasis on cultural subjects as unsound and unsuited to the people, and attempted by stressing vocational training to change at once the whole purpose of Choctaw education. He censured the boarding schools for the great proportionate cost of their maintenance and the limitation of their service to a selected group.[79]

When the Council convened, indignant resolutions were passed against the "interference of the said Secretary of the Interior without authority of law," and the Board of Education was "ordered and instructed to proceed at once to open up and conduct the schools of the Choctaw Nation according to the Choctaw Laws." A petition was also sent to Congress against the projected consolidation of all the territorial schools into one system, on the ground that "it would be a wrong against modest pride to wrest from the Choctaws and Chickasaws their schools, their highest edifice. Our present school system is the work of many years of earnest effort and steady improvement; and to take

[77]*Report Commissioner of Indian Affairs*, 1899, p. 507; 1903, p. 166; 1904, pp. 188-89; Acts of the Choctaw Nation, 1899, Inspector Zevely to National Secretary Homer regarding validity of certain warrants.
[78]*Report Commissioner of Indian Affairs*, 1899, pp. 87-89; 1900, p. 156.
[79]*Ibid.*, 1899, pp. 90-97; 1900, pp. 154-57, 159-60.

from us an institution cherished in its growth to close attachment would be at least unfair. Our system of management of the schools has proved satisfactory as is attested by results."[80]

Benedict visited the Council with Indian Inspector Wright and attempted to satisfy the Choctaw leaders, but no settlement was made; the Interior Department for the most part continued to manage the schools, but the Choctaw Board of Education employed teachers and tried to exercise a rival authority.[81]

When the Council convened in the Fall of 1900, the fight to regain control of the schools was reopened. Resolutions were passed against the usurpations of the Secretary of the Interior, and the Board of Education was instructed to take possession of the boarding schools and administer them under Choctaw laws;[82] but since the Department controlled the revenues, and since tribal laws were subject to presidential veto, the Choctaw officials could do little except protest. The dispute was finally settled during the Summer of 1901 by an agreement entered into by Superintendent Benedict and the Choctaw Board of Education and subsequently adopted by the Secretary of the Interior. The Department retained control of the schools, but the supervisor for the Choctaw Nation was to be assisted by an official, nominated by the Chief with the approval of the Board of Education and appointed by the Secretary of the Interior.[83] This concession to Choctaw pride ended the controversy, and the school system definitely passed out of tribal control. The office of district trustee was abolished by the Council the following Fall and the superintendent's position was discontinued two years later.[84] Under the new régime the boarding schools became vocational schools for the training of fullbloods.[85]

Under the regulations of the Department, systematic provision was for the first time made for the education of white children. The incorporated towns began to establish public schools as soon as the oppor-

[80]Acts of the Choctaw Nation, October 11, October 31, 1899.

[81]*Report Commissioner of Indian Affairs*, 1900, pp. 92-93, 156-57; Acts of the Choctaw Nation, October 24, 1900; October 29, October 30, 1901.

[82]Acts of the Choctaw Nation, October 25, October 26, October 30, October 31, 1900.

[83]*Report Commissioner of Indian Affairs*, 1901, pp. 127-28.

[84]*Ibid.*, 1903, pp. 77, 79; *Report Select Committee*, I, 926-30; Acts of the Choctaw Nation, November 4, 1901; October 22, 1903. The act abolishing the office of district trustee was vetoed by Chief Dukes, but the fact that it was filed by the National Secretary indicates that it passed over his veto; moreover, the item for the salaries of these officers was dropped from the appropriation bill—*see* Acts of the Choctaw Nation, November 30, 1905.

[85]*Report Commissioner of Indian Affairs*, 1909, pp. 441, 444; 1911, pp. 459-62.

tunity was given for taxation, but the rural communities were unable for a time to levy taxes because of the absence of self-government and because the land was all owned by Choctaws. The Department therefore admitted white children to Choctaw neighborhood schools upon the payment of tuition. In 1902 Supervisor Ballard reported that only thirty neighborhood schools had no white children in attendance, and that the total enrollment was 3,074 Indian and 6,244 white.[86] In 1904 the Federal Government began to make appropriations for the support of schools in the Indian Territory. This money was used mainly for the education of white children in the rural districts, and for the establishment of schools for the Negroes, who had been neglected since the tribal control had ceased and the schools had come to be supported by the royalties, in which the freedmen owned no interest. When the neighborhood schools became a part of the state school system of Oklahoma, the local taxes upon personal property and the increasing amount of alienated land were supplemented from these Congressional appropriations, and the Department for a time continued to exercise control. But the local trustees and county superintendents elected according to the new state school code resented the interference of the Federal Government, and the Department withdrew its support. The schools were then supported entirely by taxation, and tuition was paid out of tribal funds for the Indian children who attended.[87]

While the schools were passing out of tribal control other functions of the Choctaw government were gradually being relinquished. The tribal courts existed for a time, with limited authority, which was reduced still further in 1904 when Congress placed probate matters under Federal jurisdiction.[88] They were finally abolished by the Indian Appropriation Act of 1907, and all civil and criminal cases on the dockets were transferred to the Federal courts.[89] In 1905 the Council upon the recommendation of Chief McCurtain provided for the liquidation of the county and district governments. An auditing committee, consisting of the four national officers, examined the books and passed on the validity of all outstanding obligations, which were thereupon rejected

[86]*Ibid.*, 1901, p. 138; 1902, p. 127; *Commission to the Five Civilized Tribes, Annual Report*, 1902, p. 273.
[87]*Report Commissioner of Indian Affairs*, 1904, p. 90; 1908, p. 219; 1909, p. 451; 1910, p. 227; 1911, pp. 463-64.
[88]*Ibid.*, 1904, pp. 521-22, text of law, enacted April 28, 1904.
[89]*Report Select Committee*, I, 885-89; Kappler, *Laws and Treaties*, III, 278, law enacted March 1, 1907.

or assumed by the central government.[90] The county and district officers ceased to function in 1906.[91]

While the other branches of the government were gradually fading out, the power of the Principal Chief for a time continued to increase, partly because of the many details calling for executive direction, and partly because of the extraordinary ability of Green McCurtain, who remained at the head of the administration from his election in 1902 until his death in 1910. During this stage of transition he was not so much the chosen ruler of a self-governing people as he was the agent of vast and complicated corporate interests which it was his duty to administer. His opinion was listened to with respect by Federal officials and followed almost slavishly by his Council. His private secretary's salary was raised in recognition of the more detailed duties of his office, and his contingent fee was increased to give him greater independence in administering tribal interests. One of the most paradoxical duties that ever fell to the lot of a great administrator — the abdication of his own authority and the surrender of the institutions of his own people — came more and more to be carried out in the light of his individual judgment.[92]

When it became apparent that the division of the common estate would not be completed before the date fixed for the termination of the tribal government, the Choctaws became uneasy at the prospect of having no voice in determining policies in which their interests were so deeply involved. In 1905 the Council attempted to provide for this emergency by placing the full authority of carrying on the government in the hands of Green McCurtain and two associates whom he should appoint, but the President vetoed the bill, on the ground that Congress was making a similar provision.[93] McCurtain and other leaders were called to Washington to consult with the Federal officials, and a joint resolution of Congress provided that the tribal government should continue temporarily after March 4.[94]

The law which provided for the final winding up of tribal affairs was enacted by Congress on April 26, 1906. It provided that the rolls

[90]Union Agency Files, Choctaw—Principal Chief, special message of Chief McCurtain, Fall of 1905; Acts of the Choctaw Nation, October 4, 1905; February 28, 1906; October 8, 1909.

[91]Acts of the Choctaw Nation, February 21, October 16, 1907.

[92]*Ibid.,* March 23, 1899; October 22, 1900; October 23, 1902; October 30, 1903; November 1, 1904.

[93]*Ibid.,* July 3, November 25, 1905.

[94]*Ibid.,* February 16, February 28, 1906; *Report Commissioner of Indian Affairs,* 1906, p. 147.

288

should be closed on March 4, 1907, and that illegitimate children should take the status of their mother. It gave the President power to appoint and remove the Principal Chief and to pass on every act of the Council except motions for adjournment. It placed the tribal schools and the tribal revenues under the control of the Secretary of the Interior, and abolished all tribal taxes retroactively from December 31, 1905. It provided for the reservation of coal and asphalt lands until the expiration of the leases, and for the sale of surplus lands. It protected the Indians against the contingent railroad grants by stating that the tribal lands should never become the public property of the United States.[95] With the passage of this act the tribal government in every real sense ceased to function,[96] although it has continued to exist in a shadowy form even to the present time (1933).[97]

As soon as the Choctaws consented to surrender their separate political existence they became involved in statehood projects. The Atoka Agreement had held out the creation of a state embracing the five tribes as the ultimate goal set for the termination of the tribal governments. It had also provided that the Choctaws and Chickasaws should then become citizens of the United States, but in 1901 Congress anticipated this provision by granting citizenship to every Indian in the Territory.[98]

The white people living in the Choctaw Nation were not willing to wait until 1906 for the creation of a government in which they should be represented. As soon as the Atoka Agreement was ratified they began to agitate for the establishment of a territorial government embracing the five Indian nations or for union with Oklahoma and immediate admission as a state.[99] The Choctaws, on the other hand, believed that the liquidation of tribal affairs should proceed under Federal control during the eight-year period specified in the Atoka Agreement,

[95]Kappler, *Laws and Treaties*, III, 169-81; *U. S. Statutes at Large*, XXXIV, 137.

[96]*See* for example, Acts of the Choctaw Nation, February 26, 1907.

[97]The Choctaws do not now have a General Council. Their officers are the Principal Chief, appointed by the President of the United States; a National Attorney, employed by contract between him and the Principal Chief and approved by the President; and a Mining Trustee, appointed by the President, upon the recommendation of the Principal Chief and the Governor of the Chickasaw Nation. Chief Ben Dwight to Angie Debo, November 29, 1933.

[98]*Report Commissioner of Indian Affairs*, 1897, p. 414, Atoka Agreement; *Commission to the Five Civilized Tribes, Annual Report*, 1904, p. 394, text of law, enacted March 3, 1901.

[99]*See* for example, *Report Commissioner of Indian Affairs*, 1898, p. 156, and *Antlers Democrat*, January 5, 1900.

and that the Indian Territory should then be admitted to the Union as a separate state without passing through any territorial stage.

The Choctaws joined in several inter-tribal movements to accomplish their purpose. They addressed petitions to Congress and to President Roosevelt quoting treaty provisions that guaranteed that they should never be included within the territory of any state, and giving statistics of the wealth and population that they felt made Indian Territory deserving of separate statehood. They sought to enlist the support of religious and temperance organizations throughout the country, saying that the liquor traffic was "nowhere more arrogant than in Oklahoma," and that "if exposed to the whiskey influence of Oklahoma, our present high standard of morality and religion will be lowered."[100] They joined in the movement that culminated in the so-called Sequoyah Convention, when in 1905 delegates from all parts of the Indian Territory met in Muskogee and drafted a constitution which it was hoped would be accepted by Congress as the basic law of a separate state.[101]

But Congress had determined that the Indian Territory should be joined with Oklahoma. The Enabling Act was passed in 1906 and the new state was admitted to the Union in 1907. With these events the Choctaw Nation may be said to have passed out of existence as a separate political entity, and the history of the Choctaw people became fused with the greater history of the State of Oklahoma.[102]

[100]Acts of the Choctaw Nation, December 17, 1902; October 23, December 20, December 30, 1903; November 1, 1904; Union Agency Files, Choctaw—Foreign Relations, expense accounts of delegates to inter-tribal conferences.

[101]Clinton M. Allen, *The Sequoyah Convention* (Oklahoma City, 1925).

[102]After writing this book I made a study of the liquidation of the tribal affairs of the Choctaws and their neighbors and the situation of the separated individuals within the society of Oklahoma; and I followed it by a survey of the fullblood settlements at a later period. See Angie Debo, *And Still the Waters Run* (Princeton, 1940) and *The Five Civilized Tribes of Oklahoma* (Philadelphia, 1951).

BIBLIOGRAPHY

SOURCE MATERIAL

I. *Manuscript Material*

Acts of the Choctaw Nation, 1857, 1869-1910. Phillips Collection, University of Oklahoma. Norman, Oklahoma.

Official Papers, Civil Service and Interior Department. Manuscript Division. Library of Congress. Washington.

Indian Office Files. Office Commissioner of Indian Affairs, Department of Interior. Washington.

Indian Office Land File. Office Commissioner of Indian Affairs, Department of Interior. Washington.

Letters Indian Affairs, Secretary's Letter Book. Office Commissioner of Indian Affairs, Department of Interior. Washington.

Ross, John. Manuscripts and Papers. Phillips Collection, University of Oklahoma. Norman, Oklahoma.

Union Agency Files. Office of Superintendent for the Five Civilized Tribes. Muskogee, Oklahoma.

II. *Official Documents*

1. FEDERAL DOCUMENTS

Cases Decided in the Court of Claims of the United States, Vols. XLV, LIV, LIX, LXII (Washington, 1911-1927).

Commission to the Five Civilized Tribes, Annual Report, 1894-1904 (Washington).

Commissioner to the Five Civilized Tribes, Annual Report, 1908, 1909 (Washington).

Congressional Record, Vol. XXIX, Part 2 (Washington, 1897).

Extra Census Bulletin, The Five Civilized Tribes in Indian Territory (Washington, 1894).

House Exec. Docs., 40 Cong., 2 Sess., Nos. 133, 204; 43 Cong., 2 Sess., No. 47; 47 Cong., 1 Sess., No. 36.

House Misc. Docs., 30 Cong., 2 Sess., No. 35; 42 Cong., 2 Sess., Nos. 46, 51; 42 Cong., 3 Sess., No. 94; 43 Cong., 1 Sess., Nos. 88, 294; 44 Cong., 1 Sess., No. 40; 45 Cong., 1 Sess., No. 14; 45 Cong., 2 Sess., No. 251, Vol. II; 46 Cong., 1 Sess., No. 13, Vol. I.

House Reports, 42 Cong., 3 Sess., No. 94; 45 Cong., 2 Sess., No. 251; 47 Cong., 1 Sess., No. 934; 52 Cong. 2 Sess., No. 2544; 71 Cong., 2 Sess., No. 1693.

Indian Removal (Senate Docs., 23 Cong., 1 Sess., No. 512), Vols. I-V (Washington, 1834-1835).

Kappler, Charles J. *Indian Affairs, Laws and Treaties,* Vols. I-IV (Washington, 1904-1929).

Laws of the Colonial and State Governments Relating to Indians and Indian Affairs from 1633 to 1831 inclusive (Washington, 1832).

Morse, Jedidiah. *Report to the Secretary of War of the United States on Indian Affairs* (New Haven, 1822).

Official Opinions of the Attorneys General of the United States, Vol. VIII (Washington, 1872).

Report of the Committee on Indian Affairs of the United States Senate (Report No. 1278, 49 Cong., 1 Sess.), Vols. VIII and IX (Washington, 1886).

Report of the Productions of Agriculture, Tenth Census (Washington, 1883).

Report of the Select Committee to Investigate Matters Connected with Affairs in the Indian Territory (Report No. 5013, 59 Cong., 2 Sess.), Vols. I and II (Washington, 1907).

Reports, Indian Affairs (War Department, Interior Department, Commissioner of Indian Affairs, *Annual Reports*), 1829-1860, 1864-1912.

Revised Statutes of the United States, Passed at the First Session of the Forty-Third Congress (Washington, 1878).

Richardson, James D. *Messages and Papers of the Presidents,* Vol. VII (Washington, 1898).

Schoolcraft, Henry R. *Information respecting the History, Condition, and Prospects of the Indian Tribes of the United States,* Vol. II (Philadelphia, 1852).

Senate Exec. Docs., 47 Cong., 1 Sess., No. 15.

Senate Misc. Docs., 41 Cong., 2 Sess., Nos. 106, 143; 42 Cong., 2 Sess., No. 53, Vol. I; 44 Cong., 1 Sess., No. 34; 45 Cong., 2 Sess., Nos. 8, 59; 45 Cong., 3 Sess., No. 52.

Senate Reports, 35 Cong., 2 Sess., No. 374; 45 Cong., 3 Sess., No. 714, Vol. II; 49 Cong., 2 Sess., No. 1978.

Speeches on Passage of the Bill for the Removal of Indians (New York, 1830).

Statutes at Large of the United States of America, Vols. I, II, III, IV, VII, XI, XIV, XVI, XVII, XVIII, XXI, XXII, XXIX, XXXII, XXXIV (Boston, Washington, 1854-1907).

United States Reports, Cases Adjudged in the Supreme Court, Vols. CXIX, CCLXXII (New York, 1905 —Washington, 1927).

War of the Rebellion, Compilation of the Official Records of the Union and Confederate Armies, First Series, I, III, XXII, XXX, XXXIV, XLVIII; Fourth Series, I, LIII (Washington, 1880-1901).

2. CONFEDERATE DOCUMENTS

The Statutes at Large of the Provisional Government of the Confederate States of America (Richmond, 1864).

3. CHOCTAW DOCUMENTS

Acts and Resolutions of the General Council of the Choctaw Nation, 1852-1857 inc. (Fort Smith, Arkansas, 1858).

Acts and Resolutions of the General Council of the Choctaw Nation at the Called Sessions thereof held in April and June 1858, and the Regular session held in October 1858 (Fort Smith, Arkansas, 1859).

Acts and Resolutions of the General Council of the Choctaw Nation for the year 1859 (Fort Smith, Arkansas, 1860).

Acts and Resolutions of the General Council for the Regular Session of 1860, and the Called Session of 1861. Mutilated and undated copy in Phillips Collection, University of Oklahoma. Norman, Oklahoma.

Complete Roll of all Choctaw Claimants and their Heirs (St. Louis, 1889).

Durant, A. R. *Constitution and Laws of the Choctaw Nation together with the Treaties of 1837, 1855, 1865, and 1866* (Dallas, Texas, 1894).

Folsom, Joseph P. *Constitution and Laws of the Choctaw Nation with the Treaties of 1855, 1865, and 1866* (New York, 1869).

Journal of the Third Annual Session of the General Council of the Indian Territory (Lawrence, Kansas, 1872).

Journal of the Adjourned Session of the Sixth Annual General Council of the Indian Territory (Lawrence, Kansas, 1875).

III. *Translations and Compilations of Source Material*

Bourne, Edward Gaylord. *Narratives of the Career of Hernando de Soto,* Vols. I & II (New York, 1922).

Choctaws et Al. vs. *United States* et Al. Vols. I-VII. Phillips Collection, University of Oklahoma. Norman, Oklahoma.

Corden, Seth K., and Richards, W. B. *The Oklahoma Red Book,* Vol. I (Oklahoma City, 1912).

Draper Collection, Tecumseh MSS. Phillips Collection, University of Oklahoma. Norman, Oklahoma.

Lewis, Anna. "Oklahoma as a Part of the Spanish Domain," *Chronicles of Oklahoma*, Vol. III (Oklahoma City, 1924).

Miscellaneous Documents Relating to Indian Affairs, Vols. II, XV, XXV. Indian Office Library, Department of Interior. Washington.

Robertson, James Alexander. *Louisiana under the Rule of Spain, France, and the United States*, Vols. I & II (Cleveland, 1911).

Swanton, John R. *Source Material for the Social and Ceremonial Life of the Choctaw Indians, Bulletin No. 103 Bureau of American Ethnology* (Washington, 1931).

IV. *Contemporary Periodicals*

1. MAGAZINE ARTICLES

Crawford, W. D. "Oklahoma and the Indian Territory," *New England Magazine*, Vol. II (Boston, 1890).

Hinton, R. J. "The Indian Territory, its Status, Development, and Future," *American Review of Reviews*, Vol. XXIII (New York, 1901).

King, Henry. "The Indian Country," *Century Magazine*, Vol. XXX (New York, 1885).

Niles' Weekly Register, Vols. III, XV-LXXIV (Baltimore, 1812-1848).

2. NEWSPAPERS

Antlers Democrat. Antlers, Choctaw Nation, 1900-1901.

Atoka Independent. Atoka, Choctaw Nation, 1877-1889.

Branding Iron. Atoka, Choctaw Nation, 1884.

Indian Champion. Atoka, Choctaw Nation, 1884-1885.

Indian Citizen. Atoka, Choctaw Nation, 1889-1902.

Oklahoma Star. Caddo, Choctaw Nation, 1874-1877.

Vindicator. New Boggy, Atoka, Choctaw Nation, 1872-1877.

V. *Diaries, Letters, Reminiscences, Accounts by Travelers, etc.*

Adair, James. *History of the American Indians* (Johnson City, Tennessee, 1930).

Barber, John Warner, and Howe, Henry. *Our Whole Country*, Vol. II (Cincinnati, 1861).

Beadle, J. H. *The Undeveloped West* (Philadelphia, 1873).

Benson, Henry C. *Life among the Choctaw Indians* (Cincinnati, 1860).

Bryce, J. W. (editor). "Our First Schools in the Choctaw Nation," *Chronicles of Oklahoma*, Vol. VI (Oklahoma City, 1928).

Catlin, George. *North American Indians,* Vol. II (Edinburgh, 1926).

Chamberlin, Arthur Fairfield. Personal interview (Canyon, Texas, 1932).

Christian, Mrs. Emma Ervin. "Memories of my Childhood Days," *Chronicles of Oklahoma,* Vol. IX (Oklahoma City, 1931).

Cram, George F. *Unrivaled Family Atlas of the World* (Chicago, 1886).

Cuming, Fortescue. *Sketches of a Tour to the Western Country* (Reuben Gold Thwaites, *Early Western Travels,* Vol. IV. Cleveland, 1904).

Cushman, H. B. *History of the Choctaw, Chickasaw, and Natchez Indians* (Greenville, Texas, 1899).

Dunkle, W. F. (editor). "A Choctaw Indian's Diary" (Diary of Willis F. Folsom), *Chronicles of Oklahoma,* Vol. IV (Oklahoma City, 1926).

Dwight, Ben, Principal Chief Choctaw Nation. Letters to Angie Debo, 1932, 1933.

Edwards, John. "The Choctaw Indians in the Middle of the Nineteenth Century" (John R. Swanton, editor), *Chronicles of Oklahoma,* Vol. X (Oklahoma City, 1932).

Eichenberger, Flora Paine. "A Reminiscence of a Methodist Minister's Daughter," *Chronicles of Oklahoma,* Vol. VII (Oklahoma City, 1929).

Farnham, Thomas J. *Travels in the Great Western Prairies, the Anahuac, and Rocky Mountains* (Reuben Gold Thwaites, Early Western Travels, Vol. XXVIII. Cleveland, 1906).

Foreman, Carolyn Thomas (editor). "Report of Captain John Stuart on the Construction of the Road from Fort Smith to Horse Prairie on Red River," *Chronicles of Oklahoma,* Vol. V (Oklahoma City, 1927).

Foreman, Grant (editor). *A Traveler in Indian Territory* (Journal of Ethan Allen Hitchcock, 1841-1842) (Cedar Rapids, Iowa, 1930).

Goode, William H. *Outposts of Zion* (Cincinnati, 1864).

Gregg, Josiah. *Commerce of the Prairies* (Reuben Gold Thwaites, *Early Western Travels,* Vols. XIX & XX. Cleveland, 1905).

Hackett, S. B. Personal interview. Norman, Oklahoma, 1932.

Hodgson, Adam. *Letters from North America,* Vol. I (London, 1824).

Hudson, Peter J. Personal interview. Oklahoma City, 1931.

———. Letter to Grant Foreman, September 6, 1932.

James, John. *My Experience with Indians* (Austin, Texas, 1925).

King, Edward. *The Southern States of North America* (London, 1875).

Lang, John D., and Taylor, Samuel, Jr. *Report of a Visit to Some of the Tribes of Indians Located West of the Mississippi River* (Providence, 1843).

Laracy, John (editor). "Sacred Heart Mission and Abbey" (Diary of Joseph Lanchet, 1884), *Chronicles of Oklahoma,* Vol. V (Oklahoma City, 1927).

Latrobe, John H. B. *An Address to the Choctaw and Chickasaw Nations* (Baltimore, 1873).

McCoy, Isaac. *History of Baptist Missions* (Washington, 1840).

Methvin, J. J. "Reminiscences of Life among the Indians," *Chronicles of Oklahoma,* Vol. V (Oklahoma City, 1927).

Möllhausen, Baldwin. *Diary of a Journey from the Mississippi to the Coasts of the Pacific,* Vol. I (London, 1858).

Morrison, William B. (editor). "Diary of the Reverend Cyrus Kingsbury," *Chronicles of Oklahoma,* Vol. III (Oklahoma City, 1925).

Nuttall, Thomas. *A Journal of Travels into the Arkansas Territory during the Year 1819* (Reuben Gold Thwaites, *Early Western Travels,* Vol. XIII. Cleveland, 1905).

Perry, Mrs. A. E. "Colonel Forbis LeFlore, Pioneer and Statesman," *Chronicles of Oklahoma,* Vol. VI (Oklahoma City, 1928).

Phipps, B. L. "Banking in Indian Territory during the 'Eighties," *Chronicles of Oklahoma,* Vol. VII (Oklahoma City, 1929).

Pumphrey, Stanley. *Indian Civilization* (Philadelphia, 1877).

Richardson, Albert D. *Beyond the Mississippi* (Hartford, Connecticut, 1867).

Swanton, John R. "An Early Account of the Choctaw Indians" (Translation of an old French manuscript of Louisiana), *Memoirs of the American Anthropological Association,* Vol. V, No. 2 (Lancaster, Pennsylvania, 1918).

VI. *Books in the Choctaw Language*

Byington, Cyrus. Choctaw Dictionary (*Bulletin No. 46,* Bureau of American Ethnology, Smithsonian Institution. Washington, 1915).

————. *Grammar of the Choctaw Language* (D. G. Brinton, editor. Philadelphia, 1870).

Choctaw New Testament (New York, 1857, 1871).

Choctaw Spelling Book (Richmond, ____).

Wright, Allen. *Chahta Leksikon* (St. Louis, 1880).

SECONDARY MATERIAL

I. *Books*

Abel, Annie Heloise. *The American Indian as a Participant in the Civil War* (Cleveland, Ohio, 1919).

————. *The American Indian as Slaveholder and Secessionist* (Cleveland, Ohio, 1915).

296

————. *The American Indian under Reconstruction* (Cleveland, Ohio, 1925).

————. *The History of Events Resulting in Indian Consolidation West of the Mississippi* (Washington, 1906).

Allen, Clinton M. *The Sequoyah Convention* (Oklahoma City, 1925).

Bartlett, S. C. *Sketches of the Missions of the American Board* (Boston, 1872).

Bushnell, David I., Jr. *The Choctaw of Bayou Lacomb, St. Tammany Parish, Louisiana (Bulletin No. 48,* Bureau of American Ethnology, Smithsonian Institution. Washington, 1909).

Carter, W. A. *McCurtain County and Southeast Oklahoma* (Idabel, Oklahoma, 1923).

Foreman, Grant. *Advancing the Frontier* (Norman, Oklahoma, 1933).

————. *Indian Removal* (Norman, Oklahoma, 1932).

————. *Indians and Pioneers* (New Haven, 1930).

Gayarre, Charles. *Louisiana: its History as a French Colony* (New York, 1852).

Gittinger, Roy. *Formation of the State of Oklahoma* (University of California Publications in History, Vol. VI. Berkeley, 1917).

Harman, S. W. *Hell on the Border* (Fort Smith, Arkansas, 1898).

Lewis, Anna. *Along the Arkansas* (Dallas, 1932).

Linquist, G. E. E. *The Red Man in the United States* (New York, 1923).

Malone, Jas. H. *The Chickasaw Nation* (Louisville, Kentucky, 1922).

Meserve, Charles F. *The Dawes Commission and the Five Civilized Tribes of Indian Territory* (Philadelphia, 1896).

Mohr, Walter H. *Federal Indian Relations* (Philadelphia, 1933).

Morrison, William B. *The Red Man's Trail* (Richmond, 1932).

O.Beirne, H. F. *Leaders and Leading Men of the Indian Territory,* Vol. I (Chicago, 1891).

O'Beirne, H. F., and E. S. *The Indian Territory; its Chiefs, Legislators, and Leading Men* (St. Louis, 1892).

Paulin, Charles O. *Atlas of the History of the United States* (Washington, 1932).

Semmes, John E. *John H. B. Latrobe and his Times* (Baltimore, 1917).

Seymour, Flora Warren. *The Story of the Red Man* (New York, 1929).

Stanley, E. J. *Life of the Reverend L. B. Stateler* (Nashville, Tennessee, 1916).

Swanton, John R. *Early History of the Creek Indians and their Neighbors, Bulletin No. 73 Bureau of American Ethnology* (Washington, 1922).

Thoburn, Joseph B., and Wright, Muriel H. *Oklahoma, a History of the State and its People*, Vols. I and II (New York, 1929).

II. *Publications of Learned Societies*

Abel, Annie Heloise. "Proposals for an Indian State," *Annual Report American Historical Association*, Vol. I (Washington, 1907).

Allhands, James L. "History of the Construction of the Frisco Railway Lines in Oklahoma," *Chronicles of Oklahoma*, Vol. III (Oklahoma City, 1925).

Bryce, J. Y. "Perryville at one Time Regular Military Post," *Chronicles of Oklahoma*, Vol. IV (Oklahoma City, 1926).

————. "Some Notes of Interest Concerning Early Day Operations in Indian Territory by the Methodist Church South," *Chronicles of Oklahoma*, Vol. IV (Oklahoma City, 1926).

Carter, Clarence E. "Beginnings of British West Florida," *Mississippi Valley Historical Review*, Vol. IV (Cedar Rapids, Iowa, 1917).

Condra, George Evert. "Opening of the Indian Territory," *Bulletin of the American Geographical Society*, Vol. XXXIX, No. 6 (New York, 1907).

Conlan, Czarina C. "Chickasaw Courts," *Chronicles of Oklahoma*; Vol. V (Oklahoma City, 1927).

————. "Peter P. Pitchlynn," *Chronicles of Oklahoma*, Vol. VI (Oklahoma City, 1928).

————. "David Folsom," *Chronicles of Oklahoma*, Vol. IV (Oklahoma City, 1926).

Crossett, G. A. "A Vanishing Race," *Chronicles of Oklahoma*, Vol. IV (Oklahoma City, 1926).

Culberson, James. "The Fort Towson Road," *Chronicles of Oklahoma*, Vol. V (Oklahoma City, 1927).

Culin, Stewart. "Games of the North American Indians," *Twenty-Fourth Annual Report Bureau of American Ethnology* (Washington, 1907).

Debo, Angie. "Southern Refugees of the Cherokee Nation," *Southwestern Historical Quarterly*, Vol. XXXV (Austin, Texas, 1932).

Foreman, Carolyn Thomas. "The Choctaw Academy," *Chronicles of Oklahoma*, Vols. VI & X (Oklahoma City, 1928, 1933).

Langley, Mrs. Lee J. "Malmaison, Palace in a Wilderness, Home of General LeFlore," *Chronicles of Oklahoma*, Vol. V (Oklahoma City, 1927).

Mallery, Garrick. "Picture Writing by the American Indians," *Tenth Annual Report Bureau of American Ethnology* (Washington, 1893).

Morrison, William B. "A Visit to Old Fort Washita," *Chronicles of Oklahoma*, Vol. VII (Oklahoma City, 1929).

298

————. "Fort Towson," *Chronicles of Oklahoma*, Vol. VIII (Oklahoma City, 1930).

————. "The Choctaw Mission of the American Board of Commissioners for Foreign Missions," *Chronicles of Oklahoma*, Vol. IV (Oklahoma City, 1926).

Myer, William Edward. "Indian Trails of the Southeast," *Forty-second Annual Report Bureau of American Ethnology* (Washington, 1928).

Parke, Frank E., and LeFlore, J. W. "Some of our Choctaw Neighborhood Schools," *Chronicles of Oklahoma*, Vol. IV (Oklahoma City, 1926).

Rogers, Mary M. "Notes for a Talk to Kiowa Chapter No. 650, Eastern Star," *Chronicles of Oklahoma*, Vol. IV (Oklahoma City, 1926).

Royce, Charles C. "Indian Land Cessions in the United States," *Eighteenth Annual Report Bureau of American Ethnology*, Part 2 (Washington, 1899).

Swanton, John R. "Aboriginal Culture of the Southeast," *Forty-second Annual Report Bureau of American Ethnology* (Washington, 1928).

Taylor, Baxter. "An Early Day Baptist Missionary," *Chronicles of Oklahoma*, Vol. IV (Oklahoma City, 1926).

Underwood, W. H. "The Reverend Doctor Joseph Samuel Murrow," *Chronicles of Oklahoma*, Vol. VII (Oklahoma City, 1929).

Wright, Muriel H. "Additional Notes on Perryville, Choctaw Nation," *Chronicles of Oklahoma*, Vol. VIII (Oklahoma City, 1930).

————. "Early Navigation and Commerce along the Arkansas and Red Rivers in Oklahoma," *Chronicles of Oklahoma*, Vol. VIII (Oklahoma City, 1930).

————. "First Oklahoma Oil Was Produced in 1859," *Chronicles of Oklahoma*, Vol. IV (Oklahoma City, 1926).

————. "Historic Spots in the Vicinity of Tuskahoma," *Chronicles of Oklahoma*, Vol. IX (Oklahoma City, 1931).

————. "Old Boggy Depot," *Chronicles of Oklahoma*, Vol. V (Oklahoma City, 1927).

————. "Tryphena," *Chronicles of Oklahoma*, Vol. IX (Oklahoma City, 1931).

III. *Magazine Articles*

McCurtain, B. F. "The Indians of Oklahoma," *Sturm's Oklahoma Magazine*, Vol. XI (Oklahoma City, 1910).

IV. *Newspapers*

Oklahoma City Times, Oklahoma City, Oklahoma, 1932.

INDEX

A

Aboha Kulla Humma: 45, 48.
Absentee Wyandottes: 254.
Adult education: 45, 61-62.
Adultery: 18, 45, 232.
Agricultural Wheels: 225.
Agriculture: 10, 26, 58 n, 59-60, 110-14.
Ainsworth, Napoleon B.: 111, 240, 257 ff. 259, 265, 281.
Ainsworth, Thomas: 246.
Alabama: 1, 50.
Alderson: 130, 190, 224.
Alikchi: 272.
Allotments: option under the Treaty of Dancing Rabbit Creek, 55, 69, 73, 207, 208; opposed by Choctaws, 69, 211-22; under Treaty of 1866, 89, 90; recommended by Sanborn, 100 n; favored by Dell, 103; supported by Indian agents, 195; accepted by Cheyennes and Arapahoes, 198; policy of *Indian Citizen,* 227-28; controversy with United States, 245 ff; accepted, 277-78.
American Board of Commissioners for Foreign Missions: 42 ff, 60-64.
American Revolution: 31.
Amnesty Proclamation, Lincoln's: 83.
Anderson, Wesley: 171, 253, 257 ff, 259, 262, 265.
Annuities: Treaty of 1805, 34; appropriated for education, 42, 60, 242; for lighthorsemen, 46; Treaty of 1825, 50; per caput distribution, 54, 78, 242; after Civil War, 87, 89, 94, 208; freedmen not to share in, 105; statistics of, 132-34, 146; withheld to compel repeal of permit laws, 142; omitted from appropriation laws, 196.
Anti-Christian party: 53, 54, 64-65.
Antlers: 162, 170, 172, 173, 187, 258-59, 264.
Apache reservation: 197, 202.

Appraisal: of land, 257, 276-77; of town lots, 278-80.
Appropriations: 146-47.
Apukshunnubbee: 36, 40-41, 48, 50, 151.
Arapahoes: 85, 197, 198. *See* also Cheyennes and Arapahoes.
Ardmore: 125.
Arkansas: 49, 50, 66, 68, 80, 82, 83, 122, 222. *See* also Eastern boundary.
Arkansas and Choctaw Railroad: 125.
Armstrong, Agent F. W.: 60.
Armstrong, Agent William: 59.
Armstrong Academy: 61, 76, 95, 158, 239 ff.
Asphalt: 280 ff.
Atoka: 108, 131, 158, 187, 198, 224 ff, 231, 234-35, 243, 249, 251, 255, 260, 274, 277, 279.
Atoka Agreement: 260-63, 267, 269, 275, 277-85, 289.
Atoka Independent: 226-27.
Atoka Mining Company: 130.

B

"Bald Eagles": 169.
Ball play: 8-9, 17, 47, 78, 92, 228.
Banking: 114.
Baptists: patronage of Choctaw Academy, 44; beginning work in Choctaw Nation, 64-65; Isaac McCoy, 67; conducted freedmen schools, 104; Atoka Baptist Academy, 227, 243; published *Indian Missionary,* 226; activity after Civil War, 231-32.
Baxter, Uri J.: 122-23.
Benedict, John D., Superintendent of Schools for Indian Territory: 285 ff.
Bennett, Dr. Leo E., Indian agent: fought encroachments of Choctaw Coal and Railway Co., 124-25, 137; approved Federal court at Muskogee, 186; action in election trouble, 169 ff; opposition to

301

"Choctaw beer," 190-91; appointment requested by Choctaws, 195; received complaints against Choctaws, 199.

Benton, Robert: induced Mississippi Choctaws to emigrate, 181.

Betting: 8-9.

Bill of Rights: 151, 231.

Blacksmiths: Treaty of 1801, 34; Treaty of Doak's Stand, 49, 132; Treaty of 1825, 132-33; shops in Choctaw towns, 59, 222.

Blind children: provision for, 240.

Blunt, James G.: 97, 204 ff.

Board of Education: 236 ff.

Board of Health: 235.

Boarding schools: *see* Education.

Boggy Depot: 59, 76, 81, 91, 104, 213.

Bone pickers: 5.

"Boomers": 142, 166, 218-20, 226-28.

Branding Iron: 227.

Bribery: *see* Corruption.

Bristow, Benjamin H., Secretary of Treasury: 206.

Browning, Orville Hickman, Secretary of Interior: 98.

Bryant, William, Principal Chief: fight with Missouri, Kansas, and Texas Railroad, 134-35; administration, 164; candidate for Principal Chief, 1876, 165; ordered prosecution of thieves, 192-93; question regarding Leased District, 197; sustained Net Proceeds delegation, 205; advised investigation of Cochrane contract, 206; action regarding Okmulgee Council, 214-15.

Burial customs: aboriginal, 4-5, 15; change to pole pulling, 39; feeling regarding deceased, 70; "Funeral Cry," 78, 229.

Burial mounds: 1, 6.

Burris, Lemuel C., mining trustee for Chickasaws: 281.

"Buzzards": 169.

Byington, Cyrus: 43, 62, 69–70

C

Caddo: 110, 169, 219, 224 ff.

Caddoes: 85.

Caddo Free Press: 219, 226.

Cale: platting of, 279.

California Trail: 59, 222.

Calumet: use of, 19.

Cameron: 187.

Camino Real: 27, 37.

Camp Holmes: council at, 66.

Camping: enjoyment of, 8, 61-62, 63, 78.

Camp Napoleon: council at, 84.

Canada: Indians from, 27.

Capital punishment: 47, 76-77, 94, 173-74, 177, 193.

Capitals: of Choctaw Nation, 20, 75-76, 81, 158-59, 166, 239.

Capitol: 149, 159, 167, 170-71, 265 ff.

Carolinas: claim to Choctaw country, 31.

Carondelet, Baron de: policy as Spanish governor, 33-34.

Carpenter gang: 193.

Cattle: Choctaws started to raise, 26, 40; in West, 60; losses in Civil War, 92-93; raised by Choctaws after Civil War, 93, 110-11, 113, 114; tax on non-citizen, 143-45, 284 ff.

Cattle drives: through Choctaw country, 92-93, 143-44.

Cattle thieves: 92-93, 100, 192-93.

Ceded Land Colonization Society: 219.

Census: regular tribal, 111 n., 152, 221-22; provided for Dawes Commission, 256, 270; taken by Dawes Commission, 272-76.

Chahta Tamaha: 76, 83, 85, 158.

Chaise, A. D.: 199.

Chandler, Zachariah, Secretary of Interior: 136.

Cherokee Nation: 62, 117, 254, 257, 283.

Cherokees: English relations with, 31; relations of Virginia and Georgia with, 32; Spanish intrigues with, 32; Western ——, treaty with Choctaws, 40; missionaries among, 42; language unlike Choctaw, 62; in inter-tribal conferences, 66; in Civil War, 82-83, 85, 91; refugees in Choctaw Nation, 82, 91-92; at Grand Council, 85; Choctaw jurisdiction over, 178-79; Robert L. Owen, citizen, 195; Choctaw money used for, 196; sale of Outlet, 198, 220; join protest against dissolution of tribal government, 260.

Cheyennes and Arapahoes: lands in Leased District, 197, 198, 200, 201, 246.

Chicago, Texas, and Mexican Central Railroad: 121-22.

Chickasaw District: defined, Treaty of 1855, 71; provisions regarding, constitution of 1838. 74; Choctaws living in, 222, 238, 270, 272.

Chickasaw Nation: 27, 38, 103, 118, 125, 174, 245.

302

87; upheld sale of "Choctaw beer," 169; opposition of Choctaws to, 186, 188; favored by agents, 195; citizenship cases appealed to, 254, 269-72; limited jurisdiction over Choctaws conferred by Atoka Agreement, 283; succeeded to Choctaw jurisdiction, 287. *See* also Citizenship Court, Jurisdiction.

Cox, Jacob D., Secretary of Interior: 212-13.

Crazy Snake: 267.

Creation myths: 2-3.

Creek Nation: 117, 125, 169, 186, 194, 214, 251, 283.

Creeks: relationship to Choctaws, 1; English policy toward, 30-31; Spanish intrigues with, 32; policy of Georgia toward, 32; in War of 1812, 41; in intertribal conferences, 66; in Civil War, 82-83; at Grand Council, 85; refugees in Choctaw Nation, 91-92; Choctaw jurisdiction over, 178-79; ceded lands, 197, 198, 218, 220; join protest against termination of tribal government, 260; Crazy Snake disturbance, 267.

Crime: 15, 21-22, 77, 93-94, 114, 118, 177, 191-93, 218.

Curtis Act: 262, 274, 280.

Cushing, Caleb, Attorney-General: interpretation of dual citizenship provision, 107.

Cushman, Calvin: 42-43.

D

Dances: 7-8, 16, 19, 25.

Dancing Rabbit Creek, Treaty of: *see* Treaties.

Dartmouth: Choctaw graduates of, 61.

Dawes, Henry L.: chairman of Dawes Commission, 246.

Dawes Commission: 127, 173, 220, 268, 278, 283; creation of, 246; negotiations with Choctaws, 247-59; agreements with Choctaws, 259-64; citizenship rolls, 269-79; appraisal of land, 276-77; allotment of land, 277-78.

Deaf children: 240.

Delano, Columbus, Secretary of Interior: 104, 112, 213.

Delegate to Confederate Congress: 83.

Delegate to United States: 147, 195-96.

Delegate to United States Congress: desired by Choctaws, 67-68.

Dell, V.: 103.

Democracy in government: 78, 90, 96, 101,

163, 186, 247. *See* also Elections, Popular referendums.

Democratic Party: 225.

Denison, Texas: 117, 185.

Denison and Washita Valley Railroad: 125.

De Soto: invasion of Choctaw country, 24-26.

Despotic Party: 53-54.

Destitute Choctaws: *see* Poor Choctaws.

Dinsmore, Agent Silas: 38-39.

Diplomatic ability, 27, 74, 86-87 ff, 220.

District attorney: 146, 148, 175, 176.

District Chiefs: 20-21, 47, 48, 74, 75, 105-6, 139, 146, 151-52, 155 n., 178, 212.

District courts: 175-76.

District judges: 175-76.

Districts: 20, 28, 58, 151-52, 156, 236 ff, 287-88.

Division of labor: *See* Women.

Divorce: 16, 232.

Doak's Stand, Treaty of: *see* Treaties.

Doaksville: 59, 60, 71, 76, 81, 84, 85, 104, 151, 221.

"Doctors": 6-7, 41, 46-47, 233. *See* also Magic, Physicians.

Drunkenness: *see* Intoxicating liquor.

Duels: 23.

Dukes, Gilbert W.: action during famine, 113; candidate for Principal Chief, 255; protested against legislation to end tribal government, 260; election as Principal Chief, 263; rupture with McCurtain, 264; in election trouble of 1902, 264-66; on citizenship commission, 272.

Durant, A. R.: 108, 131, 166, 167, 215, 253-54.

Dwight, S. T.: 239.

E

Eagletown: 59, 174, 250.

Eastern boundary: 208, 218; Treaty of 1825, 50; Treaty of 1855, 73; Settlement, 196-97.

Eastern Star: 225.

Eaton, John H.: negotiations with Choctaws, 51, 53, 54.

Education: beginning of schools, 42-45; establishment in West, 60-63; effect of Civil War on, 95-97; school finance, 146-48; financial difficulties, 149-50; description of educational system, 235-43; after surrender of tribal government, 259, 280-81, 285-86, 289; for freedmen, 104, 105, 109, 239 ff, 249, 287; for non-citizens, 243, 270, 280.

Edwards, Thomas: 84, 97 n.

Elections: appropriations for, 146; description of, 160-61; campaigns in *Indian Citizen*, 227.

El Reno, Oklahoma: 125.

Enabling Act, to admit Oklahoma to statehood: 290.

Enforcement officers: *see* Indian police, lighthorsemen, marshals, sheriffs.

English: traders penetrated to Choctaw country, 26; intrigues, 27-29; secured Choctaw country, 30-31; Choctaws fought, War of 1812, 41.

English language: 42 ff, 62, 157-58, 163, 165, 167, 206, 237, 248, 253, 264.

Epworth League: 225.

Eufaula: 251, 255.

Everidge, Joel: 164-65, 173, 252.

Executions: *see* Capital punishment.

Extradition: 66, 179.

F

Family life: 15-18, 43, 77, 232-33. *See* also Inheritance.

Famine: 74, 112-13. *See* also Poor Choctaws.

Farmers' Alliances: 225.

Farming: *see* Agriculture.

Faucett, Dr. H. W.: 131.

Federal Intercourse Laws: 38, 48.

Fences: 110, 118.

Finances: effect of Civil War upon, 94-95, 132 ff; duties of National Treasurer and National Auditor, 155; during transition period, 284-85; under Secretary of Interior, 289.

Fines: 76.

Fire: worship of, 6.

Fishing: 11, 112, 228.

Five Civilized Tribes: 66, 85, 147, 194, 195, 218, 245, 246, 248, 262.

Flattening of head: 14.

Flood, story of: 3-4.

Florida: 26, 31.

Flynn, Dennis: 252-53.

Folsom, Daniel: 59.

Folsom, David: escorted Tecumseh to Creek country, 41; interest in schools and missions, 42, 43, 44; helped organize lighthorsemen, 45; delegate, Treaty of 1825, 49, 50 n.; resigned as Chief of Lower Towns, 52.

Folsom family: 37, 42, 77.

Folsom, Israel: student of Choctaw legends, 2-4; president of Grand Council, 85; on Net Proceeds Delegation, 203.

Folsom, J. C.: wealth, 111; opposition to Dawes Commission, 251 ff; desired removal to Mexico, 268.

Folsom, Joseph P.: opposition to St. Louis and San Francisco charter, 123; candidate for Principal Chief, 166-67; introduced resolution regarding Indian agent, 195; delegate to Okmulgee Council, 215-16; opposition to Dawes Commission, 252.

Folsom, Nathaniel: 37, 38.

Folsom, Peter: 204 ff.

Folsom, Sampson: 97 n., 203.

Folsom, Saul: 268.

Food: 10-13, 25, 112, 114, 229.

Foreigners: in mines, 130.

Fort Coffee:,66.

Fore Coffee Academy: 60, 64-65, 95, 238.

Fort Confederation: 33-34.

Fort Holmes: 66.

Fortifications on frontiers: 1, 18-19.

Fort McCulloch: 82.

Fort Nogales: 33.

Fort Reno: 265.

Fort Tombigbee: 33.

Fort Smith: 50, 66, 82, 85 ff, 92, 97-98, 100, 124, 185 ff, 188, 196, 220, 257-58.

Fort Smith and Western Railroad: 125.

Fort Smith Council: 85 ff.

Fort Towson: 59, 63, 66, 76.

Fort Washita: 83.

Fourth of July celebrations: 225.

Fowls, barnyard: 26, 60.

Freedmen, Chickasaw: not adopted, 104; received allotments, 262.

Freedmen, Choctaw: Treaty of 1866, 89, 90; emancipation, 99-100; adoption, 101-9, 133, 165, 166, 215; schools, 102, 104, 105, 109, 239 ff, 249, 287; exclusion from Leased District payment, 200-1; interviewed by chairman of Senate Committee on Territories, 217-18; population, 221-22, 272, 276; characterization of, 244; received allotments, 249-50, 255, 259, 262, 275-78, 289.

Freedmen, United States: scheme to colonize, 84, 86-87, 101, 197; found rendezvous in Choctaw Nation, 93, 99; Choctaws tried to prevent immigration, 109. *See* also Negroes.

French: settlements in lower Mississippi valley, 26; intrigues with Choctaws, 27-29.

French and Indian War: 30.

Fullbloods: 77, 144, 163, 272, 274-76, 286.

"Funeral Cry": *see* Burial customs.

Future life: belief in, 4, 231.

G

Gaines, George S.: 37, 54.

Gaines's Trace: 38.

Games: 8-10. *See* also Ball Play.

Gardner, Jefferson: 183; nomination for Principal Chief, 162; administration, 174; assistance in taking census of 1890, 222; opposition to Dawes Commission, 249 ff; candidate for Principal Chief, 1896, 255; advised preparation of citizenship rolls, 256; employed counsel to defend citizenship rolls, 270.

Garland, D. C.: 257 ff.

Garland, John: 52.

Garland, Samuel: Principal Chief, 163; member of Net Proceeds delegation, 203 ff.

Garvin, Isaac: as Principal Chief, 142, 166, 175, 218, 219, 236.

General Council: under constitution of 1834, 1838, 1843, 74-75; under constitution of 1860, 75; white and Negro citizens ineligible to, 106, 108; appropriation for, 147; committees, 147-48, 157; description of, 155-58; special powers, 155, 182; acts made subject to Presidential approval, 259, 283; abolition, 289 n.

Georgia: claim to Choctaw country, 31-32.

Glenn-Tucker family: 183.

Gobbling: custom of Choctaws, 9.

God: belief in, 7, 231. *See* also Great Spirit, Sun.

Goodland: 249.

Goodwater: 61.

Government: primitive, 20-21. *See* also Constitution, Counties, Democracy, District Chiefs, Districts, Elections, Nominations, Political Parties, Principal Chief.

Governor: 75, 154-55.

"Governor's cabinet"; 155.

Grandpré Treaty: 28-29.

Great Seal: 75, 155, 266-67.

Great Spirit: 4.

Greer County: 202.

Griffith, Agent T. D.: 134-35, 205.

Grist mills: 112.

H

Hailey, D. M.: 260.

Hair: Choctaws distinguished by long, 14.

Haley, D. W.: 52.

Hampton, Ben: 257 ff.

Hanging: Choctaw horror of, 47, 77 n.

Harkins, A. J.: 272.

Harkins, George W.: feelings about removal, 56; successor to Greenwood LeFlore, 58.

Harkins, Dr. G. W.: 234.

Harris, Henry C.: 198 ff, 246.

Harrison, President Benjamin: opposed Leased District payment, 199-200.

Hartshorne: 170, 172, 190, 224, 234, 239, 251.

Hay: 137-38.

Hayes, President Rutherford B.: action against "Boomers," 218-19.

Hayt, Ezra A.: 142, 197.

Heald, Joseph G.: indemnity to, 98, 133.

Health: 233 ff. *See* also "Doctors," Physicians.

Henry, Amos: 257 ff.

Herring, Elbert: 48.

Herron, General T. J.: made armistice with Choctaws, 85.

Hicks, S. P.: 230.

Hodges, D. W.: 246.

Hogs: 26, 60, 113, 120.

Hollister, J. D.: 120.

Homer, Solomon J.: appointed National Secretary, 257; supported Hunter in election riot of 1902, 264 ff.

Homesteads: 100 n., 103, 142, 197, 198 ff, 201, 202, 213, 245.

Honey Springs: Choctaws took part in battle, 82.

Hopewell, Treaty of: 32.

Horses: 25, 26, 60, 78, 110, 113.

Horse thieves: 192-93.

Hotema, Solomon E.: 181, 253.

House of Representatives: 74-75, 155-56.

Houses: 12, 111.

Hudson, George: Principal Chief, 81-82, 163.

Hudson, Peter J.: 222, 239, 253.

Hunter, Thomas W.: in election riot, 1902, 264-66.

Hunting: 11, 112, 228-29.

I

Iksa: 15, 77.

Illinois: Indians helped Choctaws, 27.

Immigration: 77, 86, 87, 89, 109, 139-43, 165, 221-22, 230, 245, 279-80. *See* also Freedman, Mississippi Choctaws, Non-citizens.

Impeachment: procedure, 156; of Coleman Cole, 166, 207; of Solomon J. Homer, 266-67.

Incest: 22.

Incorporation of towns: no provision for, 224, after surrender of tribal control, 280.

Indian agent: 39, 49, 50, 78, 107, 143, 145, 178, 181 ff, 185, 187, 188 ff, 194-95, 245, 284.

Indian Champion: 192, 227.

Indian Citizen: 168, 192, 226-28, 246, 251, 264.

Indian Intercourse Acts: 38, 39, 48.

Indian Journal: 227.

Indian Missionary: 226.

Indian police: 185, 188-89.

Indians (not Choctaws), living in Choctaw Nation: 222.

Individual ownership of land: *see* Allotment.

Infanticide: 45.

Inheritance: from uncle to nephew, 15, 49, 53, 56, 58.

Inns: 38.

Intermarried citizens influence of, 37; number of, 69, 221-22; laws regulating intermarriage, 77, 179-80; ineligible to certain offices, 106; activities as "loyal Choctaws," 84, 97; under Choctaw jurisdiction, 89, 178; McAlester became one of, 128; not active in politics, 163; Negroes not accepted as, 105-6; share in division of land, 250, 255, 270, 276; alienation provisions removed for, 278.

Intermarried White Citizens' Association: 255.

Inter-Tribal councils: at Augusta, Georgia, 1763, 31; at Chickasaw Council House, 40; Camp Holmes and North Fork Village, 66; during Civil War, 80 ff; Fort Smith, 85-87, 92, 93, 97, 100, 105, 197; provided by Treaty of 1866, 89, 90; Okmulgee Council, 214-17; against "Boomers," 219-20; to resist Dawes Commission, 247-48, 251; to treat with Dawes Commission, 255, 257-58; to secure separate statehood, 290.

Intoxicating liquor: 118, 171, 178; susceptibility to, 47; laws against, 48; used to secure land cessions, 50; admitted by Mississippi laws, 52; Choctaw laws against, 65-66; sale in Choctaw country, 169, 187-88, 189-91, 226; Choctaw opposition to in new state, 258, 290.

Intruders: Choctaws protected against by Indian Intercourse Acts, 38; Creek freedmen, 102 n.; permit system, 139-45; sheriffs sold improvements, 188; removal by Indian police, 143, 189; claiming to be missionaries, 229-31; claiming to be physicians, 233 ff; trying to hold allotments, 278; end of tribal control, 284.

Invested funds and trust funds: 80, 87, 89, 98, 105, 112, 133, 242, 248, 259 ff.

J

Jackson, A. H.: 97.

Jackson, Albert: 172.

Jackson, Andrew: 39, 41, 53, 56, 64.

Jackson, Clifford L.: 190-91.

Jackson, Jacob B.: opposed railroad charter, 127; political activity, 162, 168 ff, 174, 255, 263; college training, 240; opposition to Dawes Commission, 246, 251 ff, 260, 268; forced to resign as National Secretary, 256-57.

Jails: 76, 176-77, 252.

Jefferson, President Thomas: 36.

Jeter, J. B.: 242.

Johnson, Richard Mentor: Choctaw Academy, 44.

Jones Academy: 239 ff.

Jones, Robert M.: wealth, 60; worked for Confederate alliance, 81; delegate to Confederate Congress, 83 n.; president delegation at Fort Smith Council, 85; appointed treaty delegate, 88.

Jones, Willis: 172, 268.

Jones, Wilson N.: wealth, 110; reported striking miners, 130; candidate for Principal Chief, 1888, 167; administration, 168-73, 198-99, 247, 249; helped organize Tuskahoma Party, 253; candidate for Principal Chief, 1898, 263.

Jurisdiction, Choctaw: over Cherokees, Creeks, and Seminoles, 66, 92; over Chickasaws, 71; attempt to extend to freedmen, 99, 102, 103; exposition of, 178 ff; conflicts with United States, 187-88, 190, 235.

Jury: 76, 175-76.

K

Kansas: 117, 219; settlement of Indians from, 84, 86-89, 100 n., 254; cattle drives to, 92; thief runs to, 193; inquiry from regarding Choctaw - Chickasaw land, 213.

Kansas City Southern: 125.

Kerleric, French governor: dealings with Choctaws, 29.
Kidd, Meredith H.: on Dawes Commission, 246 ff.
Kincaid, Joseph: successor to Moshulatubbee, 58; hostility to Christianity, 64.
Kingsbury, Cyrus: 42 ff, 46, 50.
Kiowas: lands in Leased District, 197, 202.
Knights of Pythias: 225.
Krebs: 129-30, 190, 224 ff, 231.

L

Labor: on farms, 111; in mines, 130; permit tax, 139 ff, 143.
Land cessions: treaties of 1802, 1805, 1816, 34; of 1820, 1825, 49-50; Dancing Rabbit Creek, 55; to Chickasaws, 71; of Leased District, 88 ff.
Land patent: 68-69, 258, 260.
Land tenure: of agricultural and grazing land, 110; exercised by freedmen, 100 n., 102, 105, 109; of coal mines, 110-11, 128-29, 168, 175; no provision for townsites, 224; opposition of Federal officials, 245 ff; negotiations with Dawes Commission regarding, 247 ff, 258 ff; faction dissatisfied with allotments, 267-68; protection against alienation, 278; summary of allotments, 283.
Lane, J. M.: 222.
Latrobe; John H. B.: 88, 90, 94, 97, 203 ff.
Law: see Jurisdiction, Legal Code, Courts.
Lawmaking: 74 ff, 155 ff.
Lea, Luke: 203 ff.
Leased District: 98, 138, 209; Treaty of 1855, 71-73; Treaty of 1866, 87-89, 94, 101-2, 105-7, 133, 168; payment for Cheyenne and Arapahoe lands, 197-203, 267; in negotiations with Dawes Commission, 248-50, 258, 262.
Leasing: agricultural, 111, 141; grazing, 144-45; mining, 124, 137, 281, 282; investigated by Dawes Commission, 254.
LeFlore, Campbell: 97, 106, 108 n., 182, 195, 208 ff, 215.
LeFlore family: 37, 42.
LeFlore, Forbis: 96-97, 240.
LeFlore, Greenwood: 45, 52-54, 56, 58, 69.
LeFlore, Louis: 37.
LeFlore, Michael: 37.
LeFlore, Thomas: 58.
Legal code: beginning, 45-48; development in West, 76; list of crimes, 177, 231-33.
Lehigh: 129-30, 188, 190, 224 ff, 231, 243.

Lehmann & Company: 205.
Leupp, Francis E.: 202, 282.
Lewis, Dixon W.: 203.
Lewis, S. E.: 272.
Lewis, Silan: 173-74, 179.
Licenses: marriage, 179-80; non-citizen physicians, 233-34.
Lighthorsemen: 45-46, 76, 132, 146-47, 178, 266.
Liquor traffic: see Intoxicating liquor.
Literacy: 62, 242-43. See also Education.
Little Boggy: 224.
Live stock: 110-12; 118-20, 135-36, 152. See also Cattle, Hogs, Horses, Sheep, Mules.
Lobbying: 158.
Locke, V. M.: 172-74, 264-65.
"Locke War": 172.
Louisiana, province of: 27, 31, 34.
Louisiana, state of: 50, 181.
Louisiana Territorial Act: 36.
Loyal Choctaws: 84-87, 89, 97-98, 133.
Lucas, Eli: 192.
Luce, John B.: 208 ff.
Lying: 23, 29.

M

McAlester: 124, 128-30, 140, 169-70, 211, 224 ff, 231, 243. See also South McAlester.
McAlester, J. J.: opened coal mine, 128; opposed Choctaw royalty law, 137.
McArthur, E. T.: 285.
McClellan, Major William: Choctaw agent in West, 50.
McCoy, Isaac: 67.
McCurtain, Cornelius; 166.
McCurtain, Daniel: 49.
McCurtain, D.C.: 264, 271.
McCurtain, Edmund: 256; wealth, 111; as Principal Chief, 161, 166-67, 182; special Net Proceeds delegate, 209 ff; favored property tax for education, 242.
McCurtain family: 43, 166 ff.
McCurtain, Green: opposed railroad charter, 127; favored public ownership of mines, 129; as National Treasurer, 145-46, 168, 267; participation in election riot of 1892, 170, 173; favored negotiating with Dawes Commission, 246, 249 ff, 253; administration as Principal Chief, 1896-1900, 113, 210, 234-35, 255-63, 270; rupture with Dukes, 263 ff; administration, 1902-10, 266-67, 279, 281, 287-88.

McCurtain, Jackson F.: 114, 256; in Civil War, 83; administration as Principal Chief, 112, 121-22, 159, 166, 193, 219; interest in Choctaw Oil and Refining Company, 131.

McKee, Henry E.: 204 ff.

McKenney, Thomas L.: 50-51.

McKennon, Captain Archibald S.: member of Dawes Commission, 127, 246 ff.

McKinney, Thompson: Principal Chief, 161, 167, 208.

Magic: belief in, 6-7, 9, 19.

Marriage: primitive customs, 16; marriage laws, 77; forbidden with Negroes, 109; with whites, 77, 179-80. *See* also Family life, Intermarried citizens, Women.

Marshals, United States: 185, 188, 191, 193.

Marston, Agent S. W.: 135, 140, 195, 231.

Masonic Lodge: 172, 225.

Medical Board: 233-34.

Medicine men: *see* "Doctors."

Methodists: 45, 52, 62 ff, 96, 172, 231-32, 237 ff.

Mexico: plan to remove to, 267-68.

Midland Valley Railroad: 125.

Migration legends: 2-3.

Militia: 93, 149 n., 154, 170 ff, 178, 193.

Miller, Attorney-General W. H. H.: 201.

Minehart, Sheriff J. H.: 102 n.

Minerals: negotiations with Dawes Commission regarding, 247 ff, 257 ff; disposition of, 277, 280-84, 289. *See* also Coal, Land Tenure, Royalties.

Miners: 130, 231, 234-35, 243.

Mining towns: 190-91, 224 ff, 234-35.

Mining trustees: 280-81, 289 n.

Minute men: 81.

Missionaries: 30, 41-45, 52, 54, 60-65, 78, 229-30, 237 ff.

Mississippi: extended jurisdiction over Choctaws: 58-59. *See* also Mississippi Choctaws.

Mississippi Choctaws: 58-59, 69-71, 73, 181, 273-76.

Missouri: 82, 92.

Missouri, Kansas, and Texas Railroad: 124, 125, 140, 142, 158, 164, 224, 279; coming of, 117-20; grant contrasted with St. Louis and San Francisco, 122-23; controversies with, 134-36, 165, 188, 189, 230; only grant under Treaty of 1866, 216 n.

Mix, Charles E.: 85 ff.

Mixed bloods: 45, 77, 144, 163, 276, 278.

Mobile: 25 ff.

Moieties: 15.

Money: 114.

Moshulatubbee: first of name, 36; successor, 40-41, 49 ff, 58, 64, 65, 69, 151.

Mules: 113.

Murder: 21-22, 77, 192.

Murrow, Reverend J. S.: 226, 231.

Muskogean linguistic stock: 1.

Muskogee: 117, 169, 185 ff, 194 ff, 227, 247, 258 ff, 274, 290.

Muskogee Agreement: 258-59, 261.

Muskogee Phoenix: 195.

N

Nail, Henry: 239.

Names: 16-17, 78.

Nanih Waya: 1-3, 6.

Nanih Waya, Council House: 74 ff, 159.

Natchez Indians: 27.

National Agent: 129 ff, 145 ff.

National Attorney: 155, 159, 289 n.

National Auditor: 146-47, 155, 159.

National Party: 162 ff, 167 ff, 255, 258-59.

National Secretary: 146-47, 155, 157, 159, 161.

National Treasurer: 146-48, 155, 159, 178.

Negroes: 221-22, 234-35, 244, 265-66. *See* also Freedmen, Slavery.

Nelson, C. E.: 108, 127, 129, 164-65, 167, 208.

Nepotism: 149.

Net Proceeds: 167, 200, 218; origin of claim, 73-74; policy of Chief Cole, 165-66; whole history of, 203-11.

Net Proceeds delegation: 73, 80, 81, 88, 165-66, 195, 203 ff.

New Boggy Depot: 164, 194, 225, 226.

New Hope Seminary: 61, 65, 96, 237 ff.

New Mexico: 193.

New Orleans: battle of, 41.

Newspapers: 59, 161 ff, 168 ff, 192, 226-28, 279.

Nitakechi: 53, 54, 58-59, 69.

Noble, John W., Secretary of Interior: 199 ff.

Nogales: 33.

Nominations: 161-62.

Non-citizens: 32, 115, 137-38; extra-territoriality, 184 ff; population, 221-22; social life, 221-28; schools, 243, 270, 280; in smallpox epidemic, 234-35; Dawes Commission established contacts with, 248-49. *See* also Immigration, Jurisdiction.

310

North Fork Compact: 66, 177-78.
North Fork Village: 66, 82, 179.

O

Oats: 113.
Odd Fellows: 225.
Oil: 130-31, 283.
Oklahoma: Choctaw purchase in, 49; war and hunting parties in, 50; origin of name, 214 n.; opened for white settlement, 125, 184, 186, 198, 220, 246, 252; Choctaws opposed union with, 258, 290; Choctaws tried to sell minerals to, 282; Choctaw Nation became part of, 75, 287, 290.
"Oklahoma Bills": 214 n., 217.
Oklahoma Star: 192, 226.
Okmulgee: 214 ff.
Okmulgee Council: 214-17.
Olmstead, Captain G. T.: 103, 212.
Orchards: 60.
Ornaments: 14, 40.
Orphans: 196, 239 ff.
Osage Coal and Mining Company: 120 n., 130, 140.
Osages: 41, 66, 85.
Owen, Robert L.: 182-83, 195, 210-11, 224, 234, 245, 257-58.
Ownby, J. W.: 173.

P

Pacific Express Company: liquor shipments by, 189.
Page, John: 88 ff.
Paris, Texas: 124, 173, 185 ff, 190 ff.
Parker, Isaac C., Federal Judge for the Western District of Arkansas: 185, 190-92, 207 n., 219.
Parliamentary procedure: 21, 40-41, 122, 157-58, 163.
Parsons, Agent Albert: 135, 195.
Pastures: law regulating size of, 110.
Patton, Robert B.: 85-86, 97 n.
Patton, William S.: 85-86.
Payne, David L.: 219-20.
Peace of Paris, 1763: 30.
Peace of Paris, 1783: 31-32.
Peace ritual: 19.
Per caput distribution: of annuities, 54, 78, 242; of Leased District award, 199, 202; of tribal estate, 80, 248, 257-60, 263, 275, 278, 280, 282.
Perkins, Edward P.: 84.
Permits: required of refugees, 92; system of taxation, 139-43, 195, 229, 242; end of, 284.

Perryville: 59, 82.
Petroleum: *see* Oil.
Phillips, S. F.: sustained Choctaw permit laws, 142.
Phillips, Colonel William A.: 83-84.
Physical traits: 23, 24.
Physicians: 233 ff.
Pike, Albert: 82, 203 ff.
Pine Ridge: 61, 64.
Pitchlynn family: 42.
Pitchlynn, John: 34-38, 40, 41 n., 42.
Pitchlynn, Peter Perkins: 3, 38, 93, 100, 112, 165-66; head of lighthorse force, 45-46; feeling regarding removal, 56; opposition to territorial government, 67; head of Net Proceeds delegation, 73, 203 ff; action in Civil War, 81, 85, 88 ff; policy regarding freedmen, 101, 104; administration as Principal Chief, 163-64; policy regarding allotment, 211-13, 217.
Plains tribes: fear of, 66.
Plantations: 60.
"Pole Cats": 169.
Political parties: 148, 160-63, 263. *See* also National Party, Progressive Party, Tuskahoma Party, Union Party.
Polygamy: 16, 77.
Ponies: *see* Horses.
Poor Choctaws: 60, 91, 111-12,‾ 280.
Popular referendums: 151, 212, 262, 264. *See* also Democracy.
Population: 30, 33, 56, 69-70, 71, 192, 221-22, 272 ff, 276.
Post offices: 59, 222, 224.
Potato Famine, Irish: Choctaw collection for, 59.
Poultry: *see* Fowls.
Prayer: 6.
Presbyterians: 42 ff, 54, 63-65, 96, 231-32, 237 ff, 243.
Principal Chief: 75, 105-6, 134, 139 ff, 143, 146-47, 156-59, 161, 173, 176, 178, 288, 289.
Prisons: *see* Jails.
Probate matters: in county court, 175.
Progressive Party: 164 ff, 255, 258-59.
Prohibition: *see* Intoxicating liquor.
Publications, official: 62, 147, 158, 227, 231.
Public debt: 94-95, 149, 150, 284-85.
Punishments: see Capital punishment, Fines, Whipping.
Pushmataha: 22, 36, 40-41, 48-50, 53, 151.

311

312

mission of Oklahoma, 290. *See* also Territorial government.

Stealing: 23, 45, 114, 136-37, 192-93. *See* also Cattle thieves, Horse thieves.

Steamboats: 60.

Sterritt: platting of, 279.

Sterritt, John A.: 279 ff.

Stevens, R. S., manager of Missouri, Kansas, and Texas Railroad: 120, 134-35, 140.

Stewart, E. B.: employed to fight citizenship cases, 270.

Stockbridge: 61, 64.

Stone: *see* Royalties.

Stone, Israel W.: "Boomer" activities, 219.

Strikes: in mines, 130, 149, 234.

Stringtown: 136.

Suffrage: refused by Chickasaws to Choctaw freedmen, 107-8; qualifications for, 160.

Suicide: 22, 26, 77.

Sun: worship of, 6.

Sunday observance: 65, 231.

"Sunday Schools": 61-62, 97.

Superintendent of Schools: 63, 236, 286.

Supplementary Agreement: adopted, 263-64; citizenship court, 271; Mississippi Choctaws, 274; allotments, 277-78; townsites, 279; minerals, 280-82.

Supplementary Agreement Executive Committee: 264.

Supreme Court, Choctaw: 75, 138, 176, 181.

Supreme Court, United States: 196, 202, 208, 210, 271.

Survey: of Chickasaw Nation, 212-13; of Choctaw Nation, 250, 253.

T

Taboos: 15-16, 77.

Taff, J. A.: 281.

Talihina: 202, 255.

Talley, Alexander: 52, 63, 64.

Tattooing: 5, 14, 20.

Taxes: on cattle, 93, 143-45; on railroad right-of-way, 122-23, 135-36; permits, 139-43; not paid by Choctaws, 242; end of tribal, 284, 289; after division of property, 280, 287.

Tecumseh: 40-41.

Telle, A.: 272.

Teller, Henry Moore, Secretary of Interior: 106.

Territorial government: guarantee against, 55; favored by United States, 66-67, 86-90, 195; opposition of Choctaws, 211-20; in Dawes Commission negotiations, 247 ff.

Texas: 59, 66, 80, 81, 92, 114, 117, 122, 134, 144, 202, 222.

Texas Trail: 59, 128, 222.

Thompson, Neely: 219.

Timber: *see* Royalties.

Towbridge, Roland E.: 208.

Towns: 19-20, 25, 59, 118, 222-25, 279-80, 286-87.

Townsites: 113, 124-25, 247 ff, 277 ff.

Traders: rivalry between English and French, 26, 28; Spanish, 32; American, 32, 37, 59 n., 78; indemnity to loyal, 89, 98; permits required of, 139-43; stores owned by, 222.

Trail drives: through Choctaw country, 92, 143-44.

Trails: early, in Mississippi, 27, 34, 37-38; in new home, 59, 128. *See* also California Trail, Roads, Texas Trail.

Transportation: 222. *See* also Railroads, Roads, Trails.

Treason: definition, 177, 252.

Treaties: with France, 28-29; with England, 31; with Spain, 32; early treaties with the United States, 32, 34, 132; with Cherokees West, 40; Doak's Stand, 49, 71, 132, 133, 151, 194; of 1825, 49-50, 73, 132-33, 196; Dancing Rabbit Creek, 54-55, 59-60, 67, 69, 71, 73, 194-95, 273 ff; with Chickasaws, 71, 133; of 1855, 71-73, 75, 98, 107, 116, 133, 138, 139, 142, 178, 179, 196, 197, 203; with Confederacy, 82, 94; preliminary treaty of Fort Smith, 86-88, 105, 197; draft treaty of Fort Smith, 87, 197; of 1866, 89-90, 97-98, 101 ff, 105, 116, 121, 127, 133, 135, 138, 139, 141, 142, 164, 178, 179, 184, 197, 200, 201, 211 ff, 229, 230, 249, 254, 275; abandonment of treaty making, 121; policy of United States to abrogate, 245 ff.

Trust funds: *see* Invested funds.

Tuberculosis: 233.

Tufts, Agent John Q.: 142.

Turnbull, T. B.: 164.

Tuscaloosa: 24-25.

Tushka Lusa: school for freedmen, 239 ff.

Tuskahoma: 74, 159, 166, 170-71, 182-83, 186, 239, 251-53.

Tuskahoma, boarding school for girls: 239 ff.

313

Tuskahoma Party: 253, 255-57, 261, 263, 264.

Twin Cities: *see* Krebs, McAlester.

Twin City Topics: 228.

U

Unallotted land: 283.

Union Agency: establishment of, 194.

Union Party: 261, 263, 264.

Union Theological Seminary: Choctaw graduates of, 61.

United States: succeeded to English interests, 31; Choctaw friendship for, 32, 36 64, 79; relations affected by Civil War 80-82, 84, 86-87; characterization of relationship, 194; determination to end tribal autonomy, 245 ff.

United States Agent: *see* Indian agent.

United States citizens: *see* Immigration, Non-citizens.

United States citizenship: granted to Choctaws, 183-84, 186, 199, 289.

United States courts: *see* Courts, United States.

United States marshals: *see* Marshals, United States.

Utensils: 10-12.

V

Vaudreuil, French governor of Louisiana: 27-29.

Vigilance Committee: to control freedmen, 99-100.

Vindicator: 226.

Vinita: 254, 269.

Vinson, C. S.: 122, 170, 171, 173.

Virginia: relations with Choctaws, 31, 32.

W

Wade, Alfred: 88 ff.

Walker, Isham: 123, 159.

Walker, Tandy: 81, 82.

Ward, Agent William: hostility to Choctaws, 69, 207, 274.

Warrants, tribal: 149, 150.

Wars: conduct of, 18-19; with De Soto, 25-26; with English, Chickasaws, and Natchez, 27-29; with Creeks, 31; in American Revolution, 31; War of 1812, 41; method of declaring war, 156. *See* also Civil War.

Watie, Stand: quartered in Choctaw Nation, 91.

Wealthy Choctaws: 60, 110-11.

Weapons: 10.

Wheat: 113.

Wheelock: 61, 64, 239 ff.

Whipping: 45, 76, 177.

White citizens: *see* Intermarried citizens.

White immigration: *see* Immigration, Non-citizens.

Wichitas: 66, 71-73, 197, 202, 262.

Wilburton: 173.

Williams, A. S.: 257 ff.

Wilson, A. M.: 197.

Wilson, W. W.: 174, 253.

Wisdom, Agent D. M.: 130.

Wister Junction: 124, 125.

Witches: 7, 22, 45-46, 177.

Wizards: *see* Witches.

Women: 9-10, 18, 77, 232-33.

Woodcraft: 11, 19.

Woods, S. H.: 159-60.

Wright, Alfred: 3, 62, 64.

Wright, Allen: 225, 231, 236, 240; in peace negotiations, 88, 90; administration as Principal Chief, 92, 93, 102 n., 164, 203-4, 212, 214; helped organize Choctaw Oil and Refining Company, 131; candidate for Principal Chief, 1876, 165; suggested name, *Oklahoma,* 214 n.; edited Choctaw section of *Branding Iron,* 227.

Wright, Dr. E. N.: 131, 168, 173, 251 ff

Wright, Reuben: 98, 133.

Y

Yale: Choctaw graduates of, 61.

Yazoo: 30, 33.